# Global Issues in Education

## Pedagogy, Policy, Practice, and the Minority Experience

Edited by Greg A. Wiggan
and Charles B. Hutchison

D1160954

ROWMAN & LITTLEFIELD EDUCATION
A division of
ROWMAN & LITTLEFIELD PUBLISHERS, INC.
*Lanham • New York • Toronto • Plymouth, UK*

Published by Rowman & Littlefield Education
A division of Rowman & Littlefield Publishers, Inc.
A wholly owned subsidiary of The Rowman & Littlefield Publishing Group, Inc.
4501 Forbes Boulevard, Suite 200, Lanham, Maryland 20706
http://www.rowmaneducation.com

Estover Road, Plymouth PL6 7PY, United Kingdom

British Library Cataloguing in Publication Information Available

**Library of Congress Cataloging-in-Publication Data**
Global issues in education : pedagogy, policy, practice, and the minority experience / edited by
Greg A. Wiggan and Charles B. Hutchison.
    p. cm.
  Includes index.
  ISBN 978-1-60709-271-1 (cloth : alk. paper) — ISBN 978-1-60709-272-8 (pbk. : alk. paper)
— ISBN 978-1-60709-273-5 (electronic)
  1. Multicultural education—Case studies. 2. Education and globalization—Case studies.
I. Wiggan, Greg A., 1976– II. Hutchison, Charles B.

  LC1099.G57 2009
  306.43—dc22                                              2009011808

# Contents

# Figures

# Tables

# Preface

Through education, increasing numbers of the tiniest villages in the remotest places on earth are learning the importance and the impact of their own agricultural and traditional practices on the world and its economy. For example, the natives of the rain forests of Brazil understand that they are partial custodians of the very atmosphere the whole world depends on, and have learned that they should preserve the rain forests for all humanity. The fishermen along the shores of the Caribbean Sea and along the Atlantic Ocean in Ghana understand that fish supplies can be, and are indeed being exhausted by the insatiable appetites of ever-larger fishing vessels that deplete regions of the sea and oceans their livelihoods depend on. Concurrently, however, commercial fishing companies from industrialized nations understand that their fishing practices are unsustainable, and that their profits depend on fragile ecosystems, many of which are in the custody of poor villages around the world. On the one hand, industrialized nations like the United States and Germany and multinational oil companies depend on small regions of the earth that produce oil to satisfy their economic needs. On the other hand, these regions of the earth view themselves as a part of the matrix that makes the global economies successful.

One only needs to visit a remote village in Africa or Asia where multitudes of people are clutched to their cell phones and texting each other in order to understand the power of globalization. With passing time, globalization has become the universal force that is passively pulling all nations of the earth toward a common destiny. Nations are learning from each other at an accelerated pace thanks to the Internet—for better or worse. As a result, people around the world are learning that they have no other option than to join in the globalization movement or be left behind.

The process of globalization is an implicit invitation to the world to participate in sharing a common global pie. Whether or not one shares the view that this pie is fixed in size and so intense competition is needed in order to have access to a good enough portion of it to be satisfied, or that the pie can be enlarged to satisfy all participating nations, there is one thread that runs across all participating nations: a common system for articulating different ideas. This system of articulation falls into the lap of education: the development of common language and expectations.

As many savvy educators already know, educating just one pluralistic nation is no small feat: it involves the alignment of life and learning traditions of different cultures whose lifestyles are contingent on deep-seated systems of beliefs or philosophies. We know that traditions die hard. Thus, the enterprise of multicultural education becomes an experiment in harmonizing or equal-yoking these different systems into a smooth-running educational engine. Enter globalization, and this educational engine faces another burden to resolve: trying to pull a heavy weight along; another car on a train, as it were. In other words, in addition to harmonizing the needs of a pluralistic society—with all its complexities—there is the added burden of addressing a new educational objective: making students globally competent.

## HOW TO READ THIS BOOK

This book addresses the complexities of global education in an interconnected manner, and this is especially evident in chapter 1. For this reason, readers will find themselves being led through different circuits of ideas and yet in a progressively directional manner. Thus, when addressing the earlier chapters of the book, readers will be referred to issues in different sections of the book and vice versa in order to offer deeper, circumspective understanding of the issues.

The layout of the chapters may be viewed as comprising three parts. In part I (chapters 1–3), the broad issues of globalization are examined. This is followed by part II (chapters 4–10), where the interface of people and issues of multiculturalism are addressed, in the context of globalization. The last section, part III (chapters 11–17), addresses the issues of minority learners in relation to globalization. As readers may recognize, these divisions are not clear-cut, since the issues addressed in the different sections flow into each other and form a continuum—or better put, an interconnected, three-dimensional matrix of human issues—a testament to the ubiquity of human sensibilities, even in the enterprise of the globalization process.

It is the hope of the authors that the issues raised in this book will help readers to understand the current and emerging educational themes of globalization from a critical perspective.

# Acknowledgments

I wish to thank my very first teacher, Mrs. Lyons, the renowned educator in Westmoreland, Jamaica, and my last teacher, the late Dr. Asa Hilliard. I owe my deepest gratitude to these two educators who have had an enormous impact on my growth and development. —Greg Wiggan

I would like to thank my wife Sandra, daughter Aba, and son Nana for accommodating my absences while working on this book. —Charles Hutchison

*Chapter One*

# Introduction:
# The Intersections of Globalization, Education, and the Minority Experience

Charles Hutchison and Greg Wiggan

Today, the images of multinational corporations like Microsoft, Sony, Citigroup, British Petroleum, General Motors, Coca-Cola, McDonald's, and Xerox span the globe and represent symbols of the global economy. Daily, these companies execute an enormous number of financial transactions across the globe, with the assumption that such transactions are understood in different languages but along the same mathematical axis, and managed in an intelligible manner by people scattered all over the world — people who live by totally different philosophies and traditions of life. At the beginning of the global economic recession that started in 2007, Citigroup, the parent company of Citibank, could boast of "some 200 million customer accounts in more than 100 countries" (Citigroup, 2008) and having employees all around the world. Citigroup is just one example of thousands of multinational companies straddling the globe that employ workers who need to have some level of international competence. Given these dynamics, one must wonder: What kind of education will prepare learners for a globalized world, not only in terms of succeeding in the marketplace, but also in becoming globally proficient in order to foster the broader interests of all humanity?

Educators across the world are saddled with the growing charge of teaching internationally competitive, culturally diverse student populations. In 2002, countries like the United States (U.S.), United Kingdom (UK), Germany, France, Australia, Japan, and Spain were, respectively, the leading host countries for international students seeking higher education. Conversely, students from these countries chose China, India, Greece, Turkey, Morocco, Algeria, Malaysia, and South Korea as some of their top destinations for study abroad (Davis, 2003). These trends were consistent in 2008, where the United States and the United Kingdom outpaced all other nations as the leading host countries for international students, while India and China led the non-Western nations as the choice destinations for study abroad (Institute of International Education, 2008). Given the globalized nature of education, educators must not only prepare themselves, but also their diverse students to become globally competent workers — a responsibility that becomes clear when teachers and students find themselves in classrooms and communities with people who are culturally and linguistically different from themselves. What kind of education should students receive in order to be proficient in an international, multicultural society? Equally importantly, what kind of knowledge should educators have in order to teach in an increasingly globalized world?

In the context of this book, globalization is defined as a social and economic process that is identifiable by growing levels of financial and technological integrations and interconnections in the world system. These factors are key developments of the second-half of the twentieth century. Globalization involves complex interactions between local and global processes, and creates social and political dialectics surrounding homogenization (One World Order) on the one hand, and differentiation (global plurality) on the other. It is concerned with the consciousness of the world being one place, where simultaneously assimilation and disintegration are taking place.

Wolfgang Sachs (1992) notes we are living in a world in which human reality has been hijacked by economics. In our attempts to understand globalization and education, Sachs would caution that in the age of globalization, the very notion of education implicitly translates as a preparation for participation in the global economy, whether or not educators and their students are aware of it. Indeed, one can argue that, just as globalized economies have convertible currencies, globalized educational systems and processes are also expected to be convertible—or portable—but against what standard?

There are multiple structural forces that shape and direct educational thought, including colonization and the homogenization of diverse populations in order to make them conform to dominant global societal standards. Whereas economics and its related issues such as politics and power constitute the invisible fabric of globalization and are more apparent in the literature, the silent issues of minority populations across the globe are only now beginning to receive well-deserved attention, and that serves as one of the primary interests of this book. The first part of this chapter largely focuses on historical formations of globalization and connects this to knowledge production and global educational issues. The second part of the chapter concentrates on the selections in the book, emphasizing the intersections of race, ethnicity, culture, and gender, and their influences on global education.

## HISTORICAL FORMATIONS:
## GLOBALIZATION AND EDUCATIONAL PROCESSES

During the twentieth century, the world encountered a series of events that resulted in macrolevel changes and overarching global restructuring in the geopolitical economy. In the last century, citizens of the world suffered two world wars, the Great Depression, and the Cold War and its related competition and rivalries between communist and capitalist countries. These rivalries stimulated great interest in comparative and cross-cultural studies focusing on social, political, and economic outcomes. In education, international competition across science programs, waged in connection with the race to see which country would be the first to probe the outer-universe, created intense international relations, especially between the United States and Soviet Union

(USSR)—a race which climaxed with the collapse of the Soviet Union and the fall of the Berlin Wall.

Notwithstanding the above, throughout the twentieth century, the Great Depression (1929–1941) still towers as one of the greatest global, social, and economic crises that the modern world has ever endured. As the global financial markets crashed, people around the world found themselves struggling to survive. During the depression, leaders across the globe were forced to be creative and strategic in their attempts to develop social and economic reform. In the United States, Franklin D. Roosevelt's New Deal legislation aimed to provide assistance to millions of Americans who were unemployed, homeless, or on the verge of losing their homes. The New Deal was purposive in trying to rebuild the United States and in addressing the economic meltdown, and it marked a period of urgency and heightened levels of government involvement in public services such as education (Fass, 1981; Gabbard, 2000).

New Deal education reforms aimed to improve the U.S. labor force and its international market position by increasing school funding, repairing outmoded buildings, and employing teachers (Fass, 1981). However, the New Deal was silent on issues of access and quality education for minority students, even though racial segregation was widespread across the country and separate schools for blacks and whites were being enforced through neighborhood processes and the judicial system (Wiggan, 2007). It was not until the 1954 *Brown versus Board of Education* case that the federal government explicitly addressed racialized aspects of American education. Nevertheless, at the end of the depression and the beginning of the post–WWII era, the international community responded to the global financial crisis and the need to restructure by launching economic recovery plans through the Bretton Woods Conference of 1944, which was headed by the United States and Great Britain, and led to the creation of the International Monetary Fund (IMF) and International Bank for Reconstruction and Development (IBRD), and later the World Bank (WB) and World Trade Organization (WTO) (Stiglitiz, 2002). At the meeting, the top priorities were to rebuild Europe, reshape the Japanese economy, and although it was not explicitly stated, to address the increasing resistance to colonialism in developing countries, which were major economic producers for colonizing nations. The United Nations also played an important role in post–WWII recovery through its universal education and peace initiatives.

During this time, there was global interest in Ethiopia because it was the only African country that was able to maintain and defend its freedom against European colonization (for example, Menelik II in the Battle of Adowa) (Marcus, 2002). People in colonized countries around the world looked to Ethiopia with a sense of pride and hope, in that it was the oldest monarchy in the world and it was a free African nation. They also looked to its leader, Emperor Haile Selassie I, as Africa's elder statesman. Haile Selassie I received international attention with his many compelling speeches before the League of Nations, where he argued for equal rights and justice for all people, especially those under colonization. A year after the Bretton Woods Conference, in 1945, scholars and leaders from developing countries organized the meeting of the fifth Pan-African Congress, which was headed by George Padmore of Trinidad and Tobago, Amy Garvey of Jamaica, Kwame Nkrumah of Ghana, Jomo Kenyatta of Kenya, and W. E. B. Du Bois of the United States, among others. At the meeting, the issue of independence and decolonization was central on the agenda, and with inspiration from an independent Ethiopia, it later helped set the stage for Ghana's independence from British rule in 1957, and subsequently many other developing countries. Prior to this, India, in 1947, had been was successful in its campaign for freedom from British colonialism.

Through the Bretton Woods Conference, the formation of new global governance institutions (IMF, IBRD, WB, and WTO) inaugurated a new era of economic redevelopment and increased levels of interconnections in the world financial systems, thereby ushering in early formations of globalization. Later, other structures of globalization were made possible through the advent and mass production of the computer and the increased levels of information and data-sharing it created, as well as its capacities for instant communication and financial "connectivities" across local and global spheres. In addition, the development of the Internet—the "information highway"—facilitated the stock market and technology boom of the 1990s, and proved to be another source of wealth for investors.

Technological advancements in the computer sciences, harnessed with corporate-friendly trade regulations (per WTO) and increasing levels of venture capital funding, along with cheap labor and natural resources from developing countries, helped make global connectivity and systems of wealth possible during the second-half of the twentieth century. However, by the beginning of 2007, concerns started to grow as the global financial markets showed signs of a meltdown and unemployment rose. As it were, the international market bubble popped, and the failures of market regulations and unfair lending practices led to a global economic crisis and recession. Given the economic hardships of the time, where failing financial and housing markets are a problem across the world, in the United States, President Barack Obama, like President Franklin D. Roosevelt, is faced with the daunting task of trying to respond to a global financial crisis and improving economic conditions, as well as addressing the concerns with perpetual wars in Iraq and Afghanistan.

In general, most Americans and people across the globe celebrated as they witnessed the first African American to win a presidential election in the United States—a victory that, given the nation's static race relations, most people doubted they would have lived to see. The world partly rejoiced at Obama's victory because they found in him a true world citizen: a person who had multiple ancestral heritages and had also lived in different places around the world and therefore had the interests of the world at heart. However, while there was a great sense of hope, the realization soon set in that Obama faces serious economic and social challenges, as well as failed policies such as a market-based education reform through the No Child Left Behind Act (2001), all of which he inherited from President George W. Bush's outgoing administration. Much like Roosevelt in the Great Depression, education is viewed as a priority for Obama as part of his plan for a sustainable path to economic recovery.

The connection between economic success and effective education policy is well understood. In December 2006, the New Commission on the Skills of the American Work Force noted that "a swiftly rising number of American workers at every skill level [were] in direct competition with workers in every corner of the globe" (p. 6).

Long before then, the oft-quoted report, *A Nation at Risk*, issued by the National Commission of Excellence in Education in 1983, implicitly proclaimed the age of globalization, as it deemed it necessary to compare American education with that of other countries. The report stated that:

> The time is long past when America's destiny was assured simply by an abundance of natural resources and inexhaustible human enthusiasm, and by our relative isolation from malignant problems of older civilizations. The world is indeed one global village. We live among determined, well-educated, and strongly motivated competitors. We compete with them for international standing and markets, not only with products but also with the ideas of our laboratories and neighborhood workshops. America's position in the world may once have been reasonably secure with only a few exceptionally well-trained men and women. It is no longer. (p. 6)

Contingent on such reports, the marriage between globalization and education was cemented.

## GLOBALIZATION AND FIRST LAYER OF EDUCATIONAL ISSUES

The fact that we are living in the age of global market forces is undeniable. However, the maturing globalization process is a structural force that demands a continued conversation across educational cultures. For global-minded educators, concepts such as *globalization* and *New World Order* comprise two useful organizing frameworks for thought. In the context of this book, these two terms may be viewed as inextricably interrelated; whereas the idea of globalization connotes a shrinking world where global financial markets are synchronized, and time and space compressions are facilitated by technological advancements, and goods and services are exchanged with relative ease, New World Order—or better put, One World Order—has become necessary, since there is the need for a common, undergirding standard or system that articulates international and cross-cultural differences. Such a system strongly implies that some level of "one-world education" is vital.

Globalization and New World Order compel several fundamental, philosophical questions, such as: What is the purpose of education? Is there a difference between local education and education for global citizenship? When people are considered "well-educated" in the local, traditional context, are they necessarily prepared for global citizenship? If not, what are the knowledge gaps, and what kinds of curricula may be useful for bridging these gaps? Given that industrialized countries tend to be more influential in modern educational policies and practices, how do local educational systems across the world address their own local needs and yet respond to emerging global trends without sacrificing their own historical and cultural traditions? Such questions constitute the first layer of issues to be resolved by global-minded educators. In chapter 2 of this book, Greg Wiggan introduces readers to globalization and its connections to former social and economic systems such as slavery and colonialism. He explores the relationship between globalization and educational policies in the modern era. Wiggan further investigates these connections as they relate to educational needs and student outcomes in the United States.

Perhaps, one of the highlights of multicultural education is that historical issues are being addressed in new ways, with relatively more open hearts and minds. For example, the African American–led U.S. civil rights movement of the 1960s gave birth to, or at least fueled the second wave of the feminist movement. Thenceforth, equality of race, ethnicity, and gender became more acceptable, and long-standing, burning-but-untouchable topics became tenable in educational discourse. In chapter 3, Greg Wiggan and Kenneth Wilburn explore social discontent arising from global processes—both old (slavery) and new (globalization)—and the role of education in mediating social tensions and in creating peace. This chapter emphasizes contemporary racializations and conflicts over *reparations* and examines how and why it has the potential to foster division. Using a homocentric perspective, they present evidence from students in a major southeastern U.S. university, supporting reparations pedagogy as a helpful method for teaching about reparations and as improving students' understanding about racial and ethnic relations. These discussions help readers to develop some insights into the first layer of educational issues in globalization.

## Globalization and New World Order: Anxieties and Hopes

Across the world, the concepts of globalization and New World Order provoke anxiety in some—generally traditionalists—who suspect that new, unfamiliar, and untested systems are displacing their time-tested, ancestral-instituted systems. In the traditional context, the proliferation of Western media images often expressing ideas of individualism, wealth, and hypersexuality incite fear and concern that new social values and beliefs are undermining older forms. For this group of people, the notion of New World Order is an indicator of a forthcoming loss of precious traditions. For example, in the United States, many traditionalists fear New World Order (a concept associated with New Age) as a new force emerging to eclipse "old time religion." These traditionalists therefore pose a resistance to changes in the status quo. In postcolonial societies, these traditionalists, however, may legitimize their concerns by citing internationally imposed influences, and in many cases, the destruction of their ancestral civilizations as colonialists took over their land, depleted their wealth, and forced them to change their names, religions, and cultures and adopt new social meanings or cultural hybrids.

On the other hand, as the traditionalists wane and are replaced by a younger generation of people who are not adequately exposed to former traditions, they wonder why their social systems are not like those of the industrialized countries, since they are inculcated with a mixture of traditional and Western educational and social systems. For this group, the concepts of globalization and New World Order are music to their ears, since they pose the promise of a future that looks more like that of the dominant Western nations, where there is an abundance of material wealth that they perceive as being lacking in their own lives. One issue, however, is that traditions are not easy to extirpate. Therefore, many previously colonized countries have educational and social systems that are hybrids of both the old and the new. Such hybridized institutions create new challenges. Thus, postcolonial citizens have identities that are contested by competing forces: the spirit of the older indigenous ethos and that of the more recent colonizer's values.

## Addressing Fundamental Issues in Global Education

The globalization phenomenon, to a limited extent, can be argued to be a natural human process, since humans have historically always engaged in international trade and had interactions with each other across ethnicities, nations, and states. However, some of the most potent factors in modern trends of globalization may be viewed, for the sake of this discussion, as the direct result of advances in navigational, communicational, and transportation technologies that fueled slavery and colonization, resulting in the need for cross-cultural integration of peoples. Once colonization had taken root, hybridization of cultures was a natural result. Since all cultures have a means of making sense in their local circumstances (via native education), the secondary consequence of colonization was that new ways of making sense of the world (that is, new educational systems) became necessary.

As the colonies assimilated the colonial systems of education, many became masters of Western educational tradition and became formidable competitors, thus creating something of an equal playing field, at least education-wise. This book provides evidence that developing nations take education seriously partly because basic literacy is increasingly viewed as a must-have, or even a human right, even in traditionalist societies. Thus, in chapters 4–8, for example, the authors relate some educational postcolonial era struggles of Ghana and the United Arab Emirates (UAE), China, and Germany, juxtaposed to Western education as a baseline.

Chapter 4 is a case study that illustrates how countries around the world are struggling to create cirricula that foster global competiveness with the right dose of local relevance—with Western educational standards kept in the background. In this chapter, Daniel Kirk explores the governmental teacher preparation programs offered in the United Arab Emirates, and examines the perceptions preservice teachers hold in relation to their perceived efficacy and utility, placed comparatively against student teachers in the United Kingdom and the United States. This chapter presents the major findings of the study, predominantly the development of teacher education in the UAE as a hybrid of Western (United States and United Kingdom) systems and regional development needs alongside the voices of student teachers who offer reflective analysis of their respective programs. Meanwhile, in Germany (per chapter 5)—as a case study of a Western nation—minority populations' struggle for better educational access precipitated increased discussions about multiculturalism, an extension of the natural momentum of globalization and the effects of the civil rights movement in the United States.

Ortloff and McCarty (chapter 5) explore the topic, "Educating for a Multicultural Germany in the Global Era." This chapter argues that although macrolevel policies, which have come about as a reaction to globalization, and recommendations, both at the European Union level and the federal level in Germany, seem to embrace the notions of diversity and multiculturalism, educational policies and practices in the various German states still cling to more outdated notions of "Germanness." Focusing on the case of Bavaria, arguably the most conservative state in Germany, and using Banks's (1997, 2006) concepts of multicultural curricula as an analytical tool, the chapter illustrates how the education of minorities is conceived and practiced in Bavaria. Ortloff's and McCarty's work indicates that although discussions of globalization and multiculturalism are a part of national and supranational rhetoric, educational policy and practice are predominantly influenced by notions of citizenship that exclude minorities.

Similar observations can be made about China. In chapter 6, Stephen Bahry, Patrick Darkhor, and Jia Luo examine the topic, "Educational Diversity in China: Responding to Globalizing and Localizing Forces," and illustrate that China's centralized education system poses an impediment to the objectives of multicultural education and to the national curriculum. They propose that whereas China wishes to establish a globally competitive curriculum that meets the international expectations of the Education for All (EFA) campaign, a monolithic, national curriculum is not able to meet the needs of its diverse populations. Therefore, school policies are evolving toward the decentralization of curriculum authority in order to compensate for shortcomings in the national curriculum (Anderson-Levitt, 2003).

In the context of globalization, since global educational standards reflect Western ideals, citizens of developing countries need to operate at some level of assimilation into the Western cultural and educational standards; they need to adapt in order to function optimally in both their native cultures and the dominant culture—that is, become *bicultural*. In chapter 7, Obed Mfum-Mensah's work, "Teaching and Learning in a Developing World Context: Understanding the Curriculum Development for Marginalized Communities in Northern Ghana" further illustrates how postcolonial nations have had to become cross-culturally proficient in order to operate, not only in their own national contexts, but also in the globalized world. This ethnographic study explores the curriculum development process of a complementary education program operating in northern Ghana. It revealed that in order to be successful, the program needed to incorporate both local and national standards of social conventions, depicting the fact that globalization has elevated the diffusion of knowledge and information sharing, and created vastly hybridized canons. Kirk and Mfum-Mensah's work add to the theme that traditional curricula are being retuned to the beat of Western drums, as a part of the educational globalization process. In chapter 8, Kwabena Dei Ofori-Attah adds to the examination of African education. This chapter, "The Past and Present States of Women, Higher Education, and Their Career Aspirations in Africa," explores education as a reflection of women's liberation activities around the world—a movement that was also an offshoot of the civil rights movement. Ofori-Attah illustrates that when global civil rights is juxtaposed to African women's civil rights, a parallel evolution is observable. It provides evidence regarding the power of the globalization process as a new paradigm that is capable of changing gendered social lives around the world.

Chapters 4–8 illustrate how nations are struggling with outmoded notions of education in the contemporary era of globalization. These authors implicitly explain that educational policy reforms aimed at issues of diversity go hand-in-hand with globalization and the need for nations to become globally competitive. Nations that wish to participate in the globalization phenomenon are forced to answer the question: If a significant portion of the population is undereducated, how effectively can they contribute to the nation—in the age of global competition?

The first part of this book indicates that although ordinary citizens of the world's nations may assess competently using the yardstick of their old worldviews, native traditions, and educational systems, modernity of life (globalization) has necessitated a new measure for assessing cultural and national competence: a situation whereby a nation's citizens need to be educationally optimized in order to effectively contribute to the national interest—and therefore make the nation more globally competitive— using a common standard: that of global education (more on this later).

With Western systems having a major global influence, the world at large has become one block of major competitors, whereby, as hinted earlier, workers of India are competing for the same jobs as their American or Peruvian counterparts, and Japanese and Korean cars are competing with German and American cars in many parts of the world. In fact, the notion of global competence has become an issue of global competition, a cue inherent in the *Measuring Up 2008* report, which compared international educational achievements as a measure of future economic potentials (The National Center for Public Policy and Higher Education, 2008). A rather curious question therefore arises: What are these competitors taught in school, and are these students being taught with the greater global human interest in mind? If so, then to what extent are they being prepared for the needs of the local and international communities, since, in African parlance, an educated person is one who is better prepared to operate in the local community, but can also navigate a cross-cultural context? Should this African notion hold true, even in the age of globalization, and at what cost—both to the world and to the local community? It is contingent on these questions that the very idea of education must be scrutinized. What is the purpose of education, and how does it differ from technical skills training? And, how do national educational systems address their own local needs and yet respond to emerging global trends without sacrificing their own historical and cultural traditions?

## Culture, Pedagogy, Policy, and School Practices

Different cultures have different interests and needs, and therefore create different educational systems to respond to their perceived needs. Because different cultures have different traditions such as rules of etiquette, the nature of teaching and learning are thereby affected. For example, traditionalist societies are noted as being "listening cultures" (Hutchison, 2006), where children are "seen but not heard," as the saying goes. Therefore, teaching is less discussion-oriented and is more lecture-based since the classroom is organized as if children are expected to sit down and listen to the wisdom of the elders. In Western societies, however, students are more likely to engage the teachers in sometimes challenging discussions, dialectically; a pedagogical style that could be translated as an affront to the dignity of the traditional elder (Hutchison, 2006). Another point of interest is the differential philosophies that impact school organization. In the United States, for example, schools are organized into districts, each with its own administration; presumably a symbol of decentralization of power and egalitarianism. In more traditionalist countries such as Nigeria and Ghana, however,

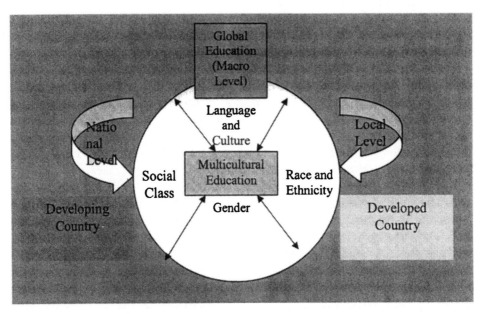

**Figure 1.1.   Global Education and Multicultural Education**

schools are organized around a hierarchical central administration from the nation's capital. In effect, cultural conventions translate into school policies and practices, and that introduces a level of complexity in globalized education.

From one perspective, global education may be viewed as the broader macrolevel framework, or hub, for multicultural education, which makes up the spokes (see figure 1.1). The first level of complexity in multicultural education is that even within the same country, different cultural groups have different interests and needs, and therefore create a challenge for intranational (within-nation) educational systems. Several chapters in this book address this complexity, including Ortloff and McCarty's "Educating for a Multicultural Germany in the Global Era" (chapter 5), and Bahry, Darkhor, and Luo's "Educational Diversity in China: Responding to Globalizing and Localizing Forces" (chapter 6). The very titles of these chapters, however, are illustrative of the second level of issues to be resolved in globalized education: situations whereby nations are not only attempting to harmonize their national educational goals across different ethnic groups, but are also concurrently attempting to respond to globalized forces that affect their economic viability.

### Cross-Cultural Conventions as Impediments in Teaching and Learning

One of the assumptions of globalization is that there is a relatively free movement of people, goods, and services across international borders. Included in these exchanges are the movement of teachers and students. In light of the pedagogical differences noted above, it comes as no surprise that when faculty engage in cross-cultural or international teaching and learning experiences, they experience not only "culture shock," but also "pedagogical shock" (Hutchison, 2006), and indeed, numerous studies support this claim (e.g., Fortuijn, 2002; He, 2002; Hutchison, 2006; Hutchison and Bailey, 2006; Kuhn, 1996; Shatz, 2002; Woods, 2001; Wu, 2002). In the book, *Teaching in America: A Cross-Cultural Guide for International Teachers and their Employers*, Hutchison (2006) notes that when teachers migrate across international borders, they are likely to experience salient and peculiar issues, including differences in communication styles, teaching styles, teacher-student relationships, school organization, and assessment. Such differences can create insurmountable challenges for effective teaching. For such reasons, Atwater and Riley (1993) contend that when teachers move into new cultural contexts, their teaching approaches should be revised accordingly.

In chapter 9, Charles Hutchison, Lan Hue Quach, and Greg Wiggan explore the topic, "The Interface of Global Migrations, Local English-Language Learning, and Identity Transmutations of the Immigrant Academician." Their work illustrates that as global migrations of both teachers and students have increased, so has the need for linguistic adaptation to the local parlance. This chapter contends that migrant educators undergo personality evolution in response to local forces, including sociolinguistic pressures. The authors argue that the intermixing of migrant educators' native identities with the host culture precipitates new identities, brewed in the crucible of educational cross-culturalisms. In chapter 10, Theresa Perez and Greg Wiggan explore the same issues as they relate to international students in U.S. schools. The authors address student migration and the linguistic and cultural challenges faced by English-language learners (ELL). The chapter also examines the *Lau vs. Nichols* case of 1974, in which the Supreme Court stated emphatically that schools were not providing equal educational opportunity by teaching only in English. This decision had great implications for bilingualism and public education. The findings reveal that the opportunities for providing bilingual education were missed as a result of post-*Lau* legislation. The chapter concludes with important classroom strategies that teachers can use to better teach and assist ELL.

It is apparent that as the globalization process matures, nations are struggling to educate their migrant populations. Whereas the migrant students are faced with the complexities of cross-cultural education, including the navigation of language barriers, host countries are increasingly facing the challenge of teaching students who do not speak the language of instruction. Often, there is a price to pay. A 2006 national study of school principals indicated that only 16 percent of their teachers were very well- or moderately well-prepared to meet the needs of their ELL (Levine, 2006). Not surprisingly, therefore, immigrant students are underrepresented in honors academic programs and are overrepresented in remedial studies. For example, the U.S. Department of Education's Office of English Language Acquisition noted that out of all high school students who were tested toward graduation in 2000, only 33.1 percent of English learners passed, as compared to 62.4 percent of all K–12 students (Hopstock and Stephenson, 2003). Furthermore, only 1.4 percent of ELL were enrolled in gifted and talented programs, as compared to 6.4 percent of all K–12 students. This trend was also found in advanced placement course enrollments.

One of the consequences of language barriers in learning among migrant students is that, as schoolwork and school social life become too challenging to navigate, they

drop out. In this respect, it is instructive to examine Hispanic (Latino/Latina) pre-high
school graduation dropout rates in the United States. In 2005, The National Center for
Educational Statistics reported that in 2002 Hispanic students between ages sixteen
and twenty-four and *born outside the United States* had a status dropout rate of 41
percent. For the same age group, in the same year, however, the status dropout rates
for *first- and later-generation* Hispanics were 14 and 11 percent respectively. The
stark difference between the educational achievement of those born outside the United
States and those born within, suggest that cultural and linguistic differences pose a
significant challenge in cross-cultural educational settings.

In a similar vein as above, international, cross-cultural students also face both
culture and pedagogical shocks when they enter foreign schools. For example, when
students from listening cultures enter conversational classrooms, they may operate
like fish out of water. They may not ask questions in classes that are often discussion-
based, and may therefore not have the opportunity to air out their misconceptions of
the subject matter in order to be corrected. In a 2008 study of instructors' perceptions
of international students in a large urban community college in a U.S. school, Isibor
(2008) finds communication and language barriers, reluctance of international students to participate in classroom discussions, and heavy reliance on textbook and rote
learning as a part of the learning challenges for international students. Such students
often end up doing double work—that is, in addition to having to resolve their communication challenges, they end up having to reteach themselves through personal
reading and peer-teaching. In fact, their communication challenges may be a part of
the reason why they are reluctant to speak up during class discussions—a common
phenomenon found among immigrant language learners.

Another issue related to cross-cultural teaching and learning is that of assessment.
Because different countries have different philosophies and objectives for assessment,
immigrant teachers and students are likely to face difficulties in gauging the best
approaches for assessing students or preparing for tests in different school contexts
(Hutchison and Bailey, 2006). In the age of globalization, such challenges constitute
a part of the knowledge base that global educators must procure.

### Globalization, Hegemony, and Cognitive Allocation

As noted earlier, the historical processes of human conquest contributed to the creation of large empires, whereby stronger states enveloped others and imposed their
traditions. Similarly, the direct result of colonization was that it brought about relationships whereby Western standards were imposed on traditional societies. In works
such as *Black Skin White Masks* (1952/1967) and *A Dying Colonialism* (1959/1967),
Frantz Fanon addresses the social psychology of living in imperialized colonial systems, and its resulting social and political consequences. Postindependence—a time
line that coincided with the end of World War II and the birth of the United Nations
and early formations of globalization—the issue of global competency emerged as a
matter of importance for the colonies.

As globalization matured, one of the notable outcomes was that new standards became necessary. Although cultural relativism was accepted intellectually, *functional
ideals* (or standards) prevailed to which any countries that wanted to participate in the

global markets were expected to aspire. Such ideals included new standards of education (generally Western), a *lingua franca* (which is generally viewed as the English language), and world trade and justice systems, mediated through the United Nations, its subsidiaries, and their affiliates such as the World Bank and the International Court of Justice. These standards, however, deserve discussion since they are not globally symmetrical in their creation and distribution of power.

As noted earlier in this chapter, after World War II the new global governance institutions were launched with the primary objective of securing the economic advantage of the West, even if to the disadvantage of colonies, their economic benefactors, which were seeking political and economic independence. The incidental or purposeful consequence of the United Nations' formation was that the West became the standard for the emerging phenomenon of globalization, or by extrapolation, the New World Order. Since Western standards became the new global standards, citizens of previously colonized nations found themselves needing to "double-pedal" in order to compete on an equal plane with their former colonial masters (Fanon, 1952/1967; 1959/1967). This disadvantageous situation can be explained by the concepts of *hegemony* and *cognitive allocation*.

Antonio Gramsci's (1971) notion of hegemony is hereby used to explain the societal phenomenon whereby the knowledge base and traditions of the members of the dominant group are accepted as the "standard" societal norms. Therefore, their cultures and matters of interest are reflected in the canon, the school curriculum, and are underlined in the mass media. In the context of student learning, the concept of *cognitive allocation* emphasizes that members of the dominant group do not need to spend their energy to adjust to the school curriculum, which is an extension of societal norms. For this reason, while the minority members of the society are struggling and using some of their energies to *adapt* to the conventions or standards which are not originally their own—in addition to tackling current tasks—members of the dominant culture have the natural advantage of allocating or focusing all their cognitive energies on current tasks (c.f., Hutchison, forthcoming).

## GLOBALIZATION AND SECOND LAYER OF EDUCATIONAL ISSUES

The second layer of global educational issues addressed in this book involves considerations that are natural components of globalization—mainly the migration or the interface of peoples: males and females of differing religious or traditional extractions, students, educators, and workers. These interactions may occur either in person or via communication technologies. No matter the form or medium through which these human interactions may occur, the prospect for assimilation into, or articulation with, new or different educational and social systems remains. Consequently, the need to address multiple educational issues across different peoples—the management of *differences*—is instructive, as inherent in the notion of *multicultural education*, a process that is aimed at fostering cross-cultural understanding and creating more inclusive, issues-conscious, progressive citizenry who are proficient in pluralistic societies. Multicultural education was borne from the struggles of the civil rights movement and seeks inclusion for all humans in a given society. Just like globalization, multicultural education is concerned with the interface of peoples along the axes of gender, race, religion, and related issues.

Closely intertwined with the second layer of educational issues are challenges regarding international achievement gaps, school reforms, minority education, and their relationships to the complex interactions of social, economic, political, and historic forces. These issues are discussed at length in the next sections, as many of the authors address the complexity of issues hereby referred to as the "minority experiences," their implications for policy, and reflections for practice.

## GLOBAL MIGRATIONS AND THE MINORITY EXPERIENCE

Global migration of people naturally creates the need for some degree of assimilation into a new local culture. It creates situations of "hybridity" along several axes, including cultural, linguistic, and educational. For example, the foreign trade policies and the heightened intracontinental migration in North America, which accelerated between the 1990s and 2000s, created one of the largest trade blocs in the world (Truett and Truett, 2007). The 1990s were years of marked economic growth, which created a great deal of wealth and inequality (Cohen, 2001). However, while the Mexican government liberalized its economy and opened its local markets to U.S. and Canadian transnational corporations, the country experienced very little sustainable growth. This resulted in increased emigration and created situations where Spanish-speaking students became a significant population in U.S. schools. Between the 1994–1995 and 2004–2005 academic years, the total English-learning K–12 enrollment in U.S. schools grew from 3,184,696 to 5,119,561, a growth of 60.76 percent (U.S. Department of Education, 2007). By the 2001–2002 academic year, English-learning students had proliferated to over 43 percent of all school districts and about half of all public schools (Zehler, Fleischman, Hopstock, Stephenson, Pendzick, and Sapru, 2003). Consequently, in the decade between the 1990/1991 and 2001/2002 academic years, the number of K–12 teachers of ELL grew three-fold, from about 15 percent to an estimated 43 percent (Zehler et al., 2003). It is therefore not a surprise that, in the United States, for example, language learning and assessment of foreign students' previous knowledge pose some of the greatest challenges in the education of foreign students.

As indicated, chapters 9 and 10 examine immigration and student-teacher language and culture issues in the classroom. Particularly, in chapter 10, Perez and Wiggan illuminate the problem of "Globalization and Linguistic Migrations: Missed Opportunities and the Challenges of Bilingual Education in the United States." This chapter explores the relationship between immigrant status and the delivery of education. It develops the social and educational challenges faced by immigrant students, more specifically Mexican immigrants, and the limited bilingual educational opportunities that they are afforded. Such challenges constitute the crucible within which the minority and immigrants' underachievement is created.

## The Minority Experience: A Wider View

The U.S. example of migration and multicultural diversity challenges mentioned above is just a reflection of a global trend. The difficulty inherent in teaching diverse populations within a nation is one that is being experienced by schools across the world. In addition to the issue of being a foreigner, female immigrant students often experience unique challenges that their male counterparts are not accustomed to. In chapter 11, J. Lynn McBrien examines the education of another group of diverse learners: refugee female students, of whom little is known about their education. Refugees are global citizens of a special category: people who have had to flee their homelands for fear of persecution, torture, or death because of their ethnicity, political affiliation, religion, or nationality. This case study examines a group of eighteen adolescent refugee girls from different countries, ethnicities, and religions. The research focused on ways in which the girls experienced discrimination, and how these experiences related to their academic motivation. In spite of numerous, regular encounters with prejudice and discrimination, the majority of the girls were motivated to succeed academically. Suggestions for providing positive support for refugee students are included in the conclusion.

Similarly, in chapter 12, Joan DeJaeghere and Shirley Miske explore the experiences of female Hmông students in Vietnamese schools. The authors highlight how these students negotiate being female and minority in Vietnam, as well as how Hmông girls and their families construct and negotiate poverty, ethnic traditions, and gender as they relate to obstacles and possibilities for continuing their education. The students' and their families' voices are compared with community practice and national policy, in an attempt to better understand how policy and practice can be negotiated in local contexts. This research is discussed in relation to the literature on Hmông students in the United States.

In mainland China, Hong Kong, and South Korea, the language and school achievement of minority nationals has been a major concern in education. This is addressed in chapter 13 by JoAnn Phillion, Yuxiang Wang, and Jungmin Lee as they explore the topic "Minority Students in Asia: Government Policies, School Practices, and Teacher Responses." Using globalization as a framework, they discuss these policies in terms of provision for heritage language maintenance, learning of new languages, cultural adaptation, and preparation for higher education. While specific issues for minorities differ regionally, analyses across areas indicates loss of first languages, low teacher expectations, neglect of culture in curriculum, early drop-out rate due to grade placement and retention in grade, and low attendance in higher education. These findings are interpreted by linking to multicultural education theories to develop a comparison to the educational landscape for minorities in the United States. Potential applications of these theories and related school practices are discussed. The authors argue that multicultural education, a process dedicated to social justice for individuals and communities, is urgently needed in Asia.

In western Japan, however, there are some interesting responses to the need for multicultural education. In chapter 14, Ruth Ahn provides insights into Dowa and

*Minzokugakkyu* educational models in Japan, and explores their broad-based implications for multicultural education. Based on over ten years of research examining
Dowa education and recent research on *Minzokugakkyu*, Ahn develops an emerging
understanding of the Dowa and *Minzokugakkyu* educational models. She observes that
specialized instruction for Buraku and Korean students in Japanese public schools
aims to offer these students a range of academic and social skills designed to alleviate
problems caused by discrimination—instructional methods reminiscent of constructs
within the framework of multicultural education in the United States. The analysis of
Dowa and *Minzokugakkyu* educational models presented and contrasted with principles of multicultural education broadens the conceptual foundations of minority
education in both countries and may lead to a global perspective of best practices for
minority education in a global age. In chapter 15, Linda Furuto extends the investigation on education in Japan and examines the mathematics achievement of Japanese
students and issues of diversity. She discusses the social and cultural context of learning, with implications for global educators in the United States and abroad. Furuto
finds that uniformity in Japanese education lead to monocultural orientations that
reproduce systemic disadvantages among the poor.

## Teaching, Learning, and Living in a Globalized World

While Japan struggles to be more inclusive of its minority population, Trinidad and
Tobago (T&T) seeks to modernize its educational system. In chapter 16, Alicia Trotman and Greg Wiggan expand the research on national education by addressing inclusive education in T&T. The authors explore how T&T's government has been trying
ambitiously to meet the UN Millennium Development Goals, and the complexities
and challenges that this developing nation faces in attempting to make education truly
inclusive. These authors' work exemplifies and corroborates the other works in this
book: the fact that the winds of change sweeping the world are changing old paradigms and instituting new ones; that the power of global forces is not only passively,
but also actively, driving the educational and political agenda of nations.

As the globalization process accelerates, so do racial, class, gender, and linguistic
diversity, as more people leave their home countries in search of opportunities in other
countries. Europe, the United States, and Canada are three of the primary destinations
for many immigrants. While migrants' home countries suffer from brain drain and inadequate policy reforms, the host countries often benefit from having diverse instructors in the classroom. For these immigrants, however, there are important personal
issues to resolve, as cross-cultural, global citizens (globizens). The outcomes of these
migrations have caught the attention of researchers, and are explored in this work.

The transmuted identities of cross-cultural migrants tend to be displayed in another peculiar way: their educational ambitions, and by extension, their educational
identities. In the final chapter, 17, Jean Walrond buttresses Trotman and Wiggan's
(chapter 16) work on T&T by examining how Caribbean parents (some from T&T)
with children in Canada's public schools perceive education, especially in a foreign
country. The findings indicate that black Caribbean families view education as being
of primary importance and as a job. Furthermore, they view education as an avenue
for the achievement of higher social status and the attainment of financial success

and self-actualization. This observation is reminiscent of American teachers' remarks about their foreign students, especially those from developing nations, who often view education as their key to a good economic future. Similar proschool attitudes are found among many African American students who view schooling as a form of resiliency (Wiggan, 2008). Using John Ogbu's (1992) theoretical model regarding society and schooling as a basic framework, chapter 17 offers some key insights into the educational experiences of Caribbean immigrants that may be helpful to teachers and administrators of diverse learners.

In a way, we have come full-circle: Whereas the studies in the last sections highlight the educational complexities for global migrants, they illustrate the multifaceted and self-looping nature of globalization issues in education: as immigrant populations struggle to adapt to new educational environments, host countries are increasingly facing a rather peculiar issue: that of teaching the minority learner, in the vein addressed in chapters 10–17. As globalization seizes the world, the world, in turn, continually seeks new solutions to new challenges. This, indeed, completes the circle!

## CONCLUSION

The advent of globalization has created a new paradigm whereby old human cultures, traditions, and institutions have become subjected to new structural forces in order to participate in the current waves of human economic and technological advances. This has created the need for the universality of the human being: a global citizen who, as it were, is locally proficient, and yet can fly into any country and still have some level of social and cultural competence. This person, however, is being created largely according to Western standards, and therefore nations around the world are seeking ways to adapt to these standards, as they prepare this global citizen. As people migrate across the globe in order to take advantage of better economies, they become reshaped by the local, dominant forces, much in the same way as racial and cultural minorities of nations. This work explores the role of diversity-sensitive education in mediating conflict and tension. It seeks to place globalization in the context of educational reforms while emphasizing minority experiences in the United States, the Middle East, Africa, Europe, Asia, and the Caribbean. This book brings together a peculiar group of international educators and scholars to discuss the intersections of globalization, education, and issues of diversity. The implications of geopolitical economy are discussed in the context of pedagogy, policy, and school processes. Emphasis is given to salient historic processes—colonial and postcolonial—and how they have contributed to contemporary issues in global multicultural education.

## REFERENCES

Anderson-Levitt, K. (Ed.). (2003). *Local meanings, global schooling: Anthropology and world culture theory.* New York: Palgrave Macmillan.

Atwater, M., and Riley, J. P. (1993). Multicultural science education: Perspectives, definitions, and research agenda. *Science Education, 77,* 661–68.

Banks, J. A. (1997). *Educating citizens in a multicultural society.* New York: Teachers College Press.

Banks, J. A. (2006). *Cultural diversity and education: Foundations, curriculum, and theory.* Boston: Allyn & Bacon.

Citibank. (2008). *Our Legacy.* Retrieved November 26, 2008, from www.citigroup.com/citi/corporate/history/index.htm.

Cohen, E. (2001). *The politics of globalization in the United States.* Washington, DC: Georgetown University Press.

Davis, T. (2003). *Atlas of student mobility.* New York: Institute of International Education.

Fass, P. (1981). *The new deal: Anticipating a federal education policy.* Institute for Research on Educational Finance and Governance, Stanford, CA: Stanford University Press.

Fanon, F. (1952/1967). *Black skin white masks: The experiences of a black man in a white world* (C. L. Markmann, Trans.). New York: Grove Press, Inc. (original work published 1952).

Fanon, F. (1959/1967). *A dying colonialism* (H. Chevalier, Trans.). New York: Grove Press, Inc. (original work published 1959).

Fortuijn, J. D. (2002). Internationalizing learning and teaching: A European experience. *Journal of Geography, 26*(3), 263–73.

Gabbard, D. (Ed.). (2000). *Knowledge and power in the global economy: Politics and the rhetoric of school reform.* Mahwah, NJ: Lawrence Erlbaum.

Gramsci, A. (1971). *Selections from the prison notebooks* (Q. Hoare and G. N. Smith, Trans.). New York: International Publishers.

He, M. F. (2002). A narrative inquiry of cross-cultural lives: Lives in Canada. In M. F. He, A narrative inquiry of cross-cultural lives: Lives in the North American academy. *Journal of Curriculum Studies, 34*(5), 513–33.

Hopstock, P. J., and Stephenson, T. G. (2003). Descriptive study of services to LEP students and LEP students with disabilities. (Special Report Topic #2). U.S. Department of Education, Office of English Language Acquisition. Washington, DC.

Hutchison, C. B. (2006). Cross-cultural issues arising for four science teachers during their international migration to teach in U.S. high schools. *School Science and Mathematics, 106*(2), 74–83.

Hutchison, C. B. (Forthcoming). *What happens when students are in the minority: Experiences and behaviors that impact human performance.* New York: Rowman & Littlefield.

Hutchison, C. B., and Bailey, L. (2006). Cross-cultural perceptions of assessment of international teachers in U.S. high schools. *Cultural Studies in Science Education 1*(4), 657–80.

Institute of International Education. (2008). *Atlas of student mobility.* Retrieved on December 22, 2008, from www.atlas.iienetwork.org/.

Isibor, T. (2008). *Instructors' perceptions of international students in a large urban community college: Students in a United States school.* Unpublished dissertation, University of North Carolina at Charlotte.

Kuhn, E. (1996). Cross-cultural stumbling block for international teachers. *College Teaching, 44*(3), 96–100.

Levine, A. (September 2006). *Educating School Teachers.* Washington, DC: Education Schools Project. Retrieved January 10, 2007, from edschools.org/teacher_report.htm (p. 4, Executive Summary).

Marcus, H. (2002). *A history of Ethiopia* (updated ed.). Berkeley: University of California Press.

National Center for Public Policy and Higher Education. (2008). *Measuring up 2008: The national report card on higher education.* San Jose: The National Center.

National Commission of Excellence in Education. (1983). *A nation at risk: The imperative for educational reform.* Washington, DC: U.S. Government Printing Office, p. 6.

The New Commission on the Skills of the American Work Force. (December 2006, pp. 6, 7). *Tough choices or tough times* (Executive Summary). National Center on Education and the Economy. Retrieved on December 20, 2006, from www.skillscommission.org/pdf/exec_sum/ToughChoices_EXECSUM.pdf.

Sachs, W. (1992). *The development dictionary: A guide to knowledge as power.* Atlantic Highlands, NJ: Zed Books.

Shatz, M. A. (2002). Teaching thanatology in a foreign country: Implications for death educators. *Death Studies, 26*(5), 425–30.

Stiglitz, J. (2002). *Globalization and its discontents.* New York: W.W. Norton and Company.

Truett, L., and Truett, D. (2007). NAFTA and the Maquiladoras: Boon or bane? *Contemporary Economic Policy, 25*(3), 374–86.

U.S. Department of Education. (2007). *The growing numbers of limited English proficient students, 1994/95–2004/05.* National Clearinghouse for English Language Acquisition and Language Instruction Educational Programs. Retrieved November 7, 2007, from www.ncela.gwu.edu/policy/states/reports/statedata/2004LEP/GrowingLEP0405_Nov06.pdf.

Wiggan, G. (2007). Race, school achievement and educational inequality: Towards a student-based inquiry perspective. *Review of Educational Research, 77*(3), 310–33.

Wiggan, G. (2008). From opposition to engagement: Lessons from high achieving African American students. *Urban Review, 40*(4), 317–49.

Woods, J. M. (2001). The barefoot teacher. *College Teaching, 49*(2), 51–55.

Wu, S. (2002). Filling the pot or lighting the fire? Cultural variations in conceptions of pedagogy. *Teaching in Higher Education, 7*(4), 387–95.

Zehler, A. M., Fleischman, H. L., Hopstock, P. J., Stephenson, T. G., Pendzick, M. L., and Sapru, S. (2003). *Descriptive study of services to LEP students and LEP students with disabilities. (Policy report: Summary of findings related to LAP and SpEd-LEP students.)* U.S. Department of Education, Office of English Language Acquisition. Washington, DC.

*Chapter Two*

# Paying the Price, Globalization in Education: Economics, Policies, School Practices, and Student Outcomes

## Greg Wiggan

Ever since the historic events of World War II (1939–1945), education has been viewed as playing an important role in national development. In the post–WWII period, as countries around the world endured severe economic hardships, fixing the global economy and improving education became top priorities for nations struggling to resuscitate their economies from the effects of the war. Globally, the post–WWII era marked the beginning of a new period of redevelopment and globalization, namely through the formation of the International Monetary Fund, the World Bank, and the World Trade Organization (IMF, WB, WTO). The United Nations (UN) also illuminated in significance as a global arbitrator, charged with the task of helping to mediate international conflicts, and with helping to safeguard against the prospects of another world war. The United Nations was also instrumental in advocating redevelopment and peace through its education platform; thus, acknowledging that the relationship between economic development and education was central for the well-being and stability of nations.

Generally, low levels of educational achievement signals to economists, politicians, educators, and citizens that the competitive advantages of having a highly qualified workforce are in jeopardy, and resulting social problems and discontents are on the horizon. Therefore, public concerns and scrutiny regarding education tends to reflect an interest in maintaining market advantage and in encouraging social stability as progressions of globalization. This chapter addresses the development of globalization and its connection to market-based school reform, and analyzes their influences on education policies such as No Child Left Behind. The chapter begins with a discussion on the historical socioeconomic dynamics that made globalization possible, and then connects its systems to global and local school reforms.

## MAPPING EDUCATION IN THE GLOBAL LANDSCAPE

In the war-torn world of 1948, following the global combat and the devastating atrocities that resulted in millions of deaths (Matanle, 1994), there was international consensus that global restructuring was needed to rebuild regions such as Eastern Europe and Asia, where countries such as Germany, Japan, and China suffered from immense bombings. With the intent of helping to achieve this goal, the United Nations through its Universal Declaration of Human Rights (UDHR), reaffirmed the dignity of all human beings to live equally as citizens of the world. The United Nations' UDHR aimed to promote respect among all nations and social groups (OHCHR, 2007). In Article 26 it emphasized education as a major area of its international focus, stating that free education is a basic, obligatory human right and that it should be afforded to all citizens (OHCHR, 2007).

Shortly after this, in the United States (U.S.), a global leader at the time, the 1954 *Brown* case brought education into the international spotlight once more when racialized patterns of exclusionary educational practices in America were challenged, and racially separate but equal schooling was presumed to be outlawed by the decision in the case (Doob, 1999; Kozol, 1991, 2006). The *Brown* case drew international attention to America's race relations, and people around the world watched attentively, especially those being colonized, as they witnessed the outcome of the case. Unfortunately, residential and school segregation continued to plague social life in the United States. The nation's education was further scrutinized when the Soviet Union, which was a major global competitor, launched Sputnik into space before the United States was able to send an equally equipped space shuttle to explore the universe (NCEE, 1983). The race to space was intense because it symbolically represented the rivalry between the major superpowers, the Soviet Union and the United States. While in 1991, the dissolving of the Soviet Union indicated that the United States was the undisputed global leader, before then, the nation always compared its achievements in math and sciences to the successful space program of its archenemy, the Soviet Union.

Similar to 1948 when the United Nations' UDHR was issued, in 2000, the United Nations' Millennium Development Goals (MDG) were announced. Set to come to fruition by 2015, the MDG were established to reduce global poverty, to globally improve education, maternal health, and gender equality, to reduce child mortality, and to help control new infections of HIV/AIDS and other diseases (MDG, 2007). In addition, a main focus of the MDG was to promote the goal of universal education for all by the year 2015. Universal education is quite a noble objective, and although resources have been lacking to make this a reality, it has been a focus of many countries.

In today's globalized world, education continues to be a principal concern as many countries view it as being foundational for a path to security and economic prosperity (Blum, 1995). A common practice of developed nations is to combine economic and educational initiatives to form a security state that is globally prepared for market competition, as well as for war and social conflicts. Spring (2006) proposes that "in an educational security state, the government attempts to mold and control the learning of children and youth for economic and military purposes, and the government incorporates educational planning into national economic and military planning" (p. 3). All of this is done to improve and protect a nation's competitive advantage in an ever-changing, globalizing world, where threats can arise from economic, political, and military realignments.

## WHAT IS GLOBALIZATION?

Since the early 1990s, globalization has been one of the most central and lively topics of discussion. While global processes existed in the old world, slave and colonial societies, in terms of complex patterns of interconnectedness that transferred labor, goods, and services across borders, creating wealth that made the Industrial Revolution possible, and laying the foundation for modern global capitalism; the contemporary emergence of transnationalizaiton and hyperized levels of capital flow are unique to the modern process known as globalization.

Sociologist Roland Robertson is one of the first persons to operationalize the term globalization. Robertson (1985) argues that "there is an emergent problem of order at the global—the emergence of that problem being a central aspect of the process of globalization. The degree to which this is related to the growth of a world economic system." (p. 34). He continues:

> If there is a higher level—a more fundamental—problem of order than that traditionally discussed in reference to societies as territorially organized and state guided sociocultural units, then, surely we have to think about the problem of societal order in global-contextual terms. (p. 34)

Robertson poses that the rapid changes in socio-cultural life are being shaped by a process called globalization, a complex social, economic, and political progression having broad macro- and microlevel effects and influences. He further argues that globalization "refers both to the compression of the world and the intensification of consciousness of the world as a whole," and that this pertains to more recent developments in global interconnections and interdependence (Robertson, 1992, p. 8). Similarly, Giddens (1994) postulates that "globalization is not only, or even primarily, an economic phenomenon. . . . Globalization is really about the transformation of space and time" (p. 4). He further states that it is concerned not only with "the creation of large-scale systems, but also the transformation of local, and even personal, contexts of social experience" (Giddens, 1994, p. 5). In sum, globalization has to do with increasing levels of economic and technological integration in the world system, which are key developments in the second half of the twentieth century, and that resulted in new patterns of social and political alignments.

## GLOBAL COMPETITION AND NATIONAL REPOSITIONING

During the last five decades, the world saw rapid changes in the global landscape, as many former colonies such as Ghana, Kenya, Sierra Leone, Jamaica, and Grenada, among many others; nations that endured three to four hundred years of European colonization were finally able to gain their "freedom" or neo-independence, meaning an assumed political independence from colonization, while simultaneously failing to achieve social and economic self-governance (Du Bois, 1946; Rodney, 1982). Although these countries are still constituted by neocolonial systems—having large amounts of foreign debt, diminishing levels of political autonomy, and experiencing economic marginalization resulting from unfair global economic policies (Offiong, 2001)—the second half of the twentieth century marked the beginning of their "freedom." During this time, the former Soviet Union collapsed, signaling to most of the world that the battle between capitalism and communism was over, and that capitalist nations were victorious in espousing a dominant system of social and economic organization. Furthermore, during the 1990s, countries like China, India, and South Korea were celebrated for their relatively high levels of outputs and for their economic growth (Friedman, 2005). However, many people overlooked the fact that most of this growth resulted from compression in the global labor market, which made outsourcing and overseas sweatshops commonplace business efficiencies for most transnational corporations.

For example, in 2007, the issue of outsourcing raised national concerns when American toy maker Mattel was forced to recall a large number of toys made in China, due to high amounts of lead paint found in most of these products (*New York Times*, 2007). Mattel outsourced the manufacturing of the toys to China simply to save money, savings consumers hardly see from toys made in Chinese sweatshops that typically use lead paint, a substance that has been banned on toys made in the United States because it has been linked to brain damage in children. Similarly, more than six million cans of dog food made in China were recalled due to toxic chemicals found in the products (CNN, 2007). These findings infuriated many Americans, especially pet lovers, but there was little discussion about market hegemony, unfair trade practices, or exploitation of overseas workers who make cheap goods for the international market. Developed countries seem to love market efficiencies so long as they work for them and make their economies strong, even when it comes at the expense of others.

Due to pressure for cheaper labor, many developing countries have become gender-export based (Wichterich, 2000), shipping goods overseas like designer clothes and other high-end products that are made by women working for low-wages in deplorable working conditions (Bhavnani, Foran, and Kurian, 2003). This creates and reproduces international gendered divisions of labor and wage inequalities that mostly benefit transnational corporations. These companies have the option of operating in developing economies that have low-wage structures, or they can take advantage of low-wage prison workers in developed countries, who work for a dollar a day much like people in low-income countries (see Angela Davis's [2001] *Prison Industrial Complex*).

Since the early 1990s, the growth and success of multinational corporations has been immense, but their benefits have not been fairly distributed among its global players. During this period, the majority of the world's citizens suffered from poverty, starvation, and preventable health-related deaths (Barnett and Whiteside, 2002; MDG, 2007). These problems persist in most developing countries that are highly indebted to international lending institutions such as the IMF and the WB, whose major stakeholders are countries that were former beneficiaries of imperial control or colonization—G-8 nations; namely, the United States, Great Britain, Germany, France, Russia, and so forth. Countries like Ghana, Nigeria, and Jamaica struggle to provide proper social services and education to their populations because of debt and overhead that they assumed in the postcolonial era (Offiong, 2001). These countries must meet structural adjustment policies, meaning loan conditionalities imposed on them through foreign lending institutions like the IMF and the World Bank, which requires large-scale privatization and often includes transferring education and other social services into the private sector (Brown, 1992; Stiglitz, 2002; 2006).

The revenue shortages in developing countries only make corruption and bribery commonplace because these nations suffer from financial constrictions. As a result, competition and conflict over scarce resources become routine. While the faces of the poor in most developing economies are majority black (African descent) and brown populations (other nonwhites), the global economy continues to be dominated by power elites who mostly live in developed countries. These extreme disparities in wealth and power are evidenced by racial and gender inequalities in the world economy, and through the process of globalization.

## GLOBAL POWER DYNAMICS AND MARKET PROTECTIONISM

Globalization, in its present form, reconstructs old power relations through its structures, institutions, and processes. It involves the rapid spread of social, cultural, and economic practices of dominant groups. Nobel Prize winner Joseph Stiglitz (2002) argues that "the West has driven the globalization agenda, ensuring that it garners a disproportionate share of the benefits, at the expense of the developing world" (p. 7). He continues:

> It was not just that the more advanced industrial countries declined to open up their markets to the goods of the developing countries—for instance, keeping their quotas on a multitude of goods from textiles to sugar—while insisting that those countries open up their markets to goods of the wealthier countries; it was not just that the more advanced industrial countries continued to subsidize agriculture, making it difficult for the developing countries to compete, while insisting that the developing countries eliminate their subsidies on industrial goods. Looking at the "terms of trade"—the prices which developed and less developed countries get for the products they produce—after the last trade agreement in 1995 (the eighth), the net effect was to lower the prices some of the poorest countries in the world received relative to what they paid for their imports. The result was that some of the poorest countries in the world were actually made worse off. (Stiglitz, 2002, p. 7)

As Stiglitz notes, developed countries have emphasized that developing countries should remove government-based market protections, yet they protect their own markets through government subsidies. Similarly, former Federal Reserve Chairman Alan Greenspan questions the high levels of U.S. subsidies allocated to the farming industry, which makes fair competition impossible (Greenspan, 2007). While this practice protects American farmers, it is antithetical to the open market ideology espoused by the government to the international community, which is the premise that affords transnational corporations greater access to developing economies and increases the flow and mobility of capital coming into high-income economies. However, wide-open markets also mean the disruption of local markets and the creation of many other undesirable outcomes.

For example, due to the competitiveness of international markets, developing countries often find themselves competing with each other for low-wage jobs. In addition, in countries like India, which tends to have better educated workers, an overseas corporation can hire a computer support technician and compensate this person at the level of a semiskilled worker in a developed country, allowing the company to obtain a competitive edge in the global labor market. While the quality of jobs offered by transnationals are often poor and unskilled in nature, and seldom improve opportunities, the global poor are forced to accept them because they otherwise have limited opportunities.

## EDUCATION AND NEOLIBERAL MARKET PRACTICES

One of the key characteristics of globalization is a focus on neoliberal market policies. Neoliberalism refers to the practice of reducing market regulations, and simultaneously opening local markets to corporate ownership, while minimizing the role of governments (Beneria, Maria, Grown, and MacDonald, 2000). Due to the focus on competition, neoliberal economic policies have been driving neoliberal education policies. This includes increasing levels of private ownership in schools, corporate sponsorship of education, aligning school curriculum with the economy, and suppressing teacher compensation. The similarities in the economic policy directions at the global and local levels, and that of public schools are interrelated. In a global context, the World Bank supports the privatization of schools in developing countries, where it is argued that private schools are more cost effective (Carnoy, 2000).

In the same way, neoliberalism has been a major public policy that has been driving school reform in the United States. Using an efficiency model of schooling, the World Bank proposes that the more schools are privatized the more efficiency they will have and the less pressure there will be on governments to fund public education. Free-market or open-market ideology is inherently antithetical to high levels of government involvement. However, governments are expected to rush to the aide of corporations with taxpayers' money as incentives to start and maintain businesses, and to provide financial bailouts in times of recession. In this way, taxpayers carry the financial burden in the success and failures of corporations, while a lack of transparency and failed regulations lead to a shrinking global middle class and the expanding of the lower class. As privatized education benefits those who can afford to pay for higher quality schooling, the lower class is often relegated to an inferior education. The stratification in schools is socially reproducing around the world and particularly in the United States, because parental social class most often determines students' access to quality education.

## SCHOOLS AS MARKETS

In the United States, the No Child Left Behind (NCLB) Act of 2001 promotes a market approach to public education, which emphasizes that all schools meet federal mandates or lose funding or ultimately face closure. As a result, an emphasis on divestment and private management of educational institutions has become widespread as states seek more efficient ways to run schools. Moreover, the emphasis on for-profit schools has led to a focus on education as a major income generator. In 2000, it was estimated that globally, the education industry was worth $2 trillion in annual revenues (UNESCO, 2000, as cited in Hill, 2005, p. 206), and in 2006 it grew to $2.5 trillion (Redden, 2006). However, only a small portion of this impacts the compensation of teachers in the United States, who are among the lowest paid professionals in a field that is gendered and female labor intensive. Through privatization, a principal aim of the private sector is to make profits from education by focusing on efficiency and cost-savings that are typically associated with a scripted curriculum, high-stakes testing, and suppression of teacher autonomy and compensation. Lieberman and Haar (2003) document the big business of education, noting that collectively more than seventy-eight million people are employed in education in the United States. The authors propose that the education industry's expenditure is estimated to be more than $700 billon nationwide at all grade levels.

Similarly, Hill (2005) makes the connection between education and for-profit, market-based education models. He argues that "proponents of liberalization claim that 'private is better than public,' that 'competition improves standards,' that privatization and other liberalizing policies and processes nationally and globally (such as free trade) improve productivity and efficiency" (p. 259). The impact of neoliberal educational policies on schools includes increasing levels of private ownership, commercialism, and corporate sponsorship of education. The major aspects of neoliberal education are:

> Deregulation and decentralisation; the importation of new public managerialism into the management of schools and colleges and education services; a fiscal regime of cuts in publicly funded schooling and further education services; commercialization of and within schools; the charging of fees; outsourcing of services to privately owned companies; and the privatization and ownership of schools and colleges by private corporations. (Hill, 2005, p. 259)

Schools are not the only institutions that are impacted by neoliberalism, there has been a move to privatize everything from public schools, social security, health care, and prisons to all other forms of public services, essentially selling off most government operations to the private sector and to corporations (Aguayo, 2001). This is a key feature of economic globalization.

For example, in Chicago, federal mandates through NCLB models high accountability, while supporting social and economic systems that are linked to globalization (Lipman, 2004). Like the rest of the nation, in Chicago high-stakes testing is used to hold teachers responsible for broad disparities in school quality and student achievement, creating a highly divided and polarized education workforce. Lipman (2004) contends that neoliberal economic policies are driving neoliberal education policies, which "shift responsibility for inequality produced by the state onto parents, students, schools, communities, and teachers" (pp. 171–72). The NCLB reform agenda, which aims to close failing schools and award students' vouchers to attend private schools, seems to do very little in the way of systemically improving school quality, or mediating racial, gendered, and class disparities in education. Furthermore, these vouchers are far from being commensurate with the full cost of private education.

In order for states to comply with Title I funding, as well as the testing and accountability standards set by NCLB, they must be prepared to deal with the finances. In a policy brief on the financing of NCLB and its assessment mandates, the following conclusions were made.

> If states use only multiple-choice questions, they would spend $1.9 billion over a six-year period (from 2002 to 2008) to develop, score, and report results. If they used all open-ended questions, they would spend $5.3 billion. Testing with the then-current mix of multiple-choice and open-ended questions would cost $3.9 billion. NCLB would provide sufficient funds to cover the costs of the multiple choice only option, but not the other two. (Bracey, 2005, p. 9)

As noted above, federal financing and assessment directives dictate the types of tests that states administer to students—multiple-choice, which are some of the most ineffective types of assessments (Hilliard, 1995, 2003). However, these are the assessments that can be easily mass-produced by private companies. The designing and scoring of tests related to NCLB are estimated to be a $400 million per year business (Lutton, 2001). In this way, the government uses taxpayers' money to pay private companies to create and score high-stakes tests. Moreover, schools are sanctioned with the prospect of losing their Title I funding through the government, if they fail to meet appropriate school achievement standards, which are presumed to be evidenced by students' scores on these exams. NCLB has an adverse effect on minority students because they are often in schools that are already of a lower quality, with less qualified teachers, who are burdened with the task of teaching to the test.

Through NCLB, schools that do not meet adequate yearly progress in increasing school achievement, which often includes school districts with large minority populations, may be denied federal funding and they may face the ultimate prospect of school closure. Furthermore, the lack of teacher training for educators of urban students, when coupled with cultural bias in testing and insufficient school funding for urban districts, creates a situation that poses severe challenges for minority students' school success. In addition, in schools these minority students are relegated to a curriculum that addresses very little of their group contributions, indirectly telling them that they are not valued.

Torres (2005) argues that high-stakes testing, accountability, and standardization of the curriculum are no longer merely national or state issues, but are a part of an "international research agenda of bilateral and international organizations like the World Bank or the International Monetary Fund (IMF), and the ideas have saturated educational discourse in most parts of the globe" (ix). Most of the focus on global education has been about strengthening students' ability to compete in an increasingly knowledge-based economy (Monahan, 2005; Tye and Tye, 1992). While it is important for students to be able to participate and compete in the global economy; however, that is a part of the end, or one of the outcomes of education. When market principles and practices are the focus of education, it restricts what teachers can teach and what students learn. The market approach to education is narrowly conceived and provides little substance in terms of nurturing critical thinking and reflection, creating democratic citizens, promoting students' growth and development (Dewey, 1916), and even encouraging opportunities for fair trade. Shifting the focus from market to quality education might just help to improve school achievement rates across the nation.

Burbules and Torres (2000) find that the performance driven goals of the marketplace and the emphasis on the bottom line are some of the same goals that are shaping the political and ideological climate of public education. Furthermore, they state:

> There is a growing understanding that the neoliberal version of globalization, particularly as implemented (and ideologically defended) by bilateral, multilateral, and international organizations, is reflected in an educational agenda that privileges, if not directly imposes, particular policies for evaluation, financing, assessment, standards, teacher training, curriculum, instruction, and testing. (p. 15)

As the authors note, the downward flow of school policies and standards and assessments are prescriptive, and they tend to deskill teachers and make the classroom disengaging. These are some of the challenges faced by schoolteachers and administrators in schools that are already failing, and where teachers are forced to teach to the test.

Due to the increasing privatization of education and the growing disparities in school quality, parents often find themselves scrambling to find good schools. Between 2003 and 2004, the most recent years that national figures were available, thirty-one thousand students in the United States exercised the option to move to higher achieving schools (Campbell, 2006). As a result, school districts receiving an influx of students were often forced to set up mobile classrooms, hire extra teachers, and reroute their school buses to accommodate new students. When the low performers leave their current schools in search of new ones, they find themselves in schools that may receive them reluctantly, knowing that these students' scores may decrease the new school's overall scores. On the other hand, when high-achieving students in low-performing schools depart in hopes of finding a better school; it leaves their old school with fewer high performers, which negatively impacts the school's overall performance. This is the way education is done in the United States, but how does the nation perform comparatively?

## U.S. EDUCATION IN A GLOBAL CONTEXT

With the increasing focus on globalization and global competition for skilled workers, there have been many concerns about American education and the readiness of its workforce to compete in the global marketplace. Cross-national studies generally indicate that U.S. students underperform relative to their counterparts in other major developed countries (Birenbaum, Tatsuoka, and Xin, 2005; Mullis et al., 1997, 2000; O'Dwyer, 2005).

In 2007, Linda Darling-Hammond, the Charles E. Ducommun Professor of Education at Stanford University, gave testimony before the House Education and Labor

Committee on the Reauthorization of NCLB. She reported that most developed countries are surpassing the U.S. school achievement levels. She found that in the Programme for International Student Assessment (PISA) study, the "U.S. ranked 19th out of 40 countries in reading," and "20th in science, and 28th in math," and was outperformed by countries like Finland, South Korea, Singapore, and Canada, among others (Darling-Hammond, 2007). She also reported that most European and Asian countries educate and graduate almost all of their students. According to Darling-Hammond (2007), from the PISA study, it was clear that countries with high achievement levels, like Singapore, had a very well-trained teacher workforce, where the top third of high school graduating students are recruited into the teaching profession. This is a major challenge in the United States, where there is a growing teacher shortage and large numbers of unqualified teachers in classrooms.

The issues of low achievement levels and poor school quality in the United States are further illustrated in the National Academies' *Rising Above the Gathering Storm* (2007) report. The report drew much concern as the findings pointed to some unique challenges regarding the continued vitality of the economy and the gap in the increasing demands of "knowledge-intensive" industries such as science, mathematics, and technology engineering; and the low school achievement and graduation rates in these areas. The recommendations focused particular attention on strengthening these fields by providing support and incentives for increased research and development. The report called on policymakers to preserve the strategic and economic position of the United States by optimizing the science and technology sectors of the economy. It also recommended improving K–12 science and mathematics education, increasing federal investment in long-term research, producing more science and engineering graduates, and ensuring continued innovation through a number of modernization and tax realignment policies.

Similarly, Margret Spellings, the former secretary of education under President George W. Bush, contends that there is insufficient preparation and completion of higher education in the United States, especially within underserved and nontraditional groups. Her report indicates that only 17 percent of graduating seniors are considered proficient in mathematics and just 36 percent of graduating seniors are proficient in reading (Spellings, 2006, p. 10). In contrast, in the United Nations' Educational, Scientific and Cultural Organization based examination of math and language tests given to third and fourth graders in thirteen Latin American countries, the results were stunning as they revealed that students in Cuba's lowest-income schools outperformed most upper-middle-class students in the rest of the region (Carnoy, 2007a, 2007b). These findings were consistent with Harvard University's examination of educational achievement rates in Cuba (Harvard, 2002). Despite having strict governmental policies, Cuba provides access to quality schooling to all of its citizens, where parental social class is not significantly related to the quality of schools students attend. These results left some people wondering about how we can better educate students in the United States, and more specifically low-income students, as well as improve education for today's globalized world. What would happen if all students in the United States could get a high-quality education regardless of their race, class, and or gender? Certainly, that would be a giant step in the way of making the nation more democratic, and the prospects for improving social mobility and global competiveness would be addressed through a more inclusive and systemic process.

What is evident is that there is an international achievement gap, and if the United States is going to improve its education it must focus on quality education for all. The nation's poor achievement levels may very well be an indication that the emphasis on a market model of public schooling is taking away from what students are actually learning in schools. While legislators and corporations focus on pushing ahead with the big business of education, the nation's children are being left behind.

## CONCLUSION

In sum, as globalization recedes the borders around nations and increases the volume and efficiency of commerce (Friedman, 2005); it creates opportunities for economic growth. Increasing financial and technological interdependence across countries makes knowledge-based economies possible. However, unregulated globalization processes have resulted in inequalities and displacements that have affected the world's poorest citizens the most. The aim of globalization was to make markets more accessible by deregulating industries and reducing governmental controls, thus providing stakeholders, small and large, with opportunities to access new markets and to improve the supply of goods and services across countries (Stiglitz, 2006). However, corporate hegemony in the privatization of markets and schools has led to the decline of not only local markets and small businesses, but through neoliberal education, it has also diminished the quality of what students are learning in schools.

The failure to educate the poor is a major concern, and that failure in the United States has been in part a result of a market approach to education. In this way, the wealthy usually benefit from access to quality schools, while the poor struggle to receive a proper education. Comparatively, even across social class lines, the education offered in the United States wanes in the spotlight of the other major developed countries, and it fails to empower students and foster excellence in education. One of the prospects for a more democratic world and a more democratic America is to shift the focus from market to excellence in education, and making quality schools accessible to all students. In turn, this can help make the world more democratic, in education, in commerce, and also in social life.

## REFERENCES

Aguayo, M. (2001). *Privatized health care: U.S. system is not the way to go*. Retrieved September 25, 2007, from www.commondreams.org/views01/021301.htm.

Barnett, T., and Whiteside, A. (2002). *AIDS in the twenty-first century: Disease and globalization*. New York: Palgrave Macmillan.

Beneria, L., Maria F., Grown, C., and MacDonald, M. (2000). Introduction: Globalization and gender. *Feminist Economics, 6*(3), vii–xvii.

Bhavnani, K., Foran, J., and Kurian, P.A. (Eds.). 2003. *Feminist futures: Re-imagining women, culture and development*. New York: Zed Books.

Birenbaum, M., Tatsuoka, C., and Xin, T. (2005). Large-scale diagnostic assessment: Comparison of eighth graders' mathematics performance in the United States, Singapore, and Israel. *Assessment in Education Principles Policy and Practice, 12*(2), 167–81.

Blum, W. (1995). *Killing hope: U.S. military and CIA interventions since World War II*. Monroe, ME: Common Courage Press.

Bracey, G. (2005 June). *No child left behind: Where does the money go? (Policy Brief)* Tempe, AZ: Arizona State University, Education Policy Studies Laboratory. Retrieved August 24, 2007, from epsl.asu.edu/epru/documents /EPSL0506114-EPRU.pdf.

Brown, R. P. C. (1992). *Public debt and private wealth: Debt, capital flight and the IMF in Sudan*. New York: St. Martin's Press.

Burbules, N., and Torres, C. A. (Eds.) (2000). *Globalization and education: Critical perspectives*. New York: Routledge.

Campbell, D. (2006, February 23). Education, chutzpah and the GOP. *USA Today*, p. 13A.

Carnoy, M. (2000). Globalization and educational reform. In N. P. Stromquist and K. Monkman (Eds.), *Globalization and education: Integration and contestation across cultures* (pp. 43–61). New York: Rowman & Littlefield.

Carnoy, M. (2007a). *Cuba's academic advantage: Why students in Cuba do better in school*. Stanford, CA: Stanford University Press.

Carnoy, M. (2007b). *Why low income children excel in Cuba*. Retrieved May 1, 2007, from www.mercurynews.com/portlet/article/html/fragments/print_article.jsp?art cleId=5754067 &siteId=568.

CNN. (2007). Dog biscuits added to recall list. Retrieved September 20, 2007, from edition .cnn.com/2007/US/04/05/pet.deaths/index.html.

Darling-Hammond, L. (2007). *Testimony before the house education and labor committee on NCLB*. Retrieved September 14, 2007, from www.forumforeducation.org/foruminaction/index.php?page=399.

Davis, A. Y. (Speaker). (2001). *Prison industrial complex* (compact disc). Oakland, CA: AK Press.

Dewey, J. (1916). *Democracy and education: An introduction to the philosophy of education*. New York: Macmillan.

Doob, C. (1999). *Racism: An American cauldron* (third ed.). New York: Longman.

Du Bois, W. E. B. (1946). *The world and Africa: An inquiry into the part which Africa has played in world history*. New York: International Publishers.

Friedman, T. (2005). *The world is flat: A brief history of the twenty-first century*. New York: Farrar, Straus and Giroux.

Giddens, A. (1994). *Beyond left and right: The future of radical politics*. Stanford, CA: Stanford University Press.

Greenspan, A. (2007) *The age of turbulence: Adventures in a new world*. New York: Penguin.

Harvard University. (2002). *Educational achievement in contemporary Cuba*. Retrieved May 15, 2007, from www.gse.harvard.edu/news/features/cuba04012002.html.

Hill, D. (2005). Globalisation and its educational discontents: Neoliberalisation and its impacts on education workers' rights, pay and conditions. *International Studies in Sociology of Education, 15*(3), 257–82.

Hilliard, A. G., III. (1995). Either a paradigm shift or no mental measurement. *Psych Discourse, 76*(10), 6–20.

Hilliard, A. G., III. (2003). No mystery: Closing the achievement gap between Africans and excellence. In T. Perry, C. Steel, and A. Hilliard (Eds.), *Young, gifted, and black: Promoting high achievement among African-American students* (pp. 131–65). Boston: Beacon Press.

Kozol, J. (1991). *Savage inequalities: Children in America's schools.* New York: Crown.

Kozol, J. (2006). *The shame of the nation: The restoration of apartheid in schooling in America.* New York: Random House.

Lieberman, M., and Haar, C. K. (2003). *Public education as a business: Real cost and accountability.* Lanham, MD: Scarecrow Press.

Lipman, P. (2004). *High stakes education: Inequality, globalization, and urban school reform.* New York: RoutledgeFalmer.

Lutton, L. (2001). Testing, testing, the mis-education of George W. Bush. InTheseTimes.com. Retrieved August, 27, 2007, from www.inthesetimes.com/issue/25/15/lutton2515.html.

Matanle, I. (1994). *History of World War II, 1939–1945.* London: Tiger Books International.

Millennium Development Goals. (2007). *United Nations Development Goals.* Retrieved June 8, 2007, from www.un.org/millenniumgoals/.

Monahan, T. (2005). *Globalization, technological change, and public education.* New York: Routledge.

Mullis, I. V. S., Martin, M. O., Beaton, A. E., Gonzalez, E. J., Kelly, D. L., and Smith, T. A. (1997). *Mathematics achievement in the primary school years: IEA's third international mathematics and science study (TIMSS).* Boston: Center for the Study of Testing, Evaluation and Educational Policy, Boston College.

Mullis, I. V. S., Martin, M. O., Gonzalez, E. J., Gregory, K. D., Garden, R. A., O'Connor, K.M., Chrostowski, S. J., and Smith, T. A. (2000). *TIMSS 1999 international mathematics report: Findings from IEA's repeat of the third international mathematics and science study at the eighth grade.* Chestnut Hill, MA: Boston College.

National Academies. (2007). *Rising above the gathering storm.* Retrieved April 4, 2007, from www.nap.edu/catalog.php?record_id=11463#toc.

National Commission on Excellence in Education [NCEE]. (1983). *A nation at risk.* Washington, DC: U.S. Government Printing Office.

*New York Times.* (2007). China signs pact to ban export of lead based Toys. Retrieved September 20, 2007, from www.nytimes.com/2007/09/ 12/business/worldbusiness/12lead. html?n=To%2fReference%2fTimes%20Topics%2fSubjec%2fT%2fToys&_r=1adxnnl=&oref=slogin&adxnnlx=1190315960-1qar5i7aX+9VwPXPvkAkIQ.

O'Dwyer, L. (2005). Examining the variability of mathematics performance and its correlation using data from TIMSS'95 and TIMSS'99. *Educational Research and Evaluation, 11*(2), 155–77.

Office of the High Commissioner of Human Rights. (2007). *Universal declaration of human rights.* Retrieved September 16, 2007, from www.unhchr.ch/udhr/.

Offiong, D. (2001). *Globalisation, post-neodependency and poverty in Africa.* Enugu, Nigeria: Fourth Dimension Publishing Co., Ltd.

Redden, E. (2006, December). No risk, no rewards. *Inside Higher Education.* Retrieved August 31, 2007, from www.insidehighered.com/news/2006/12/07/for_profit.

Robertson, R. (1985). The relativization of societies, modern religion, and globalization. In T. Robbins, W. C. Shepherd, and J. McBride (Eds.), *Cults, culture, and the law* (pp. 31–42). Chico, CA: Scholars Press.

Robertson, R. (1992). *Globalization: Social theory and global culture.* Thousand Oaks, CA: Sage.

Rodney, W. (1982). *How Europe underdeveloped Africa.* Washington, DC: Howard University Press.

Spellings Report (2006). *A test of leadership: Charting the future of U.S. higher education.* A report of the commission appointed by Secretary of Education Margaret Spellings. Retrieved

March 3, 2007, from www.ed.gov/about/bdscomm/list/hiedfuture/reports/pre-pub-report
.pdf.

Spring, J. (2006). *Pedagogies of globalization: The rise of educational security state.* Mahwah,
NJ: Lawrence Erlbaum.

Stiglitz, J. (2002). *Globalization and its discontents.* New York: W. W. Norton and Company.

Stiglitz, J. (2006). *Making globalization work.* New York: W. W. Norton and Company.

Torres, C. (2005). The globalization question. In the foreword to T. Monahan, *Globalization,
technological change, and public education* (pp. vii–xi). New York: Routledge.

Tye, B., and Tye, K. (1992). *Global education: A study of school change.* Orange, CA: Interdependence Press.

Wichterich, C. (2000). *The globalized woman: Reports from a future of inequality* (P. Camiller,
Trans.). New York: Zed Books. (Original work published in German in 1998).

## Chapter Three

# Globalization, Reparations, Education, and Social Conflicts: Toward a Reparations Pedagogy, a Homocentric Approach

### Greg Wiggan and Kenneth Wilburn

"Wretched is he who injures a poor man. If you ignore him, listeners will wish to do what you want. You will beat him through their reproof."

Ptahhotep, 2388 BCE

In an era of increasing levels of globalization, transnational corporations and overseas investors benefit immensely from high levels of efficiencies brought about through technological innovations and global policies that allow for greater market penetration in developing economies (Brecher, Costello, and Smith, 2000; Cavanagh and Mander, 2002, Chossudovsky, 1997; Chomsky, 2006; Cohen, 2001; Firebaugh, 2003). For example, in 2004, the revenues of General Motors were $191.4 billion, which was larger than the gross domestic product of more than 148 countries (Stiglitz, 2006, pp. 187–88). Furthermore, in 2005, Wal-Mart's revenues reached $285.2 billion, which was "larger than the combined GDP (Gross Domestic Product) of sub-Saharan Africa" (p. 188).

In education, globalization is receiving mounting levels of interest and concern about international competition and changes in the American population demographics, which reflect increasing trends in minorities and immigrant students in the nation's public schools. As a result, through the No Child Left Behind (NCLB) Act of 2001, states have been placing greater emphasis on accountability and preparing students for the global economy.

Since the early 1990s, globalization has been one of the most central and spirited topics of discussion. This dialogue has surrounded issues of job outsourcing, international sweatshops, corporate welfare through government incentives, and international fair trade standards (Aslandeigui and Summerfield, 2000; Bales, 1999; Chomsky, 2006; Stiglitz, 2002). While a global system was present in the old worlds, slave and colonial societies, and in the postcolonial world (Cabral, 1969/1970; Fanon, 1952/1967; Memmi, 1957/1965) in terms of complex patterns of international trade between the colonized and the colonizers (Rodney, 1982), the contemporary emergence of transnationalization and hyperized levels of capital flow are innovative and unique to the modern process known as globalization (Giddens, 1994; Robertson,

1985; Stiglitz, 2006). Globalization has to do with accelerated levels of integration in the global economy and in social and political life resulting from social and economic connectivity (Giddens, 1994). It is the process in the world system that increases economic and technological integration around the globe.

Robertson (1992) argues that although the current global economy was developed in more recent times, meaning the last two decades, it has a long genealogical history. The modern world economy is not an entirely new phenomenon; it grew out of previous systems, most notably through the transatlantic slave trade and the global interdependences that it created among colonizers and colonies between the late fourteenth and early twentieth centuries (Williams, 1944/1994). During this time, race was created as a construct to form social categories based on skin color and to produce new divisions of labor that were justified by group superiority claims. In this chapter, we use race to signify the increased sense of phenotypical differentiations and discriminations that were operationalized as a result of slavery and colonialism, and then legitimated with western theology, social science research, and through the legal system. While race merely refers to the physical appearance of an individual or group, ethnicity addresses the cultural characteristics that individuals and groups share such as language, religion, food, clothes, and political beliefs. The former is a result of the transatlantic slave trade and the dehumanization of, and prejudice toward, people who were forced to work for free.

Slavery and colonialism created systems of commerce and international flows of capital investments that went to English banks, Swiss accounts, and to the banks of other colonial and slave beneficiaries (Cohen, 2001, pp. 68–69). Due to increased forms of resistance in the slave societies and colonies, there were many attempts to change the geopolitical economy to make it more humane to human rights issues and to black and brown (other nonwhites) people in general. As a result, the world economy transitioned through racialized systems of slavery, colonialism, neocolonialism, imperialism, and then into modern global capitalism or globalization (Chossudovsky, 1997; Harvey, 1999, 2003, 2005; Wallerstein, 1974). Among the contemporary "old slave money" beneficiaries are financial institutions like Bank of America, Wachovia Bank, J. P. Morgan, and schools like Brown University and Salem College (Crews, 1998; Farmer-Paellmann, 2007). Robinson (2004) notes:

> In order to survive, capitalism requires constant access to new sources of cheap labor, land, raw materials (crops and minerals), and markets. This imperative to expand led to a period of colonialism and imperialism involving the conquest and subjugation by European power of other peoples and societies. Latin America was first conquered, colonized, and incorporated in this expanding world capitalist system between 1492 and the 1530s. In Africa this process began with the slave trade in the 1500s, and by the 1890s almost the entire continent had been formally annexed as European colonies. Asia suffered a similar fate from the 1500s into the twentieth century, as did the Middle East from the eighteenth to the twentieth century. (p. 3)

Essentially, modern global capitalism is the offspring of slavery and colonialism.

During the twentieth century, and especially between the 1990s and early 2000s, the economic success of globalization was celebrated (Eitzen and Zinn, 2006; Firebaugh,

2003; Friedman, 2005). Investors saw great increases in the flow of capital brought about by compression in the international labor market, and economic efficiencies gained through computerization and e-commerce (Friedman, 2005; Monahan, 2005). However, these gains came at great social costs in equality, and resulted in mounting conflicts over power, scarce resources, and global leadership (Huntington, 1996; Ritzer, 2004). Global integration in the modern world system has generated international resistance movements that have major consequences for the well-being of the world. For example, in the September 11, 2001, attacks on the United States, the hijackers targeted the World Trade Center, a major international financial institution, and the Pentagon, the nation's central military defense system (Ritzer, 2004). These buildings symbolically represent major establishments that pertain to global commerce and international defense, systems of globalization (Ritzer, 2004, pp. 171–74; Singer, 2002). The hijackers chose these monuments because of their significance and symbolisms in the world system.

The September 11 attacks and the subsequent war on terrorism throughout the world suggest that there are crucial opposing views to globalization and a mounting international climate of tensions over foreign policy and ideology governing economic forces. The growth in economic globalization parallels an increasing concern with conflicts and intense levels of military spending and rising global militarism. Seminal works like Benjamin Barber's *Jihad vs. McWorld* (1996) and Thomas Friedman's *The Lexus and the Olive Tree* (1999), just to name a few, have chronicled the conflicts and paradoxes of globalization and tensions over its influences.

While the economic processes of globalization are often emphasized, issues of cultural hegemony, and conflicts and countermovements receive less attention (Kaldor, 2007; Tusicisny, 2004; Yudice, 2003). Militarisms in globalization have created a globally intensified era of ethnic and racial conflicts. For example, the growing level of U.S. military presence in the Middle East has increased tensions between the Islamic world and the Western world (Kaldor, 2007). This conjures up religious, racial, and ethnic conflicts, as salient cultural and ethnic identity characteristics of each group are emphasized in a kind of xenophobia. As a result, people traveling or relocating to the West or the Middle East are greeted with suspicion when in the region of the other. For example, a seventeen-year-old student from Denbigh High School in Luton, northwest London, was suspended from school because she wore a *jilbab*, a full-length gown worn by some Muslim women (BBC, 2007; Soriano, 2006). Bombing and terror threats across Great Britain influenced the school officials' actions and they overreacted, possibly because of fear, stereotypes, and lingering racism.

In 2001, the United Nations held a world conference against racism in South Africa, a place where postapartheidism and racism remain widespread (Coomey, 2007; Manda, 2004; Maran, 2002; Pattman, 2007).[1] Among the topics raised were slavery, reparations, Zionism and racism, and xenophobia. While the general belief is that "apartheidism" has ended in South Africa and that racial struggles have subsided, the nation suffers from its past and also from contemporary structural racism through postapartheidism. Currently, South Africa is the world's leader in inequality. Fifty-seven percent of blacks live below the internationally defined poverty level of $1 a day, while white South Africans from the apartheid era continue to own 85 percent of the country's wealth. In contrast, 80 percent of the country's black population own only 5 percent of the economy (Coomey, 2007). This makes conflicts and tensions a pervasive feature of life for South Africans (Keller, 1994; Masland and Rossouw, 2005). A growing awareness of this may also engender more sympathy in the West for Robert Mugabe's controversial land redistribution program in Zimbabwe, South Africa's northern neighbor, which inherited similar inequalities from Rhodesia, the subimperial creation of South Africa's former premier, the Oxonian Cecil Rhodes.

Similarly, in the United States, the history of slavery, Jim Crow, and segregation affects race relations and perceptions among blacks and whites (Massey, 1993; Meyer, 2000). Racial differences and tensions between the groups stem from historical processes and contemporary racialized structural barriers to quality education, equal employment, affordable housing, and just treatment in the judicial system, among other things (Kozol, 2006; Massey, 1993). The 2008 presidential campaign victory of Barack Obama presents some hope of improving race relations in the United States. The first nonwhite person to become president of the United States symbolically represents the progress the nation is making in race relations. However, because the U.S. social class system can be viewed as a racial hierarchy, racialized distributions of wealth and power in the country have to be addressed and improved by President Obama and his administration. Blacks earn only 62 percent of the earnings of their white counterparts. The higher the social class, the more whites there are. In contrast, the lower class is bulging with poor black, brown, and white workers (Bullock, 2006).[2]

The nation's residential patterns reflect the racialized power relations and systems of wealth, with a shrinking middle class (Skocpol, 2000), and where segregation of wealth blocks unwanted racial interactions at the neighborhood level and through school segregation. Although school redistricting efforts across the nation have been aimed at helping to improve integration, neighborhood and school segregation are widespread and are the social norm (Kozol, 1991, 2006). Schools are one place where the dialogue on race relations and conflicts can be initiated. It is the place where a meaningful conversation can be started, as it is the space where these topics are often raised in the presence of the other (Delpit, 1995). If the nation is going to continue to improve racial and ethnic relations and create a more democratic social landscape, then schools will have to play a crucial role in facilitating this noble process. In this chapter we explore the challenges of teaching about race and ethnicity, and we present an innovative pedagogy for teaching about the sensitive topic of reparations for slavery as part of an inclusive homocentric democratic process. The following section further examines international conflicts and race relations in America. This is followed by an analysis of public education.

## RACE RELATIONS IN THE SOCIAL
## CONTEXT OF THE UNITED STATES

As suggested earlier, in the United States the tragic events of September 11 are perpetual reminders of global conflicts and terrorism. The nation's elevated terror alerts invoke concerns about international security and threats of another possible attack. In airports and other public facilities, the religious, racial, and ethnic identities of Middle Easterners raises high scrutiny, fears, and suspicion in the minds of most Americans (Chomsky, 2006; Huntington, 2004). The fears among Americans arise not only surrounding the threat of violence, but also in global leadership, as most ponder the recent growth and success of the Asian economies relative to the apparent slump in the U.S. economy (Friedman, 2005). Furthermore, job outsourcing, job scarcity, and increasing emigration have created additional conflicts between racial and ethnic groups who compete for what are perceived as limited opportunities (Green, 1997). The issue of immigration is illustrated by the debates about immigrants in the United States, and, more specifically, the presence of undocumented immigrants that come mostly from Mexico (Beyond the Border, 2007; Mexico, 2007). As new immigrants enter the shores of the United States, they find themselves in a country that is already polarized by black and white racial segregation. They enter a nation where Sunday is the most religious day of the week, and where it is the most racially segregated day. The racial lines in religious worship are striking, and intolerance of other religions and belief systems is often intoxicating.

The ideological difference between most blacks and whites is a part of the social history of the nation and its practices of exclusion. Much of this results from slavery, Jim Crow, segregation, and group suspicions and social discontents among the underserved (Meyer, 2000; Omi and Winant, 1986). In 2005, the issues of discontent and conflict were illustrated in the great challenges that arose from Hurricane Katrina in New Orleans, as seemingly large numbers of citizens, predominately African Americans, were left starving and dying weeks after the hurricane ended. With little to no response from the Federal Emergency Management Agency (FEMA) or the U.S. government, people around the world were able to see that "America, the land of opportunity," is not so opportunistic (FEMA, 2005). The world observed as thousands of black and brown residents held on for their dear lives, as they filled the New Orleans Superdome trying to escape the wrath and aftermath of Hurricane Katrina.

As the days went by, the smell of dead bodies and human excrement filled the air of New Orleans, and television cameras presented images of people who were left devastated by the hurricane and by the lack of response from the government (Katrina, 2005; Nossiter, 2007). Racial tensions surged when the images of those who were most affected, mostly black residents of New Orleans, filled television screens (Livingston, 2005/2006). Then the images shifted quickly from those of displaced residents and no governmental response, to ones of black residents looting supermarkets and neighborhood stores, recasting the issue from natural disaster to black social deviance (News24, 2005).

Both the events of September 11 and Hurricane Katrina remind us of the conflicts stemming from hegemonic power inequalities and racialization both in the United States and abroad. The government's response to Hurricane Katrina made many African Americans angry because this was yet another example of how blacks are mistreated in America. It provoked unresolved issues surrounding slavery and the lack of an official apology from the government and also the need for reparations and equity in ownership (Feagin, 2000; Kershnear, 2004).

The nation's racial stratification is evident in the distribution of wealth across the country, where much like South Africa whites are the power elites (Feagin, 2000; Masland and Rossouw, 2005). Wealth disparities are compounded by neighborhood and school segregation because most black and brown people are lower social class, and live in separate space and attend inferior schools that are affected by district- and school-level segregation (Kozol, 2006).

The issue of race and school segregation was highlighted in Jena, Louisiana, at Jena High School where a group of black students had to ask permission to occupy a tree under the white section of the school (Reuter, 2007). This invasion of space at the school was compounded by the hanging of nooses from the tree and then, subsequently, to school fights that resulted in all of the black students involved facing serious charges (Brandon, 2007). Due to the long history of whites lynching black males predominantly in the South, the hanging of nooses was a painful reminder about the approximately 3,400 black males who were murdered by lynching in the South between 1882 and 1968 (Perloff, 2000). This incident was followed by a number of noose hangings in high schools and in universities. At Columbia University, an African American professor came into work to find a noose hanging on her door (Boxer, 2007). Similar incidents occurred at the University of Maryland and other institutions of higher learning (Reuter, 2007).

## Education and Tensions about Race

In the United States, it is often difficult to introduce issues of racial justice and racial reparations because it incites anger. For this reason, there is often a public silence about the issue. Those who dare to raise the topic are quickly dismissed or sidelined by the majority and other minorities who fear that this will make most people upset. In history and sociology courses in most colleges and universities, reparations are most often left unaddressed or as a quick drive-by topic (Coates, 2004). Teachers and students may feel uncomfortable with the topic because it raises a lot of sensibilities about the history of the United States and the oppressive treatment that African Americans and other minorities have endured (America, 2000; Brooks, 2004; Feagin, 2000; Rebollo-Gil and Moras, 2006; Schedler, 1998).

Raising the topic of reparations often has consequences, infuriating those who believe that this is an issue of the past and that we need to move forward, forgetting that modern global capitalism grew out of slavery and colonialism. Others might feel a deep sense of guilt when the topic is raised. Balfour (2003) notes the backlash and reprisals from whites when the issue of slave reparations is discussed, creating a more collective hegemonic response and repositioning of power against the already afflicted (Boylan, 2002). Thus, the topic has been suppressed, especially in schools. While there has been much written on slavery, there have been very few scholarly works written on how to teach about oppression, free labor, and remunerations, and, more specifically, about reparations for slavery. There has been a silence in the literature regarding a pedagogy for reparations.

## THE STATE OF THE LITERATURE

In this research, several searches were employed to identify the available literature on reparations and education. The electronic searches were conducted using databases such as: ERIC (Education Resources Information Center), Academic Search Premiere, Education Research Complete, JSTOR, and Cambridge Scientific Abstracts, among others. The search terms included *reparations* paired with *pedagogy, education, curriculum, classroom,* and *school issues* in the abstracts and titles for the years 1954 to 2007. The search yielded fourteen documents in ERIC and Academic Search Premiere and three documents in Education Research Complete. The JSTOR database identified five documents containing the key words in the titles and abstracts when all disciplines were searched. The Cambridge Scientific Abstracts identified ten documents that met the search criteria. After excluding duplicate documents and identifying the relevance of the works, twelve documents were identified as pertinent to the topic of reparations and education. Some of the significant works included Rodney Coates's (2004) article "If a Tree Falls in the Wilderness: Reparations, Academic Silences, and Social Justice" in *Social Forces*, "Teaching Japanese-American Incarceration" by Karen L. Miksch and David Ghere (2004) published in *History Teacher*, and Andrea Smith's (2006) "Boarding School Abuses, Human Rights and Reparations" in *Social Justice*. Other pertinent references included Rita Maran's (2002) "A Report from the United Nations World Conference against Racism, Racial Discrimination, Xenophobia, and Related Intolerance, Durban, South Africa, 2001" appearing in *Social Justice*. While there were no specific scholarly works on how to teach about reparations, or a pedagogy of reparations, these articles were helpful in addressing some of the broader issues surrounding the topic. In addition, the references in these articles were explored for relevant sources.

Besides Coates (2004), the only other closest reparations literature is Miksch and Ghere's (2004) work on teaching about Japanese American incarceration, a similar but different topic. In their work, the authors argue for curriculum development aimed at addressing the treatment of Japanese Americans during World War II. They propose that students should have to read about the history of Japanese Americans in the United States. They provide suggestions for classroom adoption such as Bonnie Dry's and Dolores Danska's video, *Japan Bashing*, which can be used to provide a social context for the Japanese experience in the United States. Miksch and Ghere (2004) propose that teachers should present students with writing assignments that require them to take the position of Japanese Americans. The writings build students' critical thinking skills about the issue of social justice. In addition, the authors propose using student-led mock legal debates on the treatment of Japanese Americans to build understandings about the illegal aspects of group oppression.

While the Japanese were awarded reparations for the treatment they endured in the United States during World War II, there has not been the same logical outcome for African Americans and Native Americans. Coates (2004) argues that the primary purpose of slavery and other forms of racial discrimination was to secure profits.

Therefore, an appropriate social justice response is needed from those who profited, and from those who continue to benefit from its legacy. Like the Japanese, in the case of the Jewish Holocaust during World War II, reparations were paid to those who were affected. Through the United Nations, Germany was required to repay the Jews for years of free labor and for the Holocaust under the Nazi government (Jewish Virtual Library, 2007). In addition, most of these victims were repatriated to the Middle East as part of the remuneration. Similarly, the Japanese Americans received financial reparations for the tragic treatment they endured during World War II, in the amount of $20,000 for all those who were affected (Howard-Hassmann, 2004, p. 827).

The U.S. government acknowledged the injustice it committed against Japanese Americans during World War II. This resulted in a presidential apology and a Congressional disbursement of reparations to victims (Miksch and Ghere, 2004). In a similar case through the United Nations after Operation Desert Storm in 1991, Iraq was required to repay the Kuwaiti people for casualties and economic resources lost, namely oil, during the invasion masterminded by Saddam Hussein (Osabu-Kle, 2000).

Similarly, Smith (2006) examines the reparations movement for "American Indians" and the centuries of violence committed against them. However, there has been a roadblock in the discussion on the Native American Holocaust and also the Holocaust of Africans and African Americans and their reparations (Clarke, 1993). There have been no reparations for these two groups. Bolner (1968) argues that reparations are

> [b]enefits extended in various forms to those injured by racial discrimination practiced by, or with the acquiescence of, the government of a representative democracy. Reparations are not to be understood as an indiscriminate bonus for nonwhites, but merely as payment of damages to those nonwhites who have been injured by racial discrimination. (p. 41)

Repaying the abused for four hundred years of free labor and for racial exploitation and injustices, has been interpreted as being adverse treatment for whites (Braithwaite, 1999). Racial minorities have a justifiable claim for reparations for institutionalized racial discrimination, and from those who have benefited from their free labor like Bank of America, Wachovia Bank, and J. P. Morgan, among others (Farmer-Paellmann, 2007). "Reparations consists in the appropriate corrective justice response to injury by an offender" (Winter 2007, p. 375).

Peggy McIntosh (1995) writes about white privilege and the advantages that whites receive from direct and indirect acquiescence of years of slavery and racial discrimination. America (2000) argues that whites possess an "unacknowledged inheritance" that they received from four hundred years of practices and decision making that today benefits their social class status and social mobility. This privilege is gained through international systems that create wealth at the expense of others; in this case, in free labor, stolen inventions, and discriminatory hiring and compensation practices (Asante, 2003). All of these issues have great implications for educators and for schools.

In the next section we present an innovative pedagogy for teaching about racism and racial reparations, which seeks to mediate conflicts and tensions surrounding the issue by framing a homocentric approach. While the examples here are from university classrooms, this method can be adapted to other educational levels and classrooms dealing with diversity issues.

## METHOD

The academic environment for this project on teaching about reparations for the transatlantic slave trade is that of a major state university in the southeast with over twenty-four thousand students enrolled. This is a majority white institution with an African American population of over 15 percent, a female population of about 61 percent, and whose origin in the early twentieth century was firmly linked to teacher education. An upper-level "History of Africa" course is used in the sample. This course was selected because it is one of the more popular writing-intensive history courses, and one in which reparations is covered at length. Students passing the course may fulfill a variety of curricula requirements, such as a world history course, toward their bachelor's degree in history. In addition, the course may be taken by education majors as a general education course to satisfy three hours of their twelve-hour social science requirement. It may also fulfill requirements for a writing-intensive course, or as an upper-level history course for the history minor, or a course required in the African and African American studies major and minor. Some students also take the course out of personal interest as an elective.

The course's student population is often a bit more evenly balanced than that of the university. African Americans often have a greater interest in Africa, which would explain their larger enrollment numbers. As for female students, the university's history is steeped in teacher education, which may explain why there are sometimes more women in the course than men. This school typically educates students from working-class backgrounds. For this study, student data are used from the 2005 and 2006 academic school years. The data that are presented here are part of a larger research project aimed at understanding how teacher pedagogy can help promote social awareness and improve race relations. Because this course is taught once per year, the data were collected at the end of each year. Since African Americans generally come into the course with strong feelings supporting reparations while white students tend to be the most guarded, especially the males, the study aimed to examine how white students' perceptions about race relations and reparations were influenced by the course and by reparations pedagogy. In all, nine former students were contacted for the study and six students responded: four white males and two white females. Purposive sampling was used to target undergraduate history majors (Lincoln and Guba, 1985). The study proposed to know how white students responded to reparations pedagogy. These students gave the researchers permission to reproduce their journal reflections about race relations and reparations. The students' views on reparations were in no way attached to their grade in the course.

One of the course's primary pedagogical instruments is the summary/reaction journal. In this writing-intensive assignment students summarize in essay format and in academic English all course activities, including lectures, readings, discussions, films, and online assignments. Once the readings and class discussions for each section are completed, students have to react to content in the summary by "pulling the past into their own experience" in a paragraph or two to express the philosophy of history that the past is personally relevant. Here shy students reluctant to provoke controversy in animated class discussions can share their insights, concerns, and consternation by privately, intellectually engaging the instructor. The journals enable the instructor to share, anonymously, important points kept private during class discussions. The invaluable summary/reaction journal helps the instructor get a sense of each student's reasoning. A content analysis of the students' journal reflection was conducted, identifying themes that addressed how the students responded to the topic of reparations during the course (Strauss and Corbin, 1998). The following section discusses reparations pedagogy from a homocentric view.

## REPARATIONS PEDAGOGY, THE HOMOCENTRIC VIEW IN ACTION

In his wisdom literature, the ancient Kemetic (Egyptian) master teacher Ptahhotep (2388 BCE) argues that one of the main aims of education is to help eliminate strife and conflicts among groups and to bring harmony. In his manuscript, one of the oldest in the world, Ptahhotep provides strategies for avoiding conflict, greed, and violence in achieving unity (Hilliard, Williams, and Damali, 1987). Ptahhotep understood and espoused the virtues of having knowledge about our common human family.

In spite of the international and local conflicts and tensions surrounding different racial and ethnic groups, there is a commonality in the human experience that links us all to the same family. The homocentric view of humanity poses that "the contested history of humans" can be understood as synonymous with "the contested history of Africans," for we now know that all humans have African parentage. Kenya, Tanzania, portions of southern Africa and Ethiopia make up the "cradleland of humanity" (Oliver, 1999). Ethiopia is home to some of the world's earliest human fossil remains, including those of the 3.5 million-year-old *Australopithecine afarensis*, also known as "Lucy," or Dinkenesh, as she is called in Ethiopia, meaning "she is wonderful" (Marcus, 2002).

By homocentric, we mean human-centered. Homocentricity is based on both our human past and present—our African origins and our present-day global presence. Taking the long view of human development, homocentricity asserts that *Homo sapiens* have far more in common than ethnic, national, or socially constructed racial differences suggest.

When one sees the human past as the African past, we can appreciate that all of us in this complex world are members of the same extended African family. With our African family members in mind, we humans may more easily become arbiters in our complex sibling disputes about Eurocentrism, Sinocentrism, superiority, and inferiority claims, among other social divisions.

That we are all of African descent has profound implications. For example, in the 1960s the Africanist historian Terence Ranger was keen to liberate history in Africa from the imperial European perspective. Working in the history department at the University of Dar es Salaam in Tanzania, Ranger (1971) advised scholars to research

"African adaptation, African choice, [and] African initiative." He did not mean this in a nationalist sense that could result in court histories supporting African dictators in newly liberated colonies, but rather in comparative regional, continental, and world perspectives. Ranger's views have taken on far greater meaning than he imagined in the 1960s. Given our origins in Africa, Ranger's African initiative can now truly be understood in a global perspective—the homocentric initiative.

In the classroom, before a discussion of reparations begins, we define history, relate its meaning to Africa, examine its relationship to reparations for the transatlantic slave trade (Berry, 2005), and introduce the primary and secondary sources used in our reparations project. After introducing these themes, students are challenged to see the world's humans outside Africa in their continental contexts as African Europeans, African Asians, and African Americans. This provocative human perspective helps students see reparations as an old, serious, unresolved family dispute—brothers, sisters, and cousins wronged by their own family members. Students then learn that in international law, crimes against humanity have no statute of limitations. As Ali Mazrui (1994) once wrote when he applied international law to African tradition:

> [In Africa] if a member of one tribe was killed by another tribe, a debt was immediately created, owed by the tribe of the killer to the tribe of the victim. This debt was not subject to any statute of limitation. The debt stood until it was paid. It could be paid with heads of cattle—or with blood. If the debt was not paid there was a serious threat of long festering feud between the two tribes. Because responsibility was collective, individuals in each community themselves could be unnecessarily at risk for a killing for which they were themselves not *directly* responsible. . . . The civilized way out was to pay the debt in cows and goats. In other words, the civilized way out was to pay *reparations*. (p. 15)

Thus, our centuries-old family dispute adversely affects family harmony today, and will continue until some form of reconciliation occurs.

Perhaps there is a remedy; perhaps there are several; or perhaps there are no remedies, the instructor suggests to the class. All possibilities are on the family table to be viewed and discussed through homocentric eyes. Before that discussion can be effected at the family table, however, students engage primary and secondary sources to help them overcome the immediate stereotypical reaction many Americans have to what Randall Robinson (2000) called *The Debt*. As Congressman Chaka Fattah of Pennsylvania once wrote:

> Say the words reparations for slavery in a crowded room. Then watch the stereotypes and anxieties roll in like thunderheads: Hands move protectively over wallets or extend to receive a check; eyes scan the floor for an escape hatch or roll back in exasperation. (2001)

In 2007 the movement for reparations is twofold. One group concentrates its efforts generally on remedy for the descendants of slaves in the United States and the Diaspora. The National Coalition of Blacks for Reparations in America (N'COBRA) and the Reparations Coordinating Committee (RCC) are leaders in this movement. Within the U.S. Congress, Representative John Conyers seeks passage of House Resolution 40, named after "40 acres and a mule," which derives from General William

Sherman's Field Order 15, and calls upon the federal government to facilitate remedy (Berry, 2005; Hobgood, 2005). In the courts Deadria Farmer-Paellmann and co-counsels have achieved some success against seventeen corporations involved in the Atlantic slave trade. That case was docketed before the Supreme Court of the United States on May 22, 2007 (Farmer-Paellmann, 2002, 2007), but failed to receive a favorable decision.[3]

A second group of reparations activists seek remuneration for Africans in Africa largely due to the maleffects of colonialism, imperialism, and the oceanic slave trade. In 1992 the Organization of African Unity's (OAU) Group of Eminent Persons for Reparations led this effort. The core arguments were eloquently articulated by Ali Mazrui (1994) in his Abiola Address at the African Studies Association. The class is introduced to both movements, but discussions often focus more on the United States.

Primary and secondary resources used to prepare for discussion include books, speeches, legislation, litigation, and film. First, students read, review, and discuss Manu Herbstein's (2002) *Ama: A Story of the Atlantic Slave Trade*, which uses history and fiction to recreate African and western slavery through the eyes of a Ghanaian woman. This is truly a homocentric book because the author's ethnicity, nationalities, gender, and religion add to the mix of remedy.

Next, they read David Dennard's (2001) Southeastern Regional Seminar in African Studies paper on the historiography of reparations that spans the period between the Civil War and the present. Then they watch a visual recreation of the *Middle Passage* in a 2000 HBO film of the same name directed by Guy Deslauriers. Film sources conclude with excerpts from the Rally for Reparations that N'COBRA helped organize and sponsor on August 17, 2002, especially the impassioned poetry reading of Sister Firestarter, and the state of litigation against corporations who participated in the slave trade led by Deadria Farmer-Paellmann (Farmer-Paellmann and Sister Firestarter, 2002).

Several Congressional sources are then shared. Speeches of Congressman Chaka Fattah of Pennsylvania, the apology for slavery of Congressman Tony Hall, and Congressman John Conyers's House Resolution 40 are distributed and discussed in class. Finally, a conclusion of masters' thesis on reparations, written by John Hobgood (2005), a former student in this class who subsequently studied at the University of Dar es Salaam and earned his masters from the Peace and Development Studies of the Universitat Jaume I of Castellón (Spain), is shared with the class. Hobgood applied the Transcend Method of resolving conflict to the reparations issue and argued that remedy could be found by viewing the problem homocentrically: all acknowledge and understand the issue, all see the issue through the eyes of "the other," and all discuss a therapy for healing the festering wound.

To offer a counterview, students discuss David Horowitz's (2001) article, "Ten reasons why reparations for blacks is a bad idea for blacks—and racist too." Many students find Horowitz's arguments narrow and offensive in part because his premise assumes that the only remedy is money.[4]

Once students have engaged these sources, discussion begins in two forums, one in class and one in a private, summary/reaction journal. Students must summarize and react to all course activities, including the project on reparations. For example, they take their class notes and restate them in formal essay format, and then they react to the content by "pulling the past into their present." The journals enable the instructor to share anonymously important points kept private during class discussions. The invaluable summary/reaction journal helps the instructor get inside the minds of each student in a way no other pedagogy permits.

After five years of this project in this "History of Africa" class (and in another sociologically focused course like "Race Relations," and "Race, Class, and Gender"), the conclusion of some one hundred upper-level undergraduates is that issues of slavery affect the United States far more than most citizens realize and that if our country is to heal, remedy in some form must be forthcoming.

## FINDINGS AND DISCUSSION

What follows are excerpts from summary/reaction journals from white students (who are usually the most suspicious about reparations) that consider the project's primary and secondary sources. The students' reflection journals are given pseudonyms. These are followed by reactions to the project of reparations as a whole toward the end of the course. In response to Herbstein's *Ama* (2002), history major Darby wrote:

> The lasting effects of the slave trade are still something that America finds itself dealing with on a daily basis. The racist practices promoted during the slave trade made wounds that may never fully heal, although it seems that a little more progress is made with each passing generation. Sadly, there are still white people in America that hate black people and many cannot even give you a legitimate reason why when they are asked to explain their hate. There are also many black people that are forever suspicious of white people. I think that the only way to begin to heal our wounds is to provide forums for different races to get together and share their views with one another. Along with the racist beliefs held by many in this country, I think that America's other big weakness is its sense of superiority over other nations. Both of these weaknesses can be traced back to the slave trade. Perhaps some type of reparations are in order, not only for those who suffered in slavery, but for those in other nations that the United States has exploited and continues to exploit.
>
> [Darby later continued,] I completely agree with Herbstein's assessment that America is sick due to its failure to address its past misgivings. The thing that I found most interesting about class today is that there was a certain feeling in the room that I had never experienced before in a classroom. It seemed that all the students were on the same page and it was obvious that *Ama* had had a profound effect on all of us. It's rare that you can say about a book that it changed your life, but I think I can safely say that for everyone in the class that read the book, they are changed for the better.

Similarly, Margery reports:

> *Ama* helps in understanding the history of Africa and therefore the course, because it allows us to relate to the times and what it must have been like to experience the Atlantic Slave Trade. History is best understood when one can make it personally relevant. Now

that all of Ama's generation has passed, we must rely on stories such as this to do that. Being able to put ourselves in her place, we can try to comprehend what horrors she had to face. The history of the slave trade reveals itself through Herbstein's vivid and almost too graphic imagery in his novel, *Ama*.

*Ama* is enjoyable because it grabs your attention and disgusts you which in turn will keep you wanting to read. At some points you might not want to continue due to the graphic rape scenes. If you can somehow bear them by adopting Ama's courage, you will be able to see the true meaning of this novel and why Herbstein did put that much detail into what happened to Ama; it's because that is actually what happened to many African women taken in shackles to the new world. This is the point the author is trying to make about the millions of people who endured these circumstances. Ama's story is not a fable. Although sometimes it is hard to talk about, the Atlantic Slave Trade was a dreadful point in history that still needs to be looked at and understood by the public; just because slavery has been outlawed does not mean it's over nor have the effects of it been demolished.

On HR 40, honors undergraduate Ralph, a double major in history and religious studies, explains:

I think it is a real shame that the U.S. Congress refuses to consider H.R. 40. It is common knowledge that entities within the United States, including the Congress itself, benefited from slave labor. Considering this, why is there so much resistance to studying the impact of this phenomenon and possible restitution for it? Is it pride? Are they afraid of admitting that their forebears were complicit in the buying and selling of human beings? To [continue to] do so would be to ignore the truth. Representative Conyers is asking for eight million dollars to fund a commission. They spend more than that every day in Iraq. Our defense budget is more bloated than it has been in history. I think the Congress has a responsibility to investigate this matter if they are truly committed to equality for all Americans in all aspects of their lives.

Female honors history major, Virginia, commenting on *The Middle Passage* (the film) in the context of reparations, wrote:

I was absolutely blown away by the eloquence of the end of the film. Images such as the "courtroom of humanity" caused me to think differently about reparations than I had in the past. Someone must right the wrongs of our previous generations, and if not us, then who? This movie forces one to confront one part of our past that has been ignored for far too long. I think that it should be shown to every ethnic group in every land and in every language. Specifically, this film dealt with the Atlantic Slave Trade, but it can be interpreted for the wrongs committed on humanity as a whole throughout the existence of humankind. We forget that different ethnic groups are our brothers and our sisters, our mothers and our fathers. The pain felt in this film was a human pain and not solely a black pain. I took from it much more than I think I have taken from any film to date.

Similarly, on *The Middle Passage*, Randall notes:

The film has been an eye-opening experience. I enjoy films like *Amistad* but something about this film really speaks to me, where others do not. I think that it is the lone voice-over, by Djimon Hounsou, that makes the film so powerful. He speaks for all those who started the trip across the Atlantic, not just those that set foot in the New World but all the countless souls who entered a watery grave as well. It is as if one voice from our past, speaking for the horrors of millions, is pleading for us to remember them. I must admit that before class started, I had forgotten and I believe most of America has as well. As I watch, I can see their pain and smell the fetid cargo holds. It is difficult to watch without feeling sadness, both for the Africans and my own ancestors. I feel sorrow that one man can see another as inhuman. I understand that war is terrible and bad things can and do happen to men by men, but this is something completely different. This is Hitler-like, but with him, we had a villain, and here humanity is both the victim and the attacker. I also think this is where the reparations problem lies—there is no one to blame, because we were, and still are, all to blame.

In another reaction to HR 40, as well as Chaka Fatah's speech and Tony Hall's apology, Darby wrote:

Before reading these websites I was unaware that a formal apology had never been issued by anyone in power in this country. I think that the main reason that the issue of reparations is such a sensitive subject for 'white' people is because most feel like they should not have to atone for the sins of their ancestors, but the alternative is that the issue is not discussed at all which never resolves anything. In my American Education class we read a book by Cornel West called *Democracy Matters*, and in it West says in so many words that America's greatest weakness is its inability to seriously examine its shortcomings as a people. He means by this that we are the first on the scene when we see other people in other countries being exploited or abused, yet we have never openly dealt with the millions that were exploited and abused in this country. Imagine how much more powerful our country could be if everyone was granted the same opportunities to succeed.

Thomas also commented on the same sources. He wrote:

For me the most compelling arguments for reparations come from Chaka Fatah and Tony Hall in that they advocate reparations as a way for the entire nation to move forward and put slavery behind it once and for all. It is sad that with all that has happened in the United States since 1865 that no one has stepped up and said "Sorry." Whenever some white supremacist Nazi or KKK person speaks everyone is quick to attack them and yet we won't go one step further and apologize. An apology is not an admission of guilt; often people apologize for things they have no control over, such as slavery. But it is the point, the act of expressing sorrow and of looking at your fellow American and saying "I am sorry for what happened. I can't change it, but together we can make sure it never happens again." Until we do so we can never become the nation that I have spent the last ten years of my life defending.

After reading David Horowitz's article opposing reparations, Darby wrote:

Of all the reasons that Horowitz presents the one that most aggravated me was number eight. I think that what he says there is a slap in the face to black people in this country. Any slight advantages granted to blacks like affirmative action, educational benefits, and other things of this nature only exist because they are an attempt to level the playing field between whites and blacks. Of course there are certain situations where these programs hurt white people resulting in what people have called reverse discrimination, but I think that is a small price to pay for the many sins this country has committed against an entire "race" because of the color of their skin.

Describing our class project as a whole, Virginia wrote:

Several of my classmates made interesting points. One student pointed out that the HR 40 Committee would only cost $8,000,000 to set up, an amount that he did not consider to be a lot. Two arguments for potential reasons against reparations were then made. The idea that we "do not want to open up that can of worms" was presented. The student argued that many might feel that this would lead to more problems between ethnic groups in America because talk of reparations immediately brings out our stereotypes. Another student stated, "Giving money to people goes against American values." One of my peers discussed the types of reparations that should be given. She felt as though reparations should go into general education rather than scholarships, memorials, etc. I countered this saying that although I think money should go into the general education system, I thought that she vastly underestimated the effect that memorials have on people. I mentioned the Holocaust Museum, and Dr. Till supported this statement by explaining the powerful effect that the Viet Nam memorial has on him. In order to have the money that goes into education fix the problems we would want reparations to address, the class seemed to agree that there must be a specification that the money would go to the poorest schools. Furthermore, many agreed that classes should focus on this issue at a younger age.

Monday's class went very well. Dr. Till expressed how reparations are currently being dealt with in the court system by elaborating upon a case against several different corporations. Then, he opened the discussion to the class and many ideas were tossed around the classroom as to what must be done to start the healing process.

I think that Monday's class was easily my favorite class that we have had all semester. Honestly, I think that another period could be used to discuss reparations, because many students brought up excellent points. It was refreshing to hear the intelligent responses that my classmates made on the issue. The idea of reparations is a personal one to any American citizen, so I was a bit apprehensive as to how this discussion would go. Everyone seemed to be open to other suggestions and I think that overall, it brought our class much closer together. Had this discussion occurred earlier in the semester, prior to our learning about the issues behind reparations, I think that this would have gone much differently. The History of Africa course has stripped all of us from our preconceived notions about the idea of reparations. We no longer bring to the table our various stereotypes. We look at the facts and recognize a pain brought about by the Atlantic Slave Trade that must be healed.

Reacting to the Farmer-Paellmann case, Randall comments:

Deadria Farmer-Paellmann brings up some great points, but again responsibility seems to be the problem. Even though she, I guess, has evidence of Boston Fleet participating illegally in the slave trade, courts of biased elected officials seem to believe that the past should remain there. It appears to be just another act of dehumanizing stolen Africans and their descendants. I would like to know more about her numbers with regards to both the 35 million and 45 million figures. Also, playing Devil's advocate, I could see the "other sides" viewpoint. I researched and found that 556,082 soldiers died fighting the Civil War and according to most estimates, only about 2 percent of Africans came to British North America. That would equal to approximately 550,000 slaves. I can see why some people could say that soldiers have already paid the debt, in blood. Of course, this is assuming that the numbers are close to accurate, and we will most likely never know that answer.

Randall's comments reflect the honesty of dealing with an issue that many believe cannot be resolved or that it has already been resolved. As far as remedies for reparations, Ralph concluded:

> What form can reparations take? There could be a scholarship fund designated for the descendants of slaves, but that would be very complicated. It involves matters of proof and degree of evidence required. Similarly, money could be allotted for improving the poorest public schools in the United States. While this would primarily benefit minorities, it would in fact benefit poor children of all racial and ethnic backgrounds. This solution would create greater opportunities for those children whose parents are not financially well off. As Americans we should make it our responsibility to ensure that all children are provided with a good education. This is an issue that transcends race and ethnicity and thus goes beyond a discussion of reparations. It goes to the issue of cyclic poverty. We should be striving to ensure that equal opportunity is a fact, not just a dream.
>
> Reparations could also involve forums on race relations. This could help create greater understanding among the many diverse groups represented in America. Again, while this could help African Americans specifically with regard to relations with whites, it could also benefit all Americans. Discrimination does not take one form or target only one group. There needs to be improvement in race relations on all fronts in the United States. One way to do this is through education. As mentioned before, that could take the form of increased funding for schools to educate children, as well as forums to educate adults.
>
> There is the issue of personal responsibility that must be considered in this discussion. In order for that issue to be completely relevant, however, there must be a level playing field. All children should have the same kinds of opportunities for education and advancement. Otherwise, one cannot point to a lack of personal responsibility to explain economic disparity. If kids begin at a disadvantage, how can one honestly criticize them for not attaining the achievements of those with more opportunities?
>
> This discussion is vitally important to the United States today. While we covered many issues in this discussion, it certainly was not exhaustive. It is an ongoing discussion. It is one that will not end until there is racial, social and economic equality. In other words, it will probably never end. It is important, though, that we continue pressing the issue. If people have ideas but do not act on them, they have no value.

Virginia also concluded:

> Although the slave trade ended a century and a half ago, the effects are still evident in our country. Racism is still rampant throughout the nation, especially in the South. . . . I do not know if the human race will ever truly deal with many of these issues, but I do think that reparations are a big step in the right direction. Here, I am talking about educational reparations more than money because I do not think that money would make that great of a difference. I honestly think that classes like this one are a step in the right direction and I would push for the establishment of this course in elementary and secondary schools.

She later continued:

> Prior to reading these articles, I had no idea that [reparations] were being discussed in other forms than a check to African-Americans. Although the Atlantic Slave Trade has briefly been mentioned to me in my education, the discussion of reparations never has. I

cannot believe how completely ignorant I was of an issue that continues to go on today. In fact, as much as I hate to say it now that I have taken this class and read the HR-40, I probably would have disagreed with the idea of reparations because I did not realize how many different forms they could come in. Now, however, I am a strong advocate for reparations through education and am thankful for this class for curing my ignorance.

In another conclusion of the class project, Darby wrote:

Almost everyone in the class agreed that some sort of reparations were in order, but the form that they should take could not really be agreed upon. Some believed that the wording of HR-40 should be revised to take out the words, "compensated for efforts." The feeling was that the phrase was too close to sounding like writing a check. Others thought that a more appropriate form of reparations would be to construct a memorial or use funding for educational programs. I suggested that the money be used to fund forums or discussions dealing with "race" relations.

[The student concluded], clearly the effects of slavery have damaged this country in many ways. One of the most destructive things that slavery has done to America comes in the form of racism. I think that racism is our country's greatest weakness. Many of us are so blinded by biased thoughts against others of another "race" simply on the basis of skin color. This is a lasting ugly legacy of slavery, which is why I believe it so important to begin immediately with race relations [improvement programs] of some sort. The more that we learned about each other's "race" and culture, the less we have to fear. We should celebrate our differences and quit being afraid of those differences.

In summary, the class project on reparations convinced most students that unless treated, the open wounds of slavery and its legacy would continue to fester and pass racism from generation to generation like a genetic defect. Newly aware with familial ties and responsibilities in place, students could now envision themselves in the audience listening to the words of Brown University's Steering Committee on Slavery and Justice. In 2006 that committee wrote:

If this nation is ever to have a serious dialogue about slavery, Jim Crow, and the bitter legacies they have bequeathed to us, then universities must provide the leadership. Universities possess unique concentrations of knowledge and skills. They are grounded in values of truth seeking and the unfettered exchange of ideas. They are at least relatively insulated from political pressure. Perhaps most important, they are institutions that value historical continuity, that recognize and cherish the bonds that link the present to the past and the future.

Brown University and other educational institutions are extending invitations to the family table to discuss issues surrounding racial and ethnic relations. Furthermore, white advocates for reparations have formed an organization called Caucasians United for Reparations and Emancipation, CURE. In the organization's book *The Debtors: Whites Respond to the Call for Black Reparations* (2005), Ida Hakim addresses the need for white activism. Hakim and other whites underscore the social responsibility of those who benefit from privilege they earn from their whiteness, and at the expense of others.

Based on the findings of the project, it appeared that the students benefited from reparations pedagogy, and it helped improve their understanding of race relations. The struggles of addressing this sensitive topic came out in the students' journal reflections. In the case of Randall, the human losses of both blacks and whites during the Civil War might have just paid off the old debt, canceling everything out. Although he struggles with the issue, he comes closer to a resolve that the topic needs to be explored and discussed further in order to bring about some healing. At least this presents some prospects of continuing the dialogue on reparations. While there has been a silence in the literature regarding how to teach about reparations, the homocentric approach provides some new directions and meanings for a very sensitive subject.

## CONCLUSION

In the age of increasing globalization, which is a progression out of slavery and colonialism (Chossudovsky, 1997; Stiglitz, 2002; Williams, 1944/1994), conflicts surrounding economic benefits continue to grow. As social tensions between groups are influenced by old and new inequalities, education must continue to play a key role in creating peace and in helping to resolve social conflicts. In Ptahhotep's wisdom literature, the ancient Kemetic master teacher reminds us about how a proper education can help to bring healing and harmony in society (as cited in Hilliard et al., 1987). The homocentric view of humanity seeks to pull the human Diasporic family to the table to discuss old and new disputes surrounding slavery and modern racial discrimination. We hope that by proposing a method for raising this sensitive issue at the family table, the siblings and other family members can better appreciate their global connectivity and the need to help those who are most affected by the tragedy of slavery and its legacy in the family's affairs. Perhaps for some, electing President Obama as the first African American head of state signals the closing of the nation's chapter on racism and therefore, ends the discussion on slavery and reparations. However, for others it opens the possibilities for such discussions and creates a context for structural change aimed at improving the democratic process, as well as racial and ethnic relations. It might also reopen the dialogue on fair trade and labor standards, and international policy aimed at equal rights and justice for all.

## NOTES

1. Post-apartheidism is a racialized system of white socioeconomic and political control that endures in South Africa from the apartheid era.

2. We completely reject the use of "race" as a legitimate biological concept, but accept it as a subjective term used to describe racist views of humanity.

3. For example, see depaullaw.typepad.com/library/2006/12/7th_circuit_app.html (accessed March 22, 2007).

4. An author who eloquently takes Horowitz and other anti-reparationists to task is Roy L. Brooks (2004), *Atonement and forgiveness: A new model for black reparations*, Berkeley: University of California Press.

# REFERENCES

America, R. (2000). The last word: Reparations and higher education. *Black Issues in Higher Education, 16*(23), 104.

Asante, M. K. (2003). *The survival of the American nation: Erasing racism.* Amherst: Prometheus Books.

Aslandeigui, N., and Summerfield, G. (2000). The Asian crisis, gender, and the international financial architecture. *Feminist Economics, 6*(3), 81–104.

Bales, K. (1999). *Disposable people: New slavery in the global economy.* Berkeley: University of California Press.

Balfour, L. (2003). Unreconstructed democracy: W. E. B. Du Bois and the case for reparations. *American Political Science Review, 97*(1), 33–44.

Barber, B. (1996). *Jihad vs. McWorld.* New York: Ballantine Books.

BBC. British Broadcasting Corporation. (2007). School wins Muslim dress appeal. Retrieved October 27, 2007, from news.bbc.co.uk/2/hi/uk_news/education/4832072.stm.

Berry, M. F. (2005). *My face is black is true: Callie house and the struggle for ex-slave reparations.* New York: Alfred A. Knopf.

Beyond the Border. (2007). Beyond the border: *Más Allá de la Frontera.* Retrieved October 1, 2007, from www.pbs.org/itvs/beyondtheborder/immigration.html.

Bolner, J. (1968). Toward a theory of racial reparations. *Phylon, 29*(1), 41–47.

Boxer, S. (2007). Rally protests noose found at Columbia University. Retrieved November 12, 2007, from www.cnn.com/2007/US/10/10/columbia.noose/index.html.

Boylan, M. (2002). Affirmative action: Strategies for the future. *Social Philosophy, 33*(1), 117–30.

Braithwaite, J. (1999). Restorative justice: Assessing optimistic and pessimistic accounts. *Crime and Justice, 25*, 1–127.

Brandon, A. (2007). Throngs demand justice for Jena 6. Retrieved November 3, 2007, from www.usatoday.com/news/nation/2007-09-20-jena-rally_N.html.

Brecher, H., Costello, T., and Smith, B. (2000). *Globalization from below: The power of solidarity.* Cambridge, MA: South End Press.

Brooks, R. L. (2004). *Atonement and forgiveness: A new model for black reparations.* Berkeley: University of California Press.

Brown University Steering Committee on Slavery and Justice. (2006). *Slavery and justice.* Report of the Brown University Steering Committee on Slavery and Justice. Especially "Confronting Slavery's Legacy: The Reparations Question," 58–82. Retrieved December 15, 2006, from brown.edu/Research/Slavery_Justice/report/index.html.

Bullock, L. (2006). Economic gap widens between blacks and whites. Retrieved June 16, 2007, from news.ncmonline.com/news/viewarticle.html?articleid=b462dde8f3ffdad9fbd22f0c1a7 7bf4.

Cabral, A. (1969/1970). *Revolution in Guinea: Selected texts.* Richard Handyside (ed. and trans.). New York: Monthly Review Press.

Caucasians United for Reparations and Emancipation (CURE). (2007). Retrieved October 30, 2007 from www.reparationsthecure.org/.

Cavanagh, J., and Mander, J. (2002). *Alternatives to economic globalization: A better world is possible: A report of the international forum on globalization/report drafting Beneria committee.* San Francisco: Berrett-Koehler.

Chomsky, N. (2006). *Failed states: The abuse of power and the assault on democracy.* New York: Metropolitan Books/Henry Holt.

Chossudovsky, M. (1997). *The globalisation of poverty: Impacts of IMF and World Bank reforms.* Atlantic Highlands, NJ: Zed Books.

Clarke, J. H. (1993). *Christopher Columbus and the Afrikan holocaust: Slavery and the rise of European capitalism.* Brooklyn: A&B Publishers Group.

Coates, R. D. (2004). If a tree falls in the wilderness: Reparations, academic silences, and social justice. *Social Forces, 83*(2), 841–64.

Cohen, E. (2001). *The politics of globalization in the United States.* Washington, DC: Georgetown University Press.

Conyers, J. (1989). The commission to study reparations proposals for African American Act HR 3745 IH, 101st Congress, 1st Session, November 20, 1989. Retrieved March 18, 2007, from thomas.loc.gov/cgibin/query/z?c101:hr3745. See copy at core.ecu.edu/hist/wilburnk/Africa/Reparations/-JohnConyersHR40.htm.

Conyers, J. (2006). Statements from April 6, 2005 briefing: *The impact of slavery on African Americans today.* Retrieved March 18, 2007, from www.house.gov/conyers/news_reparations.htm.

Coomey, P. (2007, August/September). South Africa: To bee or not to bee. *New African,* 30–32.

Crews, D. (1998). *Neither slave nor free: Moravians, slavery, and a church that endures.* Winston-Salem, NC: Moravian Archives.

Delpit, L. (1995). *Other people's children: Cultural conflict in the classroom.* New York: New Press.

Dennard, D. (2001). Historiography of reparations for the Atlantic Slave Trade. Extracted from film *Roundtable on reparations.* SERSAS Fall 2001 Meeting. Director Kenneth Wilburn. Greenville, NC: SERSAS, East Carolina University, 2001. Videocassette.

Deslauriers, G. (2003). *The middle passage* [DVD]. HBO Home Video.

Eitzen, S., and Baca Zinn, M. (Eds.). (2006). *Globalization: The transformation of social worlds.* Belmont, CA: Thomson Wadsworth.

Fanon, F. (1952/1967). *Black skin, white masks.* Trans. by Charles Lam Markmann. New York: Grove Press.

Farmer-Paellmann, D. (2007). Executive director, restitution study group [Updates on litigation in the U.S. against corporations involved with slavery]. Retrieved October 30, 2007, from www.rsgincorp.com/.

Farmer-Paellmann, D., and Firestarter, S. (2002). Presentation at the millions for reparations mass rally, Washington, DC. Excerpted from private video filmed from C-Span.

Fattah, C. (2001). Extensions of remarks [copied from forward on Race Together, first published in *Philadelphia Inquirer,* May 20, 2001], *Congressional Record,* May 15, 2001, p. E981. Retrieved March 18, 2007, from core.ecu.edu/hist/wilburnk/Africa/Reparations/ChakaFattah.htm.

Feagin, J. (2000). *Racist America. Roots, current realities, and future reparations.* New York: Routledge.

FEMA. Federal Emergency Management Agency. (2005). FEMA chief relieved of Katrina duties. Retrieved November 14, 2007, from www.msnbc.msn.com/id/9266986/.

Firebaugh, G. (2003). *The new geography of global income inequality.* Cambridge, MA: Harvard University Press.

Friedman, T. (1999). *The Lexus and the olive tree.* New York : Farrar, Straus and Giroux.

Friedman, T. (2005). *The world is flat: A brief history of the twenty-first century.* New York: Farrar, Straus and Giroux.

Giddens, A. (1994). *Beyond left and right: The future of radical politics.* Stanford, CA: Stanford University Press.

Green, C. (1997). *Globalization and survival in the black diaspora: The new urban challenge.* New York: State University of New York Press.

Hakim, I. (Ed.). (2005). *The debtors: Whites respond to the call for black reparations.* Red Oak, GA: CURE Press.

Hall, T. (2003). Extensions of remarks [Resolution apologizing for slavery], *Congressional Record* 13 July 2000, p. E1223. Retrieved March 18, 2007, from core.ecu.edu/hist/-wilburnk/ Africa/Reparations/TonyHall.htm.

Harvey, D. (1999). *Limits of capitalism.* (New Edition). New York: Verso.

Harvey, D. (2003). *The new imperialism.* Oxford: Oxford University Press.

Harvey, D. (2005). *The new imperialism.* Second ed. Oxford: Oxford University Press.

Herbstein, M. (2002). *Ama, a story of the Atlantic slave trade.* New York: E-Reads. See companion website of same title: Retrieved March 18, 2007, from www.ama.africatoday .com/.

Hilliard, A., Williams, L., and Damali, N. (Eds.). (1987). *The teachings of Ptahhotep: The oldest book in the world.* Atlanta: Blackwood Press.

Hobgood, J. (2005). A peace approach to the African American reparations conflict. M.A. thesis, Peace and Development Studies under the UNESCO Chair of Philosophy of Universitat Jaume I, Castellón, Spain.

Horowitz, D. (2001). Ten reasons why reparations for blacks is a bad idea for blacks — and racist too. Retrieved March 16, 2007, from www.frontpagemag.com/Articles/- Printable .asp?ID=1153.

Howard-Hassmann, R. (2004). Getting to reparations: Japanese Americans and African Americans. *Social Forces, 83*(2), 823–40.

Huntington, S. P. (1996). *The clash of civilizations and the remaking of world order.* New York: Simon & Schuster.

Huntington, S. P. (2004). *Who are we? The challenges to America's national identity.* New York: Simon & Schuster.

Jewish Virtual Library. (2007). Retrieved June 15, 2007, from www.jewishvirtuallibrary.org/.

Kaldor, M. (2007). *New and old wars.* Second ed. Stanford, CA: Stanford University Press.

Katrina. (2005). Katrina kills 50 in one Mississippi county. Retrieved November 15, 2007, from www.cnn.com/2005/WEATHER/08/29/hurricane.katrina/.

Keller, B. (1994). Mandela's party publishes plan to redistribute wealth. Retrieved October 12, 2007, from query.nytimes.com/gst/fullpage.html?res=990CE4D81131F936A25752C09629 58260&sec=&spon=&agewanted=all.

Kershnear, S. (2004). *Justice for the past.* New York: State University of New York Press.

Kozol, J. (1991). *Savage inequalities: Children in America's schools.* New York: Crown.

Kozol, J. (2006). *The shame of the nation: The restoration of apartheid in schooling in America.* New York: Random House.

Lincoln, Y., and Guba, E. (1985). *Naturalistic inquiry.* Newbury Park, CA: Sage

Livingston, D. (2005–2006, Winter). Community rebuilding strategies: Anchor block by block. *Social Policy,* 10–11.

Manda, N. (2004). *Genocide without gunfire: Slain by IMF policy.* Baltimore: Publish America.

Maran, R. (2002). A report from the United Nations world conference against racism, racial discrimination, xenophobia, and related intolerance. Durban, South Africa, 2001. *Social Justice, 1*(2), 177–85.

Marcus, H. (2002). *A history of Ethiopia* (New ed.). Berkeley: University of California Press.

Martin, M. T., and Yaquinto, M. (Eds.). (2007). *Redress for historical injustices in the United States.* Durham, NC: Duke University Press.

Masland, T., and Rossouw, H. (2005). A good life for a few (Atlantic edition). January 24, 2005, 145, Issue 4. Retrieved March 16, 2007, from www.amren.com/mtnews/archives/2005/01/a_good_life_for.php.

Massey, D. (1993). *American Apartheid: Segregation and the making of the underclass.* Cambridge, MA: Harvard University Press.

Mazrui, A. (1994). Global Africa: From abolitionists to reparationists. *African Studies Review, 37*(3), 1–18.

McIntosh, P. (1995). White privilege and male privilege: A personal account of coming to see correspondences through work in women's studies. In M. L. Andersen, and P. H. Collins (Eds.), *Race, class, and gender: An anthology* (second ed., pp. 76–87). Belmont, CA: Wadsworth.

Memmi, A. 1957/1965. *The colonizer and the colonized.* New York: Orion Press.

Mexico. (2007). Mexico condemns immigration bill. Retrieved January 13, 2007, from www.foxnews.com/story/0,2933,179021,00.html.

Meyer, S. G. (2000). *As Long as they don't move next door: Segregation and racial conflict in American neighborhoods.* Lanham, MD: Rowman & Littlefield.

Miksch, K. L., and Ghere, D. (2004). Teaching Japanese-American incarceration. *History Teacher, 37*(2), 211–27.

Monahan, T. (2005). *Globalization, technological change, and public education.* New York: Routledge.

National Coalition of Blacks for Reparations in America (NCOBRA). (2007). Retrieved October 15, 2007, from www.ncobra.com/.

News24. (2005). Katrina: Looters turn violent. Retrieved July 17, 2006, from www.news24.com/News24/World/News/0,2-10-1462_1763752,00.html.

Nossiter, A. (2007). Whites take a majority on New Orleans's council. Retrieved November 20, 2007, from www.nytimes.com/2007/11/20/us/nationalspecial/20orleans.html?_r=1&ref=naionalspecial&oref=slogin.

Oliver, R. (1999). *The African experience: From Olduvai Gorge to the twenty-first century.* Boulder, CO: Westview Press.

Omi, M., and Winant, H. (1986). *Racial formation in the United States: From the 1960s to the 1980s.* New York: Routledge and Kegan Paul.

Osabu-Kle, D. (2000). The African reparation cry: Rationale, estimate, prospects, and strategies. *Journal of Black Studies, 30*(3), 331–50.

Pattman, R. (2007). Student identities, and researching these, in a newly "racially" merged university in South Africa. *Race Ethnicity and Education, 10*(4), 473–92.

Perloff, R. M. (2000). The press and lynchings of African Americans. *Journal of Black Studies, 3*(3), 315–30.

Ptahhotep. 2388 BCE. *The teachings of Ptahhotep: The oldest book in the World,* A. Hilliard, L. Williams, and N. Damali (Eds.). Atlanta: Blackwood Press.

Ranger, T. (1971). The "new historiography" in Dar es Salaam. *African Affairs, 70*(278), 50–61.

Rebollo-Gil, G., and Moras, A. (2006). Defining an "anti" stance: key pedagogical questions about engaging anti-racism in college classrooms. *Race Ethnicity and Education, 9*(4), 381–94.

Reuters. (2007). Jena 6 case in La spurs copycats. Retrieved November 3, 2007, from www.usatoday.com/news/nation/2007-10-09-race_N.htm.

Ritzer, G. (2004). *Globalization of nothing.* Thousand Oaks, CA: Pine Forge Press.

Robertson, R. (1985). The relativization of societies, modern religion, and globalization. In T. Robbins, W. C. Shepherd, and J. McBride (Eds.), *Cults, culture, and the law* (pp. 31–42). Chicago: Scholars Press.

Robertson, R. (1992). *Globalization: Social theory and global culture*. Thousand Oaks, CA: Sage.

Robinson, R. (2000). *The debt: What America owes to blacks*. New York: Dutton.

Robinson, W. (2004). *A theory of global capitalism: Production, class, and state in a transnational world*. Baltimore: Johns Hopkins University Press.

Rodney, W. (1982). *How Europe underdeveloped Africa*. Washington, DC: Howard University Press.

Schedler, G. (1998). *Racist symbols and reparations*. New York: Rowman & Littlefield.

Singer, P. (2002). *One world: The ethics of globalization*. New Haven, CT: Yale University Press.

Skocpol, T. (2000). *The missing middle: Working families and the future of American social policy*. New York: W.W. Norton and Company.

Smith, A. (2006). Boarding school abuses, human rights and reparations. *Journal of Religion and Abuse, 8*(2), 5–21.

Soriano, C. (2006). Muslim dress, school code clash in Britain. *USA Today*, February 10–10A.

Stiglitz, J. (2002). *Globalization and its discontents*. New York: W.W. Norton and Company.

Stiglitz, J. (2006). *Making globalization work*. New York: W.W. Norton and Company.

Strauss, A., and Corbin, J. (1998). *Basics of qualitative research: Techniques and procedures for developing grounded theory*. Thousand Oaks, CA: Sage.

Tusicisny, A. (2004). Civilizational conflicts: More frequent, longer, and bloodier? *Journal of Peace Research, 41*(4), 485-498.

Wallerstein, I. (1974). *The modern world-system: Capitalist agriculture and the origins of the European world-economy in the sixteenth century*. New York: Academic Press.

Williams, E. (1944/1994). *Capitalism and slavery*. Chapel Hill: University of North Carolina Press.

Winter, S. (2007). What's so bad about slavery? Assessing the grounds for reparations. *Patterns of Prejudice, 41*(3–4), 373–93.

Yudice, G. (2003). *The expediency of culture: Uses of culture in the global era*. Durham, NC: Duke University Press.

*Chapter Four*

# Diversity, Global Practice, Local Needs: An International Comparative Study of Preservice Teachers' Perceptions of Initial Teacher Training in the United States, England, and the United Arab Emirates

## Daniel Kirk

"Only by conversation in which experienced thinkers exchange information about their actual ways of working can a useful sense of method and theory be imparted to the beginning student."

C. W. Mills, 1959, p. 195

Teaching can be viewed differently among the many diverse cultural traditions around the world. One unifying element of what is viewed as teaching, however, is that it is regarded as the means of passing on cultural knowledge and giving members of society the skills to be able to communicate and exchange ideas. It is this social aspect of education that has meant teachers have held, and continue to hold, a central position within society. From an Anglo-European/Western perspective, teachers are educated professionals who have undergone formal training that allows them to hold the position of "teacher" within structured educational systems. However, many non-Western societies also have what are culturally recognized as teachers, yet the structural space in which they work varies greatly, often with little or no formal educational training and appointment by society rather than an organization (Layton, 1997). This variance leads us to examine how teaching is carried out, and international comparative studies of teaching and teacher education provide a starting point toward greater understandings.

Through a comparative study of teacher education in three countries, this chapter aims to report a study that examined how teachers are educated and trained in different settings and how this leads to greater knowledge and understanding between cross-cultural educational practices. The comparison will focus on teacher education in the United Arab Emirates (UAE), framed against the more familiar and established preparation of teachers in the United Kingdom (UK) and the United States (U.S.), using specific cases and institutions as examples.

# THE GLOBALIZATION OF TEACHERS AND TEACHING

Globalization has had an impact upon societies and cultures in ways that could not have been easily predicted or foreseen. The term has become globally recognized and understood to mean modernity (which in this respect could be read to mean Western) despite the overuse of the word signifying very many different meanings (Novoa, 2002). With the growth in communications technology, affordable international travel, intergovernmental cooperation and conflict, and the rise of global business and banking structures, it is hardly surprising that the field of education has also been swept away on the tide of globalization (Green, 2006). The notion of globalization as a movement or influencing system has been critiqued and questioned for the overuse of the term and the all-encompassing meaning often given to it (Vobruba, 2004). Within the sphere of education, teachers and students are far more likely to be focused on the local implications of education, such as employment options and social capital issues, rather than an often intangible international or globalized economy and workforce (Kirk, 2003). The term "globalization" is often related to the notion of a capitalist economy and the expansion of such a system worldwide (Raduntz, 2005). It is with this in mind that the globalization of education needs to be examined and discussed from a local perspective, as this is where learning becomes real, practical, and relevant for the vast majority of students.

As with any field or discipline that deals with the inexact and "messy" subjects that humans tend to be, education is shifting and altering in ways that are influenced by the local and global structures in which they exist (Cullingford and Gunn, 2005). The global movement of teachers, as well as the general role of the teacher in society, makes it all the more important to study the perceptions of student teachers, thus enabling an evaluation of current teacher education programs.

The Arab world, and in particular the Arabian Gulf, is undergoing rapid change and becoming far more global in its outlook, as well as the role it is willing to play on the international stage (Massialas and Jarrar, 1991). It could be argued that no part of the world has entered the global market more rapidly than the oil-rich states of the Arabian Gulf (Fox, Mourtada-Sabbah, and al-Mutawa, 2006). Under colonial rule, Arab states, such as Bahrain, Qatar, Oman, and what is now the UAE, reflected the colonizing power and this was also the case in the educational systems that were put in place. The educational system of the metropole (colonizing country) was at the forefront of educational provision and was often a tool used to educate the children of colonial administrators as well as instill cultural and moral values in the indigenous elite of the colonized country. This was the case, to a certain extent, in the UAE where the British government had influence and economic interest, although the area that became the UAE was never under direct rule from London. The educational system based itself firmly on the British model through the early years following the formation of the UAE (Shaw, 1993). From this point on, a system of primary and secondary education slowly developed with access to schooling gradually opening up to the general population. Until this process began, the ruling elite would send the males of the family overseas (usually the United States and Britain) to receive secondary and university level education.

Initially students in the UAE were drawn from the middle and upper classes as the rural areas of the country were not well served by schools. In 1971 the UAE spent $1,641 per pupil on schooling, yet the children of poor and agrarian families did not benefit from this as schools were not within reach (Massialas and Jarrar, 1991). Higher education was also slow to develop. Much of this had to do with the fact that the ruling family sent their sons abroad for university so there seemed, at first, no real need to provide higher education to the population. In addition, the country was poor until the discovery of oil and this prevented the creation of a state education system (Talhami, 2004). The country relied, and still relies, heavily on imported labor. In 2007, expatriates outnumbered indigenous Emiratis by nearly four to one. The wealth of the country allowed the government to import the expertise and workforce it needed to develop its oil and tourism businesses.

The use of Western school systems in the UAE has much to do with the ambitions of the country and the human resource development that is needed for these ambitions to be met (Hatch, 2006). The UAE has traditionally relied on expatriate workers to carry out both professional and manual labor work in the country (Haider, 1999). This has usually been imported and has been possible through the wealth of the country and the favorable taxation and economic structures that are in place (Findlow, 2005). As the realization that oil wealth is finite and that expatriates are transitional and do little to develop the long-term sustainability of a country, the UAE government set in place an educational system that would help meet the needs of the country through creating an educated and trained indigenous workforce (Kirk, 2007).

Alongside the need to develop a national workforce is the desire by the UAE authorities to make the country competitive on a world stage. Once the UAE was established as a nation and the British ceased overt support for the country, the government realized that an education system was needed in the country. As mentioned, historically, the leaders and elite of the UAE sent their male heirs overseas to be educated, with a favoring toward Britain and, more recently, the United States. This had implications for the design and importation of an educational structure for the UAE, as the experiences that the rulers had were shaped closely by the Western systems which they went through. Familiarity with Western educational systems made them a natural choice when selecting models for schools and universities in the UAE (Marshall and Smith, 1997). An added benefit of choosing these systems was that they were tried and tested, leading to the importation of globally recognized and competitive educational provision.

The notion of competitiveness on a global level is one that drives all that the UAE strives to do (Fox et al., 2006). The boom in oil exports led to an influx of wealth into the region that enabled the government to map out a future and build a country with the help of foreign expertise and labor. The UAE feels that it needs to compete globally in all areas of business, commerce, tourism, health care, and education.

Although the local and national economy and context is the main stimulus for education delivered through schools and the arena in which the vast majority of people will work, an understanding of the structures of education and how these are set by those in power is vital to anyone interested in looking beyond a region or system (Freire, 1970). By studying teacher training and the perceptions that preserve teachers have regarding their preparation, educators can learn and understand the commonalities and differences that exist within the sphere of teacher education globally (Kirk, 2001). It is envisaged that there will be methodological questions and concerns that are raised among the participants that are not site specific, although the resolution of such questions will be firmly situated in the context in which they occur.

## THREE SYSTEMS, ONE GOAL: THE PREPARATION OF TEACHERS

The three institutions that were the focus of my study, the University of the Southeast (UOS), Middle England University (MEU), and Northern Gulf University (NGU),[1] are in the business of educating and preparing teachers, but in very different cultural and social spaces. To begin, they exist in differing geographical, political, and cultural spaces, which add to the uniqueness of each setting.

All of these institutions have a common thread, which is they offer teacher certification programs that will allow those who complete the requirements of the course to teach in schools within the state or country of certification. All of the research sites also come under the control, in varying degrees, of the local or national government. These similarities offer a focus that can be explored to allow an examination of the practices that are carried out in each institution and the perceptions that those in the system, the students, have regarding the efficacy of their training.

## RESEARCH SITES AND PARTICIPANTS

The research sites for this study can be viewed and described from two differing angles. First, the physical and geographical location of the education program, and second, from the location and nationality of the student participants. Both need to be considered and explained to allow for the contextualization of the sites.

Each of the research sites are constructed through their unique contextual setting (Dyson and Genishi, 2005; Kazamias, 1961) and it is prudent to give a brief overview of each institution and data sets of students to allow contextual understandings to begin. As will be discussed later, the context of each research site plays an influential role in the experiences of the students

## METHOD

This study was conducted over the 2007–2008 academic years, by the author, wherein I made frequent trips to the United States, United Kingdom, and the United Arab Emirates to do field work. In order to be able to investigate the perceptions of preservice teachers in relation to their education, I identified twenty-four preservice teachers, eight from each of the three institutions, as participants in the study. All the participants spoke English, although in the UAE, these students spoke English as a second language. Thus, all the interviews were conducted in English. Participant selection is described later in the chapter. I explored their personal experiences as student teachers, which involved talking about their perceptions of their evolving professional identities, the role of the colleges of education and practice schools, professional relationships, the freedoms and constraints of their programs, their perceived efficacy of the professional training they received, and the joys and pressures they faced throughout the year. The data collection and analysis for this study occurred in five distinct phases.

During phase 1 I observed student teachers and began to gather and read course syllabi and policy documents from the three target institutions. I also selected the participants for the study and communicated with them regarding the purpose and scope of the study, as well as their involvement in it. Phase 2 involved data collection at the three sites. Data sources included digital audio recordings of a selection of interviews, transcripts of interviews, policy documents, course syllabi, institutional demographic data, a personal field journal, field notes, and promotional materials of the different institutions.

Phase 3 involved a review and analysis of the collected data. This work produced a set of emerging themes that helped focus the study more tightly and arrive at a clearer understanding of the ways in which teacher education in the three contexts was alike and different. Phase 4 consisted of a second round of data collection in all three countries and involved traveling once more to England and the UAE. The data collection took the form of further interviews with the same set of preservice teachers as well as an opportunity to clarify institutional data with administrators and faculty if needed (Tuckman, 1978). This was particularly useful in the UAE as documents and demographic data were hard to find through print and Internet sources.

Phase 5 was the final collation, coding and analysis of the data, along with further document review and e-mail communication with university personnel to fill in any missing information (such as up-to-date student enrollment figures).

## PARTICIPANTS

All of the students who participated in the study had enrolled on an undergraduate or postgraduate certification course in education, and they had all completed three years of undergraduate level course work. They formed part of a cohort of preservice teachers who were undergoing their professional certification year, which involved university-based courses in education and school-based teaching practice. The selection of the participants involved several factors. Firstly, I arranged access to preservice teachers in all locations through a contact faculty member, who facilitated access to the cohort. I then randomly selected eight students and approached them, formally asking if they would agree to take part in the study. All of the students I approached consented, and after explaining the research in detail, I asked them to read the requirements of their participation and sign consent forms. In tables 4.1, 4.2, and 4.3, I set out in tabulated form demographic and biographic data for each of the preservice teachers who participated in this study.

**Table 4.1.  University of the Southeast, United States**

| Name | Age | Gender | Biographical information |
|------|-----|--------|--------------------------|
| Jane | 20 | Female | Has always wanted to be a teacher, and moved to UOS to become an educator. From a family of teachers and wants to be an English teacher to share her passion for literature. |
| Sally | 20 | Female | Decided on teacher education program well into her undergraduate degree course. Feels teaching will give her options as career choice is limited for an English graduate. |
| Eliza | 21 | Female | Attends UOS on a scholarship. Father is a retired high-school teacher, and feels that this influenced her decision to be certified. Is looking to graduate school, and still not sure if she will go into teaching. |
| Claire | 22 | Female | Worked in retail for a year before entering university. Has a passion for literature and feels teaching is worthwhile career, although does have reservations about teaching long-term. |
| Sue | 20 | Female | She is a self-confessed "teacher," who knew she wanted to teach from a very early age. Thinks her desire to teach stems from a "brilliant and inspiring" fifth-grade teacher. |
| Tamara | 21 | Female | Admits teaching may not be the career for her, although entered program with high hopes. Had a tough time in first practice school. First-generation student, so wants to do something worthwhile for her family. |
| James | 21 | Male | Comes from a family of teachers and he chose teaching as he wants to coach sports at high school. Content with teaching English, although sees this as a way into the system, allowing him to coach. |
| David | 21 | Male | Enjoyed English at school and this led him to an English degree. David has a couple of friends who did the education course and enjoyed it, so he decided to have a go. Not sure if he will teach straight after graduation, although thinks he will end up in schools. |

## UNIVERSITY OF THE SOUTHEAST, UNITED STATES

The University of the Southeast (UOS) is a large, public university in the southeastern corner of the United States. It was founded in 1785 with a charter that set out to provide tertiary education within the state. The university is a doctoral level school and the flagship institution of the state. The university consists of a wide variety of colleges and schools, one of the largest being the College of Education, which provides undergraduate and graduate education courses and professional certification, as well as conducting educational research and consulting. In line with its status as a Research I institution, the College of Education is particularly active in examining education with a view to improving the educational experiences of youngsters in the state, and further afield. Faculty and graduate students are prolific producers of research papers and publish and present widely in various fields of education. The students who participated in this study were drawn from an undergraduate cohort of preservice teachers who were undergoing their professional certification year, which involved university-

**Table 4.2.  Middle England University, England**

| Name | Age | Gender | Biographical information |
|------|-----|--------|--------------------------|
| Ailsa | 22 | Female | From Scotland, decided to train as a teacher in England as current teacher shortage means good employment opportunities. Thinks she will teach for a few years to "pay off all the bloody student loans I have." |
| Deborah | 22 | Female | Wanted to be a teacher since before her undergraduate degree. Volunteered as a school assistant in local area. Training to be a secondary teacher, although thinks she may switch to primary level. |
| Cindy | 30 | Female | Employed in commercial and retail business for past seven years. Became disillusioned with corporate life and felt teaching would give her the change she needed. Recruited to teacher education course by central government recruiting campaign that offered significant financial incentives. |
| Caroline | 22 | Female | Wanted to be an English teacher ever since secondary school, due in part to a teacher who inspired her. Looking forward to having the opportunity to pass on her passion for literature, with the aim of teaching in an urban "high-needs" school. |
| Joanne | 23 | Female | Would like to stay in the area of MEU upon certification, with a job locally, but maybe not as a teacher. Application to the course was a last minute decision, with her feeling that career options are limited with a degree in English. Ultimate goal is to work for a publishing company. |
| Tony | 23 | Male | Went to university to study "anything," before aiming to enter the air force as an officer. Application to the military was unsuccessful, so he "fell" into teaching as an alternative option. Thinks certification will make him more marketable, and not sure if teaching is where he will head. Looking at options of substitute teaching (which pays nearly $200 a day) as a way to finance some travel. |
| Richard | 21 | Male | Has a passion for studying and decided on education as a way to remain at university for another year. Considering a master's degree in education, with a view to gaining a nonteaching role in education. |
| Phil | 24 | Male | A nontraditional student, who left school at sixteen, took an access course and entered a degree course. Is committed to teaching in a local school and giving back to his community. Volunteers at local school. |

based courses in education and school-based teaching practice where they were able to work in school settings and teach classes.

## MIDDLE ENGLAND UNIVERSITY, UK

Middle England University (MEU) is a large and established institution in the geographical heart of the United Kingdom. The university has a good reputation and

**Table 4.3.  Northern Gulf University, United Arab Emirates**

| Name | Age | Gender | Biographical information |
|------|-----|--------|--------------------------|
| Salwe | 21 | Female | Feels education is important for the growth of the UAE and that there is a need for more Emirati teachers. She has a strong sense of social justice and hopes to be able to have a positive impact on the lives of her students. |
| Lana | 20 | Female | Wanted to attend university overseas, like her brothers, but this was not allowed. Lana hoped to attend medical school, but her family chose education for her. She has slowly come to enjoy teaching. |
| Sawsan | 21 | Female | Is unsure if she will teach, and thinks that upon graduation she will return home to marry and raise a family. She has little desire to teach in government schools but thinks the course will help her as a mother. |
| Mais | 20 | Female | She is looking forward to being a teacher and thinks it is important for local schools to be staffed by local teachers. Switched to education from business major through sense of social responsibility. Hopes to become a school administrator. |
| Hala | 20 | Female | She is adamant that she will not teach upon graduation. Her courses at university were chosen by her parents. She hopes to gain high grades to allow her to get into a graduate program in business, possibly overseas. |
| Noorah | 20 | Female | Enjoys NGU and knew she wanted to be a teacher from an early age. Believes in the importance of education for the good of the country and feels there are too many foreign teachers. |
| Amy | 21 | Female | She is pleased with her decision to train as a teacher, although initially she did not want to attend university. She went to a selective private school in the UAE and wanted to go to the United Kingdom to study. Her family would not support this, but she is not ruling it out for the future. |
| Fatima | 20 | Female | Comes from a "very traditional Emirati family," which led to her being told where and what she would study at university. Does not think she will enter the workforce, but will get married instead. |

attracts students from all over the United Kingdom, Europe, and beyond, offering undergraduate and graduate degrees as well as professional training courses. The main campus is located in the heart of an historic medieval city and provides educational and social support for the surrounding population in the form of a teaching hospital and community outreach services. The School of Education is a large and well-established section of the university. It serves as one of the largest teacher education centers in the region and places hundreds of student teachers in local schools each year. The school is well-known both nationally and internationally for the undergraduate and postgraduate courses it offers, and it is home to a UNESCO center that focuses on international education. As with all teacher training institutions in the United Kingdom, the curricula offered is driven by a central set of standards which are laid out by the UK government. This ensures that all preservice teachers receive a similar experience regardless of the institution they attend. This means that many institutions specialize in graduate studies as a way to offer new and innovative programs, something the School of Education at MEU is known for. The participants for this study were all drawn from the year-long secondary school level Post Graduate Certificate of Education (PGCE), during which time the students take a minimal number of education classes and spend the large part of the academic year in their practice schools. All of the students held bachelor degrees in their subject and were taking the PGCE route to certification, as is the norm for secondary school teachers.

## NORTHERN GULF UNIVERSITY, UAE

The Northern Gulf University (NGU) was established in the oasis town of Al Ain by royal decree in 1976 under the direction of the president of the UAE. It was the first higher education institution within the newly formed UAE and was open to national citizens who sought further education. The College of Education has a faculty of over sixty professors and a student body that numbers around nineteen hundred. The demographic makeup of the undergraduate population mirrors very closely that of the national teaching force in the country with all undergraduates being female. These preservice teachers are encouraged to enter the government education sector, as the current teaching workforce in the UAE government schools is overwhelmingly made up of expatriates (97 percent). The College of Education was the first outside of the U.S. to be accredited by the National Council for Accreditation of Teacher Education (NCATE), and this is a constant point of pride for the administration at the university. The college, along with the rest of the university, is administered by the central government. The students who participated in this study were all in their final year of a bachelor of education degree and were undertaking a practice year, during which they spent the majority of the year in local schools with some courses taken at the college.

## DATA COLLECTION

The data collection involved multiple sources of data, from which it was possible to provide the *thick description* that Geertz (1983) believes to be an important element of documenting personal understandings of reality (Edwards, Holmes, and Van deGraff, 1973). The multiple data sets also allowed for triangulation (Denzin, 1989) of the data to take place, with the benefit of constant comparison providing linked evidence of themes and issues as they arose.

## INTERVIEWS

The formal interview process involved both individual interviews and group discussions. The purpose of the first round of interviews was to have the preservice teachers examine and summarize their routes into teaching and reflect on their first semester in the respective programs. These processes allowed for issues to be raised and noted as well as give useful biographic information that assisted with contextualizing the students as individuals. Bogdan and Bicklen (1992) describe an effective interview as one "in which the subjects are at ease and talk freely about their points of view" (p. 97) and which produces useable and rich data in language that reveals the views of the participants.

It was my aim to allow the twenty-four participants to talk freely and, hopefully, be at ease during the process (Robson, 1983, 1999). The use of a semistructured interview facilitated this approach. Each individual interview lasted between fifty and seventy-five minutes and detailed notes were taken, along with, when permitted, audiotaping of the session.

## FINDINGS

Through the voices of the preservice teachers, I aimed to investigate how students felt about their experiences in their education programs and how they perceived the efficacy and relevance of the preparation they had gone through. The study was designed to attempt to elicit information from the participants that highlighted their cognitive development, alongside their individual emotional journeys, as they transitioned from a student identity to that of a teacher.

## TEACHER EDUCATION IN A GLOBAL CONTEXT

An educational program deemed effective or 'good' in one situation does not necessarily mean that it can be transplanted into a different setting and work just as well. There are certain elements, however, of teacher education courses that could be viewed as generic and culturally transferable. In the UAE, for example, there has been recent debate and discussion regarding the role of reflective practice in teacher education and the way that Emiratis are employing such practice (Clarke and Otaky, 2006). This evaluation of the internal system within the state has led to an examination of wider issues, as well as a comparative look at systems globally to attempt to learn from others who have a more demographically balanced teaching workforce.

Trainee teachers, those who are undergoing their formal programs with an aim to becoming certified teachers, will experience many of the same problems and frustrations as their peers within other institutions both nationally and internationally. There are many "location specific" issues that will arise and are unique to each setting (Kirk, 2006), such as the constraints of a centralized curriculum or the conditions of the schools in which trainee teachers undertake their practice and the resources available to them. Yet it seems as if those training to become teachers have much in common with regards to the problems they face, worries they have, and their perceptions of the efficacy of their professional training.

## EMERGENT THEMES: VOICES FROM THE CLASSROOMS

The participants in the study were interviewed to allow for collection of narrative description regarding their views of the teacher education program they were undertaking. As Taylor and Bogdan (1998) state, an "interview is a form of social interaction" (p. 98). I kept this in mind as I spoke with each participant, as I wanted the exchange to be as much a discussion and conversation as an interview. I was aware that in such a situation, both I and the participant would attempt to manage our own persona and the impression that we would form of each other (Goffman, 1967). The way each of us viewed the other would have an effect on the way the discussion went, so I attempted to follow the structure of the interview questions, yet allow the participant to deviate as needed.

Through talking to the preservice teachers, several themes emerged across the three geographical locations that allowed for patterns to be traced through the words of the students. The narratives provided what Geertz (1983) terms *thick description* and it was only through coding, constant comparison, and detailed analysis of the data that themes were identified and categorized. Below I highlight some of the salient points made by the participants, which form part of a much larger data set.

## TEACHING AS WE WERE TAUGHT:
## INSPIRING AND INFLUENTIAL TEACHERS

One of the predominant reasons given for entering teaching was personal experience of an inspirational teacher whilst at school.

> He just made sense . . . the subject came alive and I think he managed to hook many of us in the class. I mean, I don't . . . umm . . . don't know how to explain but he made the subject fun and made it seem as if it was really important to us. (Claire, UOS)

Claire ascribes her desire to teach to an individual teacher who managed to make the subject matter interesting and real, and spark an interest in teaching. On further discussion about this, Caroline, another participant, recognized that she did not realize the influence of the teacher at the time, beyond the fact that she enjoyed the subject, lessons, and the teacher.

> The classes were great, always too short, especially if I'd something like maths next . . . I knew I enjoyed the teacher and the subject but at the time I never thought of teaching as something I would do, I mean, who thinks that when they're fifteen or sixteen? . . . Once I got to uni [university] I realized that I loved to learn and that I could go away and explore books on my own. . . . I found that loads of what we had done at school with Mrs. Williams [pseudonym] helped me out. I guess I kinda looked back and saw that what she gave me was a passion. . . . Later on at uni I began to think that I wanted to do that, I wanted to make kids have a passion. (Caroline, MEU)

Most of the participants stated that they had, to some extent, been influenced by a teacher that they had encountered when it came to choosing to enter an education program. Mostly, the influence of a teacher was a positive factor in the decision making, although it was far from the sole reasoning behind the decision. As shall be seen below, many other factors played a role in placing each of the participants in their education programs.

## TEACHING AS SOCIAL ACTIVITY: SOCIAL JUSTICE AND IDEALISM

Several of the preservice teachers stated that they had altruistic reasons behind their decision to enter teaching. This theme, one that deals with the practice of teaching as supporting social justice ideals, was most evident in the female participants. Although I have broadly categorized the theme as "social justice," this term encompasses a whole host of elements, as can be seen in the following comments.

> So many kids have a bad time, you know, at home and stuff and I think that school is a place where they can go and feel safe, learn, have fun, and enjoy themselves. . . . I know that teaching is going to be difficult in some places, especially in a city like London, but someone has to do it. . . . If I can help even a few kids to read and enjoy reading and this helps them have a better time, then surely that's a good thing, right? (Deborah, MEU)

The need for Deborah to seek clarification at the end of this dialogue about why she entered teaching is interesting and insightful. Deborah held strong views about teaching and her rationale for entering the profession. Yet throughout our conversations she often sought positive clarification of her views and support for the ideas and beliefs she held.

> In the UAE there is a real need for teachers who know about the students and the country. . . . We have a lot of foreign people here in our schools and many do not know about us and our country. How can our children learn from such people? . . . There are many good teacher [sic] in this country but not many enough [sic]. . . . Teachers are important to help the country grow and be better and to be strong in the world, so we need make people come teach, Emirati people. (Salwe, NGU)

Salwe had firm beliefs about the role teaching has in the development of the UAE, and she felt that such growth and development is not well served by the high number of expatriate teachers in the classrooms of government schools. Although not explicitly expressed in such language, Salwe makes reference to the issues of cultural transmission and the role schools play in this process. Several of the participants alluded to the ideas surrounding the perpetuation of sociocultural norms that teaching often supports, and this is seen later in this chapter.

## FAMILY HISTORY AND TRADITION OF TEACHING

Several of the students had personal familial ties to the teaching profession. Although none of the students went so far as to say that having a parent, sibling, or close relative who was a teacher directly influenced them to enter the profession, they all recognized, to varying degrees, that this factor would have played a part in their decision making and outlook toward the profession.

> I don't think it made me want to teach, but I would say that it probably let me see teaching as something that I could do, something that I was around from an early age. . . . My mom was an English teacher for years and she really enjoyed it. She stayed at the same school for, like, years and became well-known and liked by a lot of the students. . . . Mom went to grad school and then left the school to work at [a university in the southeastern United States]. . . . She always said how much she liked teaching, although we would see her tired and bringing work home all the time. . . . Mom always said that teaching was important but never told us that we should consider it as a job, in fact she was pretty clear that we should look at all options. . . . She now works preparing teachers and likes that and she has a lot more time to spend with the family now as well. (Jane, UOS)

Jane, by her own admission, always wanted to teach, even from an early age. She would play at being a teacher when younger and would always tell people that she wanted to be a teacher. Jane grew up surrounded by a very clear image of teachers and teaching, not only with her mother, but also friends of the family and colleagues of her mother, many of whom were teachers. Jane is not sure if her background led her to teach, or if it just gave her insight into a role that she would have taken up regardless. It is clear that Jane had well-formed preconceived ideas about the role of a teacher before entering the program, possibly more so than others with no other experience than teachers they themselves had had.

Unlike several of the students who were interviewed at both MEU and UOS, none of the participants at NGU had close family members who were teachers or in the field of education. This was an unusual situation for me to encounter, as from my own reading of the literature and working with teachers for a decade, I was always aware that familial links to teaching were an influential factor for many new entrants to the profession. Cultural differences, along with the relatively recent formation of a formal education system in the UAE, makes family ties to teaching extremely rare. Due to a number of factors—reliance on expatriate teachers, status of the profession, incentivized alternative government positions, gender inequality, small teacher education programs, minimal recruitment strategies—the teaching force of the UAE does not mirror that of the United States and England, and the students that were interviewed at NGU were devoid of any familial links that were evident in the groups from MEU and UOS.

## TEACHING PRACTICE AND ISSUES

The literature on teacher education is full of research-based accounts of the impact teaching practice has on the efficacy and development of new teachers. The students who took part in this study had strong opinions and ideas regarding their teaching practice. These ranged from very positive accounts, to more negative experiences, from debating the role of the university against the realities faced in practice schools and the relationships formed (or not) with mentor or cooperating teachers.

## THE POSITIVE AND THE NEGATIVE OF PRACTICE TEACHING

Although the participants found positive aspects of their teaching practice to talk about, the majority of time was spent highlighting challenges and experiences, along with concerns that arose. This section will highlight several of the positive aspects that were reported, and then examine the negative issues that arose.

> It was, like, strange, here I was after only a few weeks, standing in front of a class of tenth graders, saying "hello, I'm your teacher." . . . It was fun, but scary, scary in a good way, not too bad, er, good for a first time, I think. . . . My students were OK but I think they saw I was nervous and a few of them tried to make me angry and even more nervous. . . . But, I think, on the whole it was good, good for me I mean, I think it was OK for the students, you know, they have a good teacher and I am new and messing up and stuff. (Sally, UOS)

It may be stretching the reality a little too far to say that Sally enjoyed her first time in the classroom, but she certainly realized that it was a positive learning experience and one that she could build upon. What is interesting in Sally's words is that she refers to the class as "her" students: "*my* students were OK" (my emphasis). Sally has switched from a passive observer of teaching to an active and engaged practitioner, albeit new and relatively inexperienced. The language of ownership that teachers use to talk about their classes and their students highlights the personal nature and invest-ment that teachers have in their work. This is a positive aspect of Sally's first teach-ing experience and an element that should remain with her as she progresses into the profession.

> I like my students. . . . They are nice and they look at me as their teacher, which is a good thing. . . . It is little scary [sic] to be in front of room with children, but not bad, just ner-vous. . . . The students were not well behaved but this is OK as I will learn and get better at making students behave. . . . I think the time in the school has been good one for me and I better teacher now [sic]. (Noorah, NGU)

Noorah comments about her teaching practice in very personal terms, often resort-ing to speaking about the behavior of the students and how good or bad they were. Noorah sees her experience as a positive one, yet it is judged, in part, according to how the children behaved and performed. She understands that teaching practice is an im-portant element of the teacher education program and that she will grow as a teacher through the experience. Yet Noorah, in all of our discussions, focused on classroom management issues and the personalities of the students to assess how effective she had been. This superficial analysis of her development can be attributed, in part, to the structure of the education program she is undertaking, and the views of several of the faculty members who supervise and guide her practice teaching.

Most of the students also reported negative aspects of their practice teaching and these often influenced the students in terms of their overall perceptions of the teacher education program.

It was hard. . . . I don't think I was ready for how tough, how long it would be. . . . The students were tough and hard to deal with. . . . I think this has really made me think, think hard about teaching. . . . In our college education classes we're always told "reflect," think about your practice and what you are doing, try and make sense of what you're doing, well, this, this time at school has made me think about if teaching is something I want to do. (Tamara, UOS)

Tamara began to doubt if she wanted to teach from very early on in her first practice school. Tamara found the students difficult to deal with and the competing demands of juggling college coursework and the requirements of teaching for the first time. Tamara is experiencing college as a first generation student. She struggled in her undergraduate English coursework before entry into the teacher education program, and it is possible that the anxiety and difficulty she experienced during her teaching practice was a continuation of her earlier issues.

It was too much difficult [*sic*] . . . many students not behave and I had difficult time in doing planned lesson. . . . My teacher was not there and I was on my own with thirty boys, all angry and shouting. . . . My plan was good but no chance to do the class. . . . It was not nice. (Sawsan, NGU)

Sawsan had a particularly tough time in her first teaching practice as she was placed in what was termed a "difficult" school. She had a class of boys who had little interest in the subject and saw a new teacher as a source of distraction. Sawsan's issues were compounded by being assigned a mentor teacher who was often absent and left Sawsan in the class on her own for extended periods of time. Without such support early on, Sawsan's chances of succeeding were greatly diminished, along with her confidence and self-esteem.

## THEORY AND PRACTICE: A HOUSE DIVIDED?

The issue of the role between theory and practice, and the weighting given to each element by teacher education programs, has long been debated, particularly by student teachers who often are vociferous in their views. Preservice teachers often enter teacher education programs with culturally and socially defined notions of what it is that teachers do in the classroom (Lortie, 1975). This "pre-programmed" knowledge about teaching was evident in the words of the participants that I spoke to.

The stuff we did on campus, to start with, was OK because we didn't really know any better . . . it seemed like we looked a lot at what we thought a teacher was, you know, talking about what makes a teacher, characteristics of teachers and stuff like that, but to be honest, we all know what teachers do 'cos we have sat in enough classes. . . . To begin with it was interesting, but I think all of us just wanted to get out there and do some teaching. . . . It became a real pain to go into campus once we began teaching. . . . The theory and discussion didn't always relate to what I was doing in the class. . . . I know there are links, but I think that we needed more practical stuff, like classroom management and how to grade and stuff. . . . I think that in a few years, once I have settled into the job, some of the theory and research will be relevant, but not now. (David, UOS)

David seems to be expressing some frustration with the time element of the campus-based side of the program and links this with the content of what the cohort studied. Along with other participants, David often has difficulty making the link between theory and methods courses and the situation that he finds in the classroom during his practice teaching. This issue created a dichotomous relationship between what should be a coherent and unified program of study that involves both theory and practice. As David states, all he wanted to do was get into the practical teaching element of the program. This highlights an important issue that stems from teaching being a personal and practical undertaking, something that needs to be practiced, where learning is primarily experiential.

There seemed to be a sense, as I spoke to the student teachers, that they expected there to be some form of dichotomy between the theory-based programs at the university setting and the practice heavy requirements of the schools. This may be attributed, in part, to the numerous research articles and media reports that highlight teacher education and the two contrasting aspects of theory and practice. It may be that student teachers almost look for examples of how their programs and practice differ in each setting, as it has become ingrained in the literature surrounding teacher education.

The vast majority of the students I spoke to were able to give specific examples of how they saw some form of disconnect between the university instruction and the realities of the classrooms they entered as teachers. Many of the examples were related to the issues student teachers faced, such as classroom management and time management in a school setting. The student teachers could not apply much of the theory they had talked about in the university setting as, it seemed, they did not have an opportunity to remain in classes for a sustained period of time. The student teachers were, in many ways, subject to a form of culture shock that meant they were concentrating on "surviving" in the school, with little time to reflect and apply the knowledge they were developing. It was recognized, however, that once they were settled as employed teachers and had learnt to manage things in a more efficient way, then possibly the theory will begin to make more sense and become more relevant to their practice.

## TEACHER CULTURE, STATUS, AND ROLE IN WIDER SOCIETY

In each setting, there are cultural and social norms and constructions related to the profession of teaching. Teaching is a social practice and is, as Shulman argues, the property of the community in which it takes place (Shulman, 1993). This opens teachers up to criticism and public scrutiny, possibly more so than any other profession. The participants in this study were acutely aware that they were entering a profession that is often the subject of cultural, political, and social forces that shape what they do in the classroom. Interestingly, as we shall see from the comments of the participants, many of the same issues arise regardless of the cultural setting and context in which the student teachers are working.

In examining what the student teachers said in their interviews, I focused on a sociocultural theoretical and conceptual framework that allowed positioning of the student teacher within the wider social and cultural context in which they were teaching and studying. This theoretical stance allowed an understanding of what student teachers were saying from the position that they are coconstructors of their teaching practice and that teacher identities are constructed by specific societal ideals and the context in which teaching takes place (Burr, 1995).

> I guess we [teachers] are seen as pretty important but not treated that way. . . . What I mean by this is that, well, er, you know, like, money and stuff, teachers are not paid really well yet they have a real important job to do . . . people think that teachers can make kids better and stuff but that isn't the case. . . . Everyone thinks that they know what teachers do and how to teach, we spoke about this in a class on campus, 'cos everyone has been to school and seen teachers and they think, well, how hard can it be? . . . I keep hearing that teaching is a profession but so is medicine and law and look at what them guys get paid, and how they're treated, I mean, would you ever go to a doctor and question what he is saying? I doubt it, but we get it all the time, from parents and politicians and stuff. . . . It can piss you off if you think too much about it. . . . But I still think it's one of the most important jobs there is, I just wish others saw that. (James, UOS)

James has several frustrations regarding how teachers are viewed and the status of the profession. He values the role of teacher and thinks that the job is important to the wider society. Yet he is frustrated by the perceived lack of recognition, both in financial and less tangible ways. James makes the classic comparison of teaching with the fields of law and medicine, two other professions that are held in high esteem within society. While it may be true that lawyers and medical doctors are paid more than teachers, James does not make the link between private and public sector roles. Most teachers work in the public sector, where they are subject to the scrutiny of wider society and are paid from the public purse. Although James has valid concerns and observations, teachers do work in a very public space and this makes them easy prey for those seeking a scapegoat for many of the ills of society.

> In this country [UAE] teachers have lot of respect for the job they do, but it is not a job that many people from here will do. . . . The teacher is a foreigner, usually, and is seen as educated person. . . . Emirates has lots of money so we buy our experts and teachers, that is how we develop over last thirty-six years. . . . But now government want more teacher from Emirates, as they want to develop the youth of the country, this is good thing but not many people want to be teacher. . . . Teacher is seen as being woman, not a job for man, man does the business and the government, but woman should teach . . . many of the girls here [on the education program at NGU] will not go to teach, they are here because their families send them and then they will leave and get married. . . . Until teaching is seen as a good job, not many people here will do it, why, why will they when they can earn three times more working for Etisalat [national telecommunications company—owned by government] and job is easy. . . . Men want to work for government, not in school. . . . Teachers here can earn a good salary, but it is a lot of work and this is bad thing. (Lana, NGU)

Lana was in an interesting situation as she was in an education program that graduates a large number of teachers each year, yet only a small percentage take up full-time teaching positions in national schools. The cultural understanding and belief that teaching is a role for females is relatively new in the UAE, as before the introduction of formal education, teaching was preserved for men, and instruction was carried out in mosque schools. As Emiratis have prospered and the country imported labor, the national workforce has been able to pick and choose the employment opportunities that suited them. Through the Emiritization program, teaching has been heavily promoted as an option for nationals, with large incentives going in-hand with positions in good schools and rapid promotion prospects. But, as Lana mentions, teaching is still not viewed as a career of choice for nationals graduating from university.

Although many of the participants raised interesting points regarding their experience of their teacher education programs, the four themes mentioned above emerged as a coherent set of ideas that were commented on by all of the student teachers. In the following section, I will discuss the implications of the findings and outline areas of further research that would enhance this study and examine several of the themes that emerged in greater detail.

## DISCUSSION

Teacher education institutions and courses may well have the equivalent of a perception gap between student teachers, faculty, and the cooperating or mentoring teacher in schools. One theme that continues to be raised when examining the research related to student perceptions, and that is confirmed in this study, is a perceived disconnect between the university or higher education certification course and the reality of the situation encountered in the classroom during the practice phase of the course. Student teachers often cite that the university theory work has done little to prepare them for the classroom (Jones, Reid, and Bevins, 1997). There is also a difference between what student teachers perceive as theory and what academics see this as. Students often name theory as anything to do with their training that is not practical in nature, whereas faculty point to the more traditional theoretical systems as held in the literature (Burr, 1995). The main thrust of this complaint is that the student teacher is often entering a world which was never discussed in the university setting. Students often state that there was too much theory in their preparation (Labaree, 1947).

In the United Kingdom student teachers have reported that they feel the university preparation was valid, but did not focus on the wider role of the teacher and what would be expected once in the classroom (Jones et al., 1997), a situation supported through the voices heard in this study. There is a view that newly qualified teachers (NQTs, as new entrants to the profession are categorized in England) need training not only in the theory of education and pedagogy and their role as classroom managers, but also in their wider professional commitments. This highlights a possible perception gap between what the university feels that students need to know before entering the classroom and the types of information and training that the student teachers would like to have before they arrive at the school.

This concern is mirrored in studies carried out in other geographical locations. In the UAE, research carried out at the Higher Colleges of Technology, a state-sponsored college offering teacher education programs to Emirati nationals, illustrated that teacher candidates, when asked to reflect on their course and practice, often cited that they felt that they developed as educators through close reflection. For example, students stated that they benefited from a series of discussions examining how to employ reflective practice in their training and teaching (Clarke and Otaky, 2006). This practical knowledge helped teachers as they entered their full-teaching practice where they were responsible for everything that the class did as they assumed the role of the teacher in place of the regular practitioner.

The perception gap, when seen within teacher training courses, is a theme that is often mentioned by student teachers, albeit stated in different terms. Student teachers reported that they are often not able to link the theoretical training delivered by a university with the practical realities that they encounter during their teaching practice (Lortie, 1975). There is a fine balancing act to be mastered within certification courses that mix theory and practice and this is an area that many institutions are reviewing. In a university in England, an experimental teacher education curriculum is being piloted that allows students to mix practical-based courses (such as classroom management, professional expectations and behavior, and dealing with parents and other stakeholders) with the more traditional, and required, theory and methods courses (Kirk, 2006). The efficacy of such a project will not be known for some time as student teachers will be interviewed after they have entered and settled into the profession, but it does open up certification courses to a greater element of choice, something that is available in many other professional training situations.

The actual teaching practice element of teacher education is also an aspect of certification programs that preservice teachers highlighted as problematic. This, again, seems to be a concern that is reported in all three geographical locations. All of the programs that are examined in this chapter require that students undertake some form of teaching practice as they progress along the certification path and there is a general agreement that the teaching practice element of a certification course is a key aspect of any teacher education program (Beck and Kosnik, 2002). This practice varies in length, frequency, and placement in the course structure. Although the methods and structures may be different, the aim is the same: to move the trainee teacher from the theoretical "comfort zone" of the university into the reality of the school classroom. This often has surprising consequences for the student teacher and can result in a form of culture shock (Cullingford and Gunn, 2005). The problem often arises when the student teacher realizes that the teaching practice element of certification is a complex and stressful time. There are many expectations placed upon the student teacher by the university supervising staff, the cooperating teacher or mentor, and the students within the classes that are to be taught (Hobson et al., 2004). This can often become overwhelming, as Feiman-Nemser (2001) points out: "New teachers really have two jobs to do—they have to teach and they have to learn to teach" (p. 8).

This double expectation can be difficult to overcome and student teachers often feel that they are underprepared for all that they are expected to do. This is particularly difficult as the preservice teachers are making a shift from student to teacher, which calls for a new and different way for them to approach their studies.

## SUMMARY

The state of the higher education system in the UAE raises some questions regarding the direction that it is moving in and the way that it wants to develop over the coming years. Does the UAE still want to develop an indigenous higher-education system that will not only act as a way to educate the youth of the country for the demands of the future but also have elements of the transferring of culture and values through the curricula? Or does the country head in the direction suggested by the mission statements of many of the higher education institutions in the country, as an aspiring actor on the global stage, a regional powerhouse and international force? Whichever of these directions is followed, or maybe a hybrid of the two can be reached, the fact remains that the higher education system is still firmly rooted in the imported provisions from the West and, to some extent, the methods of Egypt's Western-influenced education system.

Through this study it would be hoped that there could be closer ties between institutions internationally, so that the practice in each setting would help inform the other. Through such exchanges, a greater understanding and awareness of minority issues in education may be examined, from the perspective of those in such positions. The use of student-teacher exchanges, faculty collaboration, and the sharing of ideas and research would be of great benefit in the training of teachers (Wilson et al., 2001). Although a lofty and ideal aspiration, closer cooperation may well have benefits for all institutions as the global marketplace for students becomes more competitive each year, and closer links with overseas institutions would help promote the work being carried out.

## NOTE

1. All participants and institutions have been allocated pseudonyms.

## REFERENCES

Beck, C., and Kosnik, C. (2002, Spring). Components of a good practicum placement: Student teacher perceptions. *Teacher Education Quarterly, 29*(2), 81–98.

Bogdan, R. C., and Bicklen, S. K. (1992). *Qualitative research for education.* Boston: Allyn and Bacon.

Burr, V. (1995). *An introduction to social constructionism.* London: Routledge.

Clarke, M., and Otaky, D. (2006). Reflection "on" and "in" teacher education in the United Arab Emirates. *International Journal of Educational Development, 26,* 111–22.

Cullingford, C., and Gunn, S. (Eds.). (2005). *Globalization, education and culture shock.* Aldershot, UK: Ashgate.

Denzin, N. K. (1989). *Interpretive interactionism.* Newbury Park, CA: Sage.

Dyson, A., and Geneshi, C. (2005). *On the case. Approaches to language and literacy research.* New York: Teachers College Press.

Edwards, R., Holmes, B., and Van deGraff, J. (Eds.). (1973). *Relevant methods in comparative education.* Hamburg: UNESCO Institute for Education.

Feiman-Nemser, S. (2001). Helping novices learn to teach: Lessons from an exemplary support teacher. *Journal of Teacher Education, 52,* 17–30.

Findlow, S. (2005). International networking in the United Arab Emirates higher education system: Global-local tensions. *Compare, 35*(3), 285–302.

Fox, J., Mourtada-Sabbah, N., and al-Mutawa, M. (Eds.). (2006). *Globalization and the Gulf.* London: Routledge.

Freire, P. (1970). *Pedagogy of the oppressed.* New York: Continuum.

Geertz, C. (1983). Thick description: Toward an interpretive theory of culture. In R. M. Emerson (Ed.), *Contemporary Field Research* (pp. 37–59). Boston: Little, Brown.

Goffman, E. (1967). *Interaction ritual.* Garden City, NY: Doubleday.

Green, A. (2006). Education, globalization and the nation state. In H. Lauder, P. Brown, J. Dillabough, and A. H. Halsey (Eds.). *Education, Globalization and Social Change* (pp. 192–97). Oxford: Oxford University Press.

Haider, A. (1999). Emirates pre-service and in-service teachers' views about the nature of science. *International Journal of Science Education, 21*(8), 807–22.

Hatch, T. (2006). *Into the classroom. Developing the scholarship of teaching and learning.* San Francisco: Jossey-Bass.

Hobson, A., Tracey, L., Kerr, K., Malderez, A., Pell, G., Simm, C., and Johnson, F. (2004). *Why people choose to become teachers and the factors influencing their choice of initial teacher training route: Early findings from the Becoming a Teacher (BaT) project* (Research Brief No. RBX08-04). London: Department for Education and Skills.

Jones, L., Reid, D., and Bevins, S. (1997). Teachers' perceptions of mentoring in a collaborative model of initial teacher training. *Journal of Education for Teaching, 23*(3), 253–62.

Kazamias, A. M. (1961). Some old and new approaches to methodology in comparative education. *Comparative Education Review, 5*(2), 90–96.

Kirk, D. (2001). Curricular approaches to student disaffection: Providers' aims and student perceptions. Unpublished Master of Arts thesis, University of Sunderland, England.

Kirk, D. (July 2003). *Bermudian English: An isolated language.* Paper presented at the meeting of the International Federation for Teachers of English, University of Melbourne, Australia.

Kirk, D. (2006). Bermudian English: An isolated language. How the language shift in the classroom is leading to a rethinking of teacher preparation and training. In N. Popov, C. Wolhuter, C. Heller, and M. Kysilka (Eds.), *Comparative education and teacher training* (pp. 138–46). Sofia, Bulgaria: Bureau for Educational Services and Bulgarian Comparative Education Society.

Kirk, D. (April 2007). *Global education for a local population: An international study of pre-service teachers' perceptions of professional training in the United States, United Kingdom and United Arab Emirates.* Paper presented at the conference School Reform: Challenges and Aspirations, United Arab Emirates University, Dubai, United Arab Emirates.

Labaree, D. (1947). *The trouble with Ed schools.* New Haven, CT: Yale University Press.

Layton, R. (1997). *An introduction to theory in anthropology.* Cambridge: Cambridge University Press.

Lortie, D. (1975). *Schoolteacher.* Chicago: University of Chicago Press.

Marshall, J., and Smith, J. (1997). Teaching as we're taught: The university's role in the education of English teachers. *English Education, 29*(4), 245–71.

Massialas, B., and Jarrar, S. (1991). *Arab education in transition: A source book.* New York: Garland.

Mills, C. W. (1959). On intellectual craftsmanship. In C. W. Mills, *The sociological imagination* (pp. 195–226). Oxford: Oxford University Press.

Novoa, A. (2002). Ways of thinking about education in Europe. In A. Novoa and M. Lawn (Eds.), *Fabricating Europe; The formation of an education space* (pp. 131–56). Dordrecht, Netherlands: Kluwer.

Raduntz, H. (2005). The Marketization of education within a global capitalist economy. In M. W. Apple, J. Kenway, and M. Singh (Eds.), *Globalizing education: Policies, pedagogies and politics* (pp. 231–45). New York: Peter Lang.

Robson, C. (1983). *Real world research: A resource for social scientists and practitioner-researchers.* Oxford: Blackwell.

Robson, C. (1999*). Experiment, design and statistics in psychology.* Harmondsworth, UK: Penguin.

Shaw, K. E. (1993). Higher education and development in the lower Gulf States. *The Higher Education Review, 25*(3), 36–47.

Shulman, L. (1993). Teaching as community property: Putting an end to pedagogical solitude. *Change, 25*(6), 6–7.

Talhami, G. (2004). *Women, education and development in the Arab Gulf Countries.* Abu Dhabi: Emirates Center for Strategic Studies and Research.

Taylor, S. J., and Bogdan, R. (1998). *Introduction to qualitative research methods. A guidebook and resource.* New York: John Wiley and Sons.

Tuckman, B. W. (1978). *Conducting educational research.* New York: Harcourt Brace.

Vobruba, G. (2004, May 22). *Globalization, European integration and welfare states. Sorting out the relations.* Paper presented at Reforming Social Protection Systems in Europe. Nantes, France: COST Conference.

Wilson, S. M., Floden, R., and Ferrini-Mundy, J. (2001). *Teacher preparation research: Current knowledge gaps and recommendations.* Seattle: Center for the Study of Teaching and Policy.

*Chapter Five*

# Educating for a Multicultural Germany in the Global Era

## Debora Hinderliter Ortloff and Luise Prior McCarty

In Germany, citizenship laws, policies, and practices had, until recently, institutionalized discrimination against non-Germans on the basis of the conceptually unclear standard of belonging to the German "Volk" (people). According to Brubaker (1992), the resulting ethnocultural standard illegitimately preserved a monocultural German identity that was white, European, German-speaking, and Christian—despite the nation's realities of a growing linguistic, religious, racial, and ethnic diversity. Manifestations of globalization, the impact of integration policies of the European Union, and the need for population growth have brought about significant legal reforms that have redefined Germany as a multicultural nation desiring and needing immigration.

However, despite actual changes in citizenship laws, which allow people who were not born German citizens but were long-term residents to attain that status if they met government conditions, discussions of multiculturalism as a national ideal remain, for the most part, macrolevel rhetoric in Germany. This has to do, on the one hand, with politicians accepting Europeanization (discussed in more detail below) and globalization—understood as an intensification of global connectedness—as economic and social realities that are advantageous for Germany. On the other hand, the inevitability of globalization was also used at the federal level as an ideological device to impose unpopular policies and legal changes onto reluctant states. As such, globalization was used both as a positive and a negative justification to persuade the German public that Germany had no choice but to accept its new status as a multicultural society. Public schools were recognized as one of the primary vehicles to turn this rhetoric into reality.

What is unique and particularly interesting regarding the study of the German case is the connection between citizenship and multiculturalism, as well as the acceptance of globalization and resistance toward multiculturalism. The latter has to do with a successful political campaign to associate multiculturalism with segregation. During the reforms of the immigration laws in the late 1990s, dual citizenship was considered for all minorities settled in Germany. However, this raised fears that if dual citizenship was to be granted to Germany's minority groups, it would lead to segregation rather than the desired goal of integration. Thus, multiculturalism became negatively linked to debates on citizenship. The right of minority groups to hold two passports was defeated. Therefore, Germany presents a unique case of interlinking the ideals of multiculturalism with citizenship rights of minorities. Unfortunately, neither education policy nor practice has systematically tried to create a lasting space for minorities in citizenship education in Germany.

We hope to illustrate that although macrolevel policies and recommendations, both at the EU level and the federal level in Germany, seem to embrace the notions of diversity and multiculturalism, education policies and practices in the various German states still cling to more outdated notions of "Germanness." Focusing on the case of Bavaria—arguably the most conservative state in Germany—and using Banks's (1997, 2006) conceptualization of multicultural curricula as an analytical tool, we will demonstrate how the education of minorities is conceived and practiced. Based on an investigation of changes in textbooks and state curricula over twenty years, as well as teacher interviews, our study reveals how an ethnocultural—rather than a legal standard of the German citizen—prevents a full-fledged multicultural education for all children in a global world.

## RESEARCH DESIGN

Bavarian social studies textbooks published from 1988 to 2006 for use in grades six to eight at the *Hauptschule* and *Realschule* (two middle school forms which prepare students for vocational training after completion) were examined for their framing of citizenship and inclusion of ethnic non-German stories.[1] We use John Rawls's notion of citizenship as a relation of free and equal citizens within a democratic society which they enter at birth and through which they exercise ultimate political power as a collective body (Rawls, 1999, p. 136).

Examination was based on framing analysis (Ortloff, 2006) and followed general validity guidelines for content analysis as outlined by Krippendorf (2004). At least one edition of each of the textbooks on the Bavarian Ministry of Education's list of approved books for use in schools was used in this study. (A list is included in appendix 5.1.) In addition, fifty-eight social studies teachers (from these two school forms) were interviewed from all parts of the state of Bavaria. The teacher selection followed purposive sampling guidelines (Creswell, 2007). Schools were contacted and asked if they would like to participate. Care was taken to balance the urban centers with the more rural areas of Bavaria. In general, however, *Hauptschulen* and *Realschulen* are located in larger towns and metropolitan areas, and students take public transportation from outlying areas to attend such schools. There has been a general trend, over the last twenty years, to close community schools except at the elementary school level.[2] Since non-German residents are not allowed to be state employees (civil servants), there is practically no diversity in terms of race or ethnicity in the teaching pool in Bavaria. Therefore, no efforts were made to construct a diverse sample in these terms. We did, however, for the purposes of this project, make sure to construct a sample that represented a wide-range of teachers in terms of years of experience.

Insofar as years of experience translate to age, we felt it was important to make sure the data did not represent primarily one age group. Instead, our main aim was to collect a broad range of voices from social studies teachers in these two school forms (see appendix 5.1 for a table of participants). In these interviews, we asked teachers how they used state guidelines and state-mandated textbooks in their teaching about citizenship (pseudonyms are used in the narratives). We also asked them about their own views on citizenship and teaching citizenship skills—such as how to participate in democratic or community-based processes, or how to deal respectfully with a nonnative person. These two types of data, the officially mandated use and teachers' own perspectives, were intended to present a more complex picture of the interaction between federal and state policies with actual teacher practice.

Our data indicate that textbooks and curricula reproduce the white, Christian construction of being German. Likewise, teachers, although often well-intentioned, understand a good foreigner to be an assimilated foreigner. They, too, make little space for alternative means of understanding an expanded notion of citizenship or the creation of what Walzer (1990) calls a hybridized identity, one in which one's loyalty to the state or nation as a citizen is not in conflict with one's ethnic, racial, or religious affiliation. One of the negative results of our study is the insight that ideas of globalization and Europeanization become, what Papastephanou (2005) in her discussion of cosmopolitanism calls, the "secret accomplice of ethnocentrism" (p. 547). European citizenship becomes the acceptable substitute for a deeper embrace of global or multicultural membership.

The chapter concludes with a discussion of whether the U.S. experience of multicultural education in a globalized world could have a positive bearing on the current German situation. Likewise, the contradictions of citizenship and diversity politics in Germany might shed light on the difficulties and plight of illegal immigrants to the United States.

## Macrolevel Changes: From Blood Relative to Multicultural Citizen

Germany, as suggested above, faces an especially complex task of redefining German citizenship (Brubaker, 1992; Gosewinkel, 1998) in light of its goals to become a multicultural society. The previously held ethnocultural standard excluded all non-Germans from democratic participation. Citizenship laws, policies, and practices institutionalized discrimination against non-Germans on the basis of the conceptually unclear standard of "being German" and "belonging to the German Volk."

This enforced monoculturalism has been challenged, both through global economics and societal pressures and lawmaking over the past fifteen years. Since 1990, approximately 1.8 million ethnic Germans have relocated to Germany. This group, known as the *Aussiedler*[3] or Russian Germans, claimed access to German citizenship as a consequence of post–World War II policies, which recognized ethnic Germans living in the Soviet Union as a persecuted people. This designation preserved their right to return to Germany and to become German citizens.[4] Russian-Germans are now the second largest minority population in Germany, just slightly less than the two million Turkish Germans. During the economic boom of the 1960s, Germany offered lucrative employment to so-called guest workers, primarily from southern Europe, with the idea that these guest workers, mainly male, would eventually return to their home country. Turkish citizens, mostly of Muslim faith, became the largest guest worker group. Not only did they not return to Turkey, but they also brought their families and settled in Germany. These Turkish Germans, as well as all other immigrant groups, have traditionally had no right to German citizenship, even if their children or their children's children were born in Germany.

In addition to the unique case presented by the migration of the Russian Germans, Europeanization and pressure from the growing percentage of non-German permanent residents, created enough political pressure in the 1990s to revise the citizenship law and to conceive of immigration in more lasting terms. The Law on Nationality went into effect on January 1, 2000, and allows children born in Germany to foreigners, under certain conditions, to receive German citizenship. It does not allow for dual citizenship.

## Supranational Influences

Europeanization has also affected the conceptualization of citizenship and belonging in Germany. In 1992, during the same time that Germany was beginning to grapple with the effects of massive *Aussiedler* immigration, the Treaty of Maastricht codified EU citizenship in order to encourage free movement of people within the union, to reduce the European Union's perceived democratic deficit, and to support the creation of a European identity (O'Leary, 1998).

The process of Europeanization in turn challenged Germans to define themselves in more international terms. In particular, we see this through EU support of European minority rights, which seek to preserve the linguistic and cultural heritage of small-language groups. Articles 17–18 of the European Communities Treaty regulate European citizenship and make it dependent on holding national citizenship in one of the member states of the European Union. The Maastricht European Citizenship clause clarifies this point in stating that "*Citizenship of the Union shall complement and not replace national citizenship.*" However, in reality, the existence of EU citizenship affects national citizenship policymaking because of the interdependence created—if one country, France, for example, grants citizenship to an Algerian immigrant, then that immigrant now has the right to work and live in Germany. As Hansen and Weil (2001) observe, "throughout Europe the politics of immigration have become the politics of nationality" (p. 1).

Further, and of particular importance to the German case, the regulation of third-country citizens residing within the European Union is brought into question. European citizenship, in its attempt to bring the people of Europe closer together, necessarily disenfranchised any non-European, or so-called third-country resident, living in the European Union.[5] The situation of foreigners (in particular Turks) living in Germany became the most blatant example of disenfranchisement within the European Union. Hansen and Weil (2001) explain that it was the general consensus of most member states that if EU citizenship was to rest on member state citizenship, then national citizenship needed to be equitably accessible to long-term residents. This was not the case in Germany (Joppke, 2001). Rostek and Davies (2006) argue that the adoption of the 2000 citizenship reform measures, at least in part, was in response to this EU pressure and the need to have laws harmonious with Germany's neighbors. Indeed, the German government claimed the adoption of the new citizenship standards as meeting EU standards (Federal Ministry of the Interior, 2006). Yet it should be pointed out that the European Union has introduced a powerful discourse about minority rights in Europe (Joppke, 2001). Germany has ignored or rejected this discourse, as well as attempts by the European Union to regulate third-country immigration (Joppke, 2001).

Luchtenberg (2004), for example, argues that Europeanization has allowed Germany to address diversity in nonthreatening ways that do not engage the country's racial, ethnic, and religious complexity. Moreover, when considering the changes in citizenship and immigration laws and how they have invoked a negative sense of multiculturalism internally, it appears that diversity is acceptable at the European level but only in regard to European "natives" and not to immigrants. The question remains whether and how these political changes have been reflected in creating citizenship education, which equally attempts to include diversity, particularly immigrant experiences. The next section will contribute to answering this last query.

## THE GERMAN EDUCATION SYSTEM

As outlined above, Germany has protected its *ethnocultural* membership standard primarily through citizenship and immigration laws. These laws have served as a means of continued cultural categorization into immigrants and Germans. Understanding how this plays out in education policy and practice requires us to first examine traditions of schooling in Germany and of the Bavarian state in particular. Education is the purview of the individual federal state, but each state must recognize the education credentials of the other fifteen states and, as such, there is still considerable similarity from state to state. Bavaria is considered by most to be one of the most conservative states in Germany. As such, it is arguably more resistant to multiculturalism than other states. Likewise, its ruling conservative party—in power since the establishment of post-WWII Germany—has been consistently in favor of state involvement in EU affairs and has viewed globalization as opening up great opportunity. Our choice of this state is to show one end of the continuum of how citizenship education policy is being implemented for a multicultural Germany in a global era.

Beyond state level control of education, the most pervasive feature of the German school structure is the tripartite division into different school forms after primary school—in most states, after fourth grade. There are three distinct school forms: *Hauptschule, Realschule,* and *Gymnasium.* Both the *Hauptschule* and *Realschule* are generally accompanied or followed by vocational training. The *Gymnasium,* however, is preparation for the university.

Ertl and Phillips (2000) explain that this tripartite schooling system aligns with German notions of what it means to be educated and what the perceived needs of society are in terms of three different strata of workers. The differentiation, based on a psychological typecasting of so-called talent, remains a central feature of education in

Germany. It is also a cornerstone for the variety in content and outcomes in the three school forms (Ertl and Phillips, 2000).

Despite fairly consistent criticism on the grounds of elitism and inequality, as well as the inability of the *Hauptschule* to meet the demands of contemporary society (cf. Führ and Tapia, 1997), the tripartite system remains. Furthermore, tracking of students into these schools has been shown to reproduce class structure, and more recently, has been shown to place non-Germans and Russian-Germans into lower school forms at a disproportionate level (Aurenheimer, 2006). In Bavaria, 75 percent of non-Germans attend *Hauptschule* or *Realschule* (Aurenheimer, 2006).

Overall, throughout Germany, roughly 9.2 percent of pupils are foreigners. This number does not include repatriates who possess German citizenship, but who often do not speak German as a native language (KMK, 2002). However, in Bavaria 12.2 percent of students are non-Germans. This number also does not include repatriates who resettled in Bavaria in higher numbers than in other states. Figure 5.1 shows the distribution (by percentage) of non-German versus German pupils into various school forms in Germany as a whole and in Bavaria in particular.

In the Bavarian case, just under 70 percent of German children attend *Hauptschule* and *Realschule,* compared to 80 percent of non-Germans (excluding repatriates).

Our next step provides concrete examples of how this population of pupils of non-German background is depicted in curricular material and textbooks used in citizenship education.

Percentage of German versus Non-German Student Enrollment by School Form in Germany as a whole and Bavaria in particular in 2000*

| School Form | Germany | | Bavaria | |
|---|---|---|---|---|
| | German | Non-German | German | Non-German |
| *Hauptschule* | 16.3 | 48.8 | 36 | 66 |
| *Realschule* | 21.1 | 17.4 | 23 | 13 |
| *Gymnasium* | 38.7 | 18.9 | 38 | 18** |
| Special Education Schools | 4.0 | 6.6 | 2.5 | 3.5 |

** 85 % of which come from E.U. countries or other European countries.

Figure 5.1.  **German versus Non-German Student Enrollment**

## CITIZENSHIP EDUCATION IN GERMANY

Education is a primary instrument of the state for the purpose of, on the one hand, initiating or supporting social change, and on the other, guaranteeing social stability and reproducing social traditions and social order. Citizenship education prepares students through schooling to participate in the political process and teaches them how to practice democratic values, such as social justice, but also those that sustain a state, such as obedience to its laws. The Prussian educational philosopher Johann Gottlieb Fichte articulated this social engineering function of schooling in his early nineteenth-century writings. He stated that it is only through formal education that students can be socialized into the common values of the state, including loyalty, patriotism, and commitment to the social. Thus, even in its predemocratic history, Germany incorporated ideas of *politische Bildung* (political education) as a core of its educational philosophy. It is important to note that at times during German history, particularly during the Nazi regime and in East Germany during its communist era, citizenship education, paralleling Fichte's point, was used as a means of socializing students into fascism and socialism, respectively. Indeed, in its modern form, citizenship education was introduced by the Allies (United States, Britain, and France) during the reorganization of schools directly following Germany's defeat in World War II. It was a key aspect of the Allies' policy of denazification (Giesecke, 1993). While it was a successful piece of the Allies' educational policy overall, it was an imposed policy. As Wilde (2004) points out, this creates an interesting contradiction: "Citizenship and political education in Germany suffers from the paradox of having been, initially at least, imposed on the respective systems, without due democratic deliberation and discussion" (p. 8). This is important to consider in light of the findings we will present, which indicate that teachers neither question state imperatives nor view themselves as part of a democratic process aimed at creating citizenship education policies and practices.

For the most part, citizenship education in Germany is not a separate subject, but rather it is an overarching topic in social studies. Bavaria recognizes the development of legally mature or actualized (*mündige*) citizens as a main and overarching goal of the entire *Hauptschule* and *Realschule* curricula, and as such, is a common thread in every subject area. Haendle, Oesterreich, and Trommer (1999) report that the integration of non-Germans is considered a critical goal. Likewise, discussion of the European Union and Europeanness as an aspect of citizenship is viewed as key. Yet these two areas—integration and Europeanness—which are fundamentally values-oriented, were recognized by experts as being less effective than other parts of the curriculum. The study by the International Association for the Evaluation of Educational Achievement (IEA) on civics education (Torney-Purta et al., 2001), which is the most often cited comparative citizenship education study, concludes that German students view being a good citizen as voting and participating in community service. With regard to diversity, only 71 percent of German students surveyed believe foreigners in Germany should have equal rights as others who live in Germany (Torney-Purta et al., 2001). This is well below the international average of the other twenty-eight countries including the United States, France, Great Britain, and Denmark that participated in the IEA survey. This begs the question: Why, when integration of non-Germans is viewed as a fundamental goal of citizenship education, do such attitudes persist? Haendle, Oesterreich, and Trommer (1999) provide a possible answer in their argument that the hidden curriculum is more important than the actual curriculum.

## GLOBALIZATION AS CHALLENGE TO CITIZENSHIP EDUCATION

Although often defined in a variety of ways or invoked to mean anything from strictly economic to more broadly social and cultural changes brought by increased migration, Arnove's (1999) description of globalization as a dialectic between the local and the global is useful for education. Law (2004), interpreting this dialectic, notes the influence of transnational and international discourses on national education policies. He suggests that students have to be prepared to think beyond their local or even national borders. This challenges the exclusivity inherent in citizenship education, which has been mainly aimed at preparing students to be national citizens, for example, in our case to be German. The following section will provide concrete descriptions and content examples of citizenship education in Bavaria by first analyzing textbooks that are used in social studies classes from grades 6–8. Second, teacher interviews give voice to the current practices, perceived difficulties, and rationalization of failures of teaching multiculturalism.

## CITIZENSHIP EDUCATION IN BAVARIA: GOOD CITIZENS AND GOOD FOREIGNERS

An important clue to changes in perceptions of progress toward a multicultural society can be gleaned from the study of textbooks over time. Textbooks are artifacts of educational policy reforms and political tools intended to bring about change in actual classrooms. One emergent topic in German social studies textbooks is the inclusion of foreigners in discussions of citizenship education. Particularly revealing is who this foreigner is and how he or she is depicted. Other emergent topics are migration and Islam.

Prior to 1993, there was little to no mention of Islam as a force within Germany or Europe, and any discussion of Islam was reserved for religion classes. Since Catholic and Evangelical churches oversee the required religion curricula where students are divided according to their religion (with non-Christians being relegated to an ethics class), adding Islam to the social studies curriculum greatly expanded the discussion. Additionally, migration to Germany becomes a topic for the ninth grade textbook; globalization is tackled in the tenth grade *Realschule* textbook. While these "foreign" topic chapters provide some of the only inclusions of non-Germans in the textbooks, the attention to teaching students about Islam recognizes that students in German schools will be working and living with citizens who are Muslims. This is one of the few examples of intercultural learning being directly interwoven into the textbooks. Curiously, there is no mention of any other religion in social studies texts, although students do learn about world religions in religion class. Yet it is noteworthy that, much like the examples of non-Germans that are included in the texts, Muslims, and in particular Turkish-Muslims, remain the only identified foreigners. There are of course Jews, Sikhs, Hindus, Buddhists, and a host of other religious and ethnic minorities in Germany, but Turkish Germans serve to represent all of them.

In the earliest textbooks (see appendix 5.1) that we analyzed, migration is treated as a phenomenon that happens, for the most part, outside of Germany. Starting in the late 1990s, textbooks present both asylum and economic migration as part of the German experience. The texts relate the experiences of refugee children who live in Germany, or picture refugees from the Yugoslavia conflict first fleeing from war and then finding peace in Germany. The experiences of *Aussiedler* are also included in this section, and this group is expressly identified as foreign, although their German heritage is explained. The difficulties of learning German and of finding work are presented as part of their story. In every textbook after 1998, integration is presented as something difficult but necessary. The stories profile youth (always Muslims) who have to live between two worlds.

The representation of Muslims should be seen as a positive development toward presenting Germany and belonging in Germany as pluralistic. In a sense, we can understand the development of chapters and curricular standards on Islam and migration as invoking Banks and Banks's (2001) second stage, "Heroes and Holidays," in curriculum change. While neither heroes nor holidays are mentioned, these chapters in the textbooks function in a similar manner by encapsulating non-German minority depictions in the "Islam" or "Migration" chapters. A notion of the exotic underlies this and, therefore, difference and exclusion are still primary forces.

Yet, as Banks and Banks argue, the transformation of curricula is a process that we here utilize analytically to show historical shifts in what is deemed important to understanding changes in society. While there has been a sizable Muslim population living in Germany since the 1960s, and migration has been a part of the modern German state since its inception, textbooks lag far behind in capturing social realities. This is evidenced, for the Bavarian case, in the fact that both Islam and migration have been added to the topics discussed in all social studies classrooms only in the late 1990s as part of multicultural education. It illustrates that both Islam and migration are now considered an inevitable part of understanding the current realities of German society and a necessity for citizenship education.

Despite the presence of depictions of non-Germans and of new topics mentioned above, textbooks remain for the most part Eurocentric. While each of the examples above represents aspects of Banks and Banks's stages in multicultural curricula transformation, even engaging at times with the final stage "Multicultural Social Action and Awareness" (Banks and Banks, 2001), there is still a serious gap or absence of intertwining diversity with citizenship. Indeed, the distinct categories of German and Non-German that are used in the textbooks indicate an attitude of "us and them." Even the more politically correct words, such as *Mitbürger* (cocitizen) or Turkish German, which themselves still draw lines, remain unused in the textbooks. The non-German, while growing in presence within the textbooks, is still a foreigner.

# TEACHER PERCEPTIONS AND THE DIVERSITY PROBLEM

Teachers at schools with high non-German enrollment connect diversity to citizenship education because they view it as necessary. In particular, teachers at schools which had a large number of repatriates (meaning their schools had become more diverse in the last ten years), talked about having to think about multicultural citizenship education and education for integration because they had no choice. Pedagogically, this present diversity allows teachers to engage students in discussions of mandated topics, such as Islam or migration. In contrast to some teachers who view multiculturalism as something only for dealing with the foreigner problem, a few see real value in integrating their students' experiences into the classroom. Brigitte,[6] a *Realschule* teacher with twenty years of teaching experience, focuses on the issue of resettlement since her family was transplanted from German regions of Poland, expelled after the close of World War II:

> Uprooted and newly replanted. Many of our students come from Eastern Europe, they came with their parents and they can really share their experiences. And they explain: how is it when one has to move? How does one feel? What kinds of problems does one have. What is it that makes setting down new roots difficult. Especially the Aussiedler children, many say very clearly: I would have rather stayed there or have just fallen over and died it was so hard. Then the others finally ask: why?

This emphasis on using students in the classroom was the most common way teachers talked about engaging in discussions of diversity. They also directly linked these activities to the state curricula. As one teacher, Michael, explains: "It is nice when we have a good Turkish student in the classroom or something, then I can have them talk about their experiences when we do the Islam section in the textbook." Yet even here in an explicit example of providing opportunity for diverse experiences, there is still a normative claim about when those experiences are appropriate. Turkish students should share their experiences, but only on the appointed day. We see, as in the textbooks, that recognition of diversity remains confined to Banks and Banks's notion of "Holidays and Heroes" (2001), or in this case, when it is time to discuss the Islam chapter.

## Tolerance and Transformation

Three teachers (two female and one male) that we interviewed at one small school with a high percentage of Russian immigrants, who all had between eight and fifteen years of teaching experience, present some of the more enlightened insights about the problems of integration and multicultural education. They did reflect on the inclusion of diversity as a part of preparing future citizens, German or non-German. Susanne summed it up well when she said:

> It is very important for us, because we have students from many nationalities. One must know something about the other, especially customs and maybe also about religion. One must know in order to not be afraid of difference and in order to be able to deal with it. In the 9th grade we have Islam as a theme. I have my Turkish students do reports. It is

better when the victim (Betroffener) tells their own story. They read from the Koran. I think it affected the students. For the first time they really come into contact with Islam. I think that through such activities people lose their fear of the other most quickly. They think: "I have seen that before, I know that is a nice fellow student, so this Islam thing cannot be so bad."

These teachers' talk embodies education as transformative, a notion that is essentially absent in all other reflections. Tolerance regarding difference and the idea that multicultural education is important for German and non-German children are grounded in these few teachers' reflections. Another teacher, Angela, from this same group, regards these issues within a larger framework:

There is the state on the one side and reality on the other side. Islam in the curriculum in sixth and ninth grade. I think it is very important that German children have some exposure to it, it is a foreign world. There are a lot of misunderstandings and false understandings [that] can be traced back to ignorance. For me it is important, also to go beyond the textbooks and do more than the curriculum dictates. I am very interested in history and for me that is the key aspect of social studies. I try to make the students see Judaism as the root of Christianity and Western thought. And they don't know anything at all, let alone about the relation Islam has to all this. But it is only through knowledge that there is any chance for tolerance.

That it is important to recognize diverse voices and, furthermore, to let the victims or those marked as different speak, contributes to the transformative aspect of these teachers' reflections. However, pedagogically, they still relegate inclusion of diverse experiences to the chapters in the textbooks or via the social studies curriculum. These teachers did directly connect citizenship education with diversity education, citing tolerance and ability to work with diverse people as normal and a routine part of their work in preparing future citizens. While there is more reflection about how German students can be influenced by hearing diverse voices, normatively, the voice of the other is still depicted as acceptable or appropriate only on a designated day.

## Community Involvement

When asked to discuss the most successful experience they have had teaching about tolerance and multiculturalism, however, these three teachers all described projects in which the whole community became involved. In each case, they discussed projects, such as building a traditional outdoor oven for baking bread or opening a youth center, which were external to curricula and textbooks. Below, Peter, the most senior of these three teachers, explains a community-based project that he believes is the school's only example of integrated learning:

Everybody was involved, the school psychologists, the director of the guidance center, the representative of the mayors office for foreigner affairs. We really wanted to tackle this problem of violence and help parents figure out how to deal with their own children. It was called Action Plan for "Border town—Children want rules and boundaries." We realized you have to educate the parents first. And then we realized that this required integration. This was not just a problem in the Russian-German families, although it is more obvious there, it is a societal problem. We developed a whole action plan from the Kindergarten through the schools. The best result was the youth center. A place where the Russian-German kids can go, sometimes the German children too. No alcohol, no violence, and they help run it too. It took the whole community though, not just the school.

It is important to stress that these community-based projects were described by the same three teachers who really focused on the importance of tolerance in educating all future citizens of Germany. In each case, regardless of the projects' scope, there was an immense personal commitment to the project on the part of the teacher, and in each case the projects were borne out of what was seen as a crisis—in the above example the incidence of violence in the school particularly involved Russian Germans. Yet the presence of such projects and the more reflective nature of the teachers' talk about multiculturalism and citizenship do point to the fact that such understandings and programs could be fostered in all teachers. Fundamentally, despite the presence of the more transformative talk, much of the discussions of diversity and examples of inclusion of multicultural voices were tied to fulfilling state requirements. And importantly, these examples came only from teachers working at schools where there were a high number of non-German students. In short, the presence of non-Germans in the school was a prerequisite for such discussion. In schools, whether because of school form or geographic location, where the percentage of non-Germans was less than 3 percent, a rejection of diversity as relevant emerges. Diversity becomes recognized as important, at least in certain units, only when it is demographically undeniable.

## I Don't Know the Point of Teaching It

For the most part, the recognition mentioned here preceded a discussion of why diversity education and integration had been ineffective within citizenship education. There are two important overall explanations for this failure. On the one hand, immigrants are characterized as not being able to learn about Western values and, on the other hand, state structures are typified as constraining. The idea of non-German students not being able to truly benefit from diversity education is, ironically, often linked to rudimentary understanding of immigrant groups' cultures. Below is one veteran teacher's view. With twenty years of practice, Roland demonstrates his skepticism regarding a change of attitudes:

> I try, of course, to bring about understanding. But then I have to wonder if there is even a point to it. I mean does it make sense that I learn about work ethic here at school, when Allah has already predetermined everything for me. And then really a German employer should not be surprised when his Turkish employee just lets some things slide because he is just going to say: it is Kismet. I don't know if anything I can do here is going to have an effect since this is how they think. But maybe it will help the Germans understand it.

Likewise, it is with very few exceptions, and always with reference to Islamic students who were cited as examples, that teachers doubted the feasibility of these educational efforts. With some consistency, the home life in Islamic families was given as a reason why diversity and multiculturalism education are ineffective. Relations between men and women, the position of women in Islamic society, and the lower overall educational level of the parents, were named as reasons why the values needed to become a citizen in a multicultural society cannot be held by non-German students. In nearly every school, for example, teachers talked about how the school offered German courses for Turkish women and very few people participated because "the Turkish men won't let their women learn German." Manfred, a senior teacher, stated:

> The intercultural and integration learning does not work the way I want it to because most of the Turkish families are not willing to be integrated. And if they are willing they are rejected by the others. The parents don't speak German or just enough to get by. Everything else that has to do with education, the language knowledge is just not there. The class of foreigners who come to this school are just too comfortable. And they don't let their children even speak German after they are thirteen or fourteen. Then it is all about Turkish traditions and mostly they are even worse than if they were in Turkey itself.

Manfred's comments are representative of the disparity between abstractly held norms and subjectively drawn conclusions. The idea of a German citizen who should be tolerant and respectful of difference is forwarded, but it is connected to a subjective judgment that non-German values make being this ideal citizen unattainable for foreigners. Being tolerant is something a good citizen should be, but a foreigner cannot be a good citizen.

Teachers, particularly those who felt more should be done to diversify the citizenship education practices, blamed structural constraints to true integration of multicultural activities into their classrooms. For the most part, time, lack of resources, and the expectation to cover too much material that "cannot really be thought of interculturally" are given as considerable barriers. Teachers often admitted to not really engaging in multiculturalism or to ignoring it at times other than when "we have to talk about Islam" or "deal with the globalization chapter." But they felt that if money for bringing in speakers or assistance from a social worker to develop projects were available, then more attention could be paid to multicultural themes. Most significantly though, teachers—again at schools with higher levels of non-German enrollment—pointed to a lack of training and support in German as a second language and intercultural education as extreme problems. Below, Maria, an experienced teacher who had been at this school for more than twenty years, describes how her school responds to students who don't speak German as natives:

> Here at this school there were always just teachers who would privately help students, giving them extra work to try to help them learn German. Unfortunately we don't have anybody who studied German as a second language. It is just an extra university subject. Then one does not know if one is doing it right, maybe using the wrong method despite good intentions. And one must really say that in Bavaria we have really tried to conserve resources in the wrong area. That unfortunately really must be said about our Minister President Edmund Stoiber. He is always very in favor of education, but then cuts the funding in the wrong area. And many citizens, including parents, are very taken with him.

German as a foreign language is not a required subject in teacher training, and there are no dedicated language teachers available at schools. Many teachers, such as Maria above, recognized this fundamental lack in their professional education as contributing to their inability to do much to help immigrant students. They also cited this as a reason that citizenship education, which seeks to include diverse experiences, is unrealistic. Over and over again, teachers explained that you cannot teach about being a part of German society if students do not even have the minimum requirement, a basic knowledge of the German language, to participate in it. Teachers mostly blamed the immigrant children and their parents. However, as the discussion of state constraints reveals, many teachers also criticized the education system. The following excerpt, again from Maria's interview, was typical of the overall commentary about state shortcomings:

> This is just the way the system works in Bavaria. One always waits for people who have sympathy and therefore become involved or offer help. Or that the parents know someone or have money to pay for after school help. Or, more likely, the teacher gets loaded up with work and it is said: so you are going to do this now. I am not trying to complain, there are also good things, and here in Bavaria we are well off, but we get by with what is already available.

Quite a number of teachers, both junior and senior, expressed frustration with the whole system, citing dependence on teachers to "just make schools work" somehow. While this can be interpreted as showing dissatisfaction with the state's education policies, it does not constitute resistance to them or to its inherent vision of citizenship education. We conclude that the prevailing philosophy underscoring teacher practices regarding citizenship education is ultimately anti-multiculturalism. This conclusion is modified when we compare the emergence of multiculturalism in teacher reflections to the emergent themes in our textbook analysis. For the most part, only teachers who are faced with a highly diverse classroom view the idea of multiculturalism as crucial. Mirroring state-level policies, the inclusion of non-German voices, when present, is only prevalent when the class is studying diversity chapters. In this sense, multiculturalism is, as in the state level policy, reduced to a narrow ethnocultural belief in superiority and privilege of nation and culture.

Interestingly, Europeanization provides an opportunity for teachers to address diversity without engaging with the messy issues of integration and diversity within Germany. This is very much in line with Luchtenberg's (2004) findings and serves to supplant the image of the ethnocultural German with that of the European. In either case, multiculturalism as the politics of mutual respect cannot develop fully. It would require that the neighbor, the stranger, and the family must all be treated equally. There is some recognition of the importance of this idea abstractly, particularly when we consider the voice of a minority of teachers who are concerned with tolerance. However, the manner in which multiculturalism is talked about by teachers, and their reasons for its failure to influence citizenship education, in our opinion, reveal skepticism, blame, superficial engagement, paternalist sentiment, and, ultimately, a disrespect for otherness.

Globalization is an even more abstract concept for both teachers and students. While they study and teach chapters on globalization, addressing such topics as the effects of wars on displacement of populations and migration, or the effects of pollution on the environment on a more global scale, the topic is relegated to a chapter rather than discussed more holistically. It is made concrete for the students at the European level, as when they discuss immigrants from Kosovo during the Yugoslavian conflict, or the Chernobyl nuclear disaster. Positive images of global connectedness mainly get mentioned in relation to food—that is, going to an Indian restaurant or buying exotic fruit in the winter. Human rights and cosmopolitan ethics as a commitment to a shared humanity are discussed as a global topic but they get interpreted as founded in a Christian ethic. As such, the boundaries between the familiar and the foreign are occasionally expanded to the European level. On the one hand, this expanded perspective is superficial: you might develop a sense of being part of the European community with regard to having the same currency and being able to travel without constraint across borders. But deeply held ethnocultural attitudes and values prevail when it comes to unwanted immigrants who try to enter on boats from Africa. Then the prejudicial wall of nationalist and European-centered sentiments is raised against the strangers.

## DISCUSSION: MULTICULTURALISM AND
## THE U.S. EXPERIENCE WITH MINORITY EDUCATION

Law (2004) argues that no country has abandoned local and national citizenship education in favor of a purely cosmopolitan or global education. That is, nations still insist on the primary commitment of its citizens to the state rather than to a global society. Globalization has influenced educational reform and discourse. One of the most critical areas of influence has been in the coupling of citizenship and multicultural education as areas of educational inquiry.

Torres (2001), in writing about Latin American experiences with democracy education, notes that multiculturalism must be considered when examining citizenship and education, particularly in a democracy. Yet it is only recently that this area of inquiry, that is, the exploration of the connection between multiculturalism and citizenship education, has become a more consistent part of the education literature. The majority of scholarship on multiculturalism, multicultural education, or diversity education comes out of the United States and is consequently focused largely on issues of European American privilege and the resulting disenfranchisement of nonwhites. Indeed, because of the literature's origins in the American civil rights movement, some authors have argued that the literature has been dominated by issues of race, in particular black and white relations (cf. Suarez-Orozco, Qin-Hilliard, and NetLibrary Inc., 2004). The literature, in particular Banks (1997, 2004), has been very influential in education because it has focused on curricular, textbook, and teacher training reforms, which seek to ensure that the histories, values, and experiences of nonwhite groups are interwoven into learning. Further, Banks, as well as other scholars such as Nieto (2004) and Soto (1996), have argued that multicultural education must seek to recognize oppression, and use education as a tool of empowerment.

The idea of education as empowerment and as a means of opposing oppression is clearly applicable beyond the U.S. context. But until recently, multicultural education has not included a comparative or international perspective. However, with globalization and the influence, in particular, of immigration, this has begun to change. Literature coming out of the United States has begun to include non-U.S. contexts in discussions of multicultural education. The intertwining between citizenship education and diversity are being made more directly in this literature. Indeed, Sutton (2005) argues that the field of multicultural education is beginning to "mature" as it has started to include comparative perspectives. Levinson's (2001) study of a Mexican middle school probes, among other questions, the relationship between educational equity and ethnic background. Ryan (2006), also focusing on Mexico, examines the question of interculturality and citizenship education. Several scholars (cf. Law, 2004; Leung and Lee, 2006; Martin and Feng, 2006) have contributed studies on Asia's experiences with citizenship education and diversity. Also beginning to appear are studies focusing on the countries of Europe, which have often self-identified, and been identified by others, as homogeneous despite long-standing diversity. These studies, connecting citizenship and diversity through education, are also beginning to appear (Geyer, 2005; Guilherme et al., 2006; Michaels, 2007; Schissler and Soysal, 2005; Stevick, 2006; Walat, 2006).

Indeed, in surveying recent publications about citizenship education, such as those cited above, it becomes clear that influences of globalization have refocused scholars' attention on citizenship education, multiculturalism, and interconnected areas of inquiry. Sutton (2005) argues that throughout the world, and in a wide variety of educational systems, multicultural education has become a larger part of the educational reform discourse:

> Loosened from its mooring in the U.S. civil rights movement, multicultural education has become a rubric—or foil—for a certain arena of educational reform discourse around the world. . . . [T]he "epochal" dimensions of globalization such as wide-scale human migration and intensification of global communication have complicated social identities within many nations and so stimulated public debate on how pluralism is recognized in the curriculum and pedagogy of national school systems. (Sutton, 2005, p. 2)

In Germany, as this study indicates, this recognition of the relative importance of multiculturalism comes after years of denying the existence of diversity. But the influence of global forces, particularly Europeanization and migration, have indeed brought issues of multicultural education, as a critical part of citizenship education, to the forefront. While Germany still has a long way to go to fully identify itself as a multicultural society, our investigation has attempted to document the process, the problems, the successes and failures, so far, of this path. Citizenship education and multicultural education are crucial elements in this transformation.

## APPENDIX 5.1

### Interview Participants used in this Study

In the *Hauptschule*, much like in U.S. elementary school, teachers lead classes and teach all subjects. Thus, we list what grade-level they teach. In the *Realschule*, teach-

**Table 5.1.** **Participants**

| Teacher | School Form | Subjects Taught/Grade level | Years in Service |
|---------|-------------|-----------------------------|------------------|
| 1 | Realschule | History, German, and Social Studies (H, G, SS) | 15 |
| 2 | Realschule | H, G, SS | 1 |
| 3 | Realschule | H, G, SS | 8 |
| 4 | Realschule | H, G, SS | 12 |
| 5 | Realschule | H, G, SS | 16 |
| 6 | Realschule | H, G, SS | 3 |
| 7 | Realschule | H, G, SS | 22 |
| 8 | Realschule | H, G, SS | 9 |
| 9 | Realschule | H, G, SS | 18 |
| 10 | Realschule | H, G, SS | 14 |
| 11 | Realschule | H, G, SS | 32 |
| 12 | Realschule | Religion, History, Social Studies (R, H, SS) | 7 |
| 13 | Realschule | R, H, SS | 8 |
| 14 | Realschule | R, H, SS | 13 |
| 15 | Realschule | R, H, SS | 9 |
| 16 | Realschule | R, H, SS | 4 |
| 17 | Realschule | R, H, SS | 6 |
| 18 | Realschule | R, H, SS | 28 |
| 19 | Realschule | R, H, SS | 7 |
| 20 | Realschule | R, H, SS | 4 |
| 21 | Realschule | Religion, German, Social Studies (R, G, SS) | 14 |
| 22 | Realschule | R, G, SS | 16 |
| 23 | Realschule | R, G, SS | 4 |
| 24 | Realschule | R, G, SS | 3 |
| 25 | Realschule | History and Social Studies | 21 |
| 26 | Realschule | Religion and Social Studies | 12 |
| 27 | Hauptschule | 5 | 3 |
| 28 | Hauptschule | 5 | 9 |
| 29 | Hauptschule | 5 | 17 |
| 30 | Hauptschule | 5 | 28 |
| 31 | Hauptschule | 5 | 4 |
| 32 | Hauptschule | 5 | 16 |
| 33 | Hauptschule | 6 | 24 |
| 34 | Hauptschule | 6 | 12 |
| 35 | Hauptschule | 6 | 19 |
| 36 | Hauptschule | 6 | 3 |
| 37 | Hauptschule | 6 | 5 |
| 38 | Hauptschule | 6 | 16 |
| 39 | Hauptschule | 6 | 12 |
| 40 | Hauptschule | 7 | 2 |
| 41 | Hauptschule | 7 | 2 |
| 42 | Hauptschule | 7 | 2 |
| 43 | Hauptschule | 7 | 18 |
| 44 | Hauptschule | 7 | 24 |
| 45 | Hauptschule | 7 | 17 |
| 46 | Hauptschule | 8 | 8 |
| 47 | Hauptschule | 8 | 11 |
| 48 | Hauptschule | 8 | 6 |
| 49 | Hauptschule | 8 | 23 |
| 50 | Hauptschule | 8 | 33 |
| 51 | Hauptschule | 8 | 13 |
| 52 | Hauptschule | 9 | 15 |
| 53 | Hauptschule | 9 | 3 |
| 54 | Hauptschule | 9 | 6 |
| 55 | Hauptschule | 9 | 13 |
| 56 | Hauptschule | 9 | 12 |
| 57 | Hauptschule | 9 | 15 |
| 58 | Hauptschule | 9 | 23 |

ers teach specific subjects to all grade-levels, therefore we note their subject areas. The participants are illustrated in table 5.1.

## TEXTBOOK SERIES USED IN STUDY (GRADES 5–10 FOR THE *HAUPTSCHULE* AND GRADE 10 FOR THE *REALSCHULE*)

1. Begegnungen Geschichte, Sozialkunde, Erdkunde.; Karl Filser. Munchen, OldenbourgAmbros Brucker; 2005, 1999, 1998, 1997.
2. Demokratie verpflichtet. Andreas Mack; Munchen, Oldenbourg, 2003, 1995, 1984 (used through 1994).
3. Durchblick/Bayern/Hauptschule. Hanne Auer, Braunschweig; Westermann, 2004, 2001, 1999, 1998, 1997.
4. Forum: Sozialkunde, Realschule Bayern. Braunschweig: Westermann, Grundwissen Okonomie/Christine Fischer, 2004.
5. Geschichte, Sozialkunde, Erdkunde. Klett-Perthes (Terra). Harald-Matthias Neumann., 2004, 1999, 1998, 1997.
6. Politik-nicht ohne mich! Bamberg: Buchner, 2003.
7. Politik-Wie? So! Rainer Dorrfuss. Bamberg: Buchner, 1995.
8. Geschichte-Sozialkunde-Erdkunde: GSE; Hauptschule. Regensburg: Wolf, 1997, 1998 and 1999.
9. Sozialkunde/Bayern/Hauptschule: Regenburg: Wolf, 1994,1995
10. Menschen, Zeiten, Raume/Barern/Hauptschule. Berlin: Cornelsen. 1999, 1998, 1997.
11. Trio/Bayern/Hauptschule: Geschichte/Sozialkunde/Erdkunde, Norbert Autenrieth; Hannover; Schroedel, 1994, 1997, 1998 and 1999, 2004.
12. ZeitRaume: entdecken, erfahren, orientieren. Norbert Horberg. Stuttgart: Klett, 1997 and 1998.
13. Burger und Politik: ein Lehrund Arbeisbuch fur Sozialkunde, politische Bildung. Eduard Steinbugl. Darmstadt: Winklers Verl. Gebr. Grimm, 1995.
14. bsv-Sozialkunde. Ingrid Ziegler. Munchen: Bayer. Schulbuch-Verl., 1991 and 1992.
15. Denkanstosse: Sozialkunde fur die Hauptschule. Gunter Neumann. Kulmbach: Baumann, 1986 and 1987 [used through 1998].
16. Politisch denken, urteilen and handeln: ein Lehr- und Arbeitsbuch fur den politischen und sozialkundlichen Unterricht. Von Roland Herold. Wolfenbuttel: Heckner, 1982 [used through 1994].
17. Sozialkunde/ bearb. Oskar Buhler. Schulerarbeitscheft. Ansbach: Ansbacher Verl., Ges., 1986 [used through 1995].
18. Sozialkunde fur Hauptschulen in Bayern. Dieter Grosser. Braunschweig: Westermann, 1988 [used through 1995].
19. Burger und Politik: e. Lehr-u. Arbeisbuch fur Sozialkunde, polit. Bildung. E. Steinbugl. Darmstadt: Winkler, 1984 [used through 1992].

## NOTES

1. We focused on *Hauptschulen* and *Realschulen* because they have a formal social studies curriculum which is not the case at the elementary level.

2. Elementary schools were not closed due to the belief that young children are better educated in their neighborhood school.

3. This term, which literally translates to out-settler, is actually a legal term that refers to all people who settled in areas east of the German Empire (Ingenhorst, 1997). For the purposes of this essay, we simplify the language and use the term *Aussiedler* or Russian German to refer to the large group of people who settled in Germany between 1990 and the present.

4. Article 116 of the German Basic Law determines German citizenship to be heritage-based. *Deutscher im Sinne dieses Grundgesetzes ist vorbehaltlich anderweitiger gesetzlicher Regelung, wer die deutsche Staatsangehörigkeit besitzt oder als Flüchtling oder Vertriebener deutscher Volkszugehörigkeit oder als dessen Ehegatte oder Abkömmling in dem Gebiete des Deutschen Reiches nach dem Stande vom 31. Dezember 1937 Aufnahme gefunden hat.* (A German is, in the sense of this Basic Law unless otherwise legally regulated, a person who possesses German national citizenship or who is a refugee or displaced person of German heritage or his spouse, or descendent, who has been admitted to the area of the German Empire as of December 31, 1937).

5. See for example: Council Directive 2003/109/EC of 25 November 2003 Concerning the status of third country nationals who are long-term residents.

6. All names are pseudonyms.

## REFERENCES

Arnove, R. F. (1999). Introduction: Reframing comparative education: The dialectic of the global and the local. In R. F. Arnove and C. A. Torres (Eds.), *Comparative education: The dialectic of the global and the local* (pp. 1–23). New York: Rowman & Littlefield.

Aurenheimer, G. (2006). The German education system: Dysfunctional for an immigration society. *European Education, 37*(4), 75–89.

Banks, J. A. (1997). *Educating citizens in a multicultural society.* New York: Teachers College Press.

Banks, J. A. (Ed.). (2004). *Diversity and citizenship education.* San Francisco: Jossey-Bass.

Banks, J. A. (2006). *Cultural diversity and education: Foundations, curriculum, and theory.* (fifth ed.). Boston: Pearson/Allyn and Bacon.

Banks, J. A., and Banks, C. A. M. (2001). *Handbook of research on multicultural education.* San Francisco: Jossey-Bass.

Brubaker, R. (1992). *Citizenship and nationhood in France and Germany.* Cambridge and London: Cambridge University Press.

Creswell, J. W. (2007). *Educational research: Planning, conducting, and evaluating quantitative and qualitative research.* Columbus, OH: Merrill.

Ertl, H., and Phillips, D. (December 2000). The enduring nature of the tripartite system of secondary schooling in Germany: Some explanations. *British Journal of Educational Studies, 48*(4), 391–412.

Federal Ministry of the Interior. (2006). *Bericht zur Evaluierung des Gesetzes zur Steuerung und Begrenzung der Zuwanderung und zur Regelung des Aufenthalts und der Integration*

*Unionsbürger und Ausländer (Zuwanderungsgestetz)* [Report about the evaluation of the regulation and limitation of immigration and the regulation of the residency and integration of citizens of the union and foreigners (Immigration Act)]. Retrieved on January 11, 2009, from www.fluechtlingsrat-nrw.de/2371/.

Führ, C., and Tapia, I. (1997). *The German education system since 1945.* Bonn: Inter Nationes.

Geyer, M. (2005). World history and general education: How to bring the world to the classroom. In H. Schissler and Y. N. Soysal (Eds.), *The nation, Europe and the world: Textbooks and curricula in transition* (pp. 193–210). New York: Berghahn.

Giesecke, H. (1993). *Politische bildung: Didaktik und methodik fuer schule und jugendarbeit.* Munich: Juventa.

Gosewinkel, D. (1998). Citizenship and nationhood: The historical development of the German case. In U. Preuss and F. Requejo (Eds.), *European citizenship, multiculturalism and the state* (pp. 125–36). Baden-Baden: Nomos Verlagsgesellschaft.

Guilherme, M., Pureza, J. M., Paulos da Silva, R., and Santos, H. (2006). The intercultural dimension of citizenship education in Portugal. In G. Alred, M. Byram, and M. Fleming (Eds.), *Education for intercultural citizenship* (pp. 213–32). Clevedon, UK: Multilingual Matters.

Haendle, C., Oesterreich, D., and Trommer, L. (Eds.). (1999). *Aufgaben politischer bildung in der sekundarstufe I: Studien aus dem projekt civic education.* Opladen: Leske and Budrich.

Hansen, R., and Weil, P. (2001). *Towards a European nationality. Citizenship immigration and nationality law in the EU.* New York: Palgrave.

Ingenhorst, H. (1997). *Die Russland-Deutschen: Aussiedler zwischen tradition und moderne.* Frankfurt/Main: Campus Verlag.

Joppke, C. (2001). The evolution of alien rights in the United States, Germany and the European Union. In T. A. Aleinikoff and D. Klusmeyer (Eds.), *Citizenship today: Global perspectives and practices* (pp. 36-62). Washington, DC: Brookings Institution Press.

[KMK] Kultusministerium. (2002). *Statistische veroeffentlichungen der kultusministerkonferenz: Auslaendische schueler und schulabsolventen 1991–2000.* Bonn: Sekretariat der Ständigen Konferenz der Kultusminister der Länder in der Bundesrepublik Deutschland.

Krippendorf, K. (2004). *Content analysis: An introduction to its methodology* (second ed.). Thousand Oaks, CA: Sage.

Law, W. W. (2004). Globalization and citizenship education in Hong Kong and Taiwan. *Comparative Education Review, 48*(3), 253–73.

Leung, W. S., and Lee, W. O. (2006). National identity at a crossroads: The struggle between culture, language and politics in Hong Kong. In G. Alred, M. Byram, and M. Fleming (Eds.), *Education for intercultural citizenship* (pp. 23–46). Clevedon, UK: Multilingual Matters.

Levinson, B. A. U. (2001). *We are all equal : Student culture and identity at a Mexican secondary school, 1988-1998.* Durham, NC: Duke University Press.

Luchtenberg, S. (2004). Ethnic diversity and citizenship education in Germany. In J. A. Banks (Ed.), *Diversity and citizenship education* (pp. 245–72). San Francisco: Jossey-Bass.

Martin, S., and Feng, A. (2006). The construction of citizenship and nation building: The Singapore case. In G. Alred, M. Byram, and M. Fleming (Eds.), *Education for intercultural citizenship* (pp. 47–68). Clevedon, UK: Multilingual Matters.

Michaels, D. (2007). *Transcending the nation-state in Education? Supranational and national narratives of identity in socialist and post-socialist Czechoslovak school textbooks.* Paper presented at the Comparative International Education Society.

Nieto, S. (2004). *Affirming diversity.* Boston: Pearson.

O'Leary, S. (1998). The options for the reform of European Union citizenship. In S. O'Leary and T. Tiilikainen (Eds.), *Citizenship and nationality status in the New Europe* (pp. 84–86). London: Sweet and Maxwell.

Ortloff, D. H. (2006). Becoming European: A framing analysis of three countries' civics education curricula. *European Education, 37*(4), 35–49.

Papastephanou, M. (2005). Globalisation, globalism and cosmopolitanism as an educational ideal. *Educational Philosophy and Theory, 37*(4), 533–51.

Rawls, J. (1999). *The law of the peoples.* Cambridge, MA: Harvard University Press.

Rostek, K., and Davies, G. (2006, July). The impact of Union citizenship on national citizenship policies. *European Integration Online Papers, 10.*

Ryan, P. (2006). Interculturality, identity and citizenship education in Mexico. In G. Alred, M. Byram, and M. Fleming (Eds.), *Education for intercultural citizenship* (pp. 11–22). Clevedon, UK: Multilingual Matters.

Schissler, H., and Soysal, Y. N. (2005). *The nation, Europe and the world: Textbooks and curricula in transition.* New York: Beghahn Books.

Soto, L. D. (1996). *Language, culture, and power: Bilingual families and the struggle for quality education.* Albany: State University of New York Press.

Stevick, D. (2006). *Civic education policy and practice in post-Soviet Estonia: From global influences to classroom practice.* Unpublished dissertation, Indiana University.

Suárez-Orozco, M. M., Qin-Hilliard, D., and NetLibrary Inc. (2004). *Globalization culture and education in the new millennium.* Berkeley: University of California Press.

Sutton, M. (2005). The globalization of multicultural education. *Indiana Journal of International Legal Studies, 12*(1), 97–108.

Torney-Purta, J., Amadeo, J.-A., Lehmann, R., and ERIC Clearinghouse for Social Studies/Social Science Education. (2001). Civic knowledge and engagement at age 14 in 28 countries results from the IEA civic education study [microform].

Torres, C. A. (2001). Education, social class and dual citizenship: The travails of multiculturalism in Latin America. In C. A. Grant and J. L. Lei (Eds.), *Global constructions of multicultural education: Theories and realities* (pp. 337–54). Mahwah, NJ: Lawrence Erlbaum.

Walat, M. (2006). Towards an intercultural frame of mind: Citizenship in Poland. In G. Alred, M. Byram, and M. Fleming (Eds.), *Education for intercultural citizenship* (pp. 164–86). Clevedon, UK: Multilingual Matters.

Walzer, M. (1990). What does it mean to be an American? In D. A. Hollinger (Ed.), *The American intellectual tradition: Vol. II* (pp. 387–99). New York: Oxford University Press.

Wilde, S. (2004). *Citizenship education in Germany: Not doing it by the book.* Oxford: Symposium Books.

*Chapter Six*

# Educational Diversity in China: Responding to Globalizing and Localizing Forces

Stephen Bahry, Patrick Darkhor, and Jia Luo

In recent years, the question of globalization has come to the fore in discussions on political, cultural, and economic change, a debate in which China is no bystander. Indeed, many within China see the recent educational changes as in part responses to globalization. China requires a "world-class curriculum" with national educational objectives (Wu, 2003), and so the Ministry of Education (2002a) justifies the latest curriculum reform in China as a response to three major global forces: (1) the rapid rise of the information economy, (2) the intensification of global economic competition, and (3) the increasing degradation of the natural environment. In this light, the Education for All (EFA) campaign cosponsored by the United Nations Educational, Scientific and Cultural Organization (UNESCO), United Nations Children's Fund (UNICEF), and World Bank has led to more countries passing regulations, as China has done, to achieve compulsory primary and junior secondary education (UNESCO, 2000).

To what degree has universal basic education spread to China? On quantitative measures of the achievement of EFA objectives such as enrollment, attendance, dropout, and completion figures, China made huge strides in spreading basic nine-year education; however, when these measures are disaggregated by gender, region, and ethnicity, the picture is much more complex, for there remain significant disparities in completion of basic education between male and female students, among regions and ethnicities (UNESCO, 2000).

This chapter deals with the complexity of change in education in China and its responses to local, national, and global influences. The first section draws on the results of the most recent national census to illustrate the complex interaction of region, ethnicity, and gender on educational attainment throughout geographic and social space in China. Next the chapter addresses two contrasting conceptions of quality education in China's national curriculum that lie behind recent curriculum reforms, which include limited decentralization of curriculum authority to the local and school level. A review follows of approaches to linguistic, cultural, and environmental diversity within China through bilingual education, multicultural education, and environmental education. Finally, a comparative perspective on approaches to diversity in Chinese education is provided, drawing parallels and contrasts with North American education.

We draw on field research in China on culturally relevant local curriculum for Tibetan-speaking areas in rural northwest China (Jia Luo), on stakeholders' perceptions of the role of the mother-tongue and bilingual education in the revitalization of an endangered minority language in rural northwest China (Bahry), and of teachers' perceptions of development of school-based curriculum for environmental education in urban northeast China (Darkhor). In addition, we discuss relevant primary documents and statistics published in Chinese and secondary research published in English and Chinese.

## EDUCATIONAL DIVERSITY IN CHINA

During the Cultural Revolution (1966–1976), China embarked upon a radical mass-education policy, which was achieved in several ways: by the opening of many non-formal "people-run" schools using unqualified or partially qualified teachers, which greatly increased access to schooling particularly at the village level; by restricting the practice of holding back students who performed poorly on tests; by rescinding the use of entrance examinations to control promotion from primary to junior secondary and from junior to senior secondary education (Hawkins, 1992; Lewin, Xu, Little, and Zheng, 1994; Pepper, 1990; Price, 2005). According to Suzanne Pepper, China's intellectuals opposed the populist approach to education, which in their view, sacrificed quality for the sake of valueless quantity, summing up this viewpoint as "no school was preferable to a low-quality school" (1990, p. 31 ). Thus, Pepper argues, educational policy after 1977 was radically reoriented from a "mass education" model to an "elite education" model. As a result of this policy shift, many schools were closed and the numbers of youth not continuing in school increased (Pepper, 1996).

Statistics from the 2000 census permit a concrete illustration showing the scale of the reduction in secondary level education. As is evident from table 6.1, which displays the percentage of each five-year age cohort from 1936–1940 to 1981–1985 who were able to complete junior and senior secondary school, fewer students in the 1966–1970 cohort completed secondary education than the previous cohort. The decrease was particularly stark at the senior secondary level, 8 percent for males and 5.2 percent for females. Indeed, by 2000, male senior secondary completion levels had still not reached the completion rates achieved during the 1970s.

Of course, this begs the question: what is a quality school, a quality teacher, a good student? The answer of Chinese society at large is that the central criterion is high scores on the *GaoKao* national college entrance examination (CEE), which is the measure of student quality, teacher quality, and school quality. This powerful influence of entrance examinations on curriculum and pedagogy extends down the line: a good junior secondary school prepares students well to pass key senior secondary school entrance examinations (Epstein, 1993; "Harmful key school system," 2006; Huang, 2004; MOE, 2002a).

Furthermore, quality of schools and education depends on financial resources, which vary considerably among regions, as illustrated in figure 6.1, which displays

**Table 6.1. Population with Complete Junior and Senior Secondary Education (2000 Census) (Percentage of Five-Year Age Cohorts from 1936–1985)**

| Years Born | Age in 2000 | Junior Secondary | | | | Senior Secondary | | | |
| | | Years 13–15 | Male | Female | | Years 16–18 | Male | Female |
|---|---|---|---|---|---|---|---|---|
| 1936–1940 | 60–64 | 1949–1955 | 32.1 | 13.6 | | 1952–1958 | 9.2 | 3.3 |
| 1941–1945 | 55–59 | 1954–1960 | 42.3 | 22.0 | | 1957–1963 | 10.0 | 4.4 |
| 1946–1950 | 50–54 | 1959–1965 | 44.5 | 24.5 | | 1962–1968 | 9.7 | 4.3 |
| 1951–1955 | 45–49 | 1964–1970 | 56.5 | 33.5 | | 1967–1973 | 14.3 | 7.0 |
| 1956–1960 | 40–44 | 1969–1975 | 71.8 | 50.1 | | 1972–1978 | 26.5 | 17.6 |
| 1961–1965 | 35–39 | 1974–1980 | 79.5 | 63.0 | | 1977–1983 | 25.4 | 17.7 |
| 1966–1970 | 30–34 | 1979–1985 | 74.6 | 61.2 | | 1982–1988 | 17.4 | 12.5 |
| 1971–1975 | 25–29 | 1984–1990 | 78.4 | 68.7 | | 1987–1993 | 18.6 | 14.7 |
| 1976–1980 | 20–24 | 1989–1995 | 84.0 | 78.0 | | 1992–1998 | 21.4 | 17.1 |
| 1981–1985 | 15–19 | 1994–2000 | 87.2 | 83.2 | | 1997– | 22.6 | 18.6 |

Source: Calculated from China (2002).

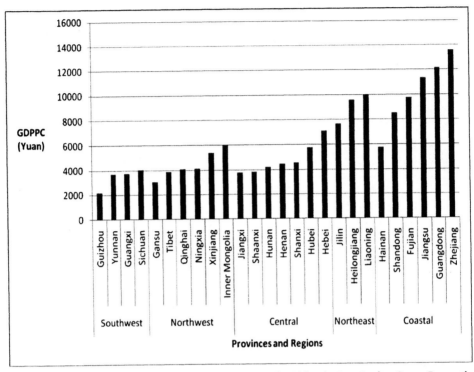

**Figure 6.1.** Regional and Interprovincial Differences in China in Per Capita Gross Domestic Product

the gross domestic product per capita (GDPPC) for 2003 by province and region. As might be expected, educational attainment in China varies greatly according to where students live. City residents complete more schooling than town dwellers, who in turn receive more education than those in township centers and villages (see figure 6.2). Similarly, there is broad variation in years of schooling by region, as is evident from figure 6.3, which indicates average total years of schooling by province. Clearly, although areas of low income and low educational attainment do not coincide exactly, there is considerable overlap between the two.

Beyond rural-urban and provincial disparities, educational attainment also varies considerably among ethnicities. As can be seen from figure 6.4, most minority languages in China are found in southwestern, northwestern, and northeastern China, again showing a considerable amount of overlap with figures 6.1 and 6.3. Mean figures averaging educational attainment figures for all minorities together fail to capture the complexity of the situation. For example, while from 1990 to 2000, the mean proportion of China's population age 6 and above with higher education rose from 2 to 3 percent, when China's ethnic groups are compared, there is a great deal of diversity. For example, the average proportion of the population with higher education in 1990 and 2000 among Koreans was well above average, 5.25 percent and 8.38 percent respectively; among Tibetans, 1.68 percent and 1.34 percent, well below average; and among the majority ethnicity, the Han, 2.03 percent and 3.82 percent, close to the national average (China, 2002).

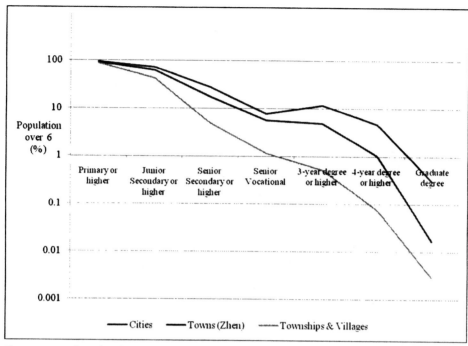

**Figure 6.2.  Educational Attainment and Residence in China: Cities, Towns, Countryside**

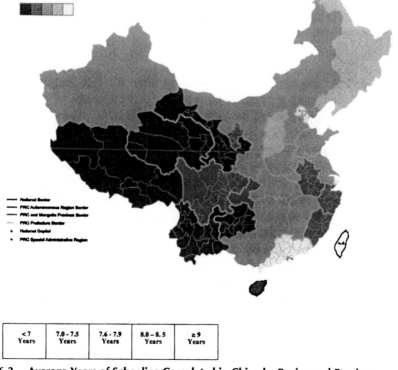

**Figure 6.3.  Average Years of Schooling Completed in China by Region and Province**

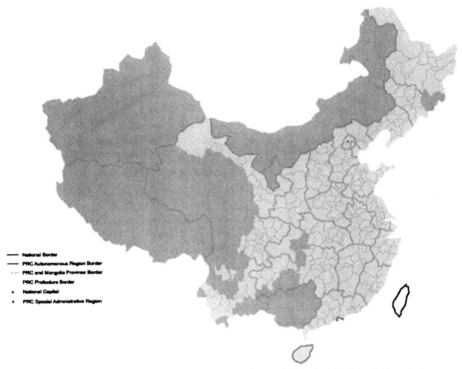

**Figure 6.4.** **Administrative Divisions in China Based on Ethnic Minority Population: Autonomous Regions and Districts (in dark grey)**

This variability becomes even more complex when we disaggregate statistics on educational attainment by gender. Relative gender balance exists for primary education, where universal completion has now been virtually achieved, and the gender gap in senior secondary completion is decreasing (UNESCO, 2000; China, 2002). Nevertheless, gender, region, ethnicity, and attainment interact, not necessarily in the same way at each level of schooling or for each ethnicity. From figure 6.5, it is evident that educational attainment is greater in most regions for males than females, but the gap in most regions is fairly small. However, there is considerable variation among regions, such that females' educational attainment levels in one region may be as high as or higher than male attainment levels in another region.

Similarly, among most ethnicities educational attainment levels are higher among males than females, but that is not to say that female educational attainment is uniformly low. In fact, educational attainment for females of one ethnicity may be higher than those of males for another ethnicity. For example, as can be seen from figure 6.6, as of 2000, completion rates are higher for Korean females than Han males and for Han females than Tajik males. This suggests that cultural attitudes toward the importance of state education for males and females are not uniform in China, but may differ among ethnicities. Hansen (1999) finds that among the Dai of southwest China, for example, a traditional Buddhist education was highly valued for males and not for females, so that many boys would drop out of government schools at some point to

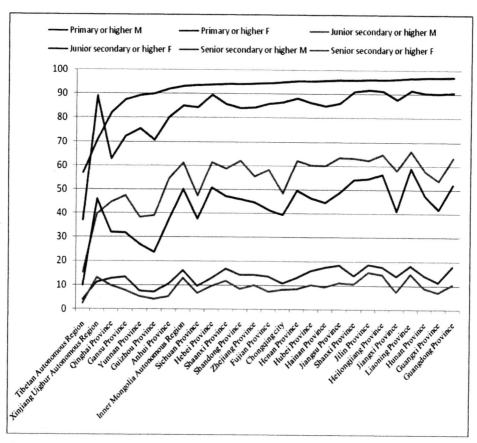

**Figure 6.5.** Educational Attainment in China of Population Aged Six and Higher by Region and Gender

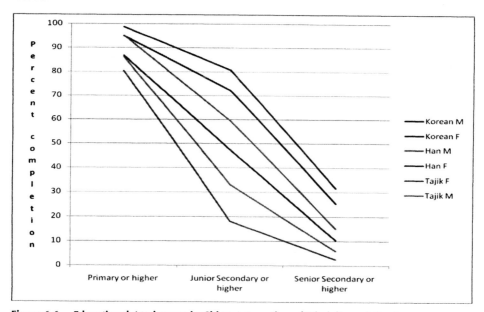

**Figure 6.6.** Educational Attainment in China: Interaction of Ethnicity and Gender

attend a monastery school, whereas for girls state schooling was the only means to continue their formal education.

For higher levels of schooling, residence may take priority over gender. As is evident from table 6.2, town females more often complete junior and secondary schooling than do countryside males; similarly, city females more frequently graduate from junior and secondary schooling than do town males.

## CURRICULUM REFORM IN CHINA: WHAT IS QUALITY EDUCATION?

The Ministry of Education (MOE) (2002a) has recently produced a strong critique of the elite model of Chinese education in force after 1977, calling this approach both *examination-oriented education*, in reference to its overdependence on examinations to determine curriculum and pedagogy, and also *promotion-oriented education*, due to the overemphasis on promotion to the next level of the education system as the main measure of quality of schools and pedagogy. It is argued that *examination-oriented education* aimed mainly at college preparation for urban students, focusing excessively on intellectual development, and neglecting the development of other important qualities of students. The Ministry of Education has proposed instead, *education for essential qualities*. By *essential qualities*, they mean innate and acquired characteristics of students. The aim of this reform is to foster students' "all-round development," which is explained as balancing the development of not only knowledge, but also practical skills and positive attitudes: providing not only intellectual training, but also physical, moral, esthetic, and labor education. Learners are no longer expected simply to receive and faithfully reproduce knowledge from authoritative sources, but are also expected to show practical problem-solving skills, creativity, innovation ability, independent learning skills, and positive attitudes toward learning, all areas that *examination-based education* is said to have neglected.

The MOE (2002b) has also criticized the *uniformity* of knowledge in the single unified standard curriculum for all China oriented mainly to large urban centers on the coast. This centralized curriculum presented lessons that were far from the experience of most Chinese, failing to connect to the curriculum the prior knowledge of the majority of the country's children, who live in rural areas. Under *examination-based*

Table 6.2.  Percent of Population with Complete Primary, Junior, and Senior Secondary Education by Residence and Gender (2000 Census)

| | Primary | | Junior Secondary | | Senior Secondary | |
|---|---|---|---|---|---|---|
| | *Male* | *Female* | *Male* | *Female* | *Male* | *Female* |
| All China | 94.7 | 86.0 | 58.1 | 46.2 | 14.6 | 10.0 |
| Cities | 97.6 | 92.3 | 76.3 | 69.2 | 31.2 | 25.2 |
| Towns (Zhen) | 96.5 | 89.7 | 67.9 | 58.0 | 21.6 | 14.4 |
| Townships and Villages | 93.2 | 82.8 | 49.1 | 34.8 | 6.8 | 3.2 |

*Source:* Calculated from China (2002).

**Table 6.3. New National Basic Education Curriculum**

| Year | Primary | | | | | | Junior Secondary | | | % of Nine-Year Total Hours |
|---|---|---|---|---|---|---|---|---|---|---|
| | 1 | 2 | 3 | 4 | 5 | 6 | 7 | 8 | 9 | |
| | National Curriculum | | | | | | | | | |
| Subjects | Language | | | | | | | | | 20–22 % |
| | Mathematics | | | | | | | | | 13–15 % |
| | Arts, or Music & Fine Arts | | | | | | | | | 9–11 % |
| | Physical Education | | | | | | Physical Education & Health | | | 10–11 % |
| | Moral Character & Life | | Moral Character & Society | | | | Thought & Moral Character | | | 7–9 % |
| | | | Science | | | | Science, or Biology, Physics & Chemistry | | | 7–9% |
| | | | Foreign Language | | | | | | | 6–8% |
| | | | | | History & Society | | | | | 3–4 % |
| | Other Curriculum | | | | | | | | | |
| | Local and School-Based Curriculum | | | | | | | | | 10–12% |
| | | | Comprehensive Practice Activities | | | | | | | 6–8% |
| Hours/ Weeks | 26 | 26 | 30 | 30 | 30 | 30 | 34 | 34 | 34 | 274 |
| Annual Hours | 910 | 910 | 1050 | 1050 | 1050 | 1050 | 1190 | 1190 | 1122 | 9522 |

*Source*: Adopted from Ministry of Education (2002a, p. 24).

*education*, the majority of China's students were "failed" students, who not only did not succeed in the college-bound curriculum, but also failed to learn any practical knowledge and skills useful in their local area outside school, seriously affecting their ability to find suitable employment and to make a positive contribution to their local community. As a result, the MOE has introduced three levels of curriculum management: the national curriculum, local curriculum, and school curriculum, and requires up to 10–12 percent of classroom time be spent on local and school curriculum, and 6–8 percent of time be spent on comprehensive practical activities decided at the local and school level. Local and school-based curricula are intended to compensate for weaknesses of the national curriculum in the local context (Ministry of Education, 2002a, 2002b; Huang, 2004; Su, 2002; UNESCO, 2000). Table 6.3 summarizes the new curriculum in tabular form.

## ADAPTING CURRICULUM TO LOCAL LINGUISTIC DIVERSITY: BILINGUAL EDUCATION IN CHINA

Article 4 of China's constitution has enshrined "the right to use and develop minority languages in minority communities" (Zhou, 2004, p. 79). Article 36 of the People's Republic of China (PRC) Regional Autonomy Law for Minority Nationalities states that "schools mainly enrolling minority students should adopt textbooks in minority languages and scripts when available and use minority languages as the medium of instruction; in upper grades in primary schools or in secondary schools Chinese courses should be offered and Mandarin should be used." Article 36 applies, however, only in special territories granted limited autonomy to protect minority culture and language (China, 1998, cited in Zhou and Sun, 2004, p. 78). Furthermore, since Article 36 states a preference rather than requirement for minority language schooling, it leaves the choice of implementation mode to local authorities, producing a wide range of practices.

Zhou (2004) concludes that local interpretation of policy depends on contingent factors, arguing, for example, that minorities with established traditional scripts generally receive mother-tongue or bilingual education, since they strongly resist Mandarin-only education, whereas for ethnicities without traditional scripts, Mandarin-only education is pervasive. Zhou (2004) also argues that ethnic minorities are more likely to receive bilingual education if their population is numerous and located in strategic border areas. Thus, while central language-in-education policy is the same for all China, implementation of policy for language-minority children is manifested in a range of possibilities as can be seen in table 6.4. The models range from monolingual Mandarin instruction, to five different forms of bilingual education.

Thus, China's policies include both rights-based elements (Skutnabb-Kangas, 2006), in that the possibility of minority language education is enshrined in laws and regulations, and norms-based elements (Patten and Kymlicka, 2003), in that standard Mandarin-medium education is treated as the norm, with compensatory policies and programs provided for minority learners who have difficulty in mainstream schooling. Compensatory policies that focus on reducing minority difficulties in college admission include:

(a) the option to write college entrance exams in a minority language;
(b) lowered CEE cut-off scores for college admission for minority applicants; and
(c) quotas for minimum numbers of minority students to be admitted (Sautman, 1999).

Chinese minority language-in-education policy also follows both a "territoriality principle" and a "personality principle" (Patten and Kymlicka, 2003, p. 22), in that while the right to use a minority language is granted to all without limitations as to location (personality principle), minority language schooling is only granted in designated areas of concentrated minority population (territorial principle). Thus, outside of these territories, minority language education is unavailable, for example, in urban centers. Like Ogbu's "voluntary minorities" (1991), migrant minority parents do not

**Table 6.4. Approaches to Minority Language Provision for Minority Learners in China**

| | Approach | Function of Mandarin | Function of Minority Language |
|---|---|---|---|
| 1. | Mandarin Submersion | All formal curriculum, textbooks & instruction in Mandarin | No support for minority language; local environment may support minority language use |
| 2. | Minority Language + Mandarin | Mandarin taught as subject only | Mother-tongue education medium of instruction for all subjects except second language |
| 3. | Mandarin + Minority Language | Medium of instruction for all subjects except mother tongue subject class | Minority language as subject only |
| 4. | Mixed Bilingual Education | Formal instruction in Mandarin | Informal oral explanation to supplement Mandarin instruction |
| 5. | Transitional Bilingual Education | Subject in early grades; later shift to main medium of instruction | Medium of instruction in early grades; later occasional use; rarely used in senior secondary |
| 6. | Maintenance Bilingual Education | Medium of instruction for some subjects throughout schooling (usually sciences) | Medium of instruction for some subjects throughout schooling (usually humanities) |

*Source:* Adopted from Blachford, 1997; Dai & Cheng, 2007; Zhou, Q., 1991, in Stites, 1999; Zhou, M., 2004; Teng & Wang, 2001.

expect the state to provide for their children to be taught in their heritage language (Iredale, Bilik, and Wang, 2001).

## DEBATES WITHIN CHINA ON IDEAL MODELS OF LANGUAGE(S) OF INSTRUCTION

According to Ma (2007), there are two main schools of thought among officials in ethnic minority areas and minority parents about language of instruction for minority children:

> Those who want to emphasize minority-language instruction stress the idea that when minority students who have no understanding of Chinese are put in a situation where they must start learning it directly, the results are not good. . . . There are some teachers, parents of students, and even some students themselves who believe that since placement examinations, especially college entrance examinations, are not written in the minority language, nor is the minority language one of the subjects on the examinations, rather than being like "the blind person who wastes wax by lighting a candle," it is better to invest the time allocated for learning the minority language in studying mathematics, physics and chemistry. (Ma, 2007, p. 20, 22)

Badeng Nima (2001), and Teng and Wang (2001), for example, argue for the first view, criticizing transitional bilingual education for shifting prematurely to all Mandarin-medium instruction. He claims that too early introduction into exclusive Mandarin instruction leads to low literacy in both the minority language and Mandarin. This argument has considerable support in bilingual education research outside China, which has found that maintenance bilingual education typically leads to higher proficiency in both the first and second language than does transitional bilingual education (Abadzi, 2006; Baker, 2001; Benson, 2004; Cummins, 2000, 2001; Hovens, 2002; Pattanayak, 2001; UNESCO, 2005; Willig, 1985).

Supporters of the second view reason from several "commonsense" assumptions about the nature of language, learning, education, and society: that Mandarin is more important than mother tongue proficiency to minority children's life chances, that effective learning of Mandarin requires maximum exposure to a Mandarin language environment, and that mother tongue learning interferes with Mandarin learning, and that modern knowledge is best learned through Mandarin (Jiang, 2002; Ma, 2007). This line of reasoning, based more on "folk psychology" and "folk pedagogy" (Olson and Bruner, 1998) than research, leads one to see minority languages as hindrances to minority children's learning, which further leads to favoring transitional over maintenance bilingual education; early over late transition to Mandarin, and even to a preference for second language submersion over bilingual education.

Such differing attitudes toward language have been named "Language as Problem" and "Language as Right" and the more positive "Language as Resource" view (Ruiz, 1990). Where language is seen as right and problem, linguistic diversity itself is seen as a problem, "Language X is a child's right; but Language Y is a problem, barring access to Language X." Thus, one camp sees Mandarin as a problem for minority children to be able to access their right to their native language; the other sees minority language as a problem blocking minority children's right to learn the common lingua franca of China—Mandarin. Neither view is informed by the language as resource view supported by current research that suggests that minority children can develop strong proficiency and literacy in two languages using maintenance bilingual education (Cummins, 2000, 2001).

The view of Mandarin as right and minority language as problem together with the low average educational attainment and Mandarin proficiency levels of many minority children have led to the proposal that minority children can benefit from being sent to boarding schools in urban Mandarin areas. Wang and Zhou (2003) and Postiglione, Jiao, and Manlaji (2007) have studied Type 3 programs for Tibetan children in an urban Mandarin environment, where students studied one course on Tibetan language and the remainder of the curriculum in Mandarin. Both studies found that these programs led to increased Mandarin proficiency, but to moderate oral and low written proficiency in Tibetan, such that graduates have insufficient Tibetan proficiency to work in their communities, except as teachers of Chinese and mathematics, commonly taught in Mandarin (Postiglione, Jiao, and Manlaji, 2007; Wang and Zhou, 2003).

Wan and Zhang (2007) moreover, conducted a study in a Tibetan-speaking district of Gansu province that found no significant differences between students' mean scores on tests of Mandarin and Tibetan proficiency in Type 2 Tibetan-dominant and Type 3 Mandarin-dominant bilingual education programs. Wan and Zhang found, however, that scores on mathematics tests were significantly higher in the Mandarin-dominant program, which the authors ascribe to the better conditions in Mandarin-dominant schools.

Discussion of dual language maintenance bilingual education, in which students study in two languages during their secondary education and even into higher education, is noteworthy by its absence from the literature, although such programs do exist in China (Zhou, 1991, cited in Stites, 1999, p. 108). Perhaps, as Ding Wenlou argued in 1990 (cited in Stites, 1999, p. 110), lack of implementation of quality bilingual education is due to a lack of social consensus on its value either socially, culturally, or educationally.

## ADAPTING CURRICULUM TO LOCAL CULTURAL DIVERSITY: LOCAL AND MULTICULTURAL CURRICULUM

National primary curriculum promotes pan-Chinese identity, emphasizing love of the land of China, its nationalities, the responsibilities of citizens toward each other and to the state, and the importance of becoming a builder of socialism with Chinese characteristics. The model of pan-Chinese identity (*Zhonghua minzu*) presented to children is based on Fei Xiaotong's concept of *duo yuan yi ti*, or diversity in unity, with every ethnic group, including the majority Han, seen as participating equally in a larger organic whole, in which all are valued, and none need give up their individual ethnic identity. China is likened to a flower garden, where each bloom is unique in size, color, and fragrance, yet contributes to a beautiful and harmonious whole (Wang and Wan, 2006; Zhou, 2003). Wang and Wan further note the similarities of the view of Chinese society as a flower garden to the western image of a diverse society as a cultural mosaic, in contrast to views of cultural fusion that stress uniformity, such as the traditional American concept of the *melting pot*.

Nevertheless, in practice curriculum and pedagogy in minority areas frequently emphasize the whole (*unity*) more than its parts (*plurality*), so that curriculum lacks relevant local content, and is not reflective of the social reality in the area for which it was designed (Chen, 2004, pp. 11–12; Wang and Wan, 2006).

The national curriculum, even when delivered in the mother tongue, is difficult for children, and even for many teachers, in remote minority areas to understand. National textbooks for example contain none of the distinct flora and fauna found in mountainous regions or grasslands. In response, Minggang Wan, Badeng Nima, and Jia Luo (1999) and Jia Luo (2003) have prepared Tibetan Mandarin bilingual textbooks that attempt to reflect the local environment and culture, incorporating for example traditional riddles and language games as means to stimulate creativity and advanced oral literacy. Surveys of local teachers, parents, and students where these textbooks have been used report a generally positive response to this approach (Jia Luo, unpublished field notes).

Another line of research has begun to explore how the schooling experience influences minority children's development of identity, utilizing the concept of the *hidden* curriculum (Apple, 2004; Jackson, 1968). Qian (2007) applies this concept in a qualitative comparative case study of students from the Baoan, Salar, and Yughur minorities of northwest China and finds that boarding school students removed from their families and familiar cultural environment drop out more often than students who travel from home to school. A Yughur researcher, Tiemuer (2006), sums up the experience of a minority child in a minority district in a Mandarin-only program:

> Everything you study and come into contact with is from an extremely different culture; for more than ten years of education, the teacher will not say a single word about your nationality, language, history or culture. Thus, this kind of lopsided education fosters students whose spirit and individuality are similarly lopsided. (2006, p. 41)

Some researchers have investigated how minority students engage with views of their culture encountered in schools. Building on Ogbu's "folk theories of success" (1987), Harrell and Ma (1999) argue that in some cases minority students construct an identity in which they have as much chance or even more chance of educational and career success as any other ethnicity. Zhu (2007) similarly explores how Tibetan students in boarding schools in Mandarin-speaking regions negotiate their identities, sometimes accepting, at other times resisting stereotypes they may encounter in schools about their minority.

The MOE recommends close study of the local community, its beliefs and cultural practices in the preparation of school-based curriculum (MOE, 2002b). Chen (2004) extends this argument to multilingual, multiethnic districts, and concludes that multicultural education is needed in China. Chen argues that multicultural education has several benefits in a multiethnic society such as China: it strengthens minority students' school achievement and sense of their own ethnic identity, and can lead students of different ethnic backgrounds to develop increased mutual understanding and respect.

Similarly, Wang and Wan (2006) provide a critical appraisal of multicultural education programs in the United States, Canada, the United Kingdom, and Australia, and an assessment of its utility in the Chinese context, particularly the northwest, which is more multiethnic than China's eastern and central regions. Wang and Wan note that despite more than twenty years of debate and experiment in multicultural education, social prejudice and inequities in education continue. They feel that a major challenge in adapting this approach to China's education is its insufficiently clear meaning: does it focus on minorities, and not the mainstream; does it differ from bilingual education? Nevertheless, Wang and Wan conclude overall that this approach has great potential to inform curriculum development in China, as long as it does not blindly follow foreign models. In fact, what they call for is sinicization of multicultural education on the national scale, combined with localization.

Wan (2003), however, points out the formidable obstacles in developing a multicultural education approach in poor minority areas of China, where the gap between western, central, and coastal regions exists not only in economy and ecology, but is also embodied in society, culture, and education. The key issue in western China is how to simultaneously rapidly reduce poverty, develop the overall school system, and develop minority education. Wan raises for discussion the study of models of compensatory education implemented earlier in the United Kingdom and United States that provided extra investment to subsidize educational development within disadvantaged regions and social groups, such as western China and its minority areas.

Zheng (2003) similarly points out that successful implementation of the national policy of developing China's western regions economically requires putting minority education in these areas in first place in order to develop local human resources to assist in the development strategy. However, for most minorities in western China, the entire way of life is closely integrated with the physical environment, and thus a culturally sustainable education for minorities must also incorporate environmental education.

## ADAPTING CURRICULUM TO THE ENVIRONMENTAL DIVERSITY: ENVIRONMENTAL EDUCATION IN CHINA

Understanding of China's environmental problems is mounting among international policymakers at the highest level, and so is the pressure, both nationally and globally, to fix them. In industrial and urban areas in the central and eastern regions, the single most serious problem is air pollution from factories and vehicles (Lee and Tilbury, 1998). Pan Yue, China's deputy head of the State Environmental Protection Administration (SEPA), views air pollution as a "bottleneck constraining economic growth in China" (Xie, 2004). At the same time, in western China, a major threat is environmental degradation: water shortages, erosion, and desertification of agricultural and pasture lands. Rising temperatures have led to glaciers shrinking by about a meter a year, increasing desertification, with 10–20 percent of grasslands used for grazing livestock, the traditional economic activity there, considered degraded in one minor-ity county in Gansu (World Bank, 2003, p. 7; Yin, Clinton, Luo, and Song, 2008, p. 95). Environmental education (EE) in China is a local response to environmental threats, and was introduced during recent education reforms, partly modeled on EE curricula in the United Kingdom. However, the national, provincial, and local materi-als that were produced following international EE curricular models proved unsuitable not only for younger students, but also for many teachers in China. EE's innovative curricular organization required schools to prepare practical activities synthesizing theoretical knowledge from many disciplines with practical local problem-solving activities and subject teachers to incorporate EE in their lessons so that EE would permeate the entire curriculum (Lee and Tilbury, 1998).

One approach to this integrative approach at the school level is the Green School movement, which originated as a practical response to the immediate school environ-ment: school grounds were bare and needed landscaping, but given limited resources, so children were involved in planting and caring for their own "adopted" trees in the schoolyard, while at the same time, participating actively in practical learning about the environment. Now children in Green Schools learn about animals and plants na-tive to their communities through class research and group projects featuring environ-mental hands-on activities, integrating knowledge from diverse sources, and applying them in actively solving concrete local problems. The local and school-based Green School approach to EE provides an active, experiential, inquiry-based component lacking in "examination-based education" and supports recent MOE goals of fostering problem-solving skills and creativity, and so it encourages the spread of this move-ment by granting Green School certificates to any schools that meet their EE guide-lines (Jiao, Zeng, and Song, 2004; MOE, 2002a; Sterling, 2004).

Nevertheless, implementing local EE remains a challenge for teachers, who are re-quired not to transmit knowledge from one discipline, but facilitate students' activity-based learning of knowledge integrated from several disciplines and application of this knowledge to the solution of practical problems in the community, which requires them to take on roles for which their teacher education does not prepare them. Thus, teachers may retain an earlier orientation toward teaching and learning. In a large industrial city of northeast China, traditional teacher-centered instruction was still dominant in grades 7 and 8 and geography lessons, which closely followed national textbooks that ignored the role of individual teachers and students in environmental protection and local decision making (Darkhor, 2005). Thus, while there is evidence that students respond positively to new EE approaches to their learning (Niu, 2001, in Darkhor, 2005), the exclusion of EE from major examinations means that EE is marginalized:

> Environmental education, if included at all, is usually accorded low priority and [consid-ered] something only to be concerned with after examination courses are ensured. (Zhu, 1995, p. 106, in Darkhor, 2005, p. 33)

Thus, many obstacles to innovative curriculum and pedagogies, such as inquiry-based learning, exist, particularly in rural areas (Zhang et al., 2003).

## Environmental Education in Rural Minority Areas

Rural schools are strongly recommended to integrate knowledge of agriculture, science, the environment, business, and management in their curriculum, allotting a suggested 10–12 percent of hours to local and school-based curriculum and 6–8 percent of hours to comprehensive practice activities (China, 2002). Knowledge about the environment is especially relevant to pastoralist herders, where desertification of grasslands threatens their way of life, and local herders' ignorance of the consequences of their practices is part of the problem (World Bank, 2003; Yin et al., 2008). Two cultural strategies exist among pastoralists to cope with environmental unpredictability: opportunism and conservatism, with conservative strategies far less stressful on the local ecology (Sandford, 1982). Sandford further argues that where "an ideology of performance and competition in respect of income, wealth or status predominates," unsustainable opportunistic strategies are more likely, while the aim of maintenance of the group "as a coherent social unit" (p. 74), is more likely to lead, not only to cultural maintenance, but also to more sustainable ecological conservatism.

Clearly, for rural minority pastoralists to be able to make informed choices about the care of their herds and the protection of their pastures implies, as Squires (2001) argues, not only indigenous knowledge about the local landforms, flora, fauna, and weather, but also relevant knowledge of modern biology, meteorology, geology, economics, business, and management, all of which must be synthesized to allow effective creative problem solving to be applied to the challenges at hand. A curriculum that included all such knowledge would be beneficial in preparing children of minority herders to meet many of the actual life challenges that will face them in their district. At present, national curriculum does not provide enough knowledge relevant to the local surroundings, and the development of local and school-based curriculum, including environmental education, has only recently begun in China. At the same time, EE in China is largely an urban and eastern phenomenon, and is combined in some cases with prestigious English bilingual education programs (Li, L., 2006). While many Green Schools have opened in urban centers throughout the country, none had yet opened at the county level or lower in the entire western region (Jiao, Zeng, and Song, 2004, p. 52.). Furthermore, developing environmental education is not a component of expert recommendations for dealing with the problem in recent reports on managing environmental degradation in western China (World Bank, 2003; Yin et al., 2008).

While a well-organized approach to integrating environmental education with local and school curriculum is highly relevant to education in minority areas, particularly in the west, that face multiple environmental challenges, it is also clear that environmental education, multicultural education, and multilingual education are not opposed concepts; moreover, they need to interact with each other. Therefore, multiple sources of knowledge are required to be integrated in local and school curriculum: scientific and indigenous knowledge, and languages of wider communication and indigenous languages — all have a place and can be mutually enriching.

## DIVERSITY IN CHINA'S EDUCATION
## IN COMPARATIVE PERSPECTIVE

China presents an exceedingly varied linguistic, cultural, and environmental landscape comparable in scale and complexity to North America's complex multicultural
societies. Approaches to this diversity in education have, therefore, been diverse and
fluid over time and space. Key features are the broad range of approaches to identity, views of culture, and views of language, as well as differing views on the place
of diverse perspectives on identity, culture, and language in the school, and a lack
of consensus on the purpose of education itself. Finally, there is a tension between
views of unity deriving from *uniformity*, whereas others see uniformity as *rigidity* that
weakens society.

Parallels with North American experience exist as well. First, globalizing forces
have been seen as threatening to identity. In the late nineteenth century, modernizers
strove to balance traditional and foreign knowledge with the formula, *zhong wei ti,
xi wei yong*, "Chinese learning for fundamental principles, Western learning for use"
(Pepper, 1996, p. 55). Similarly, Zhang (1997) has argued for traditional Confucian
values in quality education as a counterbalance to the excessive individualism of recent years. The balance of ethnic and pan-Chinese identity is also debated. Assimilation of minorities to become Han is against policy (Zhou, 2004); however, there are
two major interpretations of pan-Chinese identity. We summarize the two perspectives based on Wang and Wan (2006) as:

1. *ronghe*, or *fusion*, whereby China's ethnic groups mutually interact, leading to creation of a new, stronger, but essentially *uniform* identity, formed out of elements
   from each, but primarily from the majority nationality; this interpretation proceeds
   from diversity *into* unity: comparable to the North American *melting pot* image;
   and
2. a multiple identity, illustrated by the metaphor of China as a flower garden with
   many distinct flowers, so all citizens' identity is simultaneously on two levels, individual ethnic identity plus pan-Chinese nationality; incorporating both diversity
   *and* unity at the same time: comparable to the North American *cultural mosaic*
   image. (pp. 1–3)

As we have seen, more scholars are increasingly concerned about the effects of
negative stereotypes about students' culture and the the lack of minority contributions
and experiences in the curriculum. Thus, they call for greater inclusion of minority
culture(s) in the curriculum, in order to combat feelings of cultural inferiority and to
develop pride in unique aspects of minority culture.

Much work has been done on differences in cultural expectations of behavior
and communication among ethnicities in the United States, and how this might affect minority students' response to pedagogy, such as the responses some minority
children have to white middle class teachers' speech, the cultural use of questions as
orders, which some children may understand as choices rather than demands, or as
the teacher's lack of authority (Delpit, 1988). Cummins (2001), for example, concurs

with Delpit that minority students may require direct instruction to demystify such aspects of mainstream sociolinguistic behavior in order to understand what some majority culture students understand implicitly. A fruitful extension of research on identity construction of minority children in Chinese schools and their responses to ethnographic and sociolinguistic investigation of language, culture, and interaction in schools is important for building understandings about why minority students are labelled as they are, and how the process of schooling can be demystified for them. Indeed, it may be that not only do students need to learn about mainstream language and culture, but that mainstream teachers need to learn more about the languages and cultures of their minority students.

In formal terms, minorities have more linguistic rights in China than in the United States. However, in China the right to the use of minority languages is granted in the constitution, but the right to their use in education is granted collectively, within designated territorial limits, and is granted provisionally, where numbers warrant, and where local government authorities consider it worthwhile and feasible. In the United States, access to minority language instruction in state-funded education has been guaranteed by law where it has been deemed necessary in order to provide the more fundamental right of equal access to education (Lam, 2005; Zhou, 2003; Ricento, 1998). Burnaby and Ricento (1998) in a comparison of Canadian and American language policy in education, agree that local implementation of minority education may differ widely from policy pronouncements, just as minority education in China is implemented in many forms, despite the same general policy guidelines for the entire country (Zhou, 2004).

Beyond language policy, there is tension between views about language as neutral instrument of communication or as an essential component of cultural identity. Among some minorities in China experiencing rapid language shift at the same time as great increases in children's Mandarin proficiency and educational attainment rates, there is an anxiety that ethnic identity will completely disappear if their language is lost (Bradley, 2005).

Chinese debates between uniformity of curriculum and local adaptations to central curriculum parallel debates in the United States, where attitudes toward diversity in the curriculum range from those who believe in educational uniformity, providing the same curriculum content to all; to those who support some form of multicultural education that adapts the curriculum to reflect current social diversity, incorporating both mainstream knowledge and reflective of a broad range of cultures (Cummins, 2000; Duhaney, 2005).

There is great controversy over the use of Black English Vernacular (BEV) (Labov, 1969/2000), or Ebonics (Duhaney, 2005) in the United States. African American children's learning can benefit through their greater potential comprehension and comfort with bidialectal instruction, but this approach is rejected by many whites and some African Americans as socially inappropriate in school, and without socioeconomic utility (Delpit, 1988). The Ebonics debate parallels the case of those minority languages in China with no historical script and written literature of their own, hence without a tradition of formal literacy-based schooling in their language, and whose oral languages and newly devised scripts are seen as not suitable for the school setting (Bahry, field notes; Zhou, 2003).

Many minority parents in China are influenced to send their children to monolingual dominant language programs rather than mother tongue or bilingual programs by "facts," such as the apparent greater number of graduates of dominant-language schools who continue to higher education. In this situation, research methods that can control for differences in conditions between programs are needed; otherwise, it is difficult to know whether the "superiority" of one program or another is related to the program itself or extraneous factors, such as better resources and conditions of mainstream schools. One of the first attempts in China to conduct such a comparative evaluation is Wan and Zhang (2007). Evaluation based on examination scores may be invalid, as well, since the content of these examinations may also exhibit cultural and linguistic bias that favors students in mainstream schools and groups (Cummins, 2000, 2001; Wang and Wan, 2006).

Banks (1994) argues that multicultural education is for all ethnicities, majority and minority alike, and that majority students are enriched educationally by greater inclusion of diversity of knowledge and culture in the classroom. Wang and Wan (2006) agree with Banks that multicultural education in China should be intended not only for minority students, but also for majority Han students. Moreover, research on bilingual and trilingual education suggests that two or three languages of instruction can be used in a school successfully, where all students take some courses in another language (Cummins, 2000). However, although majority Han settlers in minority districts often develop some oral proficiency in minority languages (Ma, 2007; Hansen, 2005), there is little precedent for majority students using a minority language as the medium of instruction, which could be a barrier to developing two-language maintenance bilingual education (Baker, 2001).

In recent fieldwork in a minority district of China, when stakeholders were asked about their attitude toward the inclusion of minority knowledge, culture, and language in local and school-based curriculum, there was broad support among parents and teachers, regardless of ethnicity, for greater local minority cultural content studied *through* Chinese. Moreover, there was also broad agreement in principle that minority language instruction was useful *for* minority students. However, many adults, regardless of ethnicity, when asked whether minority language instruction would be interesting to students of other ethnicities, replied that it was *only* useful for children of that group. Yet when primary school children were asked whether they would like to learn stories and songs in a local minority language, most children of all ethnicities responded that they would be interested (Bahry, unpublished interview transcripts). Ultimately, educational research alone cannot completely settle debates about diversity in education, but as Grant and Millar (1992) point out in the context of the United States, scholarship can make major contributions toward strengthening inclusive approaches to language and culture in education (1992).

As Wang and Wan (2006) and likeminded scholars forcefully argue, the plurality in unity concept of Chinese identity, although fruitful, and even necessary for the harmonious development of China, particularly in its most linguistically and culturally diverse western regions, presupposes much greater devotion of resources toward research, curriculum, and materials development, teacher development, program implementation, and evaluation related to approaches to education which embody diversity.

Increased dialogue of educators, education scholars, and policymakers both within China and internationally will assist the process of deliberation, experimentation, and implementation of models of education in China that can both maintain and revive minority language and culture, while permitting participation within the broader society that does not involve the loss of their language and culture, and simultaneously enriching mainstream education by broadening its perspectives (Chen, 2004; Feng, 2007; Wang and Wan, 2006).

Such change implies a complex process involving much discussion, disagreement, and some resistance, particularly if changes reflecting diversity in education are perceived as weakening students' chances to succeed in the mainstream national curriculum with the ultimate goal of passing the CEE and being admitted to college. However, while local and school curriculum are less valued by many, due to their perceived lack of relevance to the main educational goal of passing the CEE, this same lack of connection to the exam should permit local and school curriculum development greater flexibility to experiment with diverse knowledge perspectives and pedagogies that support stronger forms of bilingual and multicultural education. However, research on bilingual education in China deals more with prestigious Mandarin-English bilingual education programs in the urban east than minority-Mandarin bilingual education in the rest of the country (Feng, 2005). Squires's (2001) advice in dealing with desertification among indigenous populations seems equally apt as a prescription for educational renewal among a culturally diverse population in environmentally fragile areas of China:

> Knowledge should simultaneously flow to and from rural communities. A new relationship has to be built between those who create and use scientific knowledge and those who support and finance it, and those concerned with its application and impacts. Efforts should be made to sustain traditional knowledge systems through active support to the societies that are keepers and developers of this knowledge, their ways of life, their languages, their social organization and the environments in which they live, and fully recognize the contribution of women as repositories of a large part of traditional knowledge. Governments should support cooperation between holders of traditional knowledge and scientists to explore the relationships between different knowledge systems and to foster inter-linkages of mutual benefit. (2001, p. 258)

## CONCLUSION

From the above discussion, it is clear that many educational debates in China mirror global debates on education. First, while China's unity has traditionally been emphasized through *uniformity* of curricula, there is increasing recognition among the MOE, Chinese, and international scholars of the extent of the nation's social, geographic, cultural, and linguistic diversity, and the relationship of this diversity to continuing differences in educational participation and achievement. As the national curriculum responds more to global forces, for example, by expanding English courses, the gaps between curriculum needs of urban coastal China and the central and western regions may widen. Globalization or modernization is increasingly seen as leading to the weakening of traditional local knowledge, culture, and values. This perception can be found everywhere in China, but is more common in rural areas, minority districts, and interior provinces, since their experience is farthest from global knowledge and culture. One factor leading to resistance toward education is the external imposition of uniform knowledge and values without local participation or adaptation, without which youth may become alienated, whether they stay in school or not.

In this situation, the new division of curriculum authority into three levels: national, local, and school is a welcome response to the above challenges. While all students should have access to national and international knowledge and skills, it should not need to come at the expense of local culture and identity. Thus, the preservation of local culture and identity should not imply a romantic turning to the past and refusal to engage with modernity and the outside world.

Nevertheless, many well-intentioned and potentially beneficial reforms worldwide have withered on the vine. Thus, the new curriculum system requires a great deal of support of various types: first, research on similar cases and successful models of sustainable locally relevant education: for poor rural areas, there are multigrade and nonformal education models found in Escuela Nueva schools in rural Colombia, and village schools for girls in rural Bangladesh (Farrell, 2007; Stromquist, 2007); for pastoralists, there are models of education that adapt to nomadic lifestyles and the grassland and mountain environment (Krätli, 2000); for linguistic minorities, there are many examples of successful models of maintenance bilingual education to draw on in China and abroad (Benson, 2004; Cummins, 2001; Feng, 2007; UNESCO, 2005). Furthermore, the research on China is broadening to incorporate a range of methods including qualitative research, ethnography, and educational anthropology as well as greater use of experimental and quasi-experimental methods to enrich perspectives on education. Nevertheless, research needs to interact with practice, practitioners, and communities. MOE encouragement of teachers to take on roles as curriculum developers is a welcome step, particularly if education researchers work in tandem with local stakeholders, although the recent reform is a case of top-down empowerment of the lower levels of the school system, not necessarily desired by local educators: the attitude toward school-based curriculum initiatives was expressed by one educational administrator of a minority county as "not to encourage, nor to oppose or to concern ourselves [with this]" (Li, D., 2006, p. 262).

Clearly, the success of local and school-based curriculum reform requires considerable attention to developing research capacity and teachers' professional development. Yet, the financing of education and educational research is insufficient to provide such support (Postiglione, 2006). Funding based on a per capita formula according to number of students regardless of location or type of school would go a long way to providing general schools, rural schools, remote schools, and minority schools with resources to support the greater needs of students in these areas.

Wan (2003) and Wang and Wan (2006) go further than this, invoking cases from the United Kingdom and the United States of special compensatory funding programs for education among minority groups and in areas where low achievement and high drop-out rates were frequent. They argue that equitable financing is not sufficient to improve education in poor, remote, and minority areas in China, but that compensatory financing is required. The final word goes to Yang (2006) who cautions against uncritical globalization of Chinese research in Western methods and paradigms, advising that Chinese educational researchers

> need to develop their unique perspectives and values based on rich local experience and an awareness of their local society and culture. This is to grasp the meaning of locality in the situation when nation-states experience transnational destabilisation. Such a sense of locality would allow them to seize the initiative in identifying the real needs of their local societies and in setting up their own research agendas and targets. (p. 218)

*Figure 6.1 is adapted from Herrmann-Pillath et al. (2006); figures 6.2, 6.3, 6.4, 6.5, and 6.6 are calculated by the authors from 2000 census data in China (2002 and 2003).

## REFERENCES

Abadzi, H. (2006). *Efficient learning for the poor: Insights from the frontier of cognitive neuroscience.* Washington, DC: World Bank.

Apple, M. W. (2004). *Ideology and curriculum* (third ed.). London: RoutledgeFalmer.

Badeng Nima. (2001). Problems related to bilingual education in Tibet. *Chinese Education and Society, 34*(2), 91–102.

Baker, C. (2001). *Foundations of bilingual education and bilingualism.* Clevedon, UK: Multilingual Matters.

Banks, J. A. (1994). *An introduction to multicultural education.* Needham Heights, MA: Allyn and Bacon.

Benson, C. (2004). *The importance of mother tongue-based schooling for educational quality.* (EFA Global Monitoring Report 2005). Stockholm: Centre for Research on Bilingualism, Stockholm University.

Blachford, D. R. (1997). Bilingual education in China. In J. Cummins and D. Corson (Eds.), *Encyclopedia of language and education. Vol 5: Bilingual education* (pp. 157–65). Dordrecht, Netherlands: Kluwer.

Bradley, D. (2005). Language policy and language endangerment in China. *International Journal of the Sociology of Language, 173,* 1–21.

Burnaby, B., and Ricento, T. (1998). Conclusion. In B. Burnaby and T. Ricento (Eds.), *Language and politics in the United States and Canada: Myths and realities* (pp. 331–34). Mahwah, NJ: Lawrence Erlbaum.

Chen, Y. (2004). Shaoshu minzu diqu shishi xiaoben duoyuan wenhua jecheng chutan [A tentative study of offering school-based-multicultural courses in ethnic minority regions]. *Minzu Jiaoyu Yanjiu, 15*(1), 11–15

China (2002). *Tabulation on the 2000 population census of the People's Republic of China.* Beijing: China Statistical Publishing House.

China (2003). *Tabulation on nationalities of 2000 population census.* Beijing: Minzu Chubanshe.

Cummins, J. (2000). *Language, power and pedagogy: Bilingual children in the crossfire.* Buffalo and Toronto: Multilingual Matters.

Cummins, J. (2001). *Negotiating identities: Education for empowerment in a diverse society* (second ed.). Los Angeles: California Association for Bilingual Education.

Dai, Q., and Cheng, Y. (2007). Typology of bilingualism and bilingual education in Chinese minority national regions. In A. Feng, *Bilingual education in China: Practices, policies and concepts* (pp. 75–93). Buffalo, NY: Multilingual Matters.

Darkhor, P. (2005). *China's strategy towards environmental governance: an examination of the interaction between pedagogy and practice of environmental education in creating and achieving objectives for sustainable development.* Unpublished doctoral dissertation, Ontario Institute for Studies in Education of the University of Toronto.

Delpit, L. S. (1988). The silenced dialogue: Power and pedagogy in educating other people's children. *Harvard Educational Review, 58,* 280–98.

Duhaney, L. M. G. (2005). Fostering equity curriculum and pedagogy: Educating students with dialectal variations. In R. Hoosain and F. Salili (Eds.), *Language in Multicultural Education* (pp. 95–114). Charlotte: IAP.

Epstein, I. (1993). Class and inequality in Chinese education. *Compare, 23*(2), 131–48.

Farrell, J. P. (2007). Equality of education: A half-century of comparative evidence seen from a new millennium. In R. F. Arnove and C. A. Torres (Eds.), *Comparative education: The dialectic of the global and the local* (pp. 129–50). Lanham, MD: Rowman & Littlefield.

Feng, A. (2005). Bilingualism for the minor or the major? An evaluative analysis of parallel conceptions in China. *International Journal of Bilingual Education and Bilingualism, 8*(6), 529–51.

Feng, A. (2007). Intercultural space for bilingual education. In A. Feng (Ed.), *Bilingual education in China: Practices, policies and concepts* (pp. 259–86). Buffalo and Toronto: Multilingual Matters.

Grant, C. A., and Millar, S. (1992). Research and multicultural education: Barriers, needs and boundaries. In C. A. Grant (Ed.), *Research and multicultural education: From the margins to the mainstream* (pp. 7–18). London and Washington, DC: Falmer Press.

Hansen, M. E. (1999). *Lessons in being Chinese: Minority education and ethnic identity in Southwest China.* Seattle: University of Washington Press.

Hansen, M. (2005). *Frontier people: Han settlers in minority areas of China.* Vancouver: UBC Press.

Harmful "key school" system must be ended. (2006, February 27). *China Daily.* Retrieved March 3, 2008, from www1.china.org.cn/english/China/159391.htm.

Harrell, S., and Ma, E. (1999). Folk theories of success: Where Han aren't always the best. In G. A Postiglione (Ed.), *China's national minority education* (pp. 213–41). New York: Falmer Press.

Hawkins, J. N. (1992). China. In P. W. Cookson, Jr., A. R. Sadovnik, and S. F. Semel (Eds.), *International handbook of educational reform* (pp. 97–114). New York: Greenwood Press.

Herrmann-Pillath, C., Sheng, Z., Du, J., Xiao, T., Li, K., and Pan, J. (2006). *The evolution of regional disparities in China, 1993–2003: A multi-level decomposition analysis* [Social Science Research Network]. Retrieved April 17, 2008, from ssrn.com/abstract=949072.

Hovens, M. (2002). Bilingual education in West Africa: Does it work? *International Journal of Bilingual Education and Bilingualism, 5*(5), 249–66.

Huang, F. (2004). Curriculum reform in contemporary China: seven goals and six strategies. *Journal of Curriculum Studies, 36*(1), 101–15.

Iredale, R., Bilik, N., and Wang, S. (Eds.) (2001). *Contemporary minority migration, education and ethnicity in China.* Cheltenham, UK: Edward Elgar.

Jackson, P. W. (1968). *Life in classrooms.* New York: Holt, Rinehart, Winston.

Jia Luo. (2003). *Tibetan culture readers: Grades 1–3.* Beijing: Minzu Chubanshe.

Jiang, M. (2002). A study of ethnic minority middle and elementary boarding schools in China. *Chinese Education and Society, 35*(3), 23–46.

Jiao, Z., H. Zeng, and X. Song. (2004). An overview of "Green School" development in China in 2001. *Chinese Education and Society, 37*(3), 49–54.

Krätli, S. (2000). *Education provision to nomadic pastoralists: A literature review.* Brighton, UK: University of Sussex Institute of Development Studies.

Labov, W. (2000/1969). The logic of non-standard English. Reprinted in L. Burke, T. Crowley, and A. Girvin (Eds.). *The Routledge Language and Cultural Theory Reader* (pp. 456–66). New York: Routledge.

Lam, A. S. L. (2005). *Language education in China: Policy and experience since 1949.* Hong Kong: Hong Kong University Press.

Lee, J. C.-K., and Tilbury, D. (1998). Changing environments: The challenges for environmental education in China. *Geography, 83*(3), 227–36.

Lewin, K. M., Xu, H., Little, A. W., and Zheng, J. (1994). *Educational innovation in China: Tracing the impact of the 1985 reforms.* Harlow, UK: Longman.

Li, D. (2006). *Xibei minzu diqu xiaoben kecheng kaifa yanjiu* [*Research on school-based curriculum development in northwestern minority districts*]. Lanzhou: Gansu Educational Press.

Li, L. (2006). Environmental education curriculum in a bilingual education school in China. *The Social Studies, 97*(4), 145–51.

Ma, R. (2007). Bilingual education for China's ethnic minorities. *Chinese Education and Society, 40*(2), 9–25.

Ministry of Education (MOE). (2002a). *Zoujin xin kecheng yu kecheng shishizhe duihua* [*Entering the new curriculum: A dialogue with curriculum implementers*]. Beijing: Beijing Normal University Press.

Ministry of Education (MOE). (2002b). *Shui lai jueding women xuexiao de kecheng: tan xiaoben kechengde kaifa* [*Who will decide our schools' curriculum? On the development of school-based curriculum*]. Beijing: Beijing University Press.

Niu, L. (2001). Hand in hand earth village. Centre for Environmental Education and Communication, State Environmental Protection Administration. Retrieved March 19, 2008, from www.iges.or.jp/en/phase2/ee/pdf/china.pdf.

Ogbu, J. U. (1987). Variability in minority school performance: A problem in search of explanation. *Anthropology and Education Quarterly, 18*(3), 312–34.

Ogbu, J. U. (1991). Immigrant and involuntary minorities in comparative perspective. In M. A. Gibson and J. U. Ogbu (Eds.), *Minority status and schooling: A comparative study of immigrant and involuntary minorities* (pp. 3–33). New York: Garland.

Olson, D. R., and Bruner, J. (1998). Folk psychology and folk pedagogy. In D. R. Olson and N. Torrance (Eds.), *The handbook of education and human development: New models of learning, teaching and schooling* (pp. 9–27). Cambridge: Blackwell.

Pattanayak, D. P. (2001). Educational use of the mother tongue. In B. Spolsky (Ed.), *Language and education in multilingual settings* (pp. 5–15). Clevedon, UK: Multilingual Matters.

Patten, A., and Kymlicka, W. (2003). Introduction. In A. Patten and W. Kymlicka (Eds.), *Language rights and political theory: Context, issues, and approaches* (pp. 1–51). Oxford: Oxford University Press.

Pepper, S. (1990). *China's education reform in the 80s: Policies, issues and historical perspectives.* Berkeley: Institute of East Asian Studies, University of California.

Pepper, S. (1996). *Radicalism and education reform in 20th century China: The search for an ideal development model.* New York: Cambridge University Press.

Postiglione, G. (2006). Schooling and inequality in China. In G. Postiglione and S. Rosen (Eds.), *Education and social change in China: Inequality in a market economy* (pp. 3–24). Armonk, NY: M. E. Sharpe.

Postiglione, G., Jiao, B., and Manlaji. (2007). Education in rural Tibet: Development, problems and adaptations. In A. Feng, *Bilingual education in China: Practices, policies and concepts* (pp. 49–71). Buffalo and Toronto: Multilingual Matters.

Price, R. F. (2005). *Education in Modern China*. London: Routledge.

Qian, M. (2007). Discontinuity and reconstruction: The hidden curriculum in schoolroom instruction in minority-nationality areas. In G. E. Postiglione (Ed.), *Sociology of Education Part II*. Proceedings of the First International Conference of Education, Beijing University, March 2006. *Chinese Education and Society, 40*(2), pp. 60–76.

Ricento, T. (1998). National language policy in the United States. In T. Ricento and B. Burnaby (Eds.), *Language and politics in the United States and Canada: Myths and realities* (pp. 85–112). Mahwah, NJ: Lawrence Erlbaum.

Ruiz, R. (1990). Official languages and language planning. In K. L. Adams and D. T. Brink (Eds.), *Perspectives on official English: The campaign for English as the official language of the USA* (pp. 11–25). Berlin: de Gruyter.

Sandford, S. (1982). Pastoral strategies and desertification: Opportunism and conservatism in dry lands. In B. Spooner and H. S. Mann (Eds.), *Desertification and development: Dryland ecology in social perspective* (pp. 61–80). London: Academic Press.

Sautman, B. (1999). Expanding access to higher education for China's national minorities: Policies of preferential admissions. In G. A. Postiglione (Ed.), *China's national minority education* (pp. 173–210). New York: Falmer Press.

Skutnabb-Kangas, T. (2006). Language policy and linguistic human rights. In T. Ricento (Ed.), *An introduction to language policy: Theory and method* (pp. 273–91). Oxford: Blackwell.

Squires, V. R. (2001). Distinguishing natural causes and human intervention as factors in accelerated wind erosion: The development of environmental indicators. In Y. Yang, V. Squires, and Q. Lu (Eds.), *Global alarm: dust and sandstorms from the world's drylands* (pp. 257–65). Beijing: United Nations.

Sterling, S. (2004). *Investing in the future*. A report for WWF China Education Program Evaluation. Beijing: WWF.

Stites, R. (1999). Writing cultural boundaries: National minority language policy, literacy planning, and bilingual education. In G. A. Postiglione (Ed.), *China's national minority education* (pp. 95–130). New York: Falmer Press.

Stromquist, N. P. (2007). Women's education in the twenty-first century: Balance and prospects. In R. F. Arnove and C. A. Torres (Eds.), *Comparative education: The dialectic of the global and the local* (pp. 151–74). Lanham, MD: Rowman & Littlefield.

Su, X. (2002). *Education in China: Reforms and innovations*. Beijing: China Intercontinental Press.

Teng, X., and Wang, Y. (2001). Bilingualism and bilingual education in China. In N. Shimahara, I. Z. Holowinsky, and S. Tomlinson-Clarke (Eds.), *Ethnicity, race, and nationality in education: A global perspective* (pp. 259–78). Mahwah, NJ: Lawrence Erlbaum.

Tiemuer (2006). Mei ge minzu dou you ziji de hei xiazi [Every nationality has its own "black box"]. *Yohuer Wenhua, 1,* 41–42.

UNESCO (2000). *Education for All: The Year 2000 Assessment. Final Country Report of China*. Retrieved June 18, 2008, from www.unesco.org/education/wef/countryreports/china/contents.html#cont.

UNESCO (2005). *First language first: Community-based literacy programmes for minority language contexts in Asia*. Bangkok: UNESCO Bangkok.

Wan, M. (2003). "Jiji chabie daiyu" yu "jiaoyu youxian qu" de lilun gouxiang: Xibu shaoshu minzu pinkun diqu jiaoyu fazhan tujing tansuo [Theoretical concepts, "positive treatment of difference" and "priority areas for education": Means for exploring educational development in poor minority areas in western China]. In Tiemuer (Ed.), *Minzu zhengce yanjiu wencong* (pp. 285–94). Beijing: Minzu Chubanshe.

Wan, M., Badeng Nima, and Jia Luo (1999). *Tibetan cultural readers: Grades 4-6*. Lanzhou, Gansu: Canadian International Development Agency and Gansu People's Publishing House.

Wan M., and Zhang, S. (2007). Research and practice of Tibetan-Chinese bilingual education. In A. Feng (Ed.) *Bilingual education in China: Practices, policies and concepts* (pp. 127–44). Buffalo and Toronto: Multilingual Matters.

Wang, C., and Zhou, Q. (2003). Minority education in China: From state's preferential policies to dislocated Tibetan schools. *Educational Studies, 29*(1), 85–104.

Wang, J., and Wan, M. (2006). *Duoyuan wenhua jiaoyu bijiao yanjiu [Comparative research on multicultural education]*. Beijing: Minzu Chubanshe.

Willig, A. C. (1985). A meta-analysis of selected studies on the effectiveness of bilingual education. *Review of Educational Research, 55*(3), 269–317.

World Bank (2003). China Gansu and Xinjiang pastoral development project. Report No: 25703-CHA. Washington, DC: World Bank.

Wu, Z. (2003). Quanqiuhua beijing xia de Zhongguo jichu jiaoyu kecheng gaige [Globalization and the background of China's basic education curriculum reform]. *China Education and Research Network*. Retrieved April 3, 2008, from www.edu.cn/gai_ge_272/20060323/t20060323_76272_1.shtml.

Xie, Z. (2004). Integrating rapid growth and environmental protection: A challenge for China. *Environment matters 2004: Annual Review 2003–2004* (pp. 12–13). Washington, DC: World Bank.

Yang, R. (2006). What counts as "scholarship"? Problematising education policy research in China. *Globalisation, Societies and Education, 4*(2), 207–21.

Yin, Y., Clinton, N., Luo, B., and Song, L. (2008). Resource system vulnerability to climate stresses in the Heihe river basin of western China. In N. A. Leary (Ed.), *Climate change and vulnerability* (pp. 88–114). London: Earthscan.

Zhang, B., Krajcik, J. S., Sutherland, L. M., Wang, L., Wu, J., and Qian, Y. (2003). Opportunities and challenges of China's inquiry-based education reform in middle and high schools: Perspectives of science teachers and teacher educators. *International Journal of Science and Mathematics Education, 1*(4), 477–503.

Zhang, S. (1997). Quality education cannot be separated from traditional culture. *Chinese Education & Society, 30*(6), 40–42.

Zheng, C. (2003). Lun xibu minzu diqu jiaoyu de fazhan yu renli ziyuan de kaifa [On western minority areas education development and the development of human resources]. In Tiemuer (Ed.), *Minzu zhengce yanjiu wencong [Anthology of Nationality Policy Research]* (pp. 325–43). Beijing: Minzu Chubanshe.

Zhou, M. (2003). *Multilingualism in China: The politics of writing reforms for minority languages 1949–2002*. Berlin: de Gruyter.

Zhou, M. (2004). Minority language policy in China: Equality in theory and inequality in practice. In M. Zhou and H. Sun (Eds.), *Language policy in the People's Republic of China: Theory and practice since 1949* (pp. 71–95). Norwell, MA: Kluwer.

Zhou, Q. (1991). Zhongguo shuangyu jiaoyu leixing [Varieties of bilingual education in China]. *Minzu Yuwen, 3*, 65–66.

Zhu, H. (1995). Education and examination: A major constraint hindering environmental education in the People's Republic of China. *International Research in Geographical and Environmental Education, 4*(2), 106–7.

Zhu, Z. (2007). *State schooling and ethnic identity construction in the school context: The politics of a study of a Tibetan Neidi boarding school in China*. Lanham, MD: Lexington Books.

*Chapter Seven*

# Teaching and Learning in a Developing World Context: Understanding the Curriculum Development for Marginalized Communities in Northern Ghana

## Obed Mfum-Mensah

How might an examination of the curriculum development process of an education program in rural northern Ghana[1] provide a new perspective for theorizing curriculum development and understanding how schools serve as arenas for interrogating values, beliefs, and practices? This chapter is based on an ethnographic study aimed to investigate the curriculum development process of School For Life (SFL), a complementary education program which was implemented in northern Ghana to promote school participation. It examines the factors that shaped the curriculum elements—the aims and objectives, the content, the teaching and learning activities, the assessment methods, and the process of monitoring and evaluation; the stages of the curriculum development process; and the stakeholders and their roles at each stage. I define curriculum in this chapter as "a set of purposeful, intended experiences that start by imagining how to draw together the processes and encounters that make for good learning" (Knight, 2001, p. 375). The term "School For Life" is used to denote the organization operating the complementary education program as well as the program itself. The scope of the chapter includes the historical background, analytical framework, context of education in Northern Ghana and the School For Life program, research method, findings, discussion, and conclusion.

Globalization has been a major force in the quest of the last two decades to promote universal education in developing countries. The 1990 Jomtien World Conference on Education for All (WCEFA) and subsequent planetary meetings which were organized by transnational advocacy groups, were premised on the globalization ideology to promote education for all children by 2015.[2] One of the manifestations of the global education initiative is the mass implementation of complementary education programs (CEP) in communities and groups that are "hard to reach" and "hard to teach" [rural and impoverished urban communities, girls, children orphaned by the HIV/AIDS epidemic, or belonging to communities displaced by natural and man-made disasters] in the sub-Saharan Africa subregion. The assumption is that providing literacy to these marginalized groups will enable them to participate fully in the globalization of society.

## DEFINING "COMPLEMENTARY EDUCATION PROGRAMS"

The definition of Complementary Education Programs (CEP) is ambiguous in the literature (Balwanz, Moore, and DeStefano, 2006; Farrell and Mfum-Mensah, 2002; Hoppers, 2005; Mfum-Mensah, 2003; The United Nations Children's Fund, 1993). Some scholars distinguish between CEP and other alternative primary school programs, but others view them as the same.[3] A close examination of CEP and programs categorized as community schools, alternative primary education programs, and nonformal primary education programs, reveals that they are not significantly distinct from one another. Therefore, I have used the term Complementary Education Programs in the chapter to include programs categorized under any of the programs. I also use the definition provided in The UN Children's Fund's dossier (1993) for non-formal school programs. The dossier defines the programs as follows:

> A set of complementary programmes for the unreached or poorly served, [and as] an approach to education . . . leading to greater flexibility in organization and management of educational programmes with a decentralized structure and less authoritarian management style. It also promotes adaptation of programmes to needs and circumstances of learners, a learner-centered pedagogy, creative ways of mobilizing and using educational resources, community participation in planning and management of programmes, and learning content and methods related to life and environment of learners. (p. 1)

The UN Children's Fund dossier sets out the major characteristics for CEP including school coverage, organization, management, pedagogy, and relationship with the community.

## THEORETICAL FRAMEWORK

Curriculum scholars agree that the curriculum development process requires attention to at least five major elements: aims, objectives, outcomes or statement of intent, content statements, teaching and learning activities, assessment methods, and processes of monitoring and evaluation (Alpren and Baron 1973; Harden, 2001; Knight, 2001; Posner, 1998; Prideaux, 2007). The curriculum literature identifies many perspectives on curriculum development, but two are pervasive, one based on the Tyler rationale, and another based on the critical perspectives. The Tyler rationale has dominated curriculum development theorizing. Theorists like Hilda Taba, Joseph Schwab, John Goodlad, and Mauritz Johnson used the Tyler rationale as a platform and point of departure to refine their own perspectives on curriculum planning (Posner, 1998). The Tyler rationale focuses on elaborate *technical* and *management* approaches to curriculum development. It posits that an intentional approach to curriculum development requires attention to key elements, which include the selection of educational purposes, the determination of experiences, the organization of experiences, and the provision of evaluation.

The critical perspective emphasizes flexible, fluid, interactive, and critical participatory approaches to curriculum development (Doll, 1993; Freire, 2003; Knight,

2001; Posner, 1998). While the critical perspective answers procedural questions with a step-by-step approach to curriculum planning (Posner, 1998), the major emphasis is to empower, emancipate, and foster participatory and critical approaches to curriculum development (Posner, 1998). Doll (1993) points out that, unlike the Tyler rationale approach which places power at the top with education bureaucrats, the critical perspective is an interactive curriculum development approach that empowers both teachers and learners by creating an environment where they engage in continuous dialogue, and where teachers and learners develop their own curriculum through continuous interaction and where the process of evaluation is interactive. The critical perspective advocates the decentralization of power to where learning is actually taking place (teachers and learners).

Even though most scholars separate the two perspectives, some argue that curriculum planning actually requires and/or incorporates both perspectives (Posner, 1998; Knight, 2001). Posner (1998) argues that due to the complexity of the learning enterprise and an increasingly eclectic, pluralistic, and cultural society, curriculum planners need to engage in both the technical and critical perspectives in the curriculum development process. Knight (2001) posits further that both approaches provide a purposeful intended experience. The SFL curriculum development process was rational and had guiding principles, was highly critical and participatory, and involved the local communities in shaping the elements of the curriculum. Accordingly, in this study, I applied an analytic framework that draws on both technical and critical perspectives to understand the curriculum development process. In the next section, I discuss the context of educational development in northern Ghana and the rationale for implementing SFL.

## THE CONTEXT OF EDUCATION IN NORTHERN GHANA

Colonization and globalization are forces that have contributed to the campaigns for schooling in Ghana. The campaign for mass schooling began in Ghana (then Gold Coast) in the nineteenth century by the Christian missionaries and received further push from the colonial and successive postcolonial governments in the middle and late twentieth century. The campaign was strengthened in the 1980s and 1990s by transnational governing bodies and bilateral agencies including the World Bank, the International Monetary Fund (IMF), and the U.S. Agency for International Development (USAID). The manifestations of the transnational groups in the Ghanaian society are evidenced from the aids and economic policies like the Structural Adjustment Programs and the Education Sector Adjustment programs of the 1980s and 1990s, which led to the buzzword "efficiency," as well as policies and practices that hinge on decentralization in the Ghanaian educational system (Dei, 1993).

In spite of the campaigns for mass schooling in Ghana in the nineteenth century and the subsequent egalitarian ideology that has led to the ideals of universal education over the past two decades, school participation in northern Ghana is still marginal. Northern Ghana lags behind the rest of the nation in enrollment, retention, and graduation, and the effort to address the problem has not yielded the intended result

(Akyeampong, 2004; Atakpa, 1996; Casely-Hayford et al., 2003; Ministry of Education and Sports, 2005; Ministry of Education, 1999). The Ministry of Education (1999) laments that 66 percent of eligible children in the upper east region, 32 percent of eligible children in the upper west region, and 30 percent of children in the northern region are not attending school.

The marginal school participation in Ghana is attributed to the Christian expansion agenda, the vestiges and imprints of colonization, context of northern Ghana, and the inequities in the Ghanaian school system (Atakpa, 1996; Blakemore, 1975; Bray, 1993; Folson, 1995; Mfum-Mensah, 2005). Bray (1993) points out that the implications of colonialism (and expansion of Christianity) may be as complex and far-reaching for education as they are for other sectors. To set the context, it is expedient to know that Islam came to northern Ghana long before the Christian missions started their operation in the south in the nineteenth century. The Moslem communities operated Qu'ranic schools before the mission schools were introduced in the north. The mission schools, which had a proselytizing and indoctrination agenda, were viewed in the north as a threat to the Islamic culture and religion (Atakpa, 1996; Mfum-Mensah, 2005). Furthermore, the Moslem communities viewed colonial and postcolonial schools as "de facto" Christian apparatus for proselytizing their children (Atakpa, 1996). Therefore, the effort to expand schooling during colonial and early postcolonial era was resisted and repudiated in most of the Moslem communities in the north.

Atakpa (1996) and Blakemore (1975) also explain the marginal school participation in northern Ghana as stemming from apathy to formal schooling in some communities, where children play an important role on family farms. Atakpa proposes that the early postcolonial government's use of scholarship schemes, law enforcement personnel, and provision of food to promote school participation in northern Ghana was unsuccessful. In addition, Folson (1995) and Mfum-Mensah (2003) explain that the high rates of illiteracy and marginal school participation are due to the inequities in the Ghanaian educational system. Mfum-Mensah (2003) for instance argues that the distribution of educational services has always skewed in favor of the south. The north has few schools, many of which are in deplorable condition and lack qualified teachers.[4] He explains that the problem was created by Christian missions and subsequent colonial governments who tended to focus on the south to the neglect of the north.

## THE TWO COMMUNITIES

The study was conducted in two rural northern Ghanaian communities in Tamale[5] Rural District, between May and June of 2006. The communities have access to amenities such as public schools, health centers, police stations, communication centers, and a post office because of their close proximity to Tamale. However, despite their close proximity to Tamale, the community members are poor subsistence farmers and animal herders who depend on the little income they get from their yearly farming produce and their animal herds for their economic survival. The farmers' yearly produce in northern Ghana depends on the sporadic and unpredictable rainfall. Due to the communities' economic situation, parents heavily involve children in their socioeconomic activities—a practice that inhibits many children from enrolling in the formal school (Mfum-Mensah, 2003; Stephens, 2000). Children assist their parents on the farm. During the dry season when water is scarce, children walk for long distances to fetch water for the family's use. Community members emphasize a gendered division of labor for children. Families that have animal herds are semi-nomadic, and the males in such families are responsible for taking the animal herds to graze. Girls help with the household chores and take care of younger siblings when the parents go to farm or go to the market. Most girls also sell the families' produce in the market. In addition, some of the boys and girls go to Tamale to work as porters during the day to supplement the family's income.

## SCHOOL FOR LIFE CASE STUDY

The plan to implement SFL dates back to 1993, when some local members of Dagbon Traditional Area[6] formed a group to implement a flexible educational program to help address the high illiteracy rates in the area. This group asked the Dagbon Traditional Council[7] to lend its support in their plan to seek financial support from the Danish government through the Danish Consortium.[8] The Danish government approved the financial request in 1994 and SFL began operating in 1995 as a local nongovernmental organization. Presently, SFL has a three-tiered management structure that includes the head office, the area office, and the district office which all liaise the organization's stakeholders, such as the Danish Consortium in Denmark, the District Assemblies, Ghana Education Service (GES), other nongovernmental organizations (NGOs), donor partners, and the beneficiary communities. SFL also works with the beneficiary communities through parent teacher associations (PTA) and school management committees (SMC).

The name School For Life was adopted for the organization's educational program. The program has flexible school schedules to accommodate children's roles in the economic survival of the family—selling in the market and/or engaging in menial jobs to earn money to support the family, helping their parents on the farm, helping with domestic chores, baby-sitting, and shepherding. It provides nine months of classes to children and then reintroduces them into grades three, four, or five in the public primary schools, depending on the child's performance when she or he is assessed upon reentry into the public school. Volunteers, who are recruited from the community to be facilitators or instructors, receive a monthly allowance of GHCedis 7.00 [US $8.00]. SFL uses the vernacular as a medium of instruction in an educational system that has an all-English medium of instruction.

## RESEARCH METHOD

This study is an ethnographic case study. My objective to understand the elements of the curriculum, the participatory process, and how the different stakeholders influenced the process necessitated an approach that incorporates interviews, observations, and document analyses in understanding the issues being investigated (Denzin and Lincoln, 2000; Merriam, 1988; Yin, 1984).

I conducted formal interviews with twelve participants who included the SFL director, the deputy director of operations, the education specialist, the principal education specialist, and gender coordinator, two area coordinators, one district coordinator, one key curriculum planning committee member (local member), one Ghana education service officer (local member), and two SFL facilitators. These participants were purposefully sampled because most of them were either members of the original group that formed SFL or have worked with it since the early stages of its formation. Three of the participants were females. They included the education specialist, gender coordinator, and a facilitator. Informal interviews also served as a major source of information, which helped to clarify and illuminate the data gathered. Formal interviews with participants were tape-recorded.

I organized two focus group interviews in the two communities to help me understand the nature of community participation and empowerment in SFL. Participation in the focus groups was open to any community member who wanted to join the discussion. Over forty community members (about 60 percent were females and 40 percent were males) participated in each of the focus group interviews. In addition, I observed two classrooms during instruction to assess the facilitators' interactions with students, approaches to instruction, assessment, and classroom management. I conducted the formal interviews in English and the focus group interviews in Dagbani[9] and English concurrently through an interpreter. I have provided participants' perspectives to illuminate the themes and issues arising from the interviews. For purposes of anonymity and confidentiality, I have omitted the personal details that may reveal the identity of the participants. I replaced the real names of the participants with pseudonyms. The actual positions held by the participating SFL personnel have been deliberately replaced with the term "administrator" in the study to preserve their identity.[10]

The data were reviewed on a daily basis to make sense of the themes that were emerging. I transcribed all the recorded interviews, examined the data several times, and sorted, categorized, evaluated, compared, and synthesized the information with the use of diagrams, charts, and matrices. The discussions that follow in the next section are based on the themes that emerged from the formal interview with participants, the focus group interviews, and informal conversations with stakeholders, document analysis, classroom observation, and analysis of the field notes. In the following section(s), I highlight the themes and provide illustrative excerpts from the transcripts.

## SCHOOL FOR LIFE CURRICULUM DEVELOPMENT PROCESS

Many curriculum theorists (see Alpren and Baron, 1973; Beauchamp, 1972; Harden, 2001; Prideaux, 2007; Walkington, 2002) assume that any rational curriculum development is primarily technical in that the process specifies goals and objectives, outlines curriculum instruction, and then proceeds to the assessment of learning.

Evaluation and revisions occur as needed to improve the system.[11] However, some theorists (Doll, 1993; Knight, 2001; Posner, 1998) argue that while the process generally addresses the procedural question rationally, it is also critical because it involves different stakeholders with different interests and levels of power in the process.[12] This study outlines the "technical" and "critical" processes of the SFL curriculum development process. The study outlines the four stages of SFL curriculum development process, namely, deliberation, design, implementation, and outcome stages. It highlights the different actors, the stage they were involved in, their roles, and how they arrived at their decisions.

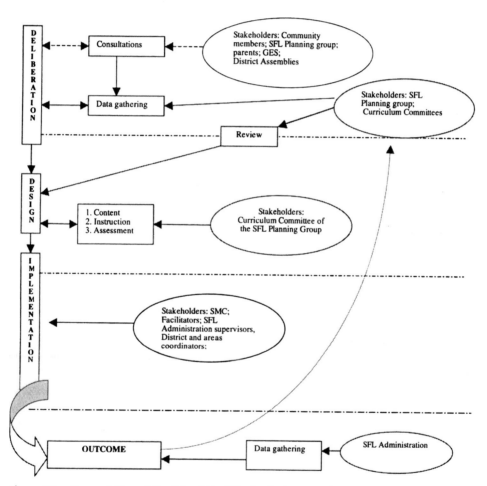

**Figure 7.1.  Concept Map of the School For Life Curriculum Development Process**

## DELIBERATION STAGE

The *deliberation* stage is the initial phase of the curriculum development process. The stakeholders that were involved in this phase included the local group, the district assembly, and Ghana Education Service (GES), that both played consultative roles (see figure 7.1). Activities at this stage included forming the SFL planning group and establishing the literacy and numeracy committees. Also considered at this stage are the aims and objectives and the language to be used for instruction. The SFL planning group and the community also held meetings at this stage to seek community input, and to begin to orient the community to the program.

After the group of local members submitted the application to seek financial help to initiate SFL in 1993, it registered SFL as a grassroots, nongovernmental organization and education program, with the original group serving as the ad hoc planners. The ad hoc planners invited some educationists from the community to assist them with developing the SFL curriculum. The ad hoc planners and the educationists evolved into the SFL planning group. The planning group organized a series of meetings with the local community leaders, parents, and community members. The issues discussed at the meetings included how to address the high rate of illiteracy, and how to encourage educational participation and get support for the program. The meetings further helped to sensitize the community toward the need for the program, and explain their potential roles and responsibilities in the initiative. The grassroots participatory critical approach is necessary in the northern Ghanaian context where communities and parents greatly influence children's schooling (Mfum-Mensah, 2003; Stephens, 2000). The discussions between the planning group and the community blended both technical and critical approaches in their SFL curriculum planning.

## Deciding the Aims and Objectives of the Curriculum

After the planning group met with the community, they held a series of meetings to decide the aims and objectives of the SFL curriculum. The meetings were contentious because members of the planning group had diverse views about what curriculum elements to include. The first issue was whether to use the formal school curriculum or develop an entirely new curriculum. About half of the planning group members passionately wanted the SFL team to use the regular public school curriculum. The others suggested that the planners develop a new curriculum. However, Musah, a local educator who also served on the literacy committee and is currently one of the SFL administrators, pointed out that after much deliberation, the majority of the members saw the utility of developing a new curriculum that focuses on the children's backgrounds but also integrates elements of the public school curriculum. (A selected list of the SFL participants whose responses are included in the chapter is presented in table 7.1.)

> The group decided to develop a new curriculum that incorporates some elements of the public school curriculum but also focuses on the children's daily activities. The objective was to give the children the flexibility to carry on their socioeconomic and sociocultural responsibilities, while allowing them to acquire literacy and numeracy skills. (Musah, curriculum committee member and SFL administrator: interviewed on June 14, 2006)

The planning group also decided that the curriculum should promote children's critical thinking by teaching them things they are familiar with and afterwards intro-

**Table 7.1. SFL Participants**

| Name | Gender | Position |
|------|--------|----------|
| Hamza | Male | SFL Area Coordinator |
| Miriam | Female | SFL Facilitator |
| Musah | Male | Curriculum Committee Member and SFL Administrator |
| Sulemana | Male | Curriculum Committee Member |
| Yusif | Male | SFL District Coordinator |

ducing them to new things. It should also affirm the children's culture, socialize them to realize a sense of self-identity, and promote morality. Similarly, the group decided to develop the curriculum to help the children acquire positive attitudes—where they will attend school, see the community's culture as important, and fulfill their assigned roles and responsibilities at home. One of the SFL area coordinators pointed out that the rationale for the emphasis on children's attitudinal changes stems from the community's negative perceptions about formal schooling.

> Northern communities view formal school with suspicion, feeling that it is a ploy to promote Christianity and indoctrinate their children. Furthermore, they believe that formal schools remove children from their cultural heritage, and make them look down upon their community. During a meeting with community members, they complained that schools in their communities observe Easter and Christmas but fail to have similar observations for the communities' farming seasons and religious holidays. (Hamza, SFL area coordinator: interviewed on June 13, 2006)

## The Language of Instruction

The language of instruction was another issue that attracted much deliberation. Even though most CEP in sub-Saharan Africa use local vernacular as the medium of instruction because of its cognitive benefits, some schools use standard vernacular for instruction due to political, economic, and sociological pressures (Andoh-Kumi, 2000; Brock-Utne, 2000; Mfum-Mensah, 2005).[13] In the SFL case, the decision to use the local language[14] as the medium of instruction was initially met with resistance from some of the planning group as well as the community members. However, Sulemana, one of the planning group members who served on the curriculum committee, noted that the group decided to use the local language with the understanding that it will help to promote the community's culture as well as literacy in the local language.

> While most of the group members initially resisted the use of vernacular for instruction, they realized that the use of local vernacular would help promote local language literacy and affirm the community's culture. (Sulemana, curriculum committee member: interviewed on June 16, 2006)

## Formation of Literacy and Numeracy Committees

After the planning group decided on the curriculum elements and language of instruction, they selected eight educators to serve on the two committees—the literacy and numeracy committees—to write the contents of the curriculum. The selection of the two committees did not take much deliberation because, according to Musah (also confirmed by Sulemana), that decision "came down to those who had the expertise to help accomplish the goal of writing the curriculum content." The group selected five members who had expertise in the local language instruction to write the literacy component, develop the facilitator's manual, and the students' assessment instrument. Similarly, the group selected three of the group members who have expertise in math to write the numeracy component and its manuals, and assessment instruments. Once the committees were formed, the planning group and its curriculum committees consulted with personnel at GES and the community on a regular basis during the deliberation stage. Notwithstanding the series of discussions with both the community and GES, the planning group and its two committees made the ultimate decisions about the scope of the curriculum, content, assessments, facilitators' manual, and preservice and in-service training.

## Design Stage

The design stage of the SFL curriculum development employed both the technical and critical approaches and included the decisions about the curriculum content, instruction, and assessment. As we can see from figure 7.1, the major actors at this stage of the process are the two committees that decided what was included in the curriculum content, the instructional methods, and the assessment model used. The curriculum committees interacted with different stakeholders and resource persons. I have organized the discussion of the design stage around the three themes: curriculum content, instruction, and assessment.

## Curriculum Content

The curriculum content is defined as the areas of knowledge that students need to master (Harden, 2001). The objective of the curriculum is to contextualize knowledge to help promote children's literacy and numeracy skills. The curriculum committees conceived that such an objective requires a content that builds on the economic, cultural, and historical context of the community, and promotes children's physical and spiritual development. Based on the above objectives, the committee included hygiene, sanitation, animal care, farming, life skills, environmental awareness, disease prevention, morality, and culture in the curriculum content. This perspective is captured succinctly in the response of Musah during the interviews.

> The objective of the curriculum is to make children aware of their environment . . . their health needs . . . to help them develop and function properly in the environment . . . embrace their culture and realize their identity as Dagbani at the early stages. (Musah, curriculum committee member and SFL administrator: interviewed on June 14, 2006)

## Instructional Methods

Due to the difficulty of recruiting teachers in northern Ghana (Akyeampong and Lewin, 2002), the curriculum committee recommended that SFL recruits delegate secondary school graduates from the community to serve as volunteer instructors (the term facilitator is used instead of instructor in the program). School For Life provides the facilitators with two to three weeks training in child psychology, teaching methods, and content instruction. Similarly, SFL provides the facilitators with a monthly stipend and some incentives. The committee recommended that the facilitators should use (a) culturally relevant instructional methods, (b) instructional strategies that would foster a friendly classroom environment, and (c) instructional approaches that would incorporate the children's local life. The committee adopted the picture code and syllabic manipulation methods as part of the culturally relevant instructional strategy to introduce children to reading and writing in the local language. The picture code method requires the facilitator to begin the literacy lesson unit with the use of pictures that are relevant to the children's lives. She or he discusses the context of the picture with the children. In the syllabic manipulation process, the facilitator selects words from the picture and breaks them into syllables and vowels and helps the children to practice them through repetition (drills). Afterwards, the children use the syllables and vowels together to form simple and complex words, and later, to form sentences. Musah explained that their goal for adopting the picture code was to contextualize learning and to make it more effective.

> We decided to use the picture code to teach the children. After all, the written part of the reading curriculum may not bring significant transformation to the children as the discussion of the picture does. Therefore, we used the picture code approach with the aim that in discussing these pictures, the facilitators will transfer knowledge to the children and hence to their parents, and change their attitudes. (Musah, curriculum committee member and SFL administrator: interviewed on June 14, 2006)

As part of the experiential learning approaches, the committee suggested that facilitators use the community as part of the children's learning resources. They invite community members to talk to the children about the community's history. The facilitators also incorporate oral traditions such as songs, stories, folktales, folklores, and plays as components of their pedagogical approaches. The goal is to foster synergy between the child, the home, the school, and the community. Similarly, the committee members underscored the need for instructional approaches that promote "a child-friendly and welcoming classroom and school environment"—an environment where children would not feel fear or anxiety. The committee members reiterated that such a classroom should encourage group work, peer tutoring, and strong classroom interactions. During the interviews, the participants shared the perspective of Yusif, one of the district coordinators, that many children in the community do not enroll in the formal school because they find it unwelcoming.

> The committee was intentional about implementing strategies that will help prevent the practices like beatings and lashings in the formal schools which have the potential to deter children from enrolling. Most of the formal schoolteachers cannot relate to their students . . . there is this widely held notion that here learning has to be painful. Learning is not fun. (Yusif, SFL district coordinator: interviewed on June 6, 2006)

*SFL Assessment Model*

One of the challenges of the design stage was how to incorporate a sensitive and non-intimidating assessment model, as opposed to the high-stakes exams that are typically used in formal schools. The committees decided to utilize a nonlinear and flexible two-level assessment model that assessed student performance at the facilitator level and at the organizational level. The facilitators' manual outlined the guidelines for student assessment by facilitators. The SFL assessment model has evolved over time and now encompasses three levels of assessment: assessment by the facilitator; organizational-level assessment; and Ghana Education Service assessment—used by formal schools to place children back into mainstream schools. The facilitators' manual stipulates that facilitators must employ different means to assess students when they complete every lesson and unit. Miriam, one of the female facilitators elaborated this further.

> I assess students at the end of every lesson to find out whether learning has occurred. I do this before I move on to another topic. If I see that most of them cannot answer the question for the lesson, I do not rush to teach a new topic but review the topic to ensure they understand. (Miriam, interviewed on June 19, 2006)

The organizational-level assessment is a pseudo norm-referenced assessment model. In this level of assessment, the SFL school district office administers the assessment to two randomly selected classes that represent the district. The average performance of the two classes is generalized to represent the performance of the district. This assessment is a data gathering process to help the SFL and curriculum planners assess the limitations of the curriculum, and the performance of the facilitators and the district. The assessment is also useful in determining specific areas for future inservice and preservice training for facilitators. The assessment follows a specific procedure. The district and area coordinator arrives, unannounced, during a normal school day, and administers an assessment package prepared by the SFL for the students. The intention is that the students take this assessment in a more relaxed atmosphere.[15] The assessment package consists of a comprehension passage for the children to read and answer, a writing component, and a numeracy component to assess children's numeracy skills. The children spend thirty minutes on each component. The SFL education department scores the students' responses afterwards and provides feedback to the facilitator, and to the area and district coordinators.

The Ghana Education Service–level assessment occurs at the end of the SFL school cycle when an SFL graduate applies to enroll in a formal school. SFL has no control over this level of assessment, which was originally not part of the SFL assessment model. This assessment became necessary for the formal schools to determine the specific class level at which to place an SFL graduate because of the differences in their ages and cognitive development.

## IMPLEMENTATION STAGE

The implementation stage details the process of using the curriculum in the classroom. The curriculum was first implemented in 1995. There are organizational-level stakeholders, school-level stakeholders, and community-level stakeholders involved in the curriculum implementation. The Deputy Director of Operations (DDO) is the overall overseer of the SFL curriculum. The DDO works with the education department of SFL to implement the curriculum. The SFL administrators interviewed explained that a few months after SFL started operating, its educational department took over the role of evaluating the curriculum including reviewing the curriculum every two years, preparing the manuals and resources, and organizing workshops for facilitators, district coordinators, and supervisors—roles that were initially played by the curriculum development committee. This perspective was further elaborated during my interview with Hamza.

> The literacy committee wrote the primers, the resources, and the manuals but the education department took over after the program began. Since then, SFL is supposed to invite editorial groups to revise the curriculum every two years . . . to discuss what they should add or leave out in the curriculum. The need to revise the curriculum depends on the changes occurring in the formal schools. (Hamza, SFL area coordinator: interviewed on June 13, 2006)

SFL education department collaborates with GES to facilitate articulation between SFL and the formal schools.[16] The area coordinators, district coordinators, and supervisors monitor, supervise, and provide continuous instructional support to facilitators. At the community-level, the local school management committee (SMC) and parent teacher association (PTA) work as partners to recruit and provide continuous monitoring of facilitators.

## OUTCOME STAGE

At the outcome stage, SFL administration assesses how the curriculum has met the goals of addressing the needs of children within their specific contexts, and providing literacy and numeracy skills. The SFL curriculum development does not culminate at the outcome stage but feeds back into the whole process again. The outcome stage helps the administration to determine the success of the other three stages, the assumption being that the four stages are intricately related and that the effectiveness of the preceding stages can be ascertained through what happens at the final stage. Sulemana pointed out that the first review of the [new SFL] curriculum occurred in 1997. He explained further that SFL's education personnel review the curriculum every two years after they have consulted with SFL's stakeholders.

> We [SFL] first reviewed the curriculum in 1997 and since then we review it every two years to check its suitability . . . before we do the revision, we consult GES, the communities, opinion leaders, and other stakeholders for their input. In two years, you are likely to get some of the stakeholders who have recommendations about some aspects of the curriculum. (Sulemana, curriculum committee member: interviewed on June 21, 2006)

During the interviews, SFL administration pointed out that they have not conducted a comprehensive review because resources were limited. They argued, however, that despite the lack of an elaborate review, the number of children SFL recruits, retains, and subsequently mainstreams into formal schools, demonstrates its impact. Similarly, anecdotal reports from the formal schoolteachers about the performance of SFL graduates, provides additional evidence regarding the impact of the program. In addition, Hamza proposes a perspective that was also shared by parents, community leaders and members, and the rest of the stakeholders during the formal and focus group interviews—namely, that the program has expanded to provide educational access, to promote school enrollment, retention, community and parental involvement, and the mainstreaming of children into formal schools.

> SFL assesses the impacts of its curriculum by how many schools we currently operate and the number of children we have recruited and who have completed the program since it began. For example, we have about 190 schools in the west district. . . . 215 schools in the east district bringing to a total of 405 schools. . . . This shows that SFL is making positive impacts in the communities. (Hamza, SFL area coordinator: interviewed on June 13, 2006)

According to the SFL administrators who were interviewed, it has succeeded in recruiting over fifty thousand children from the communities into the program. This assertion is consistent with other studies (see Akyeampong, 2004; Care International, 2003; Hartwell, 2006). Hartwell (2006) for example, reports that SFL has grown to cover 25 percent of the districts where it operates, enrolled fifty thousand students—of whom approximately 50 percent were girls—and also mainstreamed 22,090 students—representing 41 percent girls and 59 percent boys—into the formal schools. Hartwell posits that 91 percent of both boys and girls that enroll in SFL complete in nine months. Overall, 66 percent of students continue on to fourth grade in formal schools with girls matriculating at 68 percent. Hartwell also reports that about 81.2 percent of SFL pupils meet minimum standards for literacy and numeracy at third grade level after a nine-month cycle, whereas about 90 percent of public school pupils in sixth grade in the communities do not perform at the minimum level of reading.

## DISCUSSION

The study revealed that, first, both the technical and critical approaches were utilized in the SFL curriculum development process. The planning group pointed out that it was expedient to approach curriculum development in an inclusive way in rural northern Ghana, where parents and community members (more than state laws and education bureaucrats) decide whether a child goes to school (Atakpa, 1996; Stephens, 2000). The process became a platform for the marginalized communities to express their views about what they consider relevant education.

Second, the study revealed that the process was influenced by the context of the community. This is consistent with the argument that curriculum development is a social and cultural process (Doll, 1993; Prideaux, 2007). Prideaux (2007) suggests that contextual factors such as stakeholders, budget, and facilities, have an impact on the curriculum development process because, at the very least, they determine what is and what is not possible in the implementation of curriculum. Third, the study revealed that the curriculum development process was highly political, with the local communities serving as the major stakeholders or political elites (Farrell, 1999; Solomon and Geddes, 2001). The curriculum development involved different stakeholders who provided input at the different stages of the process—with the community members serving as the major actors in the process. School For Life provided an opportunity for marginalized communities in northern Ghana that ordinarily would not have the opportunity to make decisions pertaining to their children's education, to do so.

Fourth, it is clear from this case that even where the local community was involved in the curriculum development process, a small group that the community members identified as possessing the needed expertise, ultimately determined the curriculum that, in the group's estimation, will address the children's learning needs. This finding provides another perspective for analyzing "community involvement" and "decentralization" as education policy reforms in both the developing and developed nations. Decentralization was one of the World Bank's education sector reforms in Ghana in the 1990s. Education reformers make the assumption that decentralization is empowering, emancipating, and enables *all* [my italics] community members and stakeholders to participate in the education process. Decentralization is viewed as a practice that will help to address the failing educational systems and the marginal school participation in the developing world because it empowers communities to take charge of their school (Anzar, 1998; Farrell, 1998; Mfum-Mensah, 2004). However, this, and other northern Ghanaian cases (see Mfum-Mensah, 2004) reveal that participation may not necessarily empower all community members because during the process certain powerful groups or individuals are likely to emerge as elites whose input trumps all other ideas.

In the United States and Canada, decentralization is touted as an approach that enlists all constituencies to participate in the schools process. However, school practitioners ignore the fact that racial and linguistic minorities, immigrants, and the working class, participate minimally in the school because of school politics and a lack of understanding about how to navigate the education system. One remedy, for example: in an effort to promote greater participation of blacks in Toronto public schools in Ontario, Canada, the Toronto School Board has proposed an Afrocentric School (set to open in September 2009).[17]

Fifth, the study revealed that the context-specific curriculum, which addressed the lived experiences of the children, helped to promote school participation in the community. On this, Farrell (1999) points out that many times powerful policy elites who are often far removed geographically, socially, and experientially from the lived realities of marginalized and/or minority groups, nonetheless make education decisions that result in schooling practices that do not answer the educational needs of communities and therefore results in their marginal school participation. In the United States the argument that schools must incorporate students' cultural contexts and social backgrounds, is both an issue and concern in educational discourse (see Deyhle, 1986; Hall, 1986; Ladson-Billings, 1998). Hall (1986) and Ladson Billings (1998) have argued convincingly that policymakers in the United States should provide minorities, urban, and indigenous communities with schooling that is effective in addressing the children's contextual and learning needs. These discussions are particularly heuristic in this age of globalism because they provide an international perspective on the current discourse on multicultural education. In this age of increasing migration and pluralism of societies, the call for integrating the backgrounds of all groups—especially children whose backgrounds are not of the dominant groups—in the pedagogy is not only salient but also invaluable.

## CONCLUSION

This study provides another perspective on the idea of categorizing curriculum development under one model or another, as we find in the curriculum literature.[18] It shed light on critical participation and decentralization from the northern Ghanaian perspective. Furthermore, the study highlights the vestiges of colonization in Ghanaian educational discourse. The study is heuristic for educators in the West because it reveals that even in a seemingly homogeneous community in the developing world—such as the two northern Ghanaian communities—a culturally relevant curriculum became the most effective approach to address the learning needs of marginalized children.

The study has taken the lead in understanding the curriculum development process of complementary education programs. However, comparative studies that provide nuanced analyses of how the nature and the levels of stakeholders' participation affect school enrollment, students' academic success, and the overall success of complementary education programs will further illumine the benefits of critical participatory approaches to curriculum development.

## NOTES

1. Northern Ghana comprises three regions: northern, upper east, and upper west. Recent reports on the challenges of education in northern Ghana were made by the northern regional minister on May 3, 2007, which indicated that educational performance is still poor in the northern region. "Educational performance still poor in N/R." Retrieved on May 3, 2007, from www.ghanaweb.com/GhanaHomePage/NewsArchive/artikel.php?ID=123449.

2. There are over one hundred documented CEPs in sub-Saharan Africa. These programs have been extensively documented in the Association for the Development of Education in Africa, 2001; Hartwell, 2006; Hoppers 2005; Kochan, 2000; Mfum-Mensah, 2004; Miller-Grandvaux and Yoder, 2002.

3. For different definitions of CEPs, see Balwanz, Moore, and DeStefano, 2006; DeStefano, 2006, 2005; Hoppers, 2005; Farrell and Mfum-Mensah, 2002; Mfum-Mensah, 2003; The United Nations Children's Fund, 1993. While some scholars like Balwanz et al., 2006 and DeStefano, 2005 distinguish between CEPs and other alternative primary school programs, others like Farrell and Mfum-Mensah, 2002; Hoppers, 2005; Mfum-Mensah, 2003 view them as the same.

4. The 2004–2005 educational statistics reveal that the three regions in northern Ghana have a higher pupil teacher ratio than the rest of the country. For instance, the upper west region has 41:1 pupil-teacher ratio; the upper east region has 48:1 and the northern region has 37:1, compared to the national pupil-teacher ratio of 28:1.

5. Tamale is the capital of the northern region of Ghana. Tamale Rural District includes the rural communities that have become part of the Tamale metropolis due to the expansion of the area.

6. Dagbon traditional area covers about eight thousand square miles in area and has a total population of about 650,000. The area constitutes seven administrative districts in present day Ghana. These are Tamale Municipality, Tolon/Kumbungu, Savelugu/Nantong, Yendi, Gushegu/Karaga, Zabzugu/Tatali, and Saboba/Cheriponi. All the tribal and ethnic groups are popularly known as the *Dagombas.*

7. All the chiefs and some elders in Dagbon traditional area form the traditional council. The *Ya Na*, who is the paramount chief of *Yendi*, is the head of the council.

8. SFL administrators explained to the author that this approach was used because they believed the Danish government would see the credibility of the request and likely provide financial support because the traditional council was involved.

9. Dagbani is a Gur language spoken by about eight hundred thousand people in Ghana. Its native speakers are primarily of the Dagomba people of the Dagbon ethnic group of northern Ghana. Many smaller Northern Ghanaian tribes are grouped under the Dagbon ethnic group.

10. Any detailed information about participants including the position they occupy other than a generic classification will reveal the participant's identity, which is a breach of the ethical procedures.

11. Alpren and Baron, 1973; Harden, 2001; Prideaux, 2007; Walkington, 2002.

12. Doll, 1993; Knight, 2001; Posner, 1998.

13. Extensive discussion on the language of instruction has been provided by Andoh-Kumi, 2000; Brock-Utne, 2000; Mfum-Mensah, 2005; Sanou, 1990, cited in Brock-Utne, 2000.

14. The four local languages used as the medium of instruction include *Dagbani, Likpakpaaln (Konkoma), Ncaam (Bassari),* and *Anufo (Chekosi).*

15. The facilitator and SFL officers will sit and engage in conversation in a relaxed atmosphere as the children take this assessment. They do this not to intimidate the children or to create anxiety for them.

16. The reason why SFL works with GES is that the program serves as a feeder school for the formal school system in the communities.

17. *The National Post*, January 30, 2008.

18. The body of literature includes Alpren and Baron 1973; Beauchamp, 1972; Knight, 2001; Prideaux, 2007; Posner, 1974; and Walkington, 2002.

# REFERENCES

Akyeampong, K. (2004). Aid for self-help effort? A sustainable alternative route to basic education in Northern Ghana. *Journal of International Cooperation in Education, 7*(1), 41–52.

Akyeampong, K., and Lewin, K. M. (2002). From student teachers to newly qualified teachers in Ghana: insights into becoming a teacher. *International Journal of Educational Development, 22*(3), 339–52.

Alpren, M., and Baron, B. G. (1973). Procedural options in developing curriculum. *Curriculum Theory Network, 11,* 65–76.

Andoh-Kumi, K. (2000, March 8–11). Qualitative research from a university/ministry partnership: informing school language policy decisions, paper presented at the *43rd Annual Comparative International Education Society*, San Antonio, Texas.

Anzar, U. (1998). *An exploratory study of factors which have contributed to the sustainability of community participation in education in Balochistan, Pakistan.* Unpublished Ph.D dissertation. Washington, DC: American University.

Association for the Development of Education in Africa. (2001). Accelerated literacy for out-of-school youth in Francophone West Africa. Retrieved July 2, 2002, from www.adeanet.org/wgnfe/publications.

Atakpa, S. K. (1996). Factors affecting female participation in education in relation to the northern scholarship scheme. Accra, Ghana: Ministry of Education.

Balwanz, D., Moore, A-M. S., and DeStefano, J. (2006, March 27–31). EQUIP, USAID. Complementary education programs in ADEA countries. Biennale on Education in Africa, Libreville, Gabon.

Beauchamp, G. A. (1972). Basic components of a curriculum theory. *Curriculum Theory Network, 10* (Autumn), 16–22.

Blakemore, K. P. (1975). Resistance to formal education in Ghana: Its implications for the status of school leavers. *Comparative Education Review, 5*(3), 237–50.

Bray, M. (1993). Education and the vestiges of colonialism: Self determination, neocolonialism and dependency in the South Pacific. *Comparative Education Review, 29*(3), 333–48.

Brock-Utne, B. (2000). *Whose education for all? The recolonization of the African mind.* New York: Falmer Press.

Care International. (2003). Reaching underserved populations with basic education in deprived areas of Ghana: Emerging good practices. Care International Ghana/Togo/Benin.

Casely-Hayford, L., et al. (2003). *Reaching underserved populations with basic education in deprived areas of Ghana: Emerging good practices.* Accra: CARE International and USAID. Retrieved June 14, 2008, from www.dec.org/pdf_docs/PNACS140.pdf.

Dei, G. J. S (1993). Learning in the time of structural adjustment policies. *Canadian and International Education, 22*(1), 43–65.

Denzin, N. K., and Lincoln, Y. S. (2000). *Handbook of qualitative research* (second ed.). Thousand Oaks, CA: Sage.

DeStefano, J. (2005). EQUIP 2/Complementary education community schools in Zambia. Washington, DC: Academy for Educational Development.

DeStefano, J. (2006). Meeting EFA: Zambia community schools (EQUIP2 Case Study). Washington, DC: Educational Quality Improvement Program 2 (EQUIP2), Academy for Educational Development (AED).

Deyhle, D. (1986). Success and failure: A micro-ethnographic comparison of Navajo and Anglo students' perception of testing. *Curriculum Inquiry, 16*(4), 365–89.

Doll, W. E. (1993). *A postmodern perspective on curriculum.* New York: Teachers College Press.

Farrell, J. P. (1998, December 6–11) Improving learning: Perspectives for primary education in rural Africa. Paper prepared for a World Bank and UNESCO sponsored regional workshop with the support of the Norwegian Trust, Lusaka, Zambia.

Farrell, J. P. (1999). Changing conceptions of equality of education: Forty years of comparative evidence. In Robert F. Arnove and Carlos Alberto Torres (Eds.), *Comparative education: The dialectic of the global and the local.* Lanham MD: Rowman & Littlefield.

Farrell, J. P., and Mfum-Mensah, O. (2002, March). A preliminary analytical framework for comparative analysis of alternative primary education programs in developing nations. Paper presented at the Forty-Sixth Annual Meeting of the Comparative and International Education Society, Orlando, Florida.

Folson, R. B. (1995). *The contribution of formal education to economic development and economic underdevelopment Ghana as a paradigm.* Frankfurt-am-Main: Peter Lang.

Freire, P. (2003). *Pedagogy of the oppressed* (Thirtieth Anniversary Ed.). New York: Continuum.

Hall, E. T. (1986). Unstated features of the cultural contexts of learning. In A. Thomas and E. W. Plowman (Eds), *Learning and development: A global perspective* (pp. 157–76). Toronto: OISE Press.

Harden, R. M. (2001). Curriculum mapping: a tool for transparent and authentic teaching and learning. *Medical Teacher, 23*(2), 123–37.

Hartwell, A. S. (2006). Meeting EFA: Ghana school for life (EQUIP2 Case Study). Washington, DC: Educational Quality Improvement Program 2 (EQUIP2), Academy for Educational Development (AED).

Hoppers, W. (2005). Community schools as an educational alternative in Africa: A critique. *International Review of Education, 51*(2–3), 115–37.

Knight, P. T. (2001). Complexity and curriculum: a process approach to curriculum-making. *Teaching in Higher Education, 6*(3), 369–81.

Kochan, A. B. (2000). *Community projects database: An international list of community projects.* Toronto: Comparative and International Education Centre, OISE/University of Toronto.

Ladson-Billings, G. (1998). Toward a theory of culturally relevant pedagogy. In L. E. Beyer and M. W. Apple (Eds.), *The curriculum: Problems, politics and possibilities* (second ed.) (pp. 201–29). Albany: State University of New York Press.

Merriam, S. B. (1988). *Case study research in education: A qualitative approach.* San Francisco: Jossey-Bass.

Mfum-Mensah, O. (2003). Fostering educational participation in pastoral communities through non-formal education: The Ghanaian perspective. *International Journal of Educational Development, 23*(6), 661–76.

Mfum-Mensah, O. (2004). Empowerment or impairment? Involving traditional communities in school administration. *International Review of Education, 50*(2), 141–55.

Mfum-Mensah, O. (2005). The impact of colonial and postcolonial Ghanaian language policies on vernacular use in schools in two Northern Ghanaian communities. *Comparative Education, 41*(1), 71–85.

Miller-Grandvaux, Y., and Yoder, K. (2002). *A literature review of community schools in Africa.* Washington, DC: USAID, Bureau for Africa, Office of Sustainable Development.

Ministry of Education and Sports. (2005). *Report on basic statistics and planning parameters for basic education in Ghana.* Retrieved April 29, 2007, from www.edughana.net/emis%20data/html/emisdata.htm.

Ministry of Education, Ghana. (1999). Comprehensive framework for education for all. Republic of Ghana, Accra, Ghana.

Posner, G. J. (1974). Beauchamp's "Basic Components of a Curriculum Theory": A rejoinder. *Curriculum Theory Network, 4*(1), 56-60.

Posner, G. J. (1998). Models of curriculum planning. In L. E. Beyer and M. W. Apple (Eds), *The curriculum: Problems, politics and possibilities* (second ed.) (pp. 79–100). Albany: State University of New York Press.

Prideaux, D. (2007). Curriculum development in medical education: From acronyms to dynamism. *Teaching and Teacher Education, 23*(3), 294–302.

Solomon, P., and Geddes, E. L. (2001). A systematic process for content review in a public-based learning curriculum. *Medical Teacher, 23*(6), 556–60.

Stephens, D. (2000). Girls and basic education in Ghana: a cultural enquiry. *International Journal of Educational Development, 20*(1), 29–47.

The United Nations Children's Fund (1993). Reaching the unreached: Nonformal approaches
    and universal primary education: dossier prepared by UNICEF by Rosa Maria Torres. New
    York: UNICEF, Education Cluster.

Walkington, J. (2002). A process for curriculum change in engineering education. *European
    Journal of Education, 27*(2), 133–48.

Yin, R. K. (1984). *Case study research design and methods.* London: Sage.

*Chapter Eight*

# The Past and Present States of Women, Higher Education, and Their Career Aspirations in Africa

Kwabena Dei Ofori-Attah

Women all over the world have taken advantage of the new opportunities higher education credentials provide, and are consequently being increasingly employed as professionals. African women are no exception to this global trend. Today, many women in Africa have enrolled in universities and colleges all over the world, especially in the United States, Canada, Australia, and Great Britain to seek advanced education. This has offered women new life options beyond their traditional social roles as mothers and wives. Some have left the comforts of the home and entered the workforce as doctors, administrators, lawmakers, or businesswomen (UNESCO, 2006). These developments have radically changed the landscape of employment for women, and have given parents the idea that investments in the education of women can yield benefits that may be equal to, or even greater than men. The net effect is that more parents are seeking higher education credentials, not only for their sons, but also for their daughters.

The purpose of this chapter is to discuss the participation of women in higher education in Africa and its implication for global education. Five countries, namely, Egypt, Ghana, Nigeria, Kenya, and South Africa, were selected as examples in this study. Furthermore, where appropriate, references will be made to other countries and regions. These five African countries were selected to serve as models for this chapter because each of them experienced colonialism and inherited its higher education system from Britain.

## GENDER ROLES IN AFRICA

### The Traditional Model

Before coming into contact with western educational systems of schooling, traditional Africa had identified and developed certain roles that were deemed appropriate for males and females (Clignet and Foster, 1964; Sawyerr, 1971). In general, males were expected to be out in the fields hunting or preparing the land for farming and other agricultural activities. Females, on the other hand, were expected to spend most of their time at home cooking, cleaning, or caring for children. It was not easy for a female to cross the line separating male and female spheres of influence. Everyone in society became a supervisor of gender roles. Adults who failed to correct young children who crossed the gender boundaries were seen as irresponsible (Adeyemi and Adeyinka, 2003).

Although males and females are expected to play different roles in society, there are certain dispositions both sexes are expected by tradition to exhibit. These include honesty, a high sense of responsibility, and participation in community activities. By and large, the introduction of the European educational system in Africa had little influence on traditional gender roles. If anything at all, the European educational institutions provided new tools that were used to more rigidly enforce the traditional models of gender roles and worked against the interests of women (Coquery-Vidrovitch, 1997).

## Traditional African Education

Long before the introduction of Western methods of schooling in Africa, every society had established intellectual traditions for preparing young children to become responsible adults. In its rudimentary form, all adults were teachers in one way or another. For example, across West Africa, especially in Sierra Leone, the *Poro* Society had its own peculiar way of training the young boys to take their place in the community as adults. Selected adults were designated as teachers for the young children, and the training of these children lasted as long as four years (Scanlon, 1964). During the training, the children were taught several subjects, including hunting, farming, and the art of caring for a family. The modes of instruction varied from lectures to detailed demonstrations, and the students were expected to be very disciplined and attentive (Scanlon, 1964).

Similarly, women in Africa had their own education that prepared them to be responsible adults—as mothers, wives, housekeepers, and leaders. Using the Sierra Leonean example above, the women had their own secret society, just like the *Poro* Society for the men. This was called the *Sande* or *Bundu* Society. This society educated young girls aged between nine and sixteen for weeks or months at a time (Pula, 2008). Similar to the *Poro* Society, the modes of instruction varied, although the predominant mode was verbal communication. Many of the graduates of such training later became community leaders. According to Hoffer (1972), some of these women became chiefs, heads of family descent groups, and key officials of secret societies. The intellectual traditions of the *Poro* and *Bundu* Societies remained as the major means of education until the introduction of other forms of schooling in Africa by the Arabs and Europeans.

By the thirteenth century, the Arabs had set up schools in parts of West Africa to educate young children in the art of reading and writing (Hilliard, 1998a). One of the famous institutions that became a center for intellectual activities was in Timbuktu. In this community, Arab scholars set up schools where they taught the young rudiments of writing, reading, and computing. The main curriculum of their schools was focused on religion, although mathematics, science, and literature were also taught (Singleton, 2004).

Whereas old writing forms such as the Adinkra symbols were used among the Akans of West Africa, in the northern parts of the continent, many African societies had more cultivated forms of writing, and had elaborate schemes for training young children in schools that focused on literacy. For example, in the Kemet (Egypt)-Sudanese region, schools were often located in palaces or the homes of teachers who were known as scribes. In these schools, the curriculum primarily consisted of writing, memorization, and reading. Teachers implemented corporal punishment as a means to enforce discipline in the classroom. They were strict and encouraged the students to graduate with the highest possible skills in penmanship (Hilliard, 1998b; Harris, 2001). The graduates of these schools were generally employed in the service of the royalty.

## The Development of European Schools in Africa

The northern region of Africa had contact with Europe and Asia long before the establishment of European colonization. However, European interest in establishing schools in Africa reached its peak in the early twentieth century when the colonial powers started to build schools locally to train Africans for supervisory positions in their colonial empires. The aims of establishing these schools were many, but the most essential was the desire to socialize Africans with Western values and a European version of Christianity (Scott, 1938). With this in mind, each European power became responsible for the establishment of schools in its own colony or sphere of influence (Lungu, 1993). Britain, for instance, became responsible for the development of education in its territories, namely, Egypt, Ghana, Uganda, Kenya, South Africa, Nigeria, Botswana, Zimbabwe, and Gambia. France became responsible for the development of education in Algeria, Morocco, Tunisia, Mauritania, Guinea, Ivory Coast, Senegal, Togo, Gabon, and Burkina Faso, while Portugal administered the development of schools in Angola, Mozambique, and Portuguese Guinea (Brown, 1971).

Each colonial power established elementary, secondary, and higher education systems after colonizing these countries for centuries, making immense profits from the exploitation of a trained African labor force and Africa's natural resources.

In nearly all cases, the missionaries laid the foundation for Western-style schools in Africa. These included Roman Catholics, Presbyterians, Methodists, Anglicans, and the Basel Missionaries (Ayandele, 1971; Taylor, 1984; Wynne, 1971). The curriculum in all the schools followed the European model. Graduates from these schools entered a society that had little or no need for their newly acquired skills of reading and writing (Scanlon, 1964). Moreover, the contents of what students were taught in the mission schools were very much against the spirituality, values, and expectations of most African societies. Although the missionaries proffered no sound theological reasons, they considered many local African spiritual practices and customs as either fetishistic or uncivilized. Some parents were therefore eager to withdraw their children from colonial schools because they perceived a conflict between the school curriculum and their local beliefs (Grindal, 1972).

After nearly two hundred years of missionary educational activities in Ghana, Nigeria, Kenya, and South Africa, the British colonial government began to join forces with the missionaries to develop elementary and secondary education. Colonial governments were usually concerned with law, order, trade, and administrative procedures, in order to protect their interests. Therefore, the notion of *quality education* did not attract their attention as much as it did the Africans (Whitehead, 1981). This is largely because, for the Africans, Western education had ultimately become the primary avenue for socioeconomic advancement in the colonial world, since the traditional systems of education and social order had been rendered impotent.

## EARLY EUROPEAN SCHOOL SYSTEMS IN AFRICA

The early European school systems in Africa had two main models: single-sex and coeducation schools. Single-sex schools were either all male or all female. As their names imply, each model had its own characteristics and social expectations. In general, the curriculum each type of school followed was designed to produce men and women who would grow up to uphold the existing gender roles.

### All-Male Schools

Since the early schools were set up by missionaries for the education of males only, most of the early schools were designated as all-male schools. These were mostly one-room schools. Students, irrespective of age, studied in the same classroom under the tutelage of one instructor. Thus, it was common to see ten-year-old boys studying in the same classroom with fourteen-year-olds. Sometimes, the home of a teacher served as a school for boys. Most of the teachers in the boys' schools were men. Such schools were common in the rural areas.

In the urban areas, although there were some one-room schools, the missionaries built more schools to meet the rising needs of male students. Since there were no females in these schools to take on certain responsibilities, the boys performed all duties that were recognized by society as being appropriate for girls. These included sweeping and cleaning the classroom, running errands for teachers, and fetching water for the school.

In Ghana, by the middle of the twentieth century, there were ten all-male teacher training colleges, as compared to five such colleges for women, even though teaching was perceived as one of the professions where women dominated. Many of these institutions were set up by the missionaries (Hilliard, 1957). As indicated above, in all these institutions (which were generally boarding schools), all the cleaning jobs were carried out by the men, and gender roles were not evident. However, when the male students went back home during the school vacations, they evoked the gender role stereotypes and pretended as if "feminine" activities were inappropriate for them, and refused to do them.

The curriculum for all-male students in the higher institutions included science, agriculture, economics, accounting, law, mathematics, carpentry, religious education, geography, woodwork, masonry, shoemaking, and history. In particular, religious education formed the core curriculum, as can be directly inferred from the names of educational institutions that trained teachers for all public schools (Wallbank, 1934).

Generally, all the teachers working in all-male institutions were men. At that time, men did not feel comfortable learning in a class taught by a woman (Dunne, 2007).

There were also clear patterns of status, authority, and leadership models in all boarding schools. *School prefects* or leaders often enforced the rules that were designed by school authorities, such as the principal or headmaster, faculty, board of governors, or the missionaries.

Life in the boarding institutions "was strict and regulated. Students were introduced to a new concept of time, since every hour of the day was parceled into a rigid schedule" (Miescher, 2005, p. 65). All students were expected to wake up early in the morning, perform their daily chores, and prepare for classes. Students were also expected to eat at the same time in the school's dining hall. At the end of class, students engaged in different activities on campus. Some worked on the school garden, while others engaged in sporting activities such as soccer or track and field events. In the evening, after meals, students went back to class for evening studies. Students who reported late for any of these activities were punished by the school authorities. The students also had to follow dress codes and were often expected to wear prescribed school uniforms for different occasions.

## All-Female Institutions

In the female boarding schools, the girls held all the leadership positions. These school prefects included senior (i.e., school-wide) prefect, house prefects or captains, dining hall prefects, student school nurse, games captain, and entertainment prefect. These positions provided girls the opportunity to develop leadership skills. Like their male counterparts, the girls also had rules to follow. The most grievous offense a girl could commit was to exceed the time limit for returning to campus. Girls were given extra protection by school authorities while on campus. One primary concern at the time was that if a girl became pregnant, she had to drop out of school, thereby wasting the parents' educational investment in them. Parents therefore encouraged school authorities to go the extra mile to provide their daughters all the care, attention, and protection they needed while away from home.

Drawing an example from Ghana, the curriculum for girls included academic subjects and "an associated cluster of values and attitudes which the girls accepted in some cases and rejected in others" (Masemann, 1974, p. 484). The subjects taught comprised language arts, history, geography, physics, chemistry, biology, mathematics, music, art, typing, shorthand, commerce, cookery, needlecraft, and home management. Although science and mathematics courses were included in the curriculum, they did not receive the rigor and emphasis that were normally seen in all-male schools. Courses like woodwork, carpentry, masonry, agriculture, science, and mathematics were not emphasized because they were not deemed "appropriate" for the occupational aspirations for the new "ladies" that were gradually emerging in the African society. The deficiencies in science and mathematics followed the girls when they entered institutions of higher learning in search of new credentials in education.

## Coeducation

Coeducation in Africa constituted two states within a state in the sense that although both males and females formed the student body and shared some facilities, they were simultaneously segregated in terms of their location and curriculum.

By the middle of the twentieth century, coeducation was not popular in Africa. In Ghana, there were only two teacher education institutions that were coeducational. These were the Seventh Day Adventist Seminary and Ewe Presbyterian Training College. It was in the coeducation institutions that traditional values concerning gender roles resurfaced and gave the male students the opportunity to dominate the female students in school activities. Although the female students had their own leaders such as dormitory prefects and school senior prefects (of which there were separate boys and girls prefects), when the entire school met for general activities, the authority, status, and power of the male leaders overshadowed their female counterparts. As observed by Dunne (2007) when writing about a similar situation in a Ghanaian school:

> Each year equal numbers of males and females prefects were appointed. . . . [However,] male prefects had more authority and took the lead in joint activities. High-status public duties were usually performed by boys. . . . These duties would never be performed by a girl . . . as girl prefects . . . would have problems instructing or controlling male students, especially the older ones. (p. 505)

It has been argued that the colonial schools in Africa existed only to promote and perpetuate community values (Thompson, 1981). Dunne's (2007) description cited above about schools in Ghana is applicable elsewhere, and indicates that although modern schools in Africa have in some ways minimized gender roles, these changes have been very slow, and in some situations, little or no change has taken place.

## EUROPEAN POWERS AND THE
## DEVELOPMENT OF HIGHER EDUCATION IN AFRICA

After laying the foundations for elementary and secondary education in colonial Africa, the colonial powers proceeded to develop higher educational institutions. In many cases, missionaries took the lead in this endeavor. The Church Missionary Society of Britain founded the Christian Institute in 1814 in Sierra Leone. This later became known as Fourah Bay College. The British colonial government set up the University of Cape Town in South Africa in 1829, which was originally established as a high school for boys. It also established Makerere University in Uganda in 1922; a school that was originally set up as a technical college that offered courses in carpentry, medicine, agriculture, veterinary science, and teacher education. The French established Dakar University in Senegal in 1957, and the University of Abidjan in the Ivory Coast in 1958. The Portuguese did not want to be left out in the development of higher education institutions, and so in 1968 they set up *Estudos Gerais Universitários de Angola* in Angola. The United States, which was left out during the era of the scramble for Africa, established the American University of Cairo in Egypt in 1919 to offer Western-style education to students in Egypt in particular, and North Africa and the Middle East as a whole.

In many of these institutions, few or no women were originally offered admission to study. It is quite revealing that Makerere University opened its doors to fourteen day-students who studied carpentry, building, and mechanics. These courses indicate that all the initial students were boys. In a turn of events in South Africa, however, the University of Cape Town admitted women in 1886 to pursue courses in science.

In general, these higher education institutions were developed by the colonial powers to train high-level personnel locally for the new administrations that gradually evolved as a result of the introduction of foreign systems of government and monetary economy. Until the establishment of higher education institutions in Africa, all Africans who required higher education credentials had to go overseas. Most of the students sent abroad by the early European educators were men because the European educators assumed that yields from investments in the education of men were greater, as compared to women. In Egypt, Ghana, and Nigeria, the British colonial government did not promote the local development of higher education, and so students who wanted to acquire higher education credentials had to travel overseas to countries such as France, Britain, or the United States. This was the general trend on the continent until Africans took over the educational development after independence, which generally began after the late 1950s (Thompson, 1981).

## EUROPEANS AND AFRICAN PARENTS ON THE EDUCATION OF GIRLS

In their desire to provide Western education to Africans, European colonial powers often overlooked the interests of women. This, in many cases, was not the wish of the early colonial educators, since by this time the education of girls in Europe had somehow gained public acceptance in many European countries: it was the wish of the African parents. The early Christian women missionaries who came to Africa could read and write. Many of them served as teachers, school principals, or senior school administrators (Kimble, 1963). However, the interests of females in their educational establishments were overlooked because the education of girls and women did not meet the approval of many parents (Tibenderana, 1985). By all accounts, both girls and boys were needed to help with household chores, but when parents were forced to make a choice between the education of boys and girls, girls were often asked to stay home while their brothers were allowed to attend school.

What must have influenced this parental decision? One factor was obvious: Although many of the European women who followed their spouses to Africa could read and write, they were unlikely to occupy any top government positions. The highest position many of these women could aspire to was to become a principal at a girls' school. Coincidentally, the role these educated European women played was not different from what Africans considered to be the role of the African woman. Therefore, even though there was general resistance to Western education, there was a greater resistance on the part of parents to send their daughters to school because for centuries, African women had successfully managed domestic affairs without ever stepping in the classroom.

Another source of resistance to girls' education was marriage. Women who had completed elementary or secondary education entered into a new social class that placed considerable limitations on their community roles and cultural practices. Generally, women who had completed elementary or secondary school were not supposed to marry illiterate men. The general belief was that a woman with literacy skills was expected to marry a man with equal or higher literacy skills. This social restriction somehow placed unnecessary barriers on women when choosing marriage partners. Consequently, the higher the education level of the woman, the more difficult it was for her to find a husband (Rathgeber, 2003).

As the centuries passed and more parents became aware of the social and economic importance of schooling, many changed their attitude toward schooling, especially for girls. The sight of European women wearing dresses and speaking foreign languages or reading newspapers became a standard that many African parents wanted for their daughters. This standard, however, called for limited education, which a girl could acquire from the elementary educational level. Consequently, many Africans accepted elementary or secondary education for their daughters. Notably, many of the European educators shared the views of African parents themselves. Therefore, for many years, the idea of limited schooling for girls was not questioned (Peil, 1990; Taylor, 1984).

With elementary or secondary education credentials, women in Africa, like other women in less industrialized countries, continued to accept lower ranking jobs in nearly all social, political, civil, or administrative positions. This situation prevailed throughout the colonial period and even after independence. The election of Louisa Diogo in 2004 as prime minister of Mozambique and the 2007 election of Ellen Sirleaf Johnson as the president of Liberia are two major developments that have somehow breached the gender roles in Africa. These accomplishments were made possible simply because of the higher education credentials of the women. These women obtained their higher education credentials in subject areas that were once considered to be male-dominated areas. Louisa Diogo obtained her bachelor's degree in economics at the Eduardo Mondale University of Maputo in 1983, and obtained her master's degree in economics at the University of London in 1992. Ellen Sirleaf Johnson obtained her bachelor's degree in accounting at the Madison Business College in Madison, Wisconsin, in 1964; a diploma in economics from the University of Colorado in 1970; and a master's in public administration from Harvard University in 1971. These achievements highlighted the changing status of African women with higher education credentials.

## POST-INDEPENDENCE DEVELOPMENT IN HIGHER EDUCATION IN AFRICA

After Africa was regained through independence from the colonial powers, each African government made the development of education a national priority. Each introduced legislation that made the government responsible for the education of all citizens (Country Report of South Africa, 2004; Kurian, 1988; Ngome, 2003). Higher education was one area that received the greatest attention from all the newly independent nations in Africa. Ghana established the University of Cape Coast soon after independence, and developed the Kwame Nkrumah University of Science and Technology into a full-fledged university in 1961. Other African countries such as Kenya, Nigeria, Uganda, Egypt, and Zambia followed the Ghana example and gradually established and modified their higher education systems to meet the needs of their citizens. As listed by Lulat (2003), most of the post-independence universities had common characteristics. Among them were:

- The move away from a specialized single-subject honors degree in the arts to a general degree in any number of fields, including professional fields of study.
- The broadening of the disciplinary structure to include medicine and applied technology, specifically the various fields of engineering.
- The expansion of the curricula to include vocational subjects. (This was necessary in order to make available courses that would attract the interest of women.)
- The move from a three-year degree to a four-year university education, in order to eliminate the sixth-form A-level General Certificate in Education. (The new university entrance requirements would be based on the fifth form O-level examinations, thereby broadening the field of student recruitment.)
- The dedication of the first year to a general program of study with required courses (often including African studies).
- The broadening of the mission of the university to include community outreach through programs such as agricultural extension services, public health education, extramural evening courses, and long-distance correspondence courses. (p. 20)

These changes paved the way for more Africans, particularly women, to enroll in higher education.

## WOMEN AND HIGHER EDUCATION IN AFRICA

Even in modern historical terms, Africa has a long history of higher education development. North Africa in particular has a rich tradition in the development of higher educational institutions. Countries like Egypt, Tunisia, and Morocco had developed forms of higher education by the eighth century (Fafunwa, 1977; Lulat, 2003). In modern Egypt, higher education started in the Al-Azhar Mosque, which was opened in 972 CE in Cairo to offer religious education to local religious leaders. Only male students were enrolled to study religious ethics, philosophy, and law, in order to provide men the leadership skills they required to lead their communities. In 1061, it was converted to a university, and since then, its curriculum has been transformed to include secular subjects.

In the western part of Africa, the University of Sankore in Timbuktu had a long reputation as the major source of higher education in the West African subregion (Fafunwa, 1977). Despite the early development of university education in Africa, for over a thousand years, higher education in Africa continued to be off the radar of educational planners. The various colonial powers did not see the need for the development of higher educational institutions on the continent since they found it easier and cheaper to send Africans abroad for higher education. Soon after independence, however, the tide changed and all the newly independent countries saw the establishment of institutions of higher learning as key to self-reliance and national development.

Today, Africa can boast of more than two thousand higher education institutions. These include public as well as private institutions. All these universities admit women to pursue various academic programs. The net effect is that more women are enrolling in higher educational institutions to acquire new social skills, and are looking for new ways to be economically and socially independent (UNESCO, 2004, 2006).

The participation of the private sector in the development of higher education has opened another avenue for women to participate in higher education in Africa. For example, in Ghana and Nigeria, there are several private universities that routinely enroll women. In predominantly Muslim Egypt, the American University of Cairo offers women the opportunity to acquire higher education credentials. This development is instrumental for women in a nation where tradition once limited the educational opportunities for women (American University of Cairo, 2008; Ngome, 2003). Once enrolled in higher educational institutions, the questions to consider are: What are women in African higher institutions of learning studying? What are their occupational aspirations? The next sections will explore these questions.

## WHAT WOMEN ARE STUDYING IN HIGHER EDUCATION INSTITUTIONS IN AFRICA

To a large extent, gender roles determine the academic programs of African women in higher education. Generally, in Africa as elsewhere, women are expected to study courses that are deemed appropriate for their social roles. This is essentially the case because traditional gender roles "are organized so that women are more likely than men to assume domestic roles of homemaker and to be primary caretakers of children, whereas men are more likely than women to assume roles in the paid economy and to be primary family providers" (Eagly, 2001, p.1069). Therefore, as indicated in figure 8.1, women tend to concentrate in such areas as education (i.e., teaching), humanities, service areas, and "lower" programs in medicine such as nursing or doctor's aide (Rathgeber, 2003).

As revealed in figure 8.1, most women in higher education in South Africa specialize in education. For the period of study, women consistently formed the majority of students in education, comprising nearly 70 percent of the students between 2003 and 2005. In the engineering, manufacturing, and construction areas, women comprised a little over 20 percent of the students within the same time period. In the medical field, most women concentrate on "lower" programs such as nursing or doctor's aide. When they become medical doctors, few women further their education to become specialists such as surgeons, urologists, neurologists, or psychiatrists.

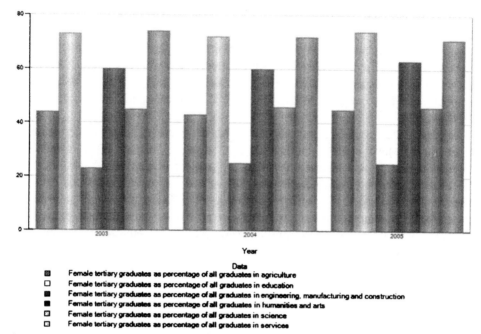

Year

Data

■    Female tertiary graduates as percentage of all graduates in agriculture
□    Female tertiary graduates as percentage of all graduates in education
■    Female tertiary graduates as percentage of all graduates in engineering, manufacturing and construction
■    Female tertiary graduates as percentage of all graduates in humanities and arts
□    Female tertiary graduates as percentage of all graduates in science
□    Female tertiary graduates as percentage of all graduates in services

**Figure 8.1.**   **Participation of Women in Higher Education in South Africa**

Similarly, a study of Nigerian University students concluded that Nigerian female students had a tendency to enroll in courses that were tagged as "female," and that such courses were generally in the humanities (Adeyemi and Akpotu, 2004). Indeed, women in institutions of higher learning in Africa and other developing countries are often kept out of science, mathematics, technology, and engineering because they are often tracked into areas like nursing and teaching (Adeyemi and Akpotu, 2004).

One argument that is used to discourage women from science and engineering is that the length of the study is likely to have a negative impact on their family status. Women in Africa tend to get minimal education so that they can spend quality time at home with their family members. There is also the "biological clock" factor: the fear that many years of schooling is likely to negatively impact the reproductive ability of a woman. Such factors combine to discourage many women from seeking academic credentials that will keep them in school for too long, especially in specialized areas such as engineering, medicine, architecture, or law. Also, the financial returns on higher education are less for women than for men, which may discourage some women.

## OCCUPATIONAL ASPIRATIONS OF WOMEN IN HIGHER EDUCATION IN AFRICA

Like women in other parts of the world, highly educated women in Africa tend to enter professions that will offer them the flexibility to spend more time at home. For this reason, they miss opportunities to take on leadership roles or assignments where they will be expected to invest extensive amounts of time in order to become successful. Thus, they are often employed by governments and other private agencies as nurses, teachers, flight attendants, administrative assistants, bank clerks, secretaries, librarians, and in other service industries such as hotel administration, front desk management, and food preparation (Biraimah, 1987; Hannah and Kahn, 1989; Maqsud, 1992).

In general, due to societal pressures and structural barriers, many women are unable to obtain high-level positions in their areas of expertise. In some cases, women with degrees in science and mathematics find employment in areas that have little to do with their academic training (Biraimah, 1987). Such societal pressures and structural barriers have the added effect of reproducing a self-fulfilling prophecy: the myth that educational investment in women is not as wise as in men, since, no matter how smart they are, their gender roles will limit the usefulness of their education, and thus limit the financial returns of such investments.

## A RETROSPECTION AND IMPLICATIONS FOR GLOBAL EDUCATION

As educational traditions become hybridized across the globe, especially with Western education, it is useful to address the inherent tensions that arise when different educational systems and philosophies become juxtaposed to each other or clash. As was noted earlier in this chapter, the contributions made by Africans toward modern school systems are often ignored or omitted by social historians. Africa has never been without teachers and scholars. Until the introduction of Western styles of education on the continent, Africa had its own educational systems. The philosophies of these educational systems or knowledge traditions were in harmony with the cultural needs of the different African societies. Consequently, the African educational system produced graduates who never looked for elusive jobs since the skills they acquired were relevant for their societies (Scanlon, 1964). In essence, the African traditional educational system had different philosophies, modes of instruction, and organization from the Western educational system that is prevalent across Africa today; such differences were a reflection of the local needs.

### Gender Equity in African Education

In terms of gender roles and social development, an analytical view indicates that African traditional education had systems in place that ensured gender equality. The *Bundu* and *Poro* societies provided men and women equal opportunities to play leadership and important societal roles. Thus, in Sierra Leone, some of the women who received training for the *Bundu* Society later became local chiefs and negotiated an important treaty in 1787 "which ceded territory to the British Crown" (Fyfe, 1962, p. 19, as cited in Hoffer, 1972, p. 151). In other situations, women played, and still play, significant roles in selecting community leaders such as chiefs or kings. Among the Akans of Ghana, for example, no man can traditionally become a king or a traditional political leader unless he is nominated or accepted by a woman, the queen mother. Such men are usually the sons or close relatives of the queen mother. Hence it is often argued in many African circles that a woman without descendants is powerless (Coquery-Vidrovitch, 1997).

From one perspective, the school systems established by Europeans and Arabs did not alter the gender divide. Rather, they introduced new concepts and ideas that kept women out of leadership positions or high-paying jobs (Coquery-Vidrovitch, 1997). Initially, women were kept out of the school systems established by the Europeans. In some cases, women had the opportunity to receive higher education after fifty or more years of waiting. They were also restricted to limited content and professional opportunities. These developments were against the basic African concept of gender equality—even in cases where "separate but equal" education was practiced. Traditionally, African women were not denied "higher education," but, like their male counterparts, they received education into adulthood, and the education they received was not limited with marriage; it was for life.

African women have historically been powerful, despite the gender divide. In the era of rapid globalization and information sharing, the roles of women in society are being continuously revised across the world, as human and women's rights movements have become a part of the globalization phenomenon. Therefore, the current changes observed in Africa about the roles of women in society are partial responses to these global trends designed by governments to help women cross the gender divide in order to promote national development—and higher education for women is a necessary part of this new equation.

## CONCLUSION

This chapter set out to discuss the participation of women in higher education in Africa, with special reference to Egypt, Ghana, Nigeria, and South Africa. In particular, it assessed the career aspirations of women with higher education credentials in Africa, and examined the changing and persisting roles of these women and the implications for global education.

Data from UNESCO and other sources revealed that although more women are enrolling in higher education, most of them still enroll in courses that will eventually place them in jobs that are traditionally deemed appropriate for their gender. On the other hand, there are a few cases where women in Africa have used higher education credentials to enter occupations that were once deemed the exclusive domain of males. The elections of Louisa Diogo as prime minister of Mozambique in 2004 and Ellen Sirleaf Johnson as the first woman president of Liberia in 2007 are classic examples of women who have changed educational and occupational aspirations for women in Africa. Incidentally, both women acquired higher education credentials in academic areas that are often considered domains for male students: economics and accounting. Their leadership roles should be expected to have a positive impact on the landscape of career aspirations for women in Africa. Bearing in mind that there are over fifty political leadership positions (presidents and prime ministers) in Africa, the position of these two women as political leaders in Africa is still insignificant. However, it should serve as a baseline for the motivation of other African women who aim at breaking the global gender divide in education and career aspirations.

Higher education credentials are essential today in all economies. Technological progress has brought the world together in a manner that is truly amazing. New, emerging occupations call for different skills, many of which can only be acquired through higher education. As globalization engulfs the world, the efforts of both men and women of all nations will be needed in order to meet the demands of competitive global markets. Societies therefore have the responsibility to encourage all their citizens, including women, to seek higher education credentials in areas that are not only highly prized by society, but will also better serve the needs of the global community.

## REFERENCES

Adeyemi, K., and Akpotu, N. (2004). Gender analysis of student enrollment in Nigerian universities. *Higher Education, 48*(3), 361–78.

Adeyemi, M. B., and Adeyinka, A. (2003). The principles and content of African traditional education. *Educational Philosophy and Theory, 35*(4), 425–40.

American University of Cairo. (2008). *Student attributes.* Retrieved March 15, 2008, from www.aucegypt.edu/ResearchatAUC/IPART/Research/Pages/StudentAttributes.aspx.

Ayandele, E. A. (1971). The coming of Western education to Africa. *West African Journal of Education, 15*(1), 21–33.

Biraimah, K. L. (1987). Class, gender, and life chances: A Nigerian university case study. *Comparative Education Review, 31*(4), 570–82.

Brown, G. N. (1971). The development of universities in Anglophone Africa. *West African Journal of Education, 15*(1), 41–44.

Clignet, R. P., and Foster, P. J. (1964). French and British colonial education in Africa. *Comparative Education Review, 8*(2), 191–98.

Coquery-Vidrovitch, C. (1997). *African women: A modern history.* Boulder, CO: Westview Press.

Country Report of South Africa. (2004, September 8–11). *The development of education. Forty-seventh international conference on education.* Geneva: UNESCO. Retrieved February 2, 2008, from www.ibe.unesco.org/International/ICE47/English/Natreps/reports/safrica_ocr.pdf.

Dunne, M. (2007). Gender, sexuality, and schooling: Everyday life in junior secondary schools in Botswana and Ghana. *International Journal of Educational Development, 27,* 499–511.

Eagly, A. H. (2001). Social role theory of sex differences and similarities. In J. Worell (Ed.), *Encyclopedia of women and gender: Vol. 4. Sex similarities and differences and the impact of society on gender* (pp. 1069–78). San Diego: Academic Press.

Exploring Africa, (2008). *Colonialism in Africa, 1914.* Retrieved April 20, 2008, from dart .columbia.edu/library/muso1097/colonialism1914.jpg?context=main.

Fafunwa, A. B. (1977). Africa, Sub-Saharan: Regional analysis. In A. S. Knowles (Ed.), *The international encyclopedia of higher education, vol. 2* (pp. 198–206). San Francisco: Jossey-Bass.

Grindal, B. T. (1972). *Growing up in two worlds: Education and transition among the Sisala of Northern Ghana.* New York: Holt, Rinehart, and Winston.

Hannah, J. S., and Kahn, S. (1989). The relationship of socioeconomic status and gender to the occupational choices of grade 12 students. *Journal of Vocational Behavior, 34,* 161–78.

Harris, C. (2001). Ancient words. *Tour Egypt Monthly: An On-line Magazine, 2*(5). Retrieved March 12, 2008, from www.touregypt.net/magazine/mag05012001/magf7.htm.

Hilliard, A. G., III. (1998a). *The reawakening of the African mind.* Gainesville: Makare.

Hilliard, C. B. (1998b). *The intellectual traditions of pre-colonial Africa.* Boston: McGraw-Hill.

Hilliard, F. H. (1957). *A short history of education in British West Africa.* London: Thomas Nelson.

Hoffer, C. P. (1972). Mende and Sherbo women in high office. *Canadian Journal of African Studies, 6*(2), 151–64.

Kimble, D. (1963). *A political history of Ghana.* Oxford: Oxford University Press.

Kurian, G. (1988). Ghana. In *World education encyclopedia* (Vol. 1, pp. 468–78). New York: Facts on File.

Lulat, Y. G. M. (2003). The development of higher education in Africa: A historical survey. In D. Teferra and P. G. Altbach (Eds.), *African higher education* (pp. 82–92). Bloomington: Indiana University Press.

Lungu, G. F. (1993). Educational-policy making in colonial Zambia: The case of higher education for Africans from 1924–1964. *The Journal Negro History, 78*(4), 207–32.

Maqsud, M. (1992). Trends in occupational aspirations of rural secondary school leavers in Bophuthatswana. *International Journal of Development, 12*(3), 205–12.

Masemann, V. (1974). The "hidden curriculum" of a West African girls' boarding school. *Canadian Journal of African Studies, 8*(3), 479–94.

Miescher, S. F. (2005). *Making men in Ghana.* Bloomington: Indiana University Press.

Ngome, C. (2003). *Kenya: Country higher education profiles.* Retrieved March 13, 2008, from www.bc.edu/bc_org/avp/soe/cihe/inhea/profiles/Kenya.htm.

Peil, M. (1990). Intergenerational mobility through education: Nigeria, Sierra Leone, and Zimbabwe. *International Journal of Development, 10*(4), 311–25.

Pula, C. M. (2008). *African Missionaries in the 1890s.* Retrieved April 14, 2008, from members.cox.net/butermohlen/africa_mission.htm.

Rathgeber, E. M. (2003). Women in universities and university-educated women: The current situation in Africa. In D. Teferra and P. G. Altbach (Eds.), *African higher education.* (pp. 82–92). Bloomington: Indiana University Press.

Sawyerr, H. (1971). The significance of the Western education experience for Africa. *West African Journal of Education, 15*(1), 45–49.

Scanlon, D. G. (1964). *Traditions of African education.* New York: Teachers College Press.

Scott, H. S. (1938). The effect of education on the African. *Journal of Royal African Society, 37*(149), 504–9.

Singleton, B. D. (2004). African bibliophiles: Books and libraries in medieval Timbuktu. *Libraries and Culture, 39*(1), 1–12.

Taylor, W. H. (1984). Missionary education in Africa reconsidered: The Presbyterian educational impact in eastern Nigeria 1846–1974. *African Affairs, 83*(331), 189–205.

Thompson, A. R. (1981). *Education and development in Africa.* New York: St. Martin's Press.

Tibenderana, P. K. (1985). The beginnings of girls' education in the native administrative schools in northern Nigeria, 1930–1945. *The Journal of African History, 26*(1), 93–109.

UNESCO Institute for Statistics. (2004). *Data center*. Retrieved March 16, 2008, from stats .uis.unesco.org/on.

UNESCO Institute for Statistics. (2006). *Global education digest, 2006: Comparing education statistics across the world*. Retrieved March 28, 2008, from www.uis.unesco.org/TEM-PLATE/pdf/ged/2006/GED2006.pdf.

UNESCO International Bureau of Education. (2006). *World data on education: Egypt*. Retrieved April 3, 2008, from www.ibe.unesco.org/countries/Egypt.htm.

Wallbank, T. W. (1934). The educational renaissance in British tropical Africa. *The Journal of Negro Education, 3*(1), 105–22.

Whitehead, C. (1981). Education in British colonial dependencies, 1919–1939: A re-appraisal. *Comparative Education, 17*(1), 71–80.

Wynne, J. G. (1971). Religious education in West African schools. *West African Journal of Education, 15*(3), 215–19.

*Chapter Nine*

# The Interface of Global Migrations, Local English-Language Learning, and Identity Transmutations of the Immigrant Academician[1]

Charles B. Hutchison, Lan Hue Quach, and Greg Wiggan

"I do not want my house to be walled on all sides and my windows to be stuffed; I want the cultures of all lands to be blown about my house as freely as possible. But I refuse to be blown off my feet by any. I refuse to live in other people's houses as an interloper, a beggar or a slave."

Mahatma Gandhi, 1921

## INTRODUCTION

In a U.S. (National Public Radio) program called "This I Believe" (January 16, 2006), Dr. Pius Kamau, a Kenya-born medical doctor related an arresting experience: When he first arrived in the United States, it dawned on him that when he was working in the hospital, he was seen as a "doctor." However, when he was outside the physical limits of the hospital, he was racialized and given the identity of "black," and was thus subjected to predetermined race relations prescribed by the American sociological machinery. (This machinery included the factors which defined the nature of the society in which he lived, including how different groups of people viewed each other.) He also reported an encounter with a white supremacist who had a swastika tattoo on his chest. Although this person was rushed into his hospital coughing up blood, the white supremacist refused to be treated by him, a black doctor. This man would rather have died than to be treated by the "wrong" kind of person. On the other hand, many international people report the warm welcome they experience as immigrants in the United States, and how they are viewed in a positive light.

When immigrant educators arrive in the classroom, however, they encounter peculiar problems which are pedagogical in nature (Hutchison, 2005). The kinds of experiences noted above bear the beacon for the broad range of issues—including linguistic and identity development—that ultimately define international educators. In this chapter, *academic cosmopolite identity* denotes the personality that evolves as the resulting product of psychosocial forces to which the immigrant academic worker is subjected. The confluence of forces that emerge during global migrations are hereby discussed, with an emphasis on how *academic cosmopolite identity* is developed in light of the pressure to conform to the local parlance. Using data collected from fifty-five student evaluations as supporting evidence, this chapter contends that academic immigrants undergo personality differentiation in response to local sociolinguistic forces.

## DEFINING THE STRUCTURAL FORCES SHAPING ACADEMIC COSMOPOLITE-IMMIGRANT IDENTITY DEVELOPMENT

People who engage in any form of international or cross-cultural travel necessarily subject themselves to certain kinds of structural forces. Such forces lie primarily on the axis of the sociocultural, and define the norms and conventions of a society. According to Bodley, there are several domain-specific aspects of culture, including the topical, historical, behavioral, normative, functional, mental, structural, and symbolic. These are the unspoken but compelling forces which drive the nature of any society (Bodley, 1997).

For people engaged in longer tours of travel, including students and academic migrants, there is a second tier of organic, structural forces to which they are exposed (Fortunijn, 2002). This group of travelers (i.e., academic migrants) enter their new assignments only to confront often unexpected differences in their new educational environments (Aikenhead and Jegede, 1999). This is not surprising, since teaching is a human enterprise that is influenced by institutional and cultural frameworks (Lemke, 2001). Related issues may include differences in teaching and learning styles, curricula, assessment, and available resources (Hutchison, 2005). In sum, academic migrants are likely to face a pedagogical culture shock from which they need to recover and reconstitute themselves.

### The Identity Development Process

One of the most powerful influences to which academic migrants become exposed is how they are defined or perceived by the local macroculture. For example, instructors from hierarchical societies would behave differently toward their students than ones where students are viewed as social equals (Hutchison, 2005). To this local definition or perception of them, they do respond—consciously or unconsciously. By this response, they would have undergone the process of identity development, in an evolutionary sense. Cross, Parham, and Helms observe that identity development occurs when minority individuals encounter the majority culture to which they feel subordinated (as cited in Cross, 1978). Although members of the majority culture may sometimes arrive at the consciousness of their majority position, they have the prerogative to confront this consciousness or avoid it if they are not comfortable with the process (Helms, 1984). However, the onus rests on minority individuals (in this case, the academic cosmopolite) to undergo the necessary adaptation process to suit the new educational environment (Hutchison, 2005).

The nigrescence model of Cross (1978) and Hardiman's (1982) model of social identity development will be used as the basis of this argument. The theory of nigresence was created to explain the identity development of African Americans as a cultural-racial minority in the United States. Specifically, Cross's model involves five separate stages which are: preencounter, encounter, immersion-emersion, internalization, and internalization-commitment. A person in the preencounter (Hardiman's naivete) stage has not begun the identity development process, since he or she has not yet been exposed to the external defining agents. They therefore exist in an unexamined identity state. Having traveled to become a minority in a cross-cultural context, individuals may arrive at Cross's encounter (Hardiman's passive and active acceptance) stage, whereby the academic cosmopolite realizes sociocultural differences and their minority status. U.S.-born minority groups have natural rights of abode and other socioemotional buffers, such as the support of close relatives. Therefore, they have the resources to move into the next stage and may be characterized by Cross's resistance aspects of the encounter stage (Hardiman's passive and active resistance stages). However, being *voluntary migrants*, academic cosmopolites necessarily conform to the local pressures with less resistance and friction. Thus, they are likely to skip the immersion-emersion stage, and arrive at the internalization and internalization-commitment stages (Hardiman's redefinition and internalization stages respectively); the stages of mutual acceptance of both the defining culture and self-definition. In this connection, Watson explains that African students in the United States go through similar identity formation processes, although they do not experience the immersion-emersion stage (Watson, 2005).

## Definition through Communication

It is vital to note that sociolinguistic forces (that is, need to relearn English in response to the local parlance) pose as issues for this population (cf. Hall, 1984, as cited in Kuhn, 1996). This includes the need for cross-cultural academic workers to conform to the local language conventions, including formal and informal language styles (i.e., verbal and nonverbal communication), accents, understand the differential use of certain specific words, expressions, technical language, and the social function of language. Ming Fan He illustrates this new academic cultural plunge as a situation whereby the international traveler may initially negotiate new experiences, become influenced by the new culture, and ultimately assume a new cross-cultural identity (He, 2000).

From a social-constructivist (and situated cognition) standpoint, teachers in cross-cultural settings may experience changes in their linguistic worldviews in several ways (Good and Brophy, 2003). First, in the school setting, their discourse and dialogue become exposed to local, conforming pressures owing to the new input from teacher-colleagues, students, and parents. These new linguistic forces may alert them to new linguistic conventions and, consequently, an expansion of their linguistic-cognitive structures. Second, they are exposed to new linguistic ideas and even traditional beliefs or other kinds of information that may contradict their native beliefs and cause them to consciously examine and restructure those beliefs, where necessary. Finally, migrants' communication with local people may force them to articulate their ideas differently in the pursuit of clarity during communication. In so doing, they would have experienced the process of assuming new linguistic identities; a parallel to the process of identity development.

Therefore, international, cross-cultural academicians necessarily present their indigenous identities to be partially eclipsed by the local forces described above. For this reason, they are inadvertently engaged in the process of academic cosmopolite-immigrant identity development.

## The Pressure to Define and to be Defined—By Language

Immanuel Wallerstein contends that to pose the question "What are you?" is to open Pandora's box (Wallerstein, 2000). He illustrates thus:

> The setting is South Africa. The South African government has by law proclaimed the existence of four groups of "peoples," each with a name. . . . Somewhere in the 1960s or perhaps 1970s—it is not clear when—the ANC slipped into using the term "African" for all those who were not "Europeans" and thus included under the one label what the government called Bantus, Coloureds, and Indians. Some others—it is not clear who—made a similar decision but designated this group as "non-Whites" as opposed to "Whites." In any case, the consequence was to reduce a four-fold classification into a dichotomy. (Wallerstein, 2000, pp. 293–94)

After living in the United States for seven years, I (Hutchison, one of the authors) decided to return to Ghana (where I was born and lived for twenty-eight years) for a visit. At the airport, one of the workers inquired if I was an African American. This got me thinking, since back in the United States, I am never mistaken for a U.S.-born native, owing to (what I thought was) my "unmistakable" African accent and parlance. It is interesting and important to note that when in the United States, I am first of all, "black" until I speak. When I speak, I become "African." This connotes that the notion of linguistics is inherently tied with locational-cultural identity. The subsequent question then becomes "What kind of African are you?"—since, as a cross-cultural teacher in the United States for thirteen years, one of the questions to almost certainly expect of students during the first day of class (if given the opportunity) is, "What part of Africa do you come from?" For academic migrants, therefore, there is a potential slipperiness of designation that becomes a part of their self-identity landscape that has to be navigated. Their shifting locational-linguistic identities can usher them into a linguistic "homelessness," whereby they can become strangers both in their native lands and their new lands. To me, the airport inquiry above by a Ghanaian as to who I was by dint of my acquired accent crystallized my linguistic homelessness: I had arrived at a social location whereby I spoke with an enigmatic accent to people both in my own native land and my adopted country. In commenting on the cross-cultural experiences of ESL students, Roth and Harama (2000) observe that

> change in language entails a change in the way we experience ourselves, and in the way we relate to others. Learning a new language and living in a new culture changes how we relate to the Other and to the world; learning a new language, therefore, changes who we are, how we experience ourselves, and, therefore, our Selves. (Roth and Harama, 2000)

Like ESL students, academic cosmopolites' need to engage with the *Other* and the consequent products of such relationships precipitate a transmutation of the immigrant academician's identity. In a Wallersteinian sense, these teachers are migrating from the periphery and semiperiphery to the core (Wallerstein, 2000).

## The Duality of Being and its Precarious Meaning

From the personal, airport narrative above, one may contend that, *to speak* is *to become*. It is hereby argued that the locus of *the process of becoming* occurs in Anderson's (1983) "social-imaginary"—a discursive space whereby one becomes reconstructed via the imaginational mechanisms of his or her observers (as cited in Ibrahim, 1999). Such imaginations are mediated by the history and cross-cultural knowledge base of the local environment, given the notion of "societal mind" or traditions (Bodley, 1997). These include how certain groups of people are viewed historically, and thus, through *symbolic interactionism*, may determine the kinds of relationships that occur among cultural groups, in the tradition of Schutz's phenomenology (Schutz, 1967).

Contingent on the above propositions, therefore, the academic immigrant is laden with the burden of cogitating the questions: Who do people think that I am? Who do I think that they think that I am? Who do I think that I am? Who really am I? (Rice and Dolgin, 2005) These kinds of questions are vital for several reasons:

(a) They help to determine the products of self-definition, self-concept, the ideal self, and therefore self-esteem (Rice and Dolgin, 2005).
(b) To be labeled as a minority (especially black) in the United States carries its own psychological burden, since one's identity may be juxtaposed against that of the majority identity, with tangible consequences (Ibrahim, 1999; Kunjufu, 1984).
(c) The very idea of one being a duality (an immigrant-American) mitigates the value of one's citizenship: it connotes a dilution of the purity of being a "full citizen."
(d) To be labeled as "African" carries a duplicitous connotation. On the one hand, being African may carry an acceptance that may even go beyond that offered to native African Americans. This is because of inherent prejudice against blacks in America (Kunjufu, 1984). On the other hand, being immigrant-African could sometimes be rather precarious. This is so because of the strong influence of the media. There have been several very popular movies such as *Mandela*, *Hotel Rwanda*, and *Tarzan* (just to mention a few), and *National Geographic* episodes of African landscapes (capturing safari scenery, including tantalizing flora and fauna) that have left long-lasting, rather exotic impressions of Africans.

Based on the above, the psychological faces of native-born Africans in the United States may therefore be approximately categorized into the Kenyan safari, the Ethiopian famished, the South African (Mandelan) freedom fighter, or simply a resurrection from the movie *Tarzan*. These are simply so because of the perennial media coverage that inadvertently serves as psychoemotional fuel for stereotypical framing, as opposed to serving as ambrosia for feeding the intellect. These media images have been burned into the psyche of many consumers, creating lasting and unintended, but erroneous images of blacks at large. Concomitant to the above, in a majority-black school, Traoré (2002) found an evident hierarchy of blackness, whereby Caribbean Americans were assigned to a higher social position than African immigrant students. Consequently, many African students spoke with a Jamaican accent (Traoré, 2002). This pathological view of blacks, however, is not a surprise, since it is a part of the legacy of slavery and forgotten history. Ironically, however, Herodotus, the Greek historian, and several historians of antiquity wrote that ancestral black Africans were the originators of the oldest known advanced civilizations. Herodotus also demonstrated that "Greece borrowed from Egypt [a colony of the then-Sudan/"Aethiopa"] all the elements of her civilization, even the cult of the gods" (as cited in Diop, 1974, p. 4). By extrapolation, and ironically therefore, the forgotten but true basis of Western civilization is black African, according to Greece's Herodotus. This fact is not only in oblivion to the larger global society, but also to many blacks in America, who therefore do not view themselves with the pride and abilities that appertain therewith.

In a psycho-logico-hierarchical sense, it may be contended that when a group of people has been psychosocially placed in a location of need—whereby even children are sympathetically compelled to empty their "piggy banks" in order to help the likes of them, this group's psychological estate or placement would thus have been lowered to the position of the "recipient" as opposed to the "donor." The defined recipient would then be easier psychologically viewed as a group in need of benefaction of different forms, including the linguistic. For this reason, no matter what one's level of command of English is, it may potentially be less valued, especially when there are differentiating factors such as spelling, differences in the meaning of words and idioms, accent, and so forth (Hutchison, 2005).

## Accent as a Communicational Structural Force

Speaking with an accent can influence a listener's impressions about a speaker (Giles and Powesland, 1975). Nonstandard accents are often thought of less favorably than what are considered "standard" accents. This may easily be illustrated by the fact that the "Queen's English," for example, or the British accent is deemed more admissible and even viewed as being superior to the Indian or African accent. Even when both accents are articulated with correct grammatical content, it is not likely to ask one speaking a "more admissible" English to change his or her accent, but the converse is likely.

In many parts of the world, certain regional accents lend positive or negative traits to their speakers. For example, in the United States, the midwestern accent is considered standard (or nonaccented). In Ghana, West Africa, the Fanti language spoken in the Cape Coast area is favored over that in the surrounding areas, and in England, the "standard" British English is favored over the "nonstandard" Birmingham British English (Cocks, 2002). In a research study, the way in which various Irish regional accents affected students' impressions of a man reading a passage on Irish history was investigated (Edwards, 1977). The matched-guise technique was used to record five stimuli accents. Students were asked to rate five recorded stimuli accents that had been modified using the matched-guise technique. Each accent was rated for nine qualities, including intelligence, ambition, and friendliness. It was found that regional accent indeed had a significant effect on all traits. The Donegal accent was rated most positively, and the Dublin accent rated least positively.

Given that some accents may attract prejudice against the speakers, the phenomenon of accent reduction or change is evident in several areas of the United States, especially in the broadcasting professions where the "standard midwestern" accent is deemed the "broadcaster's quality," but southern accents are less favored, and negatively captioned as "having a southern drawl." In 1993, one of the authors was advised to attend an "accent reduction program," in a well-known university in the southeastern United States. The purpose was to reduce his foreign accent in order to better reach his students. Interestingly, however, many American professionals were in attendance of this program, trying to "reduce and polish" their own accents in order to be more presentable for their current competitive jobs.

Dixon, Mahoney, and Cocks studied the negative consequences of accent prejudice. In this study, the participants were presented with an audiotape of a criminal investigation in which a person was being interrogated by the police. The race, crime-type (blue- or white-collar), and accent of the accused person were manipulated by the researchers, using the matched-guise technique. They found that the attributions of crime (i.e., the likelihood of being found guilty on a seven-point bipolar scale of *innocent* to *guilty*) increased as a function of nonstandard English (Birmingham) accent, minority race (black suspect), and blue-collar job. This inadvertent criminalization of accent by the participants is reminiscent of criminalization of race in the United States (cf. Elizabeth Loftus's works, such as *Our Changeable Memories: Legal and Practical Implications*).

In summary, accent evaluation is a compelling issue with tangible consequences. It is therefore a significant structural force in the educational environment. For academic cosmopolites, one of the strongest forces which elicit sociolinguistic redevelopment is the students of the academic cosmopolites. In the next few sections, the linguistic issues (with an emphasis on accent) faced by an academic cosmopolite are discussed as viewed by his or her own students.

## A Case in Point: An Immigrant Professor and his External Evaluators

Global travelers may be privy to cross-cultural issues on two levels. For some, cross-cultural issues are just transient, since they may be mere tourists. For this group, the challenges of bilingualism are short-lived. For the second group; those who are immigrants on a long-term basis, this is a long-term challenge which deserves an intellectual investment. For this second group, although bilingualism could be viewed as an academic strength, the linguistic differentials may emerge as a pedagogical issue of interest. The following sections describe fifty-five student evaluations of an immigrant professor's course and include analyses of these ratings. This data illuminates how his students (external assessors) viewed him—both as a person and a bilingual speaker of English, and how these perceptions may have contributed to the identity development of this immigrant academic cosmopolite.

## METHOD

Student evaluations of their professors are a common practice in U.S. higher institutions. The primary objective is to allow the students to illuminate both the areas where professors are effective and ineffective so that they can further improve their pedagogical practices. There are some public fora (a.k.a. "forums") such as, rateyourprofessor.com where students may do exactly that: discuss and rate their professors. Many universities have their "underground" networks of knowledge dissemination, whereby they can rate their professors for both noble and ignoble reasons. While the noble reasons may include how to select a professor for content of interest and teaching style that may suit different students, the ignoble reasons for rating professors may include how to find an easy professor, or resolve a personal vendetta. These ratings are generally voluntary and subjective since students' comments are not subjected to stringent guidelines. There are unofficial but comprehensive platforms where students may do this. One example is Shippensburg University's "Shipunderground" for rating professors (available at www.shipunderground.com).

Since, at this website, students voluntarily rate their professors, it fulfils the requirements of having knowledgeable sources or "key informants" and willing participants (McMillan and Schumacher, 1997; Schensul, Schensul, and LeCompte, 1999).

From the "Shipunderground" website, the database on an identified immigrant professor (whose personal information is altered for anonymity) was identified and used as the unit of analysis. This professor was evaluated by 55 of his own students. Each student was expected to declare some initial information, such as the class taught, the grade obtained, and general commentary. However, their names were not declared, thereby protecting their identity, and promoting honesty. For the ratings of each professor, they were required to fill out numerical ratings on a Likert scale of 1–10, based on the following questions:

1.  How effective was this professor? ("not effective" [with lower numerical ratings] to "very effective" [with higher numerical ratings])
2.  How easy are this professor's classes? ("very hard" [with lower numerical ratings] to "very easy" [with higher numerical ratings])
3.  How would you rate his/her availability? ("never around" [with lower numerical ratings] to "always there" [with higher numerical ratings])
4.  What is your overall rating for this professor? ("needs work": not recommended [with lower numerical ratings] to "very good": highly recommended [with higher numerical ratings])

This website was a very powerful source of data since it was easy to see how the honesty and the true feelings of the students were apparent. Even in the best ratings, the students did not hesitate to intermingle both positive and negative comments that represented their true views of, and feelings about this professor. It was also obvious that some of the other participants were aware of the other students' ratings and reacted to them, either in agreement or disagreement. For these reasons, this data source was even more powerful than other forms of data collection, whereby identifiable parties were collecting the data for a specific identifiable reason. For the purposes of this study, therefore, this data source was effectively neutral. It is apparent that this data source is meant as a site to inform students about what students truly felt about their professors and therefore an advising source for future students.

## DATA ANALYSIS

Strauss and Corbin's 1990 open, axial, and selective coding schemes were used to analyze the data (Strauss and Corbin, 1990). All the fifty-five data entries on the immigrant professor were printed out and read through several times, looking for cross-cultural issues in general. Ideas with similar meanings were used in the formation of concept clusters. Having identified linguistic issues as a clear theme, any language-related comments were highlighted in one color. Subsequently, accent-related comments were differentiated and counted. Finally, the professor's conscious or unconscious responses were sought in the light of previous research (Hutchison, 2005).

## FINDINGS

The findings from this website are grouped into two sections. The first reviews the numerical ratings of his students. The second part (voluntary comments) sheds some light on the ratings. From the website, this professor's average ratings were as follows:

Table 9.1. **Professor's Numerical Ratings**

| Item # | Question for Rating | Average Rating |
|--------|---------------------|----------------|
| 1 | How effective was this professor? | 7.27 |
| 2 | How easy are this professor's classes? | 6.21 |
| 3 | How would you rate his/her availability (outside of the classroom)? | 7.79 |
| 4 | What is your overall rating for this professor (would you recommend this professor to your friends)? | 7.88 |

### Student Comments

In analyzing the comments part of the student evaluations, it was obvious that the professor in question was generally identified not just as a professor, but one with an accent. Out of fifty-five voluntary total student entries, twenty-one of his students made a language-related (mostly accent) comment. It is important to emphasize that the issue of language was not even solicited information in the professor's evaluation; these were *voluntary* comments made by his students. On this issue, there were two factions of students: those who complained about not understanding him well (and even made a rather pejorative comment), and those who accommodated his accent (and one even commended the professor for his superior mastery of English). From the first (negative) category of students, there were comments such as the following entries:

Anonymous (Undeclared): My roommate and I had this class together and were really scared when he first started talking and sounded like Abu from the Simpsons. As it turns out, this is the easiest class I had and I HATE history. He prints out his notes for you everyday on a handout, basically gives you the test answer key to study from and his grading scale is AWESOME: 85–100=A. It is the BEST!!!

Anonymous (Comm/Journ): I stopped doing the readings after three weeks, took frequently incomplete class notes, studied the night before tests, handed in an incomplete paper for which I got a "B," and I still managed to get a "B+." While my habits of procrastination did not hurt me, I would recommend that you still do work in this class just to be safe. Dr. B— is a very effective professor. He is not only an easy grader, but operates on a very generous curve. His accent—he was born in [Africa], I believe—is quite thick, and his frequent mispronunciation of words is pretty damned funny.

The second group of students made comments such as the following:

Anonymous (Biology): Dr. B— is one of the most brilliant profs here at Ship. Throughout, the entire course, he never referred to any prepared notes. He comes to class well prepared and he is the most organized prof I have seen. He is exceedingly helpful. He goes out of his way to help students. I know for fact that he does extra work with students who don't do well in some aspects of his course. For example, I did not do well on the midterm and he asked me to see him during his office hours. Once there, I met a number of students with the same problem. Dr. B— devised a strategy for all of us to improve our grades. Yes, Dr. B— has an African accent, but he speaks excellent English, in fact, better than most American professors I know. He also prepares his students for exams, and he is very good at it. I think that that is why students do well in his course and it is not that he is easy as most of the comments here shows. Dr. B— is simply an excellent professor, someone who is committed to helping students to attain their academic potential.

And

Anonymous: Dr. B—is a good guy. He always tries his best to make things easy for you. The only thing is he is hard to understand (but that's not his fault). He gives a review sheet for the test which makes it so easy. This class is boring . . . but simple. If you can [bear] to sit through a boring class, I would recommend Dr. B—.

It is important to note that out of fifty-five students, thirty-four did not make any comments about his language issues. Four students rated him with what was classified by the website as "negative comments." Out of these four students, three of them made negative comments about this accent. The numbers involved indicate that his effectiveness as a communicator was not an issue for most of the students. This, however, does not reveal the obvious fact that his foreign accent, and therefore his foreignness was obvious to all his students. From a further analysis of the student comments, it was clear that even those who rated him positively (and many extremely positively for his superior content knowledge) put on their subject lines such entries as: "Truly an African giant," "African man man," "Brilliant African intellectual scholar," "Greatest African man I ever met," "Excellent Africa man," and "In my opinion, Dr. B— is an African who is very proud of who he is, and it comes out, as someone pointed out here, in the way he carries himself." These comments clearly indicate that the students were very conscious of his native origins in juxtaposition to his obvious accent. In fact, the professor was fully aware of this new identity as the "professor with accent," as the following comment indicates:

> Anonymous (Psychology): Dr. B— is hard to understand at the beginning of the semester, *but he will tell you that himself.* [Emphasis mine] Don't worry [because] he is willing to repeat himself many times and you will get used to his accent. He is really nice and understanding. He wants his students to do well. He gives awesome notes! You never have to do the reading as long as you go to class. He really knows what he's talking about and can answer almost any question you ask him. I definitely recommend!

As indicated earlier, the students who were less accommodating of his foreign accent were more likely to rate him worse (three of four negative comments were accent-related), thus potentially influencing his peers' perception of him as a professor, and, consequently, his potential success on the job.

## DISCUSSION

The evaluation of this professor is comparable to the social vision (see Anderson, 1983) to which he was catapulted and examined by his external assessors; his own students. The products of this vision, therefore, yielded the reactants for phenomenological interactions with him (cf. Giles and Powesland and Traoré's works). Granted that his accent was nonstandard (and he was aware of it, as noted by one of the students), he was therefore consciously subjected to the linguistic structural force to which he had to respond.

Although the voice of this professor is silent in this data set, he did respond to the local pressure partly by providing his students with copious notes on the board. He also provided print-out copies of his course notes. He also repeated himself, as some students observed. These were interesting adaptations that would mitigate any linguistic and cross-cultural pedagogical dissonance (cf. Hutchison's work).

Given that U.S. university students generally evaluate their professors each semester for each course taught, this professor was likely to receive returned copies of his students' evaluation of his teaching at the end of each semester. In these evaluation forms, it is customary—even standard—to provide areas for voluntary student comments. If students were willing to visit a voluntary website to offer comments on his linguistic issue, they are likely to do the same in their course evaluation, in anonymity. By this means, the linguistic structural force would have found a formal outlet to exact from the professor, a linguistic redevelopment or reconformation to the local tongue (cf. Hutchison, Butler, and Fuller's, and Roth and Harama's works). Given the conglomeration of the forces above, this professor would have undergone the process of academic cosmopolite identity development via linguistic redevelopment (or local English-language learning). This sociolinguistic evolution is reminiscent of Habermas's notion that since the use of language is a common denominator in society, it could also be a conduit for social inequalities, whereby external, dominating agencies may impose structural forces in specific directions (Habermas, 1979). In this work, the power of students as external agents was evident in exacting directional linguistic evolution from their professor, and thereby affirming Habermas.

## CONCLUSION

This chapter argued that to be a cross-cultural academician is to offer oneself to be analyzed on the platter of the *social imaginary* machinery. The forces exerted by this machinery remold the cross-cultural academician both consciously and unconsciously, resulting in the creation of a new personality—the *academic immigrant cosmopolite*. One of these forces is sociolinguistics. As evident from the fifty-five student evaluations (see comments above), academic immigrants may necessarily have to respond to sociolinguistic forces by relearning local English conventions. For academic cosmopolites, one of the strongest forces which elicit linguistic redevelopment is the students. To his students, this professor was reconstituted as "the professor with an accent." As demonstrated in the students' comments, accent evaluation posed as a significant communicational structural force in the context of education. The same comments also revealed that the negotiation of cultural and linguistic forces during the development of the identity of the migrant academician can be rather complex. Ultimately, it shows that the hybridization of one's native socio-culturo-linguistics and emergent cross-cultural forces have the capacity to precipitate new permutations of international, transmuted identities.

The limitations of this study are obvious. A more directed study of identity development may have provided a richer context for this study. Besides, a direct interview with the professor in question could have addressed his own responses to his students' evaluations, not to mention the richness that further elaborations of the students' comments could have provided.

## NOTE

1. This chapter was originally published in the *Forum on Public Policy Online*, Fall 2006 edition.

## REFERENCES

Aikenhead, G. S., and Jegede, O. J. (1999). Cross-cultural science education: A cognitive explanation of a cultural phenomenon. *Journal of Research in Science Teaching, 36*(3), 269–87.

Bodley, J. H. (1997). *Cultural anthropology: Tribes, states, and the global system.* Mountain View, CA: Mayfield.

Cocks, R. (2002). Accents of guilt? Effects of regional accent, race, and crime type on attributions of guilt. *Journal of Language and Social Psychology, 21,* 162–68.

Cross, W. E., Jr. (1978). The Thomas and Cross models of psychological nigrescence: A review. *Journal of Black Psychology, 5*(1), 13–19.

Diop, C. A. (1974). *The African origin of civilization: Myth or reality* (Trans. M. Cook). New York: Lawrence Hill Books.

Edwards, J. R. (1977). Students' reactions to Irish regional accents. *Language & Speech, 20,* 280–86.

Fortuijn, J. D. (2002). Internationalizing learning and teaching: A European experience. *Journal of Geography, 26*(3), 263–73.

Giles, H., and Powesland, P. F. (1975). *Speech evaluation and social evaluation.* London: Academic Press.

Good, T. L., and Brophy, J. E. 2003. *Looking in classrooms* (ninth ed.). Boston: Allyn and Bacon.

Habermas, J. (1979). *Communication and the evolution of society* (Trans. T. McCarthy). Boston: Beacon Press.

Hardiman, R. (1982). White identity development: A process oriented model for describing the racial consciousness of white Americans (Doctoral dissertation, University of Massachusetts, 1982). *Dissertation Abstracts International* 43(01A), 104.

He, M. F. (2000). A narrative of inquiry of cross-cultural lives: Lives in the North American academy. *Journal of Curriculum Studies, 34*(5), 513–33.

Helms, J. E. (1984). Toward a theoretical explanation of the effects of race on counseling: An African American and white model. *The Counseling Psychologist, 12*(4), 153–63.

Hutchison, C. B. (2005). *Teaching in America: A cross-cultural guide for international teachers and their employers.* Dordrecht, Netherlands: Springer.

Hutchison, C. B., Butler, M. B., and Fuller, S. (2005). Pedagogical communication issues arising for four expatriate science teachers in American schools. *Electronic Journal of Science Education, 9*(3). Available at wolfweb.unr.edu/homepage/crowther/ejse/ejsev9n3.html.

Ibrahim, A. K. M. (1999). Becoming black rap and hip-hop, race, gender, identity, and the politics of ESL. *TESOL Quarterly, 33*(3), 349–69.

Kuhn, E. D. (1996). Cross-cultural stumbling block for international teachers. *College Teaching, 44*(3), 96–100.

Kunjufu, J. (1984). *Developing positive self-images & discipline in black children.* Chicago: African American Images.

Lemke, J. L. (2001). Articulating communities: Socio-cultural perspectives on science education. *Journal of Research in Science Teaching, 38*(3), 296–316.

Loftus, E. F. (2003). Our changeable memories: legal and practical implications. *Nature Reviews: Neuroscience, 4,* 231–34.

McMillan, J. H., and Schumacher, S. (1997). *Research in education: A conceptual introduction.* New York: Longman.

Rice, F. P., and Dolgin, G. D. (2005). *The adolescent: Development, relationships, and culture* (eleventh ed.). Boston: Pearson Education, Inc.

Roth, W. M., and Harama, H. (2000). English as second language: Tribulations of self. *Journal of Curriculum Studies, 32*(6), 757–75.

Schensul, L. S., Schensul, J. J., and LeCompte, M. J. (1999). *Essential ethnographic methods.* Walnut Creek, CA: AltaMira Press.

Schutz, A. (1967). *The phenomenology of the social world* (G. Walsh and F. Lehnert, Trans.). Evanston, IL: Northwestern University Press.

Strauss, A., and Corbin, J. (1990). *Basics of qualitative research: Grounded theory procedures and techniques*. Newbury Park, CA: Sage Publications.

Traoré, R. L. (2002). *Implementing Afrocentricity: African students in an urban high school in America*. Unpublished doctoral dissertation, Temple University, Philadelphia.

Wallerstein, I. (2000). *The essential Wallerstein*. New York: The Free Press.

Watson, M. A. Undated. *Africans to America: The unfolding of identity*. Retrieved November 24, 2005, from www.africamigration.com/articles/watson.html.

## Chapter 10

# Globalization and Linguistic Migrations: Missed Opportunities and the Challenges of Bilingual Education in the United States

Theresa Perez and Greg Wiggan

My maternal family (Theresa Perez) is from a small village in Mexico, Encarnacion de Dios, where they lived for generations. They left Mexico for the United States during the great exodus caused by the Mexican Revolution. Like many others, they fully intended to return when the country became stable, but that was a dream that was never realized. The revolution, which began in 1910 and lasted until at least 1920, started as a revolt against the thirty-year rule of Mexico's President Porfirio Diaz. It was a social and agrarian movement against the concentration of land and power in the hands of a few people (Simpson, 1967).

The years that followed were difficult ones. My grandfather worked in the silver mines of Arizona for a time, but the mines were no longer producing much silver and the pay was meager. My family worked their way west by following the crops as migrant farm workers, and it remained their way of life for many years. The family traveled from place to place, living in migrant camps, sleeping in tents, and carrying all of their possessions with them wherever they went.

We lived this way until I was about five years old and my grandfather became too ill to work in the fields, whereupon the family moved to Fresno, California, where he could receive medical attention and my sister and I could go to school. It was during my formative years that I realized I was different. I seemed to live a bilingual life with one foot in my English-speaking school and one foot in my Spanish-speaking home. The two lives remained very separate and distinct; it was like being two people, one person at school and another at home.

Upon graduation from high school my principal told me that I was definitely not college material and should follow a path that did not involve higher education. This rather startling pronouncement caused me to see myself as lacking in intelligence and, as a result, I did not seek very challenging employment. It was many years before I felt I could succeed as a college student and enrolled in a four-year teaching program at a university.

After graduating from Fresno State College, I worked as a seventh and eighth grade middle school teacher in a school with many Spanish-speaking migrant students. The students were tracked by ability, and the lowest tracks were filled with migrants. I found these students to be intelligent and capable of doing quality work, but discouraged by the school's belief in their lack of ability. By the seventh grade most students had lost any hope in their future. I considered this unacceptable and sought out new ways to improve their skills and self-esteem by developing a relationship with them, and providing them with encouragement. I also dropped the textbooks they had been using and sought out interesting activities that would challenge students in new ways. These students taught me that by giving them hope and the right support, they could display as much enthusiasm and intelligence for school work as students in the higher tracks. I reluctantly left the middle school teaching position when I was offered a position as a lecturer in Chicano Studies at Fresno State. My university teaching load consisted for the most part of teaching courses related to Chicanos in the educational system.

During the 1960s, the justice system began providing support to minority communities by passing a series of laws that supported students' rights to receive services related to language instruction. For example, the Civil Rights Act of 1964 provided that all students regardless of their race, ethnicity, or national origin, receive an equal education. In 1968 the Bilingual Education Act was signed into law as Title VII of the Elementary and Secondary Education Act, which gave funding to support educational programs to help students become literate in English. Title VI of the Civil Rights Act outlawed discrimination by government agencies that received federal funding, including schools. If the local education agency violated the provisions, it could lose federal funding.

Finally, in the *Lau vs. Nichols* case of 1974, the Supreme Court stated emphatically that schools were not providing equal educational opportunity by teaching only in English. While the *Lau* decision did not mandate bilingual education, it left the door open to interpretation. No longer would the time-worn practice of providing English-only instruction to all students, regardless of their differences, be considered equal education or acceptable practice in public schools (Crawford, 1992, 1995).

In my fifth year of teaching at Fresno State, I was informed that I would need a doctorate to continue in my position at the university, and was given a two-year leave of absence to complete a PhD program. I applied and was accepted into the Curriculum and Teacher Education Program at Stanford University. I found my experience at Stanford to be academically rich and intellectually stimulating. It was also during this time that I began an in-depth examination of issues related to students' identity status (immigrant, race, class, and gender) in U.S. classrooms, and explored whether classroom status affects the participation and achievement of minority and low-income students.

Based on my past experience teaching migrant students in a middle school and interacting with teachers, I knew that all the students were capable of doing quality work. There was ample evidence to support ways to bring about higher levels of academic achievement among these students, but teachers were not exposed to the research or the teaching strategies. I saw the problem as one of reaching the classroom teachers with the right tools, and chose a dissertation study that examined ways to bring about change in classroom settings. Through my research assistantship at the Center for Educational Research at Stanford, I was able to examine interventions in classroom organization that lead to the success of all students.

This experience set the course for my professional life as a university professor, and I have since worked to provide classroom teachers with information on learning environments that promote high levels of academic achievement for students from second language backgrounds. Thus, the questions that are guiding this chapter are: (1) What are the challenges faced by immigrant students, more specifically Mexican immigrants? (2) What educational opportunities have we missed in providing bilingual education to these students? and (3) How can teachers better teach and assist this population? We explore the relationship between immigrant status, linguistic migrations, and education.

The chapter begins with a discussion on global and linguistic migrations, and their connections to Mexican immigrant experiences and to the historical context of public policy and issues of language rights in the United States. This is followed by an analysis of the 1974 *Lau vs. Nichols* case and contemporary post-*Lau* legislation, and their implications for English-language learners. The chapter concludes with recommendations and strategies for teachers of English-language learners.

## GLOBAL MIGRATION AND LINGUISTIC MIGRATIONS

First and second generation immigrants under age fifteen are the fastest growing segment of the U.S. population (Chapa and De La Rosa, 2004; Garcia, 2001). With increasing levels of non-English speakers in public schools, educators must be prepared to address these students' educational needs. In 2008, the U.S. Department of Education (USDE) indicated that 5,074,572 English-language learners were enrolled in preK–12 public schools and they made up 10.29 percent of total school enrollment, and between the years of 1994–1995 and 2005–2006, this population increased by 57.1 percent (USDE, 2008). Educating this ever-growing group of students has become a national concern and over a period of about forty years, many court decisions were mandated that appeared to provide some guidance for school districts. However, problems remain. Studies indicate that in 2007, only 31 percent of English-language learners in the eighth grade scored at or above basic achievement level in mathematics (NCELAL, 2008). A similar finding from the National Center for Education Statistics indicates that only 29.7 percent of students whose first language is not English in the eighth grade scored at or above basic achievement level in reading (NCES, 2008).

While many consider English to be the global language or the language of the global marketplace, transnational migration makes issues of cultural and linguistic diversities a salient concern (Spring, 2006). Mexicans make up the largest part of the Latino/Latina population in the United States and their growth is expected to continue to outpace all other groups (Chapa and De La Rosa, 2004). The counterflow of immigrants, meaning immigrants who return to live in their home country, is relatively low compared to those who remain in a country other than their own, otherwise called a destination country. In the case of Mexican immigrants, many of them make their homes in the United States. The amount of immigrant flow and the destination of the flow depend greatly on the political economy and military stability of the home country as well as the destination country. In the instance of Mexico, the North American

Free Trade Agreement (NAFTA) of 1994 signed between Mexico, Canada, and the United States, created one of the largest trade blocs in the world (Truett and Truett, 2007). The 1990s were years of marked economic growth, which created a great deal of wealth and inequalities (Cohen, 2001). While the Mexican government liberalized its economy and opened its local markets to U.S. and Canadian transnational corporations, the country experienced very little sustainable growth. Through NAFTA, duty-free imports into Mexico made local production and competition a major challenge. In addition, low-wage employment structures increased economic destabilization and have contributed greatly to the number of Mexicans who emigrate.

## MEXICO IN THE GEOPOLITICAL ECONOMY

Since as early as the mid-1800s, Mexico has been a principal interest because of its geography, natural resources, and its potential as cheap labor. This interest can be traced to the Mexican-American War of 1846 and the Treaty of Guadalupe Hidalgo in 1848, where Mexico surrendered one-half of its territory, which included most of what is now Texas, and Arizona, New Mexico, Colorado, California, Nevada, Utah, and Wyoming. Under the treaty, Mexicans retained the right to their language and customs and the right to remain on the land as citizens of the United States. These rights were soon nullified as laws were changed and English became the language of the courts. Thus, since it was against the law to testify in Spanish, Mexicans, who spoke no English, could not testify on their own behalf (Pitt, 1999). With these changes in the law, Mexicans soon lost their land, their livelihood, and their way of life. They became like strangers in their own land (Perez, 1991).

In another period of Mexico-U.S. relations, the Mexican Revolution of 1910 serves to demonstrate U.S. involvement in the affairs of Mexico and in the great migrations north. President Porfirio Diaz, who governed Mexico for thirty years, had by the beginning of the revolution become very despotic. The Revolution of 1910 was both a peasant uprising as well as a social movement by Mexican intellectuals who were dissatisfied with the Diaz administration. President Diaz, seeking money for his treasury, sold Mexican lands to foreign investors (U.S. investors owned over one-fourth of Mexico's land), and to a small powerful elite, who held both the power and the land. The discontented peasants, whose land had been confiscated and who lived in poverty, became serfs and were seeking relief from their material conditions. Disgruntled peasants and a group of new young leaders called for democratic elections to unseat the Diaz dictatorship. The armed struggle that followed lasted ten years and ended in the defeat of the government in 1920 (Simpson, 1967).

The Mexican Revolution of 1910 did not bring about sweeping reforms for the peasants. In spite of the great uprising and loss of life, their lives remained relatively unchanged. However, this was not the case for foreign investors who lost both their land and their businesses to the new Mexican government. After the revolution, these investors had to adjust to a new way of life, one where they had fewer resources and less power. Nevertheless, throughout the twentieth century, Mexico remained a principal place of economic and political interest for the international community because of its location, natural resources, and potential as cheap labor.

Today, in the contemporary era of globalization, Mexico continues to grow in importance. Graizbord and his colleagues (2005) examine the effects of globalization on Mexico City. They argue that Mexico City is a second-tier global, urban city in the world economy. The city continues to be a desirable location for national and transnational corporations because of its corporate-friendly policies and cheap labor. Automakers like General Motors, Ford, and Chrysler do much of their production in Mexico because of the reasons mentioned above, adding to the country's rural-to-urban migration flow, as people leave the countryside seeking employment in the cities. According to Graizbord and his colleagues (2005):

> Mexico City, with over 18 million inhabitants, has historically been the main destination of migrants from the rest of the country, the prime location for all types of economic activity and the center for coordination, decision-making and most economic development efforts by the Mexican government. (p. 147)

However, today, urban sprawl and congestion pose major problems for the city because of the high levels of rural-to-urban migration and insufficient employment opportunities. Graizbord and his colleagues (2005) explore problems associated with increasing concentration of international corporations, environmental damage, and poor air quality in Mexico City. They find that migrants continue to move from the countryside, seeking employment in the city, the place where most local merchandise is made. The increasing presence of transnational corporations makes this migration even more prevalent (Stern, 2007). Eventually, labor markets become saturated with a surplus of workers, which further suppresses the price of labor. In addition, transnational corporations generally widen income inequalities because most of the jobs they create pay low wages and lack long-term potential for social mobility. The city receives few benefits from globalization relative to the social, economic, and environmental costs it endures for these gains.

Graizbord and his colleagues (2005) argue that quality of life in Mexico has not improved through the government's support of globalization. Thus, many Mexicans immigrate to the United States for better employment opportunities. The migration decision-making process is often influenced by economic advantages in the destination country, the presence of international support systems (family and/or friends), location, and legalities (some countries are more sympathetic to immigrants than others).

Mexico-U.S. emigration leads to population redistribution and general geographical changes in the allocation of immigrants in the United States. Emigration affects the distribution of skills, labor, capital income, and educational attainment in Mexico and the United States. While internal migration is commonplace, several cities have become gateways for immigrants, creating national and international trends and population shifts. Cities like Houston, New York, Los Angeles, San Francisco, Chicago, Miami, and Charlotte continue to be choice destinations for Mexicans and other immigrants. They often select large metropolitan areas where there are already ethnic enclaves and where there are opportunities for employment (Singh, 2001).

Immigrants must adjust to life in the United States and to discrimination they might face from their new identity (immigrant) and from being a cultural and linguistic minority. The fear and prejudice against unpopular immigrants is sometimes alarming, but not all immigrants are treated the same way. For example, a white middle-class British immigrant in the United States is more likely to receive better treatment than a Mexican or Haitian immigrant. Similarly, Chinese immigrants might be received differently than Central and South American immigrants. The extent to which a destination country is accommodating to new immigrants depends greatly on where their originating nation falls in the perceived stratification in the status of nations. Other issues like political climate, international relations, and racial and ethnic prejudice influence the disparities in the treatment of immigrants.

The geographic concentration of immigrants resulting from chain migration helps them form support systems to assist in navigating their new social landscape and in dealing with discrimination. These support systems form what may be viewed as *migration systems*. Most immigrants, specifically those with less education, documented or undocumented (meaning those without documents that legally permit them entrance into the destination country), must be prepared to fill jobs at the bottom of the occupational ladder in the destination country. This forms *ethnic divisions of labor* whereby immigrants, in this case Mexican immigrants, fill a niche in the labor market. As a result, some low-income Americans might feel a sense of competition from the newly arrived Mexicans. This often creates resentment toward each other. Furthermore, the fear of wage compression resulting from the presence of immigrants makes laborers uneasy (Howell and Mueller, 2002). Immigrant workers often face labor exploitation and are forced to work in poor conditions. However, low-wage immigrant workers help keep labor and production cost low in developed countries, which means that they play an important role in the economy, and therefore their particular social needs must be explored.

## GLOBALIZATION, LANGUAGE, AND PUBLIC POLICY

Globalization and emigration have many consequences for immigrants and their life chances, taking these issues into the realm of public policy. The issue of immigration management has been evident in the implementation of legislation such as the 1986 Immigration Reform and Control Act, the Immigration Act of 1990, and in more recent immigration guidelines through the United States Citizenship and Immigration Services. Furthermore, policies like California's Proposition 187 attempt to block public benefits and services to Mexican immigrants—all of this coming from a state that originally belonged to Mexico. Cultural and linguistic minorities in California and across the nation find themselves at the center of a very intense struggle over language rights.

In a complex multilingual world, English is more than a language; it is generally believed to be the language of economic globalization and a principal communication tool in the global marketplace. The push to make English the official language raises the issue of identity politics and education in the context of globalization. However, with the growing number of Spanish speakers in U.S. public schools, the opportunities and challenges in educating immigrant students must be addressed. Some people view Spanish speakers as distorting the American cultural identity, and believe that schools need to reinforce the process of Americanization (Huntington, 2004). Americanization efforts seek to ensure that immigrants and speakers of other languages (including Spanish) learn English and other American cultural ethos as part of their new identity. They also seek to preserve the Anglo-American culture. However, the attempt to nationalize English is not a new phenomenon.

## HISTORICAL CONTEXT OF LINGUISTIC HEGEMONY

Historically, in the 1600s when the Pilgrims arrived in the Americas, they fought the Native Americans for their land and attempted to suppress and eradicate Native American culture, including religion and language. Hegemonic language suppression was crucial to "Anglicizing" the region, and only in more recent times have Native American words been popularized as names of National Football League teams like the Washington Redskins and Kansas City Chiefs, as names of professional baseball teams like Atlanta Braves and Cleveland Indians, and names of automobiles like Jeep Cherokee and Mazda Navajo. Similarly, where the African slaves were concerned, there were systematic attempts to suppress all African forms of life and to prohibit the use of African languages and spirituality. Although preserved through the use of modern Ebonics (a.k.a. black vernacular), language suppression was important to the aim of trying to create new identities in the Africans (Turner, 2002). Prohibiting bilingualism and making English the only acceptable language was a way of universalizing the interest of the dominant group through the machinery of hegemony, and creating new identities in the oppressed.

As a pluralistic society, the United States has always been a multilingual country. Even before the arrival of the Europeans, there were between five hundred and one thousand Native American languages. After the arrival of the Europeans, seven languages were established in the United States: English along the eastern seaboard; Spanish in the south, from Florida to California; French in Louisiana and northern Maine; German in Delaware; Russian in Alaska; Dutch in New Amsterdam (New York); and Swedish in Delaware (Liebowitz, 1971). Four languages survived: English, Spanish, French, and German; and three did not: Russian, Dutch, and Swedish (Liebowitz, 1971). The reasons for the survival of the English language are discussed later.

Similar to the treatment of the Native Americans, after the New Mexico territories were taken from Mexico in the Mexican-American War and the signing of the Treaty of Guadalupe Hidalgo in 1848, Americanization campaigns and English requirements were widespread in the newly acquired regions. As a result of the American victory in the war, the new regions needed to be Americanized. The Treaty of Guadaupe Hidalgo was very specific in terms of linguistic and cultural freedoms. However, California, which was designated as a bilingual state, quickly nullified its agreements regarding language minorities. There was a perceived conflict between the culture in the former Mexican territories and the Anglo-American culture, which permeated linguistic tensions, the English-Spanish struggle. In places like Arizona, all courses were taught in English and in all the newly acquired territories English would quickly be made the legitimate language. Similarly, in California, migration surrounding the Gold Rush of the 1800s transformed the social landscape of the state from one dominated by Mexicans, making them the minority and quickly changing the culture to Anglo-American. By the turn of the twentieth century, Mexican Americans in places like California and New Mexico were in an ensuing battle to have both Spanish and English instruction in school (U.S. Commission on Civil Rights, 1972/1992).

Native language use was also discouraged with the German immigrants coming to America during the late nineteenth and early twentieth centuries. Cohen (2001) argues that throughout the nineteenth century, German was one of the leading second languages in the United States.

In the nineteenth century, public schools in Ohio, Minnesota, Maryland, and Indiana used German either alone or with English for instruction. Some public schools in New England used French and many schools in the southwest used Spanish as the language of instruction. Until 1868, French was used in the public schools of Louisiana (Fishman, 1956). The German experiment of setting up public schools that used German as the medium of instruction was popular until World War I, at which time it was discontinued because of conflicts between the United States and Germany.

The United States acquired its multilingual character through purchase, acquisition, and annexation of territories that contained people who spoke diverse languages. Efforts by language minorities to sustain their language and culture have often been viewed as anti-American and divisive for the country (Liebowitz, 1971). Part of the reason for the survival of English as a dominant language was because it was constantly reinforced by the arrival of new settlers in the seventeenth and eighteenth centuries. The census of 1790 showed that 60 percent of the population was of English descent, 18 percent was of Scottish and Irish descent, and 9 percent was of German descent. In 1880 there was a great migration from western and northern Europe, which continued the dominance of English influence (Fishman, 1956).

By 1917 bilingual instruction in the public schools had disappeared and many states, including California, passed legislation requiring that English be the language of instruction and imposed fines on teachers and punishments on students who spoke in their native languages. The non-English-speaking students were forced to sink or swim in schools that used English as the only language of instruction. There are many stories of students being punished for speaking in their native tongue. In the southwest, schools enforced Spanish detention (Ramirez and Castaneda, 1974). The idea of assimilation was widespread, and that got translated into educational policy and theories of cultural deprivation and genetic and biological beliefs about low levels of intelligence among minority groups (Herrnstein and Murray, 1994). These theories were supported by popular literature, the mass media, social science, and bolstered by European-based IQ scores and low school performance among minority students. Thus, minority students were seen as lacking in the knowledge, skills, and values for school success, and schools found no need to assume any responsibility for the education of students who spoke little or no English. Both in schools and society, these students were viewed as having failed. When the schools did act, it was to promote ideas of compensatory education in order to make up for what these students were perceived as lacking in their home environment (Ramirez and Castaneda, 1974).

At the same time, scholars agreed that it was better to begin education in the students' native language in order to strengthen their linguistic skills (Cummins, 1981; Freeman and Freeman, 2002; Wong Fillmore, 1991). Cummins (1981) found that students who strengthened their first language made an easier transition into English and did not lose out academically. Research studies began to demonstrate that second language acquisition is not impaired by first language instruction, but rather that it enhances students' learning (Peal, 1962; Skuttnab-Kangas, 1988). Other studies by Cummins (1981) found that the better developed the first language, the more likely the learner acquires high proficiency in the second language. Scholars also found that interruption of the native language before linguistic skills are consolidated (ten to twelve years) may have a destabilizing effect on language proficiency. Therefore, the idea that a student's first language be the language of instruction (at least for a time) became more popular, and the notion that bilingualism is not detrimental to cognitive growth was established. Thus, the belief that bilingual education was a viable concept began to take hold.

## MISSED OPPORTUNITIES: POLITICS OF IMMIGRATION AND THE *LAU* CASE

During the twentieth century, there were some key social developments that impacted minorities and their educational opportunities. Between the 1960s and 1970s, the civil rights and Chicano movements led to increasing sensitivities surrounding social justice issues and equality. The 1960s created new waves of immigration policy. Toward this end, Title VI of the 1964 Civil Rights Act and the Bilingual Education Act of 1968 were created to ensure that all students were able to gain access to education and language support systems.

In 1963, a federally funded program was established in Dade County, Florida for exiled Cuban students, which attracted national attention. The following year Webb County, Texas, and San Antonio, Texas, began bilingual programs. By 1967, the U.S. Senate called for hearings on federal subsidies for bilingual education. Proponents presented a convincing case that bilingual education could improve Spanish-speaking students' chances for success in schools (Gonzalez, 1975).

In 1968, the U.S. Congress passed the Bilingual Education Act aimed at meeting the educational needs of students who spoke a language other than English. Subsequent amendments and elaborations of the Act came in 1974, 1978, 1984, 1987, and 1994. Under the Bilingual Education Act, Congress appropriated $7.5 million to bilingual education as seed money to local education agencies for new and innovative elementary and secondary programs designed to meet the needs of students of limited English ability.

In the 1970s, precedence was made for bilingual education through the legal system. In the *Lau vs. Nichols* (1974) case, Chinese families challenged the San Francisco School District. Chinese students were receiving instruction in English, a language they did not understand, and their families argued that this violated their civil rights under Title VII of the 1964 Civil Rights Act and the equal protection clause of the Fourteenth Amendment to the Constitution, which contained a provision forbidding discrimination on the basis of national origin. The parents cited language discrimination in public schools.

In 1974, in what is considered a landmark case, the U.S. Supreme Court ruled that the Chinese students were not receiving instruction in a language they could understand and were therefore not receiving an equal education. Thus, in this case, language rights were considered civil rights, and the court held the position that schools had an obligation under the law to provide non-English-speaking students with an education that would enable them to overcome their language difficulties (Crawford, 1999). According to Justice Douglas (1974) who delivered the opinion of the court:

> Under these state-imposed standards there is no equality of treatment merely by providing students with the same facilities, textbooks, teachers, and curriculum; for students who do not understand English are effectively foreclosed from any meaningful education. Basic skills are at the core of what these public schools teach. Imposition of a requirement that, before a child can effectively participate in the educational program, he must already have acquired those basic skills is to make a mockery of public education. We know that those who do not understand English are certain to find their classroom experiences wholly incomprehensible and in no way meaningful. (*Lau vs. Nichols*, p. 3)

In spite of the decision in the *Lau* case, recent legislation has focused on "English-only" mandates. The opportunities the *Lau* case presented to create social justice and linguistic rights have generally been lost, as support diminished over the years. More recent laws like California's Proposition 227, the initiative to end bilingual education, gave non-English-speaking students a one-year transition period of native language support to catch up with their native English-speaking counterparts (Crawford, 1999).

Thomas and Collier (2002) report that it takes twice as long for English-language learners to reach grade level when they have no primary language support. In spite of this evidence, in states like Virginia, Arizona, and Florida, just to name a few, measures have been passed to ensure the official use of English in schools.

In 1996, the English Language Empowerment Act was signed into law, a landmark initiative that undermined the decision in the *Lau* case, and also reversed much of the progress gained during the 1960s. Similarly, through the No Child Left Behind Act (2001), language minorities have suffered from lack of funding for programs that promote their learning. Furthermore, the emphasis on standardized testing and closing failing schools has made the perceptions of language minorities, especially Mexican students, even more problematic, as many view these students as a liability to school performance on national assessments. The perception and treatment of minority students is especially concerning in the age of globalization, and where many diverse learners come to American classrooms.

## EDUCATION, IMMIGRANT STATUS, AND BILINGUALISM

The changes arising from the world system are influencing demographic trends and the transitory nature of immigrants and immigrant students. Regional and cross-national integrations in the world system are forging many changes in the educational needs of nations and their student populations. Education is extremely important for upward mobility and immigrant and minority students are increasingly dependent on it for their economic welfare. At issue, therefore, is whether or not they have access to quality education and quality employment. Immigrant status is crucial to school processes, and frequently results in tracking and within-school segregation and stratification. Clark's (2002) study on tracking and social mobility of Latino/Latina students is revealing. His work:

> Documents the increasing problem for new Hispanic migrants for whom the traditional ethic saga of hard work is unlikely to lead to upward and outward mobility. In fact, the evidence from the study provides specific evidence, albeit ecological, of the effects of low education levels and linguistic isolation on increasing poverty in inner city neighborhoods. If this data is placed along side the anecdotal data on high drop-out rates, street gangs and inner city crime, the outcomes for these new migrants are likely, without significant social intervention, to be a long downward spiral into poverty and hopelessness. (p. 150)

Education is important if newly arriving immigrants are going to be successful in their destination country. At issue is the language barrier faced by immigrants from non-English-speaking countries (Crawford, 1992). Many people believe that Mexican immigrants are choosing not to learn English; therefore, they campaign to make English the official language (Hayakawa, 1992). However, immigrants want to learn the language. They know that low English language skills make the pathway to poverty a definite fate for them and their children. Immigrant success is contingent on language acquisition and, whereas bilingualism is viewed as social capital by employers, it is viewed as a hindrance by schools, as evidenced by "English-only" legislation.

The educational challenges faced by Mexicans and other Latino/Latina students surround issues of their English language abilities, and incongruence between the students' home and school cultures. Many Latino students come from small villages in Mexico where their families have resided for generations and they adhere to rural values that emphasize communal living (Valdes, 1996). These students are taught to identify with their families and communities, and are encouraged to give up a sense of a separate, individual identity. Their families play a central role in their lives and their needs come second to those of the family (Ramirez and Castaneda, 1974). Families function as small societies and students belong to the whole family, and can be corrected by all the adults in the family (Valdes, 1996). The struggle comes about when schools foster a sense of individualism and individual student success is celebrated (Ramirez and Castaneda, 1974). The emphasis on competition and achievement for oneself goes against the values of community and achievement for others, which are guiding principles of many Latino families.

Most Latino students develop skills in relating to others and through their social interactions. Valdes (1996) discusses how Latino students demonstrate these characteristics by noting that at home, many students are taught to be considerate and show respect for their parents, do as much as possible for themselves, and to take on the care of their younger siblings. Thus, Latino students may be more motivated in cooperative settings rather than through competitive achievement, which is often emphasized in many U.S. classrooms.

These students are often not integrated into the school culture and so they have difficulty finding a place for themselves at school, and in making connections with students and teachers. Their heritage is not part of the school experience and they are placed in separate classrooms or in pull-out programs that do not integrate them with native speakers of English. Furthermore, students' identity and self-esteem are often affected by the transition from being a majority in their home country to being the minority when they arrive in the United States. Being minority and perhaps having an undocumented status further complicates life for many students and the school environment where they might experience stigma and peer sanctioning. These students often face other obstacles such as having unqualified teachers and being in a culturally repressive classroom.

In the classroom, teachers are often frustrated with language barriers and students who cannot understand them. These students are often branded as being lazy or unwilling to learn. The lazy immigrant narrative becomes a convenient way of explaining why student performances are low. In addition, school administrators often view Mexican immigrants as having achievement deficits that negatively impact a school's overall scores. However, these are stereotypes and unhealthy perceptions; immigrant students can perform when given the opportunity.

Suarez-Orozco (1989) examined immigrant students from El Salvador, Nicaragua, and Guatemala in order to understand their experiences and the reasons for their educational motivation. He found that half of the students in his study were honor students who were succeeding despite their immigrant status. He attributed much of this motivation and success to the students' memory of the scarce opportunities in their home country, a strong belief in U.S. meritocracy reinforced by their parents, and a supportive school environment. These students outperformed many other Spanish-speaking immigrants. However, this type of success is especially challenging in today's "English-only" educational policy climate.

At issue is the fact that immigrant students must learn a new language as quickly as possible. They must assimilate and adopt the norms, language, and ethos of the host country in order to survive. However, students who acquire a new language and lose their native language are at a particular disadvantage relative to those who become bilingual. Language is a resource and therefore it must be preserved. The transition to English proficiency is important for students, and the preservation of their native language is equally important. Critics of bilingual education such as Linda Chavez have pointed to its cost and ineffectiveness, and posed that students should learn English without extra support or resources. This is more politics and xenophobia than common sense. How could one, for example, try taking a test in German or Amharic without any instruction or resources to support the transition from English to the new language? Resentment for immigrants often results from fear that the immigrant population may disrupt the national identity and the culture of the host country. Therefore, a popular belief is that they should survive on their own and assimilate into American culture with few resources or basically without support (Ravitch, 1990). Others emphasize the increasing levels of competition for work, and link lost opportunities to the presence of immigrants. With the growing number of immigrants and linguistic and cultural minorities in public schools, what can teachers do?

## WHAT CAN TEACHERS DO? IMPLICATIONS AND BEST PRACTICES

### Making the Connections Clear

Teachers should try to make connections for Latino/Latina students by using their heritage as a part of the school experience. Students should be encouraged to talk about what they know since they have rich cultural backgrounds and their family stories are important to them. Students' experiences and stories should be treated with respect in order to foster an atmosphere of community in the classroom. Effective teachers involve new immigrant students in the learning environment and help them to make connections. Because the heritage of these students has never been a part of the school, they often feel excluded and unimportant. English-language learners learn to read more easily when they make connections, and when school becomes relevant for them. Teachers can also learn Spanish through their teacher education programs or through supplemental materials (computer software and other at-home study resources). When teachers become proficient in a second language, it helps them improve the instruction they offer students. Teachers should also seek support from more experienced colleagues in their schools.

### Make Classrooms Safe Environments

Teachers must strive to make students feel comfortable enough to share their ideas. Students who speak little or no English are often apprehensive about sharing what they know for fear of ridicule from teachers and other students. Students are reluctant to share when they feel threatened, so teachers should be sensitive to students' experiences, and above all, they should treat students with respect. Students are aware of their perceived status in the classroom, as they read social behaviors very well. They need to feel that they are valued members of the classroom community. Many of these students are accustomed to responsibilities outside of school, so one way to make them feel a part of the class is to give them responsibility for carrying out classroom activities.

### Give English-Language Learners
### Opportunities to Demonstrate their Competence

Teachers should give English-language learners opportunities to demonstrate their competence, and they should seek to provide contextual clues to help students complete their learning tasks. With little knowledge of English, contextual clues, as well as hands-on activities, help English-language learners attach meaning to an assignment or activity. They also find it easier to learn materials that have social and human content, especially if it includes fantasy and humor.

## Teacher Beliefs

Some teachers often assume that students, because of their limited English skills, are inadequate in many other ways. This is normally not the case. Therefore, a belief in students' ability is an important teacher disposition to have when working with Latino students. The students may not be proficient in English, but they have many other important skills. Students are generally very sensitive about the opinions of teachers and classmates, and perform better when teachers express confidence in them. In contrast, they perform less well when teachers doubt their ability. Thus, teachers should be mindful of the negative perceptions and low expectations they have of students.

## Cooperative Groups and New Norms of Behavior

Learning new classroom norms of behavior can include helping students learn that everyone is good at something, and that no one is good at everything. This has the tendency to level the playing field when it comes to classroom status issues. No student should be perceived as being either high or low on all classroom skills. Students should see that everyone has things they do well and things they can improve upon, or that they need help to accomplish. When students see that small group activities require the support of all members of the group, and that what they bring to the setting is valued, they increase their level of engagement and class participation. If all the students believe that the English-language learners have something valuable to contribute to the group effort, this becomes reassuring for all students and it encourages them to keep putting in the effort.

## On Reading

Reading develops with interest. When students are placed in small cooperative groups and given interesting hands-on activities that they have to read in order to figure out how to accomplish a task, it encourages them to read. Teachers must integrate the English-language learners with students who can read, and over time, these nonreaders will develop their reading skills. From the small reading groups, teachers can connect reading and writing by asking students to write about what they read. At first it might feel rudimentary, but given time, students develop the habit and skill of reading and writing.

When students have to negotiate meaning among themselves, their English language skills begin to grow. This comes about through assigning activities that have high interest, and through the way in which students are grouped (in heterogeneous ability groups). Students need to learn to do their reading assignments and to work together in a respectful manner (this takes time and practice), and the dominance of some students needs to be managed so that other students can have access to the learning task. If students believe that everyone brings something important to the classroom, then dominance is reduced. Furthermore, if students are given different roles to play, the heterogeneous groups tend to have to problem-solve and to take turns in those roles, which helps encourage sharing and reduces classroom management issues.

## Other Ways to Develop Reading Skills

Teachers should be aware that there are possibilities for developing reading skills that are inherent in the context of students' prior knowledge. Thus, they should use students' background knowledge as a basis for learning new content. Allow students to discuss what they read with other students, and without teacher-directed instruction, and encourage them to negotiate the meaning of the text. Students can use their background knowledge to make inferences, find the main idea, and find sources of information to answer questions.

## Parental and Community Support

Teachers should seek to get parents involved in schools, but should not be discouraged if immigrant parents are reluctant to come to the school. Immigration concerns, language barriers, and employment issues might make it difficult or even intimidating for immigrant parents to come to the school or to Parent Teacher Association meetings. Teachers should not assume that this lack of involvement means that the parents do not value their children's education. Teachers can reach out to parents and the community in a number of ways. With regard to helping students use language, if parents speak only Spanish, they can be encouraged to use their primary language at home, explaining to them that the development of a strong first language helps second language acquisition.

Teachers can help encourage parents to use picture books to help their children develop language skills by talking about the stories in the books. Parents can also be encouraged to read with their children in their first language. Bilingual books are plentiful and one way to promote reading is for teachers to send these books home with the students so that the parents can help them with reading.

There are also many examples of ways to welcome parents to schools and to reach out to the community. One important strategy is to translate materials (school letters, Parent Teacher Association information, and upcoming school activities) that are sent home with students. Another is to have someone at the school compile a list of learning opportunities and community resources, and provide parents with this material in the home (native) language. Teachers may consider seeking assistance from a bilingual facilitator, and arranging for an orientation and tour of the school so parents can learn about the school and meet the staff. Parents and community members feel much more welcomed in schools when teachers reach out to them in these ways.

## CONCLUSION

In the age of globalization, global migration brings many new learners to U.S. public schools, and many of these students are English-language learners. With the many challenges faced by immigrant students, education presents them with hope for a better life. In the wave of recent legislation such as California's Proposition 227 and other "English-only" mandates, cultural and linguistic minority students face an educational landscape and public policy agenda that undermines their very existence. These recent laws reversed many of the gains made through the *Lau* case, which recognized that English-language learners were not being provided an equal educational opportunity. Furthermore, the ruling in the *Lau* case presented opportunities to ensure that all students gained access to education and to language support, taking language rights into the realm of civil rights. Despite the shift in recent policy regarding English-language learners, education still presents a ray of hope for immigrant students.

Educators must understand and account for linguistic and other cultural diversities in the classroom. Teachers must have a strong belief in English-language learners' abilities; that although these students' English-speaking skills might be limited, they are not lacking in cognition. Teachers often only see a little of what these students are capable of producing because they can express very little in the English language. Therefore, teachers should not assume that what they see is all the students are capable of producing. Issues of classroom status affect the participation of English-language learners, thus if teachers do not see students as strong and capable learners, this may create an even more adverse effect on their effort and performance. Teachers can capitalize on the bilingual existence of their students, thereby making schools more relevant to their lives, while bringing their experiences into the classroom. In addition, teachers can take advantage of opportunities to learn a second language. This can help teachers meet students halfway, a distance that is worth traveling.

## REFERENCES

Chapa, J. and De La Rosa, B. (2004). Latino population growth, socioeconomic and demographic characteristics, and implications for educational attainment. *Education and Urban Society, 36*(2), 130–49. Thousand Oaks, CA: Sage.

Clark, W. (2002). A comparative perspective on large-scale migration and social exclusion in US entry-point cities. In M. Cross and R. Moore (Eds.), *Globalization and the new city: Migrants, minorities and urban transformations in comparative perspective* (pp. 133–50). New York: Palgrave.

Cohen, E. (2001). *The politics of globalization in the United States*. Washington, DC: Georgetown University Press.

Crawford, J. (Ed.). (1992). *Language loyalties: A source book on the official English controversy*. Chicago: University of Chicago Press.

Crawford, J. (1995). *Bilingual education: History, politics and practice*. Los Angeles: Bilingual Education Sources.

Crawford, J. (1999). *Bilingual education: History, politics and practice* (fourth ed.). Los Angeles: Bilingual Education Services.

Cummins, J. (1981). The role of primary language development in promoting educational success for language minority students. In C. F. Leyba (Ed.), *Schooling and language minority students: A theoretical framework* (pp. 3–49). Los Angeles: Evaluation, Dissemination and Assessment Center, CSULA.

Fishman, J. (1956). *Language loyalty in the United States.* The Hague: Mouton Co.

Freeman, Y. S., and Freeman, D. E. (2002). *Closing the achievement gap: How to reach limited-formal schooling and long-term English learners.* Portsmouth, NH: Heinemann.

Garcia, E. (2001). *Hispanic education in the United States: Raices y alas.* New York: Rowman & Littlefield.

Gonzalez, J. M. (1975). Coming of age in bilingual/bicultural education: A historical perspective. *Inequality in Education, 19,* 5–17.

Graizbord, B., Rowland, A., and Guillermo Aguilar, A. (2005). Mexico City as a peripheral global player: The two sides of the coin. In H. W. Richardson and C.-H. C. Bae (Eds.), *Globalization and Urban Development* (pp. 147–64). New York: Springer.

Hayakawa, S. I. (1992). The case for official English. In James Crawford (Ed.), *Language loyalties: A source book on the official English controversy* (pp. 94–100). Chicago: University of Chicago Press.

Herrnstein, P. H., and Murray, C. (1994). *The bell curve: Intelligence and class structure in American life.* New York: The Free Press.

Howell, D., and Mueller, E. J. (2002). The effects of immigrants on African American earnings: A jobs-level analysis of the New York City labour market. In M. Cross and R. Moore (Eds.), *Globalization and the new city: Migrants, minorities and urban transformations in comparative perspective* (pp. 200–27). New York: Palgrave.

Huntington, S. P. (2004). *Who are we? The challenges to America's national identity.* New York: Simon & Schuster.

*Lau vs. Nichols,* 414 U.S. 563, 566-69, 96 S. Ct. 786, 788-90, 39 L. Ed. 2d 1 (1974).

Liebowitz, A. (1971). *Educational policy and political acceptance: The imposition of English as the language of instruction in American schools.* Washington, DC: ERIC Clearinghouse for Linguistics.

National Center for Educational Statistics. (2008). English language learners. Retrieved May 1, 2008, from www. nces.edu.gov.

NCELAL. (2008). National clearinghouse for English language acquisition and language. Retrieved May 1, 2008, from www.ncela.gwu.edu/.

Peal, E., and Lambert, W. E. (1962). The relation of bilingualism to intelligence. *Psychological Monographs, 176*(27), 1–23.

Perez, T. (1991). *Portraits of Mexican Americans: Pathfinders in the Mexican American community.* Torrance, CA: Good Apple Publications.

Pitt, L. (1999). *The decline of the Californios.* Berkeley: University of California Press.

Ramirez, M., and Castaneda, A. (1974). *Cultural democracy, bicognitve development and education.* New York: Academic Press.

Ramirez, M., and Price Williams, D. R. (1974). Cognitive styles of students of three ethnic groups in the United States. *Journal of Cross-Cultural Psychology, 5*(2), 212–19.

Ravitch, D. (1990). Multiculturalism: E pluribus plures. *American Scholar, 59*(3), 337–54.

Simpson, L. B. (1967). *Many Mexicos.* Berkeley: University of California Press.

Singh, R. B. 2001. *Urban sustainability in the context of global change.* Enfield, NH: Science Publishers, Inc.

Skuttnab-Kangas, T. (1988). Multilingualism and the education of minority students. In T. Skuttnab-Kangas and J. Cummins (Eds.), *Minority education: From shame to struggle* (pp. 9–44). Clevedon, UK: Multilingual Matters.

Spring, J. 2006. *Pedagogies of globalization: The rise of the educational security state*. Mahwah, NJ: Lawrence Erlbaum.

Stern, D. I. S. (2007). The effect of NAFTA on energy and environmental efficiency in Mexico. *Policy Studies Journal, 35*(2), 291–322.

Suarez-Orozco, M. M. (1989). *Central American refugees and U.S. high schools: A psychosocial study of motivation and achievement*. Stanford, CA: Stanford University Press.

Thomas, W. P., and Collier, V. P. (2002). *A national study of school effectiveness for language minority students' long-term academic achievement*. Santa Cruz, CA: Center for Research on Education, Diversity and Excellence.

Truett, L., and Truett, D. (2007). NAFTA and the Maquiladoras: Boon or bane? *Contemporary Economic Policy, 25*(3), 374–86.

Turner, L. D. (2002). *Africanism in the Gullah dialect*. Columbia: University of South Carolina Press.

United States Commission on Civil Rights. (1972). Language rights and New Mexico statehood. In J. Crawford (Ed.), *Language loyalties: A source book on the official English controversy* (pp. 58–62). Chicago: University of Chicago Press.

USDE. United States Department of Education. (2008). Language minority in schools. Retrieved May 1, 2008, from www.ed.gov.

Valdes, G. (1996). *Con Respeto*. New York: Teachers College Press.

Wong Fillmore, L. (1991). Second language learning in students: A model of second language learning in a social context. In E. Bialystok (Ed.), *Language processing in bilingual students* (pp. 49–69). Cambridge: Cambridge University Press.

## Chapter Eleven

# Beyond Survival: School-Related Experiences of Adolescent Refugee Girls in the United States and Their Relationship to Motivation and Academic Success

## J. Lynn McBrien

The United Nations High Commissioner for Refugees (UNHCR) estimates that nearly one-half of the world's 11.4 million refugees are children (UNHCR, 2006, 2008). Refugees[1] resettling in the United States in the past decade have fled war-torn countries such as Afghanistan, Bosnia, Iraq, Somalia, and Sudan. People arriving from these countries are of diverse ethnicities; and tribal, rural, and urban cultures. Refugees from many of these countries maintain cultural and religious practices that differ from those of European immigrant and refugee populations that arrived at the turn of the last century and immediately following World War II. Some of these practices, such as wearing *hijab* (conservative Muslim clothing), stigmatize many new refugees.

As Suhrke (1997) notes, concepts of globalization are linked to understandings of the refugee regime and to ways in which refugee flows contribute to globalization. According to Zolberg, Suhrke, and Aguayo (1989), the 1951 United Nations (UN) convention on the Status of Refugees pertained only to Europeans who were affected by events occurring before January 1, 1957. As a result, early UN organizations established to help refugees limited their assistance primarily to Europeans displaced as a result of World War II, in spite of major political and military conflicts occurring in other world regions, such as hostilities after the partitioning of India in 1947. Not until the 1967 protocol was added to the 1951 convention did international protections and rights expand to include those affected after 1950 from anywhere in the world. Political upheavals and civil wars in Africa, Asia, and Eastern Europe have led to regional migration of millions of refugees during the last three decades of the twentieth century. Since 1975, the United States has resettled more than 2.6 million refugees. The highest annual admission—207,000—coincided with the 1980 Refugee Act, which expedited refugees from the Vietnam War. The lowest number, 27,110, was the result of political factors after terrorist attacks on the United States on September 11, 2001. Since 1980, the average annual U.S. admittance rate has been 98,000 (Refugee Council USA, p. 8).

Educators have key roles in facilitating the socialization and acculturation of refugee children (Anderson, 2004; Hones and Cha, 1999). However, when they are not trained to understand the unique challenges faced by refugee children, teachers sometimes misinterpret these students' behaviors and their families' cultural practices (Birman,

Trickett, and Bacchus, 2001; Igoa, 1995; Trueba, Jacobs, and Kirton, 1990). Teachers may, for instance, interpret a Muslim boy's refusal to look into the eyes of a female teacher as disrespectful, or they may believe that parents who do not attend school conferences are not interested in their children's education. Therefore, it is critical that multicultural education for preservice teachers include sessions on experiences of refugee students, in order for teachers to respond helpfully to these children. Additionally, it would be beneficial for U.S. students to learn about refugees in multicultural education units to increase their understanding, compassion, and acceptance.

Along with cultural challenges, most refugee children have experienced trauma that can impede their ability to learn (Williams, 2001). Trauma can affect the students' attention spans, memory skills, and impulse control (Thabet, Abed, and Vostanis, 2004). Refugee children are at risk for post-traumatic stress disorder, depression, anxiety, and grief that persists over many years due to experiences of war, violence, torture, and loss through death or separation from family members and friends (Ehntholt and Yule, 2006). Frater-Mathieson (2004) finds that children react to these stressors differently than do adults, and that those from different cultures display diverse reaction patterns; thus, it may be difficult for teachers and service providers to recognize the unique coping patterns and subtle cries for help made by refugee students unless they are well informed. Igoa (1995) and Mosselson (2007) point out that such "cries" might, in fact, be in the form of silence. Silence can manifest in the form of docile obedience but nonparticipation in class, or it can take the form of high academic achievement that hides a need for psychological help.

Because refugee student numbers[2] are much smaller than children of voluntary immigrants[3] in the United States, teachers are not always informed about differences between refugees and other immigrants. They may be unaware that refugee children are frequently affected by multiple physical and psychological traumas that occurred prior to their resettlement, and that such trauma can cause children to process events in unexpected ways. For instance, routine occurrences in school, such as loud noises, yelling, and crowded hallways, can trigger seemingly exaggerated responses in a refugee child suffering from posttraumatic stress. Reynolds (2004) reports on a refugee student who would attack other children who walked near him due to prior experiences in a refugee camp where he needed to "protect his food from thieves" (p. 78). These experiences again indicate the need for teachers to have multicultural inservice workshops or preservice courses that include specific information on refugee students and how they differ from other immigrant students.

The purpose of the current research was to explore the school experiences of female adolescent refugee students in the United States and to understand how their encounters with U.S. peers and teachers related to their academic motivation and goals. Portes and Rumbaut (2001; see also Suárez-Orozco and Suárez-Orozco, 2001) have indicated that discrimination is a common experience affecting immigrant and refugee students' ability to acculturate and succeed academically. Discrimination has been shown to be a factor in lowered academic motivation and/or achievement of other minority groups, and victims of discrimination can experience lasting effects on their self-perceptions, social interactions, motivation, and achievement (Portes and Rumbaut, 2001; Rist, 1970; Steele, 1997; Suárez-Orozco and Suárez-Orozco, 2001).

## RESETTLED REFUGEES' EDUCATIONAL
## EXPERIENCES: WHAT IS KNOWN

Most U.S. educational researchers have included refugees together under the broader term "immigrant," so it can be difficult to determine the differences in their educational experiences (McBrien, 2005). For instance, Portes and Rubaut's (2001) large-scale study, Children of Immigrants Longitudinal Study (CILS), includes students from Mexico, the Philippines, and the West Indies (immigrants); Cuba and Vietnam (mostly refugees); and Nicaragua and Haiti (mostly refugees by the UN definition, although the United States has not recognized Nicaraguans or Haitians as refugees), but the researchers do not investigate differences that may be a result of voluntary immigrant versus refugee status. Gitlin, Buendía, Crosland, and Doumbia (2003) conducted research with Latino, Bosnian, Somali, and Sudanese students in a western middle school, but they referred to all of these students as immigrants and did not examine ways in which their refugee and immigrant participants might have different responses to school practices that isolated them.

Of course, there are similarities between voluntary immigrants and refugees that allow researchers to consider them in combination. In both cases, the children must leave their friends, relatives, social systems, and native countries with which they are familiar (Igoa, 1995). They are likely to encounter a society in which the language, educational system, and lifestyles of their new peers are different from the one into which they were born (Gibson, 2001). Both groups of children often encounter various levels of xenophobic attitudes and discrimination. They also have to negotiate multiple identities as they struggle to belong with their new peers but also maintain relationships with older family members who may cling more to traditional cultural values. However, given the considerable differences in refugees' and other immigrants' experiences prior to arrival in the United States, it is important to study the populations separately.

Although literature includes the themes of discrimination and depression in the lives of resettled refugee children (Lee, 2002; Trueba, Jacobs, and Kirton, 1990), studies also indicate the role of resilience in young refugees' lives. Phan (2003) finds that Vietnamese refugee children experienced depression as a result of discriminatory experiences. At the same time, discrimination seemed to raise the children's academic aspirations. Phan stated that the study participants developed a "resistance stance" to racism they faced, in part through the resilience they gained in refugee camps and through their desire to "pay back" their parents.

Some researchers have found protective factors alleviating the negative effects of trauma experienced by refugee children. Goodman (2004) finds that a collective sense of self-recognition that they were not alone in their plight—along with making meaning of their experiences and believing in a promising future through education helped unaccompanied Sudanese male youths cope with war trauma and set high goals after resettlement in the United States. Ehntholt and Yule (2006) discuss protective factors such as belief systems (which can include not only religious beliefs, but also patriotism and glorification of war); cohesive, well-adapted families; and social support systems that can also alleviate some risk factors due to trauma.

Several studies have explored specifically female refugee experiences, but the studies do not indicate a particular pattern or theme. Goldstein's (1988) ethnographic study of sixteen Hmông high school girls in a midwestern city revealed practices by both U.S. teachers and students that isolated the girls. Goldstein concludes that teachers were more concerned with classroom order than with helping the girls to acculturate. Goldstein also indicates that the girls tried to challenge boundaries of gender expectations and identity within their cultural societies, but that they experienced restrictions due to language limitations and marginalizing policies of the dominant culture. In contrast, Zhou and Bankston's (2000) study of Vietnamese refugee girls indicated that the girls were showing higher levels of achievement than their male counterparts, but not because the girls were trying to liberate themselves from traditional values. Through adapting to a new culture, Vietnamese families recognized the value of education for their children, and traditional gender roles allowed families to exert greater pressure on their daughters than their sons. Mosselson (2007) finds that Bosnian adolescent refugee girls felt isolated and depressed by student and teacher stereotypes. However, the girls worked hard to maintain high grades, in part to move attention away from themselves.

## THE CURRENT STUDY

This case study explored school-related experiences of adolescent refugee girls in a southeastern urban area. Specifically, the research addressed the following questions:

1. What kinds of school experiences are most noted by adolescent refugee girls? What are the similarities and differences between the responses by Muslim and non-Muslim participants?
2. What external supports help the girls to overcome potentially negative experiences?

Question 1 considers potential differences in experiences of Muslim and non-Muslim refugee girls because of the increased discrimination since September 11, 2001, against Muslims, Middle Easterners, and those perceived to be in those categories (Human Rights Watch, 2002). I expected that students' personal experiences would reflect the changed sociopolitical context in the United States as a result of the terrorist attacks.

I learned that all of the girls in the study were average to above average achievers, in spite of being targets of discrimination by both students and teachers. As a result, I examined factors that allowed the girls to overcome typical negative motivational responses to discrimination.

### Frameworks of Acculturation

In order to be successful, resettled refugees must negotiate and situate themselves in a new sociocultural environment that is likely to include both barriers and support systems. For this study, Bronfenbrenner's (1979) ecological systems model offers an explanation of processes that can enhance or deter positive acculturation. Feminist theory also offers valuable contexts for framing the participants' resilient responses to discrimination.

Bronfenbrenner's (1979) ecological systems model has been used previously by Hamilton and Moore (2004), in discussing interventions for refugee children. The model demonstrates how people develop depending on various nested and interactive contexts, from family, to school, to community and society. Four contexts are considered: (1) the microsystem, which describes the relationship between the child and his or her immediate contacts (such as family, neighbors, or peers); (2) the mesosystem, or a series of microsystem relationships (such as home and school); (3) the exosystem, or relationships between systems with which the child is not directly related (such as between the home and the parent's place of employment); and (4) the macrosystem, or broader culture of a society. Bronfenbrenner (1992) emphasized that environment is not a single entity, but rather numerous settings that are interconnected. In this view, self-development involves the process of adapting to changing contexts.

For the current research study, the refugee agency utilized by families and their children for after-school tutoring, summer camp, art club, and/or dance club offered every level of Bronfenbrenner's (1992) model through multiple, targeted services and the creation of a network of community social services. Altogether, these services provided individual relationships for refugee children, links between parents and schools, and bridges to employment opportunities. Additionally, programs provided increased cultural understanding for both refugee families and for native members of the community.

With Mohanty's (1988) criticism of Western scholarship, feminist theorists from the developing world began to critique the lens through which scholars viewed development. Assuming their own culture as the "norm," and, therefore, different cultures as the "other" and inferior to the norm, early Western feminist scholars stereotyped women in developing countries as "ignorant, poor, uneducated, tradition-bound, family-oriented, victimized, etc." (p. 56). Mohanty explained that this category of analysis, one that viewed women from poor countries as dependent and oppressed, denied the complexity of history and culture as well as the diverse specificity of women's life situations.

Bhavnani, Foran, and Kurian (2003) extend Mohanty's (1988) argument, asserting that women from developing countries are not universally victims. Rather, they stated, these women confront challenges in creative and effective ways, and the struggles of their existence often evoke a strong sense of agency. Bhavnani and colleagues emphasize that to understand lives of women from developing nations, "ethnicity, religion, age, and sexualities, in addition to class and gender, become aspects of women's lives that cannot be omitted from analysis or practice" (p. 8). Further, the scholars state that "lived experience, subjectivity, agency, dreams, and visions underline the centrality and embeddedness of culture in everyday life" (p. 12). In my own research, I considered religion, age, and family background as I analyzed data from interviews and observations of young refugee women from areas in Africa, the Middle East, Southeast Asia, and Eastern Europe. In this way, one can consider Bronfenbrenner's (1992) ecological systems with respect to gender.

## METHODS

The current research was a two-year instrumental case study of 18 refugee adolescent girls who participated in one or more programs offered to refugee youth by an agency I will call the Help for Refugee Families (HRF). The study relied on interviews and focus groups, observations, and academic records. The voices of the adolescent refugee girls provided the context necessary for analyzing experiences using Bronfenbrenner's (1979) and feminist frameworks, which consider the role of personal and social supports for acculturation.

### Setting

HRF was located in an old plaza store in an urban community with the second largest population of refugees in the southeastern United States. Refugee adults were also highly visible at the center, and they walked the roads nearby. Walls inside HRF were painted with brightly colored murals of animals and diverse children playing together. Portable panels separated the age groups for after-school tutoring and summer camp. Because of the open atmosphere and the presence of approximately fifty children ranging in age from six to sixteen, the environment was always noisy. Staff, along with volunteers from four universities, helped students with homework and other reading. Children often waited to use the two computers available to them to complete assignments. On nice days, the children could go outside with a volunteer to play soccer or jump rope in the parking lot of a neighboring church. During summer camp, the children received free breakfast and lunch, and they went on weekly field trips to places such as youth art museums, movies, a community garden, a zoo, and a roller skating rink.

In spite of the southern location, the black participants themselves did not bring up issues based on race. However, Muslim participants, black and white, referred to religious-based experiences of discrimination. Therefore, some discrimination in school may have been more attributable to the general post–September 11 attitude of the country (Bittle, Arumi, and Johnson, 2006). At the same time, residents working closely with the local refugee populations, such as police, health workers, volunteer tutors, and Girl Scout leaders, would often visit HRF and express positive statements about refugees. These examples lent strength both to the importance of the ecological systems layers and to barriers and resources affecting the refugee community.

### Research Participants

Eighteen adolescent refugee girls participated in the research, fitting the following selection-based criteria: all participants spoke English, all interviewed students were females between the ages of twelve to nineteen, all attended at least one of the services offered by HRF, and half of the girls were Muslim. My student participants originally came from Bosnia, Iran, Iraq, Vietnam, Ethiopia, Gambia, Sierra Leone, Somalia, and Sudan. Half were black Africans, and the remaining girls were of white European, Asian, or Middle Eastern ethnicities. Their length of time in the United States ranged

**Table 11.1. Demographic Chart of Adolescent Refugee Girls Interviewed**

| Name | Age | Grade | Religion | Race/Ethnicity | Country | 2nd Country [Exile] | Years in U.S. (2004) |
|---|---|---|---|---|---|---|---|
| Corĕ | 16 | 11 | Muslim | Kurdish | Iraq | Iran/Pakistan | 4 |
| Faduma | 16 | 11 | Muslim | Black African | Somalia | Kenya | 5 |
| Fatima | 14 | 10 | Muslim | Black African | Gambia | Senegal | 6 |
| Layla | 19 | College | Muslim | Kurdish | Iraq | Iran/Pakistan | 5 |
| Mirela | 14 | 9 | Muslim | Black African | Sierra Leone | Unknown (UNHCR camp) | 1 |
| Atifa | 19 | 12 | Muslim | Black African | Somalia | Ethiopia | 3 |
| Sadia | 13 | 7 | Muslim | Black African | Somalia | Unknown | 7 |
| Sozan | 14 | 9 | Muslim | Kurdish | Iraq | Pakistan | 4 |
| Irena | 14 | 8 | Muslim/Greek Orthodox | White | Bosnia | Switzerland, Germany | 5 |
| Anna | 18 | 12 | None | SE Asian | Vietnam | None | 6 |
| Ayana | 13 | 6 | Christian | Black African | Ethiopia | Unknown | 1.5 |
| Lulu | 13 | 6 | Christian | Black African | Sudan | Egypt | 3 |
| Mirjana | 15 | 9 | Greek Orthodox | White | Bosnia | Germany | 4 |
| Monique | 14 | 8 | Christian | Black African | Sudan | Unknown | .8 |
| Nien | 16 | 10 | Buddhist | SE Asian | Vietnam | Thailand | 3 |
| Niloofar | 13 | 6 | Bahai | Iranian | Iran | Turkey | 1 |
| Yordanos | 12 | 6 | Christian | Black African | Sierra Leone | Unknown | 1.5 |
| Maari | 12 | 6 | Christian | Black African | Sudan | Unknown | 2 |

**Table 11.2. Family Characteristics**

| Name | Adults at Home | Siblings at Home | Mother's Education | Father's Education | Education on Goals | Grades at School |
|------|----------------|------------------|--------------------|--------------------|--------------------|------------------|
| Corě | Mother/Father | 2 | Some college | Some college | College | As/Bs |
| Faduma | Mother/Father | 3 | Unknown | Unknown | College | As/Bs/Cs |
| Fatima | Mother/Father | 4 | Some HS | College degree | Grad school | As/Bs |
| Layla | Mother/Father | 2 | Some college | Some college | Med school | As |
| Mirela | Mother | 2 | Unknown | Unknown | College | As/Bs/Cs |
| Atifa | Aunt | 1 | HS grad | HS grad | College | As/Bs/Cs |
| Sadia | Mother/Father | 2 | Unknown | Unknown | Unsure | Bs/Cs |
| Sozan | Mother/Father | 2 | Some college | Some college | Grad school | As/Bs |
| Irena | Mother/Father | 1 | HS grad | HS grad | College | As |
| Anna | Mother/Father | 0 | Some HS | Some HS | College | As/Bs/Cs |
| Ayana | Mother | 0 | Some HS | Unknown | College | As/Bs |
| Lulu | Mother/Father | 0 | Unknown | Unknown | Med school | Bs/Cs |
| Mirjana | Mother/Father | 1 | Some HS | Some HS | Grad school | As/Bs |
| Monique | Mother | 3 | None | None | College | Cs |
| Nien | Mother/Father | 1 | Some HS | Some HS | College | As/Bs |
| Niloofar | Mother/Father | 1 | HS grad | HS grad | Grad school | Bs |
| Yordanos | Grandmother | 2 | Unknown | Unknown | Unsure | Bs/Cs |
| Maari | Mother | 2 | Some elementary | Unknown | College | Bs/Cs |

from less than one year to over six years. I intentionally chose mixed, rather than uniform demographics, because these attributes constituted a typical sample of this community's refugee population.

As a white female researcher, I was not someone in whom refugee youth would immediately confide. I needed to gain the trust of the girls in order for them to tell me their experiences. I volunteered as an after-school tutor during the 2002–2004 school years, and in the summer of 2003 I worked as a full-time summer camp counselor for many of the adolescent girls who participated in my study, allowing them to become comfortable with me. As such, my role was that of a participant-observer. In fact, my outsider status was also a reason for which I was ultimately unable to include boys in the study. In part due to cultural barriers, I was unable to gain the trust of enough boys to include them in my investigations.

My interview questions asked the girls to describe their favorite and least favorite teachers and school subjects, engagement with native-born peers and international peers, and examples of positive and negative experiences in school. The girls were asked to comment on their interest in school, ambitions to continue past high school, and future career aspirations. I also asked for examples of people or sources that encouraged and discouraged them.

For triangulation, I interviewed HRF staff and seven teachers, as well as conducting observations in four schools attended by the student participants. However, this chapter will concentrate on responses of the student participants. Because they emphasized their communications with teachers more than U.S. peers, this chapter will focus on the student-teacher relationships.

## FINDINGS

Responses to my questions about teachers corresponded to three themes, which occasionally overlapped: characteristics of well-liked teachers, language barriers and ridicule, and isolation. Responses from the Muslim participants reflected themes of religious stigma and negative stereotypes. Finally, answers to my second research question identified specific support systems: internal, peer, adult, and systemic. This findings section exemplifies each of these themes.

### Characteristics of Well-Liked Teachers

Many of the refugee girls picked their favorite subjects based on how well they liked the teacher rather than on how they felt about the subject, as this conversation with Faduma and Sozan shows:

*Faduma*: I used to like math. I loved math. The teacher...
*McBrien*: It had to do with the teacher?
*Faduma*: The teacher, yeah. Now I like history. The teacher, you know, he made me love it. If you don't understand it, he don't, like, yell at you. He explains til you get it.
*Sozan*: Mine used to be math, too. But the teacher kind of switched it, so now it's science.

The girls were positive about teachers who offered multiple explanations of topics, were patient and willing to review class materials, and had a sense of humor. Some of the girls used "second mother" and "second father" to describe their favorite teachers. Several also discussed teachers they found to be empathetic due to their own international experiences. Layla fondly recalled her English for speakers of other languages (ESOL) teacher who was from Russia, "so she knew how it felt to be different." Monique felt close to a teacher who had "married a man from Liberia" and frequented that country, because the teacher did not express stereotypes about Africa. In these cases the girls' microsystems with teachers offered them support. The teachers' own extended contexts created a microsystemic level of support for the refugee girls.

## Language Barriers and Ridicule

The girls had far more comments about negative experiences than positive ones regarding language difficulties. Fatima said that her teacher publicly humiliated her by loudly announcing Fatima's time to leave for ESOL class:

> One time, I did not look at the time, and she went like, "Fatima, can't you tell time? It's time for you to go." I was really embarrassed and felt at the time she thought I was really stupid.

When describing a negative experience she had with a teacher, Corě explained that when she raised her hand to answer a question, no one else raised a hand. Yet, because she mispronounced the answer, her teacher "was the first to laugh." Two girls told me they would not answer questions in class because they feared ridicule. This fear, of course, can lead to isolation. Nien believed that teachers "gave up on international students because they took too long to answer questions." Bronfenbrenner's (1992) framework provides for both positive and negative models in each layer of the model. In these cases, a lack of support at the microsystem level could create a potential failure to achieve or could reduce motivation.

## Isolation

Some of the girls' comments specifically indicated that they felt isolated by teachers. Layla said:

> Most of my teachers did not know I was a new arrival. They just thought I was a quiet student who did not want to participate in class. I made bad grades.

She also told me that she was made to take a quiz on her first day of school, though she did not read English. She got one question correct. She said: "The teacher did not even try to talk to me about why I did so poorly." Layla explained her silence as a coping mechanism she used while she struggled to understand both the language and the cultural behaviors in the school environment. She told me that the casual and noisy atmosphere in the school confused her, as her previous experiences in Pakistan had been formal and disciplined.

Anna, a Vietnamese refugee, said: "I wish I could have skipped my whole first year here. I could not communicate, and I felt so alone." Fatima, a young woman from Gambia, related her feelings of confusion and separation in an incident with a home economics teacher:

> She [the teacher] said to me, "You're not supposed to have your jacket in class." And I said, "Oh, I'm sorry." Then she said, "Stop giving me an attitude, young lady." I was confused. I wasn't giving her an attitude. I didn't know how to make myself understood.

Even Yordanos, a young participant who claimed to have no problems with U.S. peers or teachers, alluded to isolation in a song she wrote, in which the refrain was, "I wish they could see me for who I really am."

## Stigmatization of Muslim Participants

Six of the nine Muslim participants wore *hijab*, Muslim clothing intended to cover all of the body, including a head covering. Five of the six were frequently teased about wearing scarves. During summer camp one day, participants had the following conversation about wearing head coverings, reflecting both stigmatization and ridicule:

> *Faduma*: Everyone says, "Why do you wear a scarf?" I tell them a million times, and they keep saying, "Is it your religion? Do you have to? Are you bald?"
> *Sozan*: They're like, "Is there something wrong with your hair?"
> *Faduma*: I say, "If you think I don't have hair, that means I don't have hair, if that's what you think. But I'm wearing it because of my religion." They still don't get it.
> *Layla*: It's part of our religion to cover your hair. They ask, even though we have told them a million times. In their own way, they think that they're hurting you.
> *Corĕ*: They wondered, because of the scarf, whether we ever take a shower or not. Well, of course! It's like you wearing your pants or skirt.

Mirela, a refugee from Sierra Leone, wore her scarf tied tightly behind her head. She said that this was also a popular African American fashion, so she was not teased. In this case, she fit in with the dominant population, which was African American at her school.

Middle Eastern Muslim participants were associated by both some students and teachers to terrorist events, indicating a powerful sociopolitical stereotyping factor that influenced the host culture's ability to welcome these refugees. The Kurdish girls all referred to the Gulf War, the September 11, 2001, tragedies, and the subsequent war in Iraq as factors of their inflight and postflight struggles. They related stories about their being called "bin Laden's sister, "Hussein's sister," or "terrorist." This association was particularly poignant for the Kurdish sisters, whose home had been bombed by Saddam Hussein's army in the 1990s, forcing their family to flee. Layla told me that her history teacher denounced Islam in class, saying that it brainwashed its followers. She openly disagreed with him:

> And he told me that I shouldn't disagree, so the class wouldn't hear those things. It was okay for me to have my own opinion, but I shouldn't talk. But I said that was reality and everybody ought to know the truth. And he said I can keep that truth to myself.

Her sister, Corĕ, told me about her history teacher who skipped the chapter about Islamic and Middle Eastern countries:

> He said it wasn't an important subject and chapter. It was important. I'm sitting there thinking, well, we're being abused every single day by these small-minded kids, and you can't set an example, you think it's okay to just skip the chapter. He covered every single chapter except that one. He said we shouldn't waste our time.

## Negative Experiences and Motivation

In reviewing interviews with the student participants, I found that twelve out of eighteen girls connected discriminatory experiences with negative motivation. Some of the girls feigned illnesses to avoid going to school after experiencing discrimination. Some argued with their parents about continuing in school. Layla, a young woman who had run to school in Pakistan hours before it opened when her parents could not afford tuition, said, "Mom, Dad, I quit school. I'm not going anymore," after her first day in a U.S. school. Corĕ told me that she cried every day after school for months. Mirela said, "I was teased by my classmates because I did not understand English, and they had stereotyped expressions about Africa. They think Africa is a jungle and that people there do not wear clothes. This made me feel bad and I almost thought of quitting school."

In the immediacy of discrimination, then, the girls experienced lowered academic motivation in the form of preferring to avoid school. However, in the long term, not one of the girls that I interviewed ultimately chose to leave school. Since completing the research for this study, I have stayed in touch with eight of the girls in the study. One has completed a pre-med bachelor's degree at a private women's college and is applying to medical schools at the time of this writing. Five are enrolled in four-year public or private colleges or universities. Two are enrolled at community colleges. One of the undergraduates recently received a highly selective national award for exemplary community service, which included a financial award of $5,000. All but two of the eighteen had a GPA of 3.0 or above (one with a lower GPA had been in the United States for less than one year; the other has been faltering since I conducted my interviews). Their career goals include teaching, medical practice, and jobs in human rights work.

## Support Systems

Analyzing the transcripts, I found numerous themes in the girls' reflections on positive support that helped them overcome negative experiences: positive self-beliefs, religious beliefs, career goals, refugee peer support, positive and encouraging teachers, and parent and other adult support. Layla believed she was "naturally motivated; I have always loved to learn." Corĕ held to her religious identity, saying, "This is me, and I wear skirts, and that's who I'm going to be." Three of the girls had a conversation about inner strength:

*Fatima*: You have to be strong. And you have to concentrate in school and you have to know what you're there for. And just ignore it [teasing].
*Sozan*: Sometimes you can't ignore it.
*Fatima*: But you have to try.
*Mirela*: Encourage yourself. Don't think about what other people say. Just follow what you want to do, and forget about them.

Regarding religious motivation, Sozan said, "Of course, the first thing the Qur'an tells you is to educate yourself. So first read the Qur'an, and second of all, live your life in successful ways." Corĕ agreed that Islam commands Muslims to become as educated as they can.

The girls created strong bonds with one another, in spite of ethnic, racial, and national differences, due to commonalities in their refugee experiences. HRF provided them with a space in which they could relax and come together. Mirela said, "I love being here. I can relax and be with my friends. I love going to school, but my friends are here." Others told me that they missed being with refugees in their separate schools, but that they enjoyed the opportunity to come together at the center.

Many of the girls' comments alluded to their relationships with their parents, especially their mothers. During camp activities, Irena, Mirela, and Fatima frequently expressed great love for their mothers and the desire to make them "proud" of their achievements. When Layla related her comment about "quitting school," she said that her mother responded, "You can't give up on life. These things are going to happen in life, and you can't just go and run away from it." Three girls specifically discussed ways in which they saw their parents struggling in the United States. They wanted to be able to help them and to do well so that parents did not feel they left their countries in vain. Niloofar commented that her parents wanted her to have more education than they had.

Earlier in the chapter, I included examples of positive teacher models. The girls also showed their connection with the adult staff at the refugee center who modeled kindness, support, and respect. The girls showed appreciation for staff that used camp time to discuss cooperation and positive uses of power with them. They also indicated affection for their camp counselors by their handmade presents and a birthday celebration for a counselor at the end of camp. The adult models at the refugee center provided opportunities for positive observational learning.

## DISCUSSION

Interpreting the results to address my research questions, I found three major themes in the study:

1. The majority of girls in this case study experienced frequent instances of discrimination from U.S. peers or teachers, or from both groups.
2. All of the girls displayed resilience and held positive long-term goals requiring higher education in spite of discrimination.

3. Nested levels of support systems contributed to the girls' resilience and motivation.

Observations and interviews with this diverse group of adolescent refugee girls indicated that the majority experienced discrimination from U.S. peers and teachers. These repeated experiences caused many of the girls to want to avoid school in the short term. Muslim girls experienced negative comments specifically targeted at stereotypes equating Islam with terrorism.

However, unlike findings from studies in which prejudice and discrimination negatively affected students' academic motivation (Rist, 1970; Steele, 1997; Suárez-Orozco and Suárez-Orozco, 2001), the girls had high academic expectations and goals, and those I have been able to stay in touch with since the completion of this study have pursued higher education successfully. Interview comments indicated that the girls were aided by a positive sense of self as well as family support, beliefs that inspired them, and some teachers who offered encouragement.

The findings of this study concurred with past research in several important ways. Similar to Goodman's (2004) and Phan's (2003) results, my findings indicated positive factors mediating between trauma, motivation, and achievement. Like Goodman's participants, the adolescent girls in my study were making meaning from their traumatic backgrounds and planning positive futures by maximizing their opportunities for a U.S. education. The refugee girls indicated the desire to show gratitude to their parents through achievement, as did the participants in Phan's research. The students in the present study also expressed feelings of alienation and sadness, similar to the depression expressed by participants in Mosselson's (2006, 2007) work. At the same time, many of the girls in my study did not allude to present feelings of depression due, I believe, to the extraordinary support systems of HRF.

Additionally, the girls' comments highlight the agency and importance of cultural contexts for these young women from developing countries, as suggested by non-Western feminist frameworks. Their words and choices demonstrated Mohanty's (1988) and Bhavnani, Foran, and Kurian's (2003) assertions that women from developing countries ought not to be stereotyped as victims. Their attachment to their religious beliefs, their families, and one another offered them cultural and relational support systems. Their response to trauma and discrimination, to move forward with their lives and goals in spite of negative experiences, indicated their determination to succeed.

Reflections on positive influences in the refugee girls' lives show the relevance of Bronfenbrenner's (1992) systems theory in understanding resilience creation in the refugee students, beginning with the self, and moving to the institutional level. Anderson (2004) lists resilience traits that include both personal and environmental factors. Individual traits included characteristics such as an internal locus of control, problem-solving skills, a positive personality, and high intelligence. Environmental resilience factors involve supportive systems of family, friends, schools, religious institutions, and special services. The girls in my study benefited from numerous interwoven systems of support.

In particular, the role of the HRF agency provided bridges between the systems levels described by Bronfenbrenner (1992). Unlike most refugee agencies that concentrate on helping refugee adults find employment and housing for their families during their first three to six months in the country, HRF focused on long-term support for refugee children and women. The center offered extensive, specialized programs for youth, including after-school tutoring by staff and college volunteers, one-to-one tutoring for those having the greatest academic difficulties, summer camp, and dance and art clubs. Volunteers who worked as tutors were paid to attend workshops that gave them skills to work with refugee youth. A partnership with a local university provided ESOL and counseling services for youth. One of the staff members also worked as a refugee child advocate in the court system. Irena's mother became the director of a special services program for refugee youth who were in especially difficult or dangerous situations. Staff in that program created a network of community partners (such as counseling services, Planned Parenthood, the juvenile justice system, and employment services). They helped the community partners become more effective in working with refugees by providing them with training. As Frater-Matthieson (2004) suggests, even a small number of supportive volunteers can serve as a protective factor to shield children from the negative effects of trauma and loss. She also points out the importance of culturally appropriate liaisons between the school and home, a program that was extensively instituted at the refugee center.

Along with the academic services, the refugee center provided students with role models in terms of staff and college volunteers, and a place where the students could be together after the school day for companionship and support. As they progressed, the refugee youth took leadership roles at the center, where they could volunteer to tutor and read to younger children. Some took part-time jobs with pay at the center for regular tutoring duties or jobs as junior summer camp counselors. These opportunities strengthened the girls' self-esteem and increased positive identity formation. They also provided what Frater-Mathieson (2004) discusses as essential psychological processes: attachment, or the bond between a person and a place; familiarity, which addresses a person's awareness of place; and identity, which pertains to a person's self-identity developed out of one's immediate environment (see also Fullilove, 1996).

HRF staff offered a positive model of each of the layers described by Bronfenbrenner (1979). Staff and volunteers created microsystem layer relationships as supports and role models for the children. The liaison program offered culturally appropriate support between families and schools at the mesosystem layer, and the special services program created that layer for refugee youth. Language and job services for women established a positive exosystem layer, reducing potential family stress by helping women with financial support. The center also created opportunities for families to receive free vaccinations and medical care, alleviating the financial stress of some medical expenses. Finally, training services provided by liaison staff and special services staff to refugee families, teachers, administrators, and community service providers created opportunities for understanding at the macrosystem level, offering bridges between diverse cultures and allowing people to work together for positive outcomes.

## Implications for Practice

The study offers important implications for educators and other adults working with refugee youth. There is a need to reach out to refugees, to recognize their need to be understood. Irena told me that even when she had problems with English, "something as simple as a smile" helped her to feel welcomed and encouraged. Layla's surprise that her teacher did not discuss her failing quiz indicated the need for appropriate ESOL strategies for communication. Teachers, administrators, school staff, and U.S.-born students need to learn about the refugee experience and about the situations of their homelands, so that they do not rely on stereotypes. Information is available from refugee aid agencies, and many have personnel who can provide workshops for schools. Certainly a sense of safety is critical for refugee children, and this may be fostered through training sessions in which teachers and school staff learn about the refugee experience. If refugee adults were consulted and represented on school boards, this need would quickly be addressed.

An agency such as HRF is an ideal support for refugee youth and families. Unfortunately, there are few refugee agencies that have the focus of HRF. Schools can, however, work with those experienced in refugee matters to create peer support groups for refugee students, in which the students can have time away from the pressure of fitting in with their new society. Administrators can establish contacts with adult refugees, usually through refugee agencies, who can be trained to work as school liaisons. They can commit to providing inservice workshops for teachers about the refugee experience. Many refugee agencies, even if they do not have well-developed educational programs for refugee families and school systems, can provide inservice teacher professional development trainings, and they can put school administrators in touch with refugee adults who would be interested in helping with translation and cultural knowledge. Additionally, many states have information and resources available through their agencies. For example, Florida has a Division of Refugee Services through its Department of Children and Families. The division has created a network of area Refugee Task Forces in several Florida locations that offer regular meetings, updates, and information on current refugee populations in the state. Nongovernmental organizations such as the International Rescue Committee, Lutheran Services, Catholic Charities, and Jewish Family Services often have divisions that provide services for and information about refugees in their area of service. They welcome both inquiries and volunteers.

## CONCLUSION

Trauma, although it can be debilitating, does not always psychologically impede those who experience it. Particularly if strong family and social supports are in place, refugee youth may become resilient and motivated. Because of the extreme conditions that refugee youth have already endured, they know that they can succeed, and they are encouraged to do so by welcoming teachers and supportive programs. At the same time, trauma leaves scars, and "even resilient children need help and support to overcome the sadness and loss of trust resulting from their experiences" (Anderson, 2004, p. 59; see also Garmezy, 1991, and Luther, Doernberger, and Zigler, 1993).

Regional conflicts, often precipitated by the economics of globalization, remain a sad state of the world, as represented by Darfur, the Ivory Coast, Afghanistan, and other regions. New conflicts contribute to migrations from countries with new refugee populations; at the time of this writing, for example, the United States must plan for refugees from Iraq and Burma. As Pipher (2003) indicates, refugee populations continue to arrive in areas that have been relatively homogeneous for generations. Teachers who once expected they would always educate mainstream American children are being challenged to help refugee children. They will be richly rewarded if they take the time to learn about the children's backgrounds and offer them support. With encouragement, these children will succeed.

## NOTES

1. I use the UNHCR's definition of refugees: "people who are outside their country and cannot return owing to a well-founded fear of persecution because of their race, religion, nationality, political opinion or membership of a particular social group" (UNHCR, 2006, p. 8).

2. In 2007, for instance, over one million legal immigrants were accepted into the United States, but only fifty-five thousand of them were refugees, and just over eighty-one thousand were asylees (DHS, 2008). Approximately one-half of the population figures are children.

3. Recognizing that Ogbu's (1988) classifications of voluntary and involuntary immigrants are debated, I am using his definition of a voluntary immigrant as "those who have more or less willingly moved to the United States because they expect better opportunities . . . than they had in their homelands" (p. 164). I find his statement that refugees' "tourist attitude helps them to behave and talk like white Americans without fear of losing their cultural and language identity" (p. 165) highly problematic.

## REFERENCES

Anderson, A. (2004). Resilience. In R. Hamilton and D. Moore (Eds.), *Educational interventions for refugee children: Theoretical perspectives and implementing best practice* (pp. 53–63). London: RoutledgeFalmer.

Bhavnani, K., Foran, J., and Kurian, P. A. (2003). An introduction to women, culture, and development. In K. Bhavnani, J. Foran, and P. Kurian (Eds.), *Feminist futures: Re-imagining women, culture, and development* (pp. 1–21). London: Zed Books.

Birman, D., Trickett, E. J., and Bacchus, N. (2001). *Somali refugee youth in Maryland: A needs assessment.* Retrieved March 2, 2004, from 63.236.98.116/mona/pdf/somali.pdf.

Bittle, S., Arumi, A. M., and Johnson, J. (2006). *Confidence in U.S. foreign policy index: Anxious public sees growing dangers, few solutions.* Public Agenda. Retrieved September 20, 2007, from www.publicagenda.org/research/research_reports_details.cfm?list=102.

Bronfenbrenner, U. (1979). *The ecology of human development: Experiments by nature and design.* Cambridge, MA: Harvard University Press.

Bronfenbrenner, U. (1992). Ecological systems theory. In R. Vasta (Ed.), *Six theories of child development: Revised formulations and current issues* (pp. 187–249). London: Jessica Kingsley Publishers.

Department of Homeland Security. (2008). *Yearbook of immigration statistics: 2007.* Table 7. Retrieved October 25, 2008, from www.dhs.gov/ximgtn/statistics/publications/LPR07 .shtm.

Ehntholt, K. A., and Yule, W. (2006). Practitioner review: Assessment and treatment of refugee children and adolescents who have experienced war-related trauma. *Journal of Child Psychology and Psychiatry, 47,* 1197–1210.

Frater-Mathieson, K. (2004). Refugee trauma, loss, and grief: Implications for intervention. In R. Hamilton and D. Moore (Eds.), *Educational interventions for refugee children: Theoretical perspectives and implementing best practice* (pp. 12–34). London: RoutledgeFalmer.

Fullilove, M. T. (1996). Psychiatric implications of displacement: Contributions for the psychology of place. *American Journal of Psychiatry, 153,* 1516–23.

Gibson, M. A. (2001). Immigration adaptation and patterns of acculturation. *Human Development, 44,* 19–23.

Gitlin, A., Buendía, E., Crosland, K., and Doumbia, F. (2003). The production of margin and center: Welcoming-unwelcoming of immigrant students. *American Educational Research Journal, 40*(1), 91–122.

Goldstein, B. L. (1988). In search of survival: The education and integration of Hmông refugee girls. *Journal of Ethnic Studies, 16*(2), 1–28.

Goodman, J. H. (2004). Coping with trauma and hardship among unaccompanied refugee youths from Sudan. *Qualitative Health Research, 14,* 1177–96.

Hamilton, R., and Moore, D. (2004). *Educational interventions for refugee children: Theoretical perspectives and implementing best practice.* London: RoutledgeFalmer.

Hones, D. F., and Cha, C. S. (1999). *Educating new Americans: Immigrant lives and learning.* Mahwah, NJ: Lawrence Erlbaum.

Human Rights Watch. (2002). *We are not the enemy: Hate crimes against Arabs, Muslims, and those perceived to be Arab or Muslim after September 11.* Retrieved October 25, 2008, from www.hrw.org/reports/2002/usahate/usa1102.pdf.

Igoa, C. (1995). *The inner world of the immigrant child.* Mahwah, NJ: Lawrence Erlbaum.

Lee, S. (2002). Learning "America": Hmông American high school students. *Education and Urban Society, 34,* 233–46.

McBrien, J. L. (2005). Educational needs and barriers for refugee students in the United States: A review of the literature. *Review of Educational Research, 75,* 329–64.

Mohanty, C. T. (1988). Under western eyes: Feminist scholarship and colonial discourses. *Feminist Review, 30,* 51–80.

Mosselson, J. (2006). Roots and routes: A re-imagining of refugee identity constructions and the implications for schooling. *Current Issues in Comparative Education, 9*(1), 20–29.

Mosselson, J. (2007). Masks of achievement: An experiential study of Bosnian female refugees in New York City schools. *Comparative Education Review, 51,* 95–115.

Ogbu, J. U. (1988). Class stratification, racial stratification, and schooling. In L. Weis (Ed.), *Class, race, and gender in American education* (pp. 163–82). New York: State University of New York Press.

Phan, T. (2003). Life in school: Narratives of resiliency among Vietnamese-Canadian youth. *Adolescence, 38,* 555–66.

Portes, A., and Rumbaut, R. G. (2001). *Legacies: The story of the immigrant second generation.* Berkeley: University of California Press.

Refugee Council USA. (2008). *History of the U.S. Refugee Resettlement Program.* Retrieved March 12, 2008, from www.rcusa.org/index.php?page=history.

Reynolds, C. (2004, December 27). Children of war. *Maclean's, 52*(1). Retrieved October 2, 2007, from Proquest.

Rist, R. C. (1970). Student social class and teacher expectations: The self-fulfilling prophecy in ghetto education. *Harvard Educational Review, 40*, 411–51.

Steele, C. M. (1997). A threat in the air: How stereotypes shape intellectual identity and performance. *American Psychologist, 52*, 613–29.

Suárez-Orozco, C., and Suárez-Orozco, M. M.. (2001). *Children of immigration.* Cambridge, MA: Harvard University Press.

Suhrke, A. (1997). Uncertain globalization: Refugee movements in the second half of the twentieth century. In G. Wang (Ed.), Global history and migrations (pp. 217–38). Boulder, CO: Westview Press.

Thabet, A. A., Abed, Y., and Vostanis, P. (2004). Comorbidity of PTSD and depression among refugee children during war conflict. *Journal of Child Psychology & Psychiatry, 45*, 533–42.

Trueba, H. T., Jacobs, L., and Kirton, E. (1990). *Cultural conflict and adaptation: The case of Hmông children in American society.* New York: Falmer Press.

United Nations High Commissioner for Refugees. (2006). *Refugees by number 2006 edition.* Retrieved January 24, 2007, from www.unhcr.org/basics/BASICS/3b028097c.html.

United Nations High Commissioner for Refugees. (2008). *2007 global trends: Refugees, asylum seekers, returnees, internally displaced and stateless persons.* Retrieved October 26, 2008, from www.unhcr.org/statistics/STATISTICS/4852366f2.pdf.

Williams, J. H. (2001). On school quality and attainment. In J. Crisp, C. Talbot, and D. B. Cipollone (Eds.), *Learning for a future: Refugee education in developing countries* (pp. 85–108). Lausanne, Switzerland: United Nations Publications.

Zhou, M., and Bankston, C. L., III. (2000). The biculturation of the Vietnamese student. *ERIC Clearinghouse on Urban Education, 152*, 1–7.

Zolberg, A. R., Suhrke, A., and Aguayo, S. (1989). Escape from violence: Conflict and the refugee crisis in the developing world. Oxford: Oxford University Press.

## Chapter Twelve

# Constructing and Negotiating Gender Relations, Ethnic Tradition, and Poverty: Secondary School-Age Hmông Girls in Viêt Nam[1]

## Joan DeJaeghere and Shirley Miske

The globalized discourse of Education for All affects most countries' educational plans and initiatives, particularly as it relates to promoting access, quality of education, and equality for girls and other marginalized groups who generally participate at lower rates in education (Unterhalter, 2007). Viêt Nam is no exception to this global influence, as indicated by its achievement of universal primary education measured by the government's standards (70 percent enrollment), and now its attention to secondary education. These efforts to achieve universal secondary education in Viêt Nam have brought a focus to the percentage of students who are not continuing on to secondary school. Girls and boys from nonmajority ethnic groups, which include fifty-three different ethnic groups, are disproportionately enrolled in education at lower rates as compared to the Kinh majority group in Viêt Nam.

Gender disparity in Viêt Nam education parallels a global concern in educational access and outcomes for male and female students. The number of out-of-school children worldwide is disproportionately represented by girls and marginalized (ethnic, linguistic, caste) groups (Filmer, 2000; Stromquist, 2001; Wils, Carrol, and Barrow, 2005; Lewis and Lockheed, 2006). Furthermore, for many countries where secondary education is not authentically "free," wealth is shown to be the key determinant of participation. Besides wealth, gender issues play a part in educational attainment, an issue that is more glaring at the lowest income levels (Lewin, 2005). This disparity in attaining universal secondary education has its parallels in school achievement in the United States, as a comparison between migrant Asians and whites. However, a distinct characteristic of Viêt Nam is that many nonmajority ethnic students are not even enrolling in secondary education. In particular, the Hmông have the lowest enrollment rate (4.5 percent) at the secondary level of all ethnic groups, and Hmông girls enroll at an extremely low rate of 1.6 percent (Baulch, Chuyen, Haughton, and Haughton, 2004).

The attention to and pressure for providing universal secondary education also is affected by economic globalization. Viêt Nam's efforts to develop its economy and compete in a global market necessitate a more educated population. While Viêt Nam's economy has been growing at a robust pace and the proportion of the population in poverty has declined (Vietnamese Academy of Social Sciences [VASS], 2006), many regions of the country, particularly those where nonmajority ethnic groups live, are highly underdeveloped in their economy and public services, including schooling (State Committee for Ethnic Minority and Mountainous Area Affairs [SCEMMAA], 2005). In particular, many areas where the Hmông ethnic groups live have been determined by the Vietnamese government indices as the most "underdeveloped," and participation of the Hmông in the labor market and in education is extremely low. For these reasons, the government, working with international agencies on education improvement initiatives, is interested in understanding the causes of Hmông girls' and boys' low participation in schooling in Viêt Nam. This chapter is based on a larger study that aimed to understand the causes of low transition to secondary school for the Hmông, among other ethnic groups (see United Nations Children's Fund [UNICEF], 2008).

While the contexts of Viêt Nam and the United States are considerably different, there is a noteworthy and growing Hmông population in the United States, projected to be more than 368,000 by 2010 (Xiong and Tuicomepee, 2003). The U.S. Hmông population experiences different dynamics of globalization, similar challenges of retention and achievement in secondary education are discussed in the literature and among educators. According to the U.S. Census Bureau (2000), 27 percent of Hmông in the United States were high school graduates; however, that number does not represent the current enrollment rates of the secondary school-age children, which is presumably higher than previous cohorts. A significant gender gap exists overall in the U.S. Hmông population, in which 34 percent of males have completed a high school degree compared to only 20 percent of females (Pfeiffer and Lee, 2003). In recent years, Hmông girls' and women's educational attainment has increased, and this is not yet reflected in these statistics (Vang, 2003).

A considerable body of research exists on the Hmông and their interface with education in the United States, China, Laos, and elsewhere. Lee (2007) observes that much of the literature on Hmông, and particularly Hmông girls and women in the United States, characterizes the differences between Hmông and mainstream U.S. cultures, particularly noting "traditional" practices and beliefs that conflict with the educational system. These characterizations, however, do not allow for the cultural practices to be articulated and constructed by the girls or their families as social processes that are adaptive in their meanings (Ngo, 2002; Lee, 2007). This chapter utilizes a critical analytical approach to compare and contrast Hmông experiences with the discourse related to gender, ethnicity, and poverty in educational policy and practice in Viêt Nam. The experiences of Hmông girls and their parents in relation to schooling is also compared and contrasted to the literature on Hmông girls' educational experiences in the United States.

## EDUCATIONAL STATUS OF THE HMÔNG IN VIÊT NAM

Viêt Nam, the second most populous country in Southeast Asia, has fifty-four different ethnic groups. The Kinh ethnic group comprises the majority of the population; fifty-three non-Kinh ethnic groups makeup 14 percent of the population (1999

Census in Kosonen, 2004). Many of these non-Kinh ethnic groups live in remote and mountainous areas of Việt Nam (Baulch et al., 2004). These regions are geographically disadvantaged in terms of access to and opportunities for profitable agriculture, resulting in subsistence farming as a primary means of living. Low levels of education and high rates of malnutrition and poverty are prevalent for many of the nonmajority ethnic groups (Kosonen, 2004; United Nations Development Programme [UNDP], 2002). The Hmông, nearly one million in population, reside primarily in the northern mountainous region, in communes that have been determined by the government to be economically disadvantaged.

Educational attainment is high overall in Việt Nam, as suggested by the primary enrollment rates in national education indicators. However, these national statistics mask variations in enrollment and completion for the different ethnic groups, and for boys and girls within ethnic groups in the different regions. The primary enrollment rate is 93 percent for the Kinh majority group and 42 percent for the Hmông; in addition, the largest gender gap exists for the Hmông (1999 Census in Baulch et al., 2004).

Secondary enrollment rates are considerably lower than primary enrollment rates overall (see table 12.1), and are less than 20 percent for many nonmajority ethnic groups (the Gia-rai, Ba-Na, Xodang, Hmông, and Dao) (UNICEF, 2004, 2005). Data disaggregated by different ethnic nonmajority groups show greater gaps between nonmajority and majority students, as well as between nonmajority girls and boys (see table 12.2). Nearly 65 percent of the Kinh majority are enrolled in secondary education (lower and upper), whereas only 4.5 percent of Hmông children are enrolled, the lowest enrollment rate of all ethnic groups (see tables 12.1 and 12.2). The gender gap for ethnic groups overall is 13.4 percent, and the gap for Hmông is 5.9 percent, as both boys and girls enroll at very low rates (based on 1999 Census in Baulch et al., 2004).[2]

These statistics and analyses often lead to identifying instrumental barriers and policy recommendations that address issues of poverty, gender, or ethnic relations (Sutton, 2001). For example, policies specifically target ethnic groups below the poverty level in Việt Nam to provide assistance toward their educational fees (boarding and books). This strategy is aimed at addressing household poverty as a barrier to access to education. While these strategies have been effective to an extent in some countries (see Kane, 2004; Miske, Schuh Moore, and DeJaeghere, 2000; UNICEF, 2008), they do not address how families and children negotiate the tensions among poverty, gender roles, and ethnic traditions. Providing assistance to certain ethnic groups or to girls and not boys has resulted in a backlash to such efforts (see United States Agency for International Development [USAID], 2006).

**Table 12.1. Primary and Secondary Enrollment Ratios (%)**

|  | Primary | | | Lower Secondary | | |
|---|---|---|---|---|---|---|
|  | *Overall* | *Boys* | *Girls* | *Overall* | *Boys* | *Girls* |
| Gross enrollment rates | 106 | 109 | 103 | 79 | 83 | 76 |
| Net enrollment rates | 95 | NA | NA | 61 | NA | NA |

*Source*: UNESCO Institute for Statistics, 2000 data.

**Table 12.2.  Primary and Secondary Enrollment Ratios (%) by Twelve Different Ethnicities**

| Groups | Primary Level | | | | Secondary Level | | | |
|---|---|---|---|---|---|---|---|---|
| | Gross | Net Girl | Net Boy | Net | Gross | Net Girl | Net Boy | Net |
| Kinh | 113.6 | 93.4 | 93.5 | 93.4 | 80.6 | 64.8 | 65.5 | 64.0 |
| Hoa | 122.6 | 93.7 | 94.5 | 92.9 | 71.0 | 51.7 | 50.4 | 53.1 |
| Khmer | 114.5 | 76.3 | 77.3 | 75.3 | 35.9 | 22.5 | 23.8 | 21.2 |
| Central Highlands | | | | | | | | |
| Gia-Rai | 126.3 | 66.4 | 67.6 | 65.1 | 37.1 | 14.9 | 15.2 | 14.5 |
| Ba-Na | 108.9 | 57.8 | 55.0 | 60.4 | 20.0 | 8.9 | 9.0 | 8.9 |
| Xo-Dang | | | | | | | | |
| Dang | 139.3 | 62.2 | 64.7 | 59.3 | 35.2 | 10.1 | 12.7 | 7.1 |
| Northern Uplands | | | | | | | | |
| Tay | 135.4 | 94.7 | 94.9 | 94.4 | 77.0 | 51.0 | 47.1 | 55.2 |
| Thai | 135.5 | 83.9 | 87.2 | 80.5 | 55.2 | 32.1 | 33.6 | 30.5 |
| Muong | 133.4 | 94.5 | 94.9 | 94.0 | 76.7 | 52.3 | 50.8 | 53.9 |
| Nung | 136.6 | 89.3 | 89.7 | 88.9 | 61.8 | 39.2 | 37.0 | 41.6 |
| **Hmông** | **80.5** | **41.5** | **51.5** | **31.5** | **9.8** | **4.5** | **7.5** | **1.6** |
| Dao | 126.4 | 71.4 | 73.7 | 68.8 | 20.3 | 11.8 | 11.9 | 11.8 |

*Source*: Baulch et al., 2004. (Based on 3 percent enumeration sample of 1999 Census)

Studies from a critical qualitative approach at the microlevel can further problematize these factors and illustrate how children and their families construct, resist, negotiate, or enact their roles and social relations related to poverty, gender, and ethnicity. An understanding of local practices of the Hmông as they negotiate these relations should also be understood in relation to national policies. By examining the micro- and macrolevel structures and practices of gender, ethnicity, and poverty, we can potentially open the door to more effective policies for nonmajority and disadvantaged ethnic girls, particularly among the Hmông.

## METHODS

In addressing the issues of this chapter, Weis and Fine's approach (2004) was implemented with the aim of presenting a critical analysis for understanding the structural conditions of poverty, gender, and ethnicity, and how Hmông girls and their families construct and negotiate these relations in the wider social and economic environment of Viêt Nam. The analysis is informed by Amartya Sen's (1992, 1999) framework of poverty as capability deprivation, which moves beyond an instrumental approach to income deprivation and aims to achieve a broader construction in which poverty is the difference in social relations and conditions that affect individual and community well-being. Sen suggests that the relationship between low income (instrumental poverty) and low capability is variable between different communities, families, and individuals, depending on other conditions and factors, such as age, gender, social roles, and locations. Families and communities construct and enact these various relations, thus creating differing opportunities for their children. For example, income is often distributed unequally between the genders, thus impeding the well-being of girls in the family (Sen, 1999). In essence, Sen's approach prompts researchers and policymakers to consider the interconnections among poverty, gender relations, and ethnic group values and traditions.

This analysis is also informed by a critical understanding of ethnic traditions as socially constructed in relation to colonial and postcolonial discourse and practices (Vavrus, 2002), as well as the notion that gender is socially constructed, akin to ethnic/racial identity and social class relations (Hill Collins, 1990; Subrahmanian, 2002). As Vavrus (2002) argues, international development discourse, including government policymakers, has often ascribed ethnic or gender practices as impediments to schooling. This ascription of impediments to gender or ethnic traditions, however, does not account for the various ways in which girls, families, and communities negotiate and enact these aspects of their identity in relation to schooling.

In this study, we worked collaboratively with native Vietnamese researchers,[3] as part of a larger project initiated by the Ministry of Education, United Nations Children's Fund (UNICEF), and United Nations Educational, Scientific and Cultural Organization (UNESCO), Viêt Nam. The research and analysis were conducted over the course of two years, with short field visits of one to two weeks in the communities involved in the study.

The participants included primary and secondary school-age girls and boys, their parents, community leaders, village heads, school personnel, district education officials, and provincial and district People's Committee members. Girls and boys of secondary age who had been out of school for less than one year were selected to participate, along with their parents and parents of other out-of-school children. We were particularly concerned about understanding children's and parents' experiences and perspectives, and comparing and contrasting these perspectives with those held by educators and policymakers. The selection of participants from the community, school, and district and provincial levels reflected nearly equal representation of males and females. The participants were chosen based on their responsibilities for education and commune development. We interviewed forty-six in- and out-of-school Hmông girls and boys; held thirty focus groups with mothers, fathers, teachers, community members and district and provincial education officials; and conducted fourteen classroom observations in four different communes. Interviews were conducted in the Hmông language with local translators, then translated to Vietnamese and then to English.[4]

## A FOCUS ON THE HMÔNG IN NORTHERN VIÊT NAM

This chapter is based on data from four communes where Hmông ethnic group members live, in the Bac Ha district of Lao Cai province, which borders southern China.

Lao Cai province is a mountainous region in northwest Viêt Nam, about three hundred kilometers (186 miles) away from Hanoi. It has one provincial city and eight districts. The population of Lao Cai is more than a half million, and includes twenty-five different ethnic groups, which comprise 70 percent of the population. The Hmông are the largest ethnic group in the province. Agriculture and forestry contribute 78 percent of the income in this province. Most Hmông families' primary source of employment is subsistence farming of corn and rice crops.

The Lao Cai communes included in this research study were located in the Bac Ha district and were extremely disadvantaged as indicated by the government (SMCEEMA, 2005). Across the country, 35 percent of the Hmông households were classified as poor in 2003 (SCEMMAA, 2005). Poverty reduction initiatives, such as the improvement of infrastructure and roads and the provision of social services, including the building of a secondary school and health clinic, are targeted in this region (SCEMMAA, 2005). While these communes are a focus of poverty reforms, only some communes have experienced their benefits. For example, roads may not be adequately constructed in some areas (SCEMMAA, 2005). In some cases, villages in these communities may be up to thirty kilometers (nineteen miles) from the commune center and without passable roads, where the main primary and secondary schools are located.

Each of the communes has a primary school and a lower secondary school. Many villages surrounding the commune center have "branch" schools, which are community built, and serve children usually from kindergarten through third grade. The lower secondary schools in the commune centers are boarding schools, because the children have to travel from more than twenty kilometers (twelve miles) away by foot and are unable to return home each day. The boarding facilities are modest, built from local wood materials. Often, they do not have sufficient beds, private space for boys and girls, or private bathrooms. In addition, generally children do not have sufficient clothes, blankets, or food; they must prepare their own meals with few utensils. Although electricity is available in one of the schools, it is not available in the boarding areas or children's homes.

In one of the communes with 50 percent poor households, the enrollment rate of girls to boys at every grade level is less than half, and decreases in the upper grades. In grade 5, Hmông boys' enrollment rate is 3.3 times that of the Hmông girls, and in grade 9, this ratio is 5.2 times greater. In another commune—which is closer to the district center—gender parity occurs in the lower grades, but in the upper grades boys enroll at a rate of 2.5 times greater than girls (a personal communicatian with the Bac Ha District Education Office, 2006). Very few Hmông teachers work in the schools; only one of the communes had Hmông teachers, and of the fifty-nine teachers serving these areas, only five of them were Hmông, and all were in primary schools. In the other communes there were no Hmông teachers.

## FINDINGS: COMMUNITY DISCOURSE AND PRACTICES

Among the concerns discussed by girls, their parents, and community members, two themes reflect the tensions girls face in continuing their studies in secondary school—themes that are also addressed in the literature on Hmông students and families in the United States. They are financial capability and family welfare, and bilingual and culturally relevant education.

## Financial Capability and Family Welfare

Poverty is a discourse used to define these communities and households within the communities. For these Hmông families and children, being poor means that they lack the finances to provide for basic needs. Even more resources are required to attend secondary school: To study in the boarding secondary schools, children must bring rice, vegetables, firewood, and pay an additional fee. Girls in all the communes said repeatedly, "We do not have rice to eat or clean clothes to wear." One woman, Chu, a mother of three children with two younger children enrolled in school, explained:

> The family condition is so poor, we don't have enough money for them to buy vegetables and rice to bring to the boarding school. Our cultivated land is so small, and they don't have enough rice and noodles to bring along [to school]. We have no money to buy clothes. There is nobody else to look after the buffalo when the parents go to work [in the fields].

Parents and girls both emphasized the need to take rice and firewood to school—and these basic needs are not only a requirement, but also a symbol of access to school. As one father, Chan, explained, "If they go to school, they need to bring rice. But we do not have rice, and neither do we have money." Rice is a valued food among the majority population in Viêt Nam; however it may not be as valued by all ethnic groups, in particular when it is not an easily accessible commodity. Another father, who cultivates primarily maize, added: "Rice does not grow well in this soil [at this elevation]." Most Hmông families' main crop was maize, and corn is regarded as an adequate food, as one father, Xang, whose daughter had recently dropped out of school said: "If the girls stay home or study close by the house, they can eat *men men* [a finely ground maize dish]."

In addition to sufficient food for their developing bodies, adolescent girls are also aware of their need for clean and nice clothes when going to school. Within the Hmông community, adolescent girls' embroidered clothes are important symbols of maturity and position, and they prefer to wear these clothes rather than those worn by Kinh children (such as cotton skirts and shirts). With little money, they are not able to buy or make appropriate clothes. Che, a mother of one son and two daughters said: "I spend little money on my son's clothes but I need more for my daughters." She suggested that with no land nor buffalo, it is financially difficult to buy clothes for adolescent girls. She felt that financial support of rice and clothes from the school would allow her to support her daughters' education.

To have sufficient food and to provide for the well-being of the families, the Hmông, and particularly girls and women, work long hours in the home and fields. One young girl, Sun, the only daughter in her family, had dropped out after primary school. Two older brothers were married, and another brother boarded during the week at secondary school. Sun captured the responsibility she feels as a daughter to work to provide for the family and the cost of schooling: "If I go to school, I cannot help my family earn money; then we do not have money to buy clothes." Other girls echoed these same responsibilities, especially if they were the oldest family member, or the one living at home. Women, whose husbands were not able to work because of

health reasons, shared these concerns about work and providing for the family welfare. One mother, Ly, explained: "There is only me to earn money in our family, and
we have only rice and corn to eat. The money earned all week is spent on [one] son to
go to school as he will graduate this year."

The Hmông women discussed the tension they feel in wanting their children to be
educated. Most mothers expressed the desire for their girls to be educated and to work
as teachers or nurses. They also recognized the need for girls' work to support the
well-being of the family. Vang, a mother of four boys and four girls who said she had
told her daughter that studying would result in a happier life, lamented: "I also want
my daughters to study as my son. But we have no money. I sold all the horses, pigs,
and buffalos for my son's wedding." Another mother, Tung, stated she had awareness
of the benefits of school: "My daughter was just about to leave for school, and I told
her to come home soon to tend buffalo. I was wrong, I know, but we have too much
work, [and I] asked my daughter to stay home to help." A thirteen-year-old girl, Say,
who had dropped out after sixth grade, captured the tension between wanting to go to
school and the need to help her family: "My mother asked me to go to school, meanwhile my father asked me to tend the buffalo. If I go to school, it is for nothing. If I
work, I can help make money to buy clothes, and help my parents. We do not have
money."

Girls are regarded as harder workers than boys and more able to contribute to the
family welfare when they are adolescents. Doa, a mother with a severe health problem, illustrates the discourse of girls' roles: "Girls are better able to care and assist at
home." Working at home is a viable way for Hmông girls to contribute to the family
welfare, as they see few opportunities to work in the formal economy. Fathers often
suggested the need for girls to have skills that would contribute to the family and community; some fathers emphasized skills such as sewing and embroidery; others suggested farming skills. A father, Xang, whose daughter works in the fields after leaving
school, said: "[I] want her to learn skills that would help the family, such as learning
animal husbandry or farming techniques." A mother, Mang, recognized the trade-offs:
"Being educated is good. If they cannot find a job, they can apply what they have
learned to develop the household economy." Most families and girls see little opportunity for work beyond the household and farm. Parents and girls have aspirations to
learn to become teachers and doctors, as these jobs were the only opportunities they
saw for adult women in their commune.

Contributing to the family's welfare during a girl's adolescence is important for
many Hmông families, as they believe that once the daughter is married, she will
not contribute to the family. The discourse in the community suggests that Hmông
families regard "girls as daughters of others, and therefore, why should they invest in
them? After marriage, they will go to work for the husbands' families" (a community
leader restating what he regarded as a profoundly held belief). Not all Hmông mothers
or fathers, however, felt that their daughters should get married at a young age. Doa,
a woman who was seriously ill and whose two daughters quit school to help at home,
said she did not want her daughters to marry at a young age. Other mothers expressed
deep concerns about girls going to boarding schools and getting into relationships or
getting pregnant. The financial situation of children's families also affects decisions

about marriage. Chen, a girl who had recently dropped out of school and was married, captured these tensions: "I did not want to marry, but my family is too poor and accepted their [the boy's family] gifts." The village head explained that the boy's family had arranged for an early marriage mainly "to have more labor."

## Financial Capability and Family Welfare: A Wider Scope

Government policymakers are aware of the financial poverty that exists among ethnic groups, and programs are in place to address and monitor poverty reduction (Socialist Republic of Việt Nam [SRV], 2003; SCEMMAA, 2005). However, the government attributes one of the causes of ethnic minorities' poverty in Việt Nam to traditional and backward farming practices (United Nations High Commissioner for Refugees [UNHCR], 2002). The Hmông are regarded as using "slash and burn" techniques as an example of these backward agricultural traditions, and the government programs aim to change these farming practices. "Tradition" and "backward" are a part of the discourse associated with ethnic groups. The Hmông view their farming practices as being hindered by a lack of access to markets to sell their crops. They lack roads to major cities, and the most disadvantaged communes can be forty to sixty kilometers (twenty-five to thirty-seven miles) from the main city. In addition, many Hmông families do not have equipment nor have they acquired the technical skills to conduct alternative forms of farming. The most commonly farmed crop among the Hmông is corn, which is not regarded as nutritious or as valuable as rice in Vietnamese society. As noted earlier, rice is a national crop and staple, and lacking sufficient rice for food is a symbol of poverty for these families, and inhibits attendance of boarding schools. While efforts in the Lao Cai province are promoting improved agricultural production and diversification, land is scarce, markets remain unstable, and technical knowledge is needed (UNDP, 2002).

Several educational tensions arise for girls in particular when living in conditions of subsistence farming. First, when food is limited, families make decisions about whether boys or girls will get food for school, and families' discourse and practices reflect these gendered relations. Families and girls explained that if their brothers were going to school, the boys would need food first, and the girls took the rice that was available thereafter. These practices, however, are influenced by other factors. Girls are also regarded as hard workers both at home and in the fields, thus allowing the family to have more food. In a national survey on child labor, girls spend more hours working than boys, and, among the Hmông, girls work twice the number of hours as boys (Asian Development Bank, 2002).

Based on the statements and stories from parents and girls, family welfare is also related to current and future opportunities, including long-term economic support and returns that exist differentially for girls and boys. Some community leaders perceive traditional cultural practices, including early marriage for girls as a representation of different expectations, opportunities, and returns for girls and boys. The implication of these cultural practices is that boys provide long-term financial support for their parents, and, therefore, the boys need to be educated and find work to provide this support. However, beyond working in the fields, few opportunities exist for Hmông girls to be employed. For example, in the communities where this research took place, there were no Hmông female teachers.

A family's assessment of its immediate welfare and future opportunities is also reflected in the discourse and practices related to early marriage. Often, the discourse in Viêt Nam, as in the United States, is that early marriage among the Hmông reflects "traditional cultural practices" and that these practices should not be allowed under law until they have reached the age of eighteen, the legal marrying age for girls (twenty years for boys) in Viêt Nam. In 2004, 30 percent of Hmông girls in Viêt Nam were married before the age of eighteen (UNICEF, 2004), which implies that many Hmông boys also probably marry young, albeit when slightly older than the girls. Marrying at a young age is not only a "cultural" practice, but a social practice that reflects a family and community's financial situation and welfare, as well as school and work demands and opportunities. In difficult financial situations, the boy's family gains through marriage by adding labor to the family, and the girl's family gains needed income from gifts from the boy's family. Girls and family members did not express that they preferred marriage over schooling. Rather, it was apparent that they negotiated these decisions against short-term family and community welfare, and against long-term prospects for employment.

The discourse among education policymakers and practitioners is that education and advocacy campaigns can prevent early marriage by changing attitudes about marriage and stressing the importance of education. In one community meeting, a commune leader, Ho, suggested that enforcing the age of marriage was a possible solution to the problem, and when asked if this approach was working, he acknowledged that families still avoid the law and have their children married. Girls' and their families' discourse and practices suggest other reasons beyond cultural "traditions" for early marriage. These reasons should be addressed in combination with the enforcement of the law and the advocacy of education.

Research on girls' education and parental aspirations for schooling in developing countries has emphasized an economic rationale on the one hand, in which parents make educational choices based on economic returns to the family for educating girls (Buchmann and Hannum, 2001), and on the other hand, cultural norms such as early marriage, as influencing schooling opportunities (Zhang, Kao, and Hannum, 2007). Zhang, Kao, and Hannum find that both cultural attitudes about equality and educational returns affect families' decision-making. This study suggests that among Hmông girls, cultural attitudes or ethnic traditions, poverty, and gender roles are influential and interrelated constructs in family and community welfare.

## Bilingual and Culturally Relevant Education: Community Discourse and Practices

Most Hmông girls talked about liking school and wanting to go to school, but they were also conflicted because they felt they did not learn well. Two girls, Lan and Binh, who had recently dropped out capture this sentiment:

> I like school, but I do not understand, and I cannot read the lesson.
> I study without understanding, and then I do not want to go to school.

For these girls, not learning or understanding meant that they did not understand the Vietnamese language. One girl, Tung, who had dropped out at grade 5, said: "I don't understand the language the teacher speaks. The teacher teaches me, but I do not understand." Their statements were corroborated by comments from parents, teachers, and community members. Many fathers expressed concern that the teachers can only speak Vietnamese and not the ethnic language, and that the students do not understand Vietnamese. One mother in a mothers' focus group discussing their girls' learning experiences captured their collective sentiment: "It is very difficult for the children to listen to the lesson in Vietnamese; they do not understand anything." Classroom observations also revealed that many Hmông students in grades 5, 6, and 7 comprehend and use limited Vietnamese. The Hmông students often do not understand the meaning of words and sentences and they read slowly, struggling with pronunciation and meaning; they also cannot understand the questions nor provide answers to the teachers. Teachers also recognized that children were not learning well in Vietnamese, and Hoa, a secondary school teacher, said the following, in reference to a girl who dropped out: "She does not know the language, and she cannot understand what I am teaching. That leads to bad learning performance." In all class observations in the primary and lower secondary schools, teachers never used Hmông to explain concepts to students. The lack of opportunity to learn in their mother tongue and inability to learn well in Vietnamese were the Hmông community's key concerns about schooling.

Difficulty in learning in the Vietnamese language is more prevalent for girls than boys. In interviews with out-of-school Hmông girls, a local interpreter was used because the girls could not understand or speak Vietnamese. In contrast, a majority of boys could communicate in Vietnamese and very few boys needed interpreters. Some teachers felt that girls are often less fluent in Vietnamese than boys, in part because "they are more shy and timid in communication than the boys are." In a classroom observation of a combined class of grades 3 and 5, girls were often less engaged by teachers. In grade 3, there was only one girl, and she was not called to participate in the lesson or answer questions, nor did she receive assistance from the teacher. In a grade 5 reading lesson, only the boys were asked to read the lesson, not the girls. The girls were called on to answer questions and were given assistance; however, this assistance was less frequent than that given to the boys.

In addition to the language of instruction, the content and pedagogy of education is perceived by community members, parents, and children as not reflecting the economic, cultural, and gender needs of the Hmông communities. Besides, they are challenged by the pedagogical methods used in school. Classroom observations revealed that the only method used was didactic lecturing and questioning. Teachers asked the students to read the examples in the textbooks, then asked questions while students consulted their textbook for the answer. Teachers also lectured from the textbook (as observed in grade 7). Teaching aids, such as pictures, posters, and models, were not utilized in any of the lessons observed. Textbooks written in Vietnamese were the only instructional materials used by the teachers.

Girls noted that they liked learning Vietnamese, but that they also wanted to learn in Hmông as well. During interviews with girls in grades 6 and 7, one girl, Chu, said: "I like [it if] everyone speaks in Hmông." Two other girls echoed this statement. One mother, speaking in Hmông, reflected on the importance of the language of instruction: "Parents don't speak Vietnamese, so it is in vain [if our children try to tell us about school]." These Hmông parents felt they were not able to help their children with schooling because they could not understand the language of instruction. They wanted their children to learn Hmông, as they felt they could learn better and could use the language in the community. They suggested that learning in both languages is valuable. Community leaders and some teachers suggested that learning Hmông and Vietnamese would foster students' learning. A commune police officer, who was responsible for mobilizing girls and their families to attend school, suggested: "Hmông teachers would be good examples for Hmông girls so they could be a person who does advocacy best." The principal, Tam, from one of the schools recognized how learning to write in Hmông was motivating for some students, and suggested that this supported their learning.

## Bilingual and Culturally Relevant Education: A Wider Scope

In conversations with educators and policymakers, the discourse is that non-Kinh ethnic groups do not have sufficient capacity in the Vietnamese language. School educators and district officials expressed a concern for teaching Vietnamese better and at earlier ages. The Hmông parents recognized the importance of learning Vietnamese, but they were also adamant about the importance of learning in Hmông, their mother tongue. Community members strongly suggested that teachers need to teach in the mother tongue, Hmông, and in Vietnamese. These perspectives represent two different approaches in policy debates: a focus on improving the teaching of Vietnamese at earlier ages, or the provision of bilingual teaching in mother tongue and Vietnamese language. Dutcher (2004) finds that students who do not learn their mother tongue proficiently have greater difficulty learning another language well. Further, international development research has shown consistently that girls are more disadvantaged than boys in learning a language other than their mother tongue, often because of a lack of social interaction and lack of access to materials (Kane, 2004).

Likewise, the discourse and practice of teaching Vietnamese as the language of instruction reflect a perspective about ethnicity and ethnic traditions in Vietnamese society. The Vietnamese constitution and education law provide ethnic minority children the right to learn in their own language in primary school, as well as to have instruction in their second language, Vietnamese. However, bilingual education is not being implemented both in policy and practice (Chantrill, Lendon, Sit, and Thanh, 2002; Kosonen, 2004)—although UNICEF is supporting a pilot of such a model. In practice, teachers primarily instruct in Vietnamese, and a percentage of official instructional time is set aside for locally controlled instruction, which may or may not be in the local languages. This locally controlled instruction time did not appear to be developed enough to include local cultural content and language. While the policy acknowledges ethnic identity and traditions, it does so in a manner that allows for the preservation of ethnic identity through certain traditions, such as songs and dance, but it does not appear to support preservation or development of ethnic identity through effective language instruction and use.

The development of ethnic identity is particularly important for the Hmông people as they maintain a strong sense of cultural identity, given their history of forced migration across Asia (see Chan, 1994). Some regard this development of identity as "maintaining traditional culture," which may be in tension with Viêt Nam's movement to modernize the country in an increasingly globalized economy. National policies and documents that address poverty reduction in Viêt Nam also emphasize the importance of ethnic minorities to speak Vietnamese in order to participate in the labor market (Centre for International Economics, 2002). In fact, parents and students recognized this need, but they equally recognized the importance of learning and using their own language in their community and for their community development. Learning the Hmông language in school, as well as other elements of Hmông cultural identity, does not presuppose that Hmông do not make language adaptations in order to participate in the larger Vietnamese society. However, learning both Hmông and Vietnamese in a bilingual program does require specialized instruction so that both languages are learned proficiently, rather than the current situation where neither is learned well (Kosonen, 2004). This is a problem that is further complicated by the paucity of materials and teachers who speak the local languages. Insufficient language abilities are exacerbated by the poor economic situations of the schools' communities where children have little access to written material in either Vietnamese or local languages outside of school (UNDP, 2002).

## COMPARING AND CONTRASTING EDUCATIONAL ISSUES FOR THE HMÔNG IN VIÊT NAM AND THE UNITED STATES

In their review of studies on Hmông students in the United States, Ngo and Lee (2007) note that the research has often focused on cultural or structural barriers as explanations for educational participation. Cultural analyses tend to emphasize differences between the Hmông and the U.S. mainstream population. The structural barriers primarily focus on factors such as poverty or parental engagement in education. Ngo and Lee also note that the recent research is more nuanced in understanding adaptive cultural practices for success in education, while also recognizing the barriers that push Hmông students out of education.

Economic hardship has been cited in the literature on Hmông students in the United States as negatively affecting their educational opportunities, including dropping out of school (Root, Rudawski, Taylor, and Rochon, 2003). A lack of financial means is an instrumental assessment of the barriers Hmông face in being educated. However, how poverty is perceived by them and others is another approach to understanding why poverty is a barrier. For example, Lee (2001, 2005) found that Hmông students' negative experiences with poverty and with schools helps to construct some students' pessimistic views about education and their life chances in the United States. It must be noted, however, that for some Hmông students, education is viewed as a pathway out of poverty (Lee, 2007). In the U.S. context, Pfeifer and Lee (2003) suggest education as an avenue out of poverty is a real possibility,[5] as Hmông have increased their educational attainment and fewer Hmông now live below the poverty line (38 percent in 1999, a decline from 60 percent in 1990). In contrast, educational attainment for the Hmông in Việt Nam has not increased by any large measure. Poverty among all nonmajority groups has decreased, but at a much slower rate (from 86 percent in 1993 to 61 percent in 2004) than for the majority Kinh (54 percent in 1993 to 14 percent in 2004) (VASS, 2006), suggesting that a lack of economic and community development persists for nonmajority groups in Việt Nam.

Some scholars have suggested that Hmông students experience educational discrimination and racism in the United States (Thao, 2003; DePouw, 2006). Hmông students in the United States recount experiences of being perceived by teachers as members of gangs, as being untrustworthy, and being less intelligent (Thao, 2003; DePouw, 2006). As suggested in the analysis above, the Hmông in Việt Nam are perceived in the public discourse as having "backward ethnic traditions," which reflects discriminatory perceptions of them. In addition, Hmông students' discourse reflected a concern about teachers' lack of respect and concern for their ethnic identity and language, and a feeling of prejudicial treatment based on their poor financial conditions—experiences echoed in a report conducted on youth (Việt Nam Youth Association et al., 2006).

Early marriage is another issue commonly cited in the United States and Việt Nam as affecting girls' educational attainment. Research in the United States from the 1980s and early 1990s focused on the negative effect of early marriage on girls' educational attainment and opportunities. Academic difficulties for Hmông girls were attributed to "patriarchal norms," which reinforced girls' status as mothers and wives (Goldstein, 1985; Rumbaut and Ima, 1988). Ngo (2002) finds that even (Hmông) girls who had completed high school and attended college resisted educational expectations by asserting their choice to be married. Ngo suggests this is not a simple act of following "traditional" culture, but is rather a complex adaptation to U.S. social and economic norms and structures, as they negotiated their gender and cultural identities.

In Việt Nam, the Hmông girls with whom we spoke did not have the same social or economic opportunities and freedoms as those in the United States, in part due to societal structures, development, and geographical location (i.e., remote and rural). They saw little opportunity to pursue higher education or hold jobs in the labor market. In contrast, the perception in the United States is that Hmông girls are now achieving at a greater rate than boys (Vang, 2003). Also, more than 40 percent of Hmông women work in the U.S. labor market. While not at parity with males (59 percent) (Pfeiffer and Lee, 2003), this is still a considerable participation in the workforce. Hmông girls in Việt Nam are not able to negotiate their identity and power in the same way as the Hmông in the United States. For example, their early marriage in Việt Nam is not purely a function of cultural tradition. Girls' and parents' discourse suggest that it is a negotiated reality influenced by cultural practices, economic realities, and gender roles, all of which have the possibility of changing over time.

Another common issue for the Hmông in Việt Nam and the United States is language and cultural identity in relation to education. Hmông students in both societies often encounter a linguistic barrier to full participation in schooling. In Việt Nam, more girls than boys were regarded as not having sufficient Vietnamese language skills. One approach taken in the United States and Việt Nam has been to provide more opportunities earlier in life for students to learn the national language (English or Vietnamese). More recently, the literature and practice lean toward the adoption of a bilingual approach to learning (McBrien, 2005). This is particularly important for girls who may have less access to social settings where the second language is spoken (Kane, 2004).

Related to language learning are Hmông students' cultural identity and practices. These students are likely to suffer from cultural isolation in school because their culture is not represented. The lack of culturally relevant education has received attention in both the United States and Việt Nam, though less so in Việt Nam. Culturally relevant pedagogy or responsive teaching (Gay, 2000; Ladson-Billings, 1995) may be useful for addressing teachers' understanding of Hmông students' language and identity issues and also the factors involved in their acculturation to the local culture. Culturally responsive teaching in Việt Nam must also take into account the economic conditions in which the Hmông currently live. Such a pedagogical approach would emphasize high expectations for Hmông, where studies have shown that teachers have lower expectations, and as a result, Hmông students are tracked into less successful classes (Goldstein, 1985; P. Thao, 1999; Y. Thao, 2003). In Việt Nam, lower expectations have created a discourse of failure and a culture of exceptionality for secondary school enrollment among these students.

In effect, culturally responsive teaching, culturally relevant pedagogy, and bilingual instruction are positive directions for helping Hmông students to acculturate selectively. Some research indicates that Hmông students who are bicultural and adopt an approach of selective acculturation are more successful in school (Bosher, 1997; Lee, 2005). In this approach individuals from a specific cultural group may use innate characteristics of both their culture and the local culture for adaptation to a given situation. This discourse is not yet prevalent in Việt Nam, but there appears to be some movement toward it, as indicated by policies and programs oriented toward the implementation of bilingual education.

## CONCLUSION

Even though the geographical conditions, material circumstances, and penetration of globalized influences for Hmông girls in Việt Nam and the United States are different, this study suggests that the Hmông in Việt Nam face some similar educational challenges, albeit with some differing causes, as their ethnic counterparts in the United States. These challenges include limited financial resources and the consequent social pressures to contribute money to their family's welfare, and being the cultural and linguistic minority. Furthermore, they face issues related to language barriers and an overall educational experience that either marginalizes or omits their culture. The discourse, policies, and practices in the broader society in the United States and Việt Nam affect differently how Hmông children and families negotiate financial resources and family welfare, and cultural and language development related to educational opportunities in these two contexts. These issues call for policies and practices within schools aimed at creating space for understanding and helping these students develop their identities, knowledge, and skills through gender-responsive and culturally relevant education. National policies and practices related to education, such as language policies, also need to account for the differing capabilities that diverse members of society value and are able to create in their social contexts (Sen, 1999; Unterhalter, 2007).

While global institutions have given much attention is given to poverty reduction and gender equity, few studies problematize the intersections of poverty, gender, and ethnicity. Stromquist and Monkman (2000) argue that one of the outcomes arising from the increasing importance of the global markets as a result of globalization is that issues of equality in and through education for ethnic minority groups and women are losing ground to efficiency considerations. In the age of globalization, if education is to simultaneously attend to and contribute to the development of social solidarity (Stromquist and Monkman, 2000), then government policies and school practices should be attuned to issues of equality and inclusion. Examining the disjunctures among local communities' practices and national and international policies and discourses is one response to converging global discourses that can "essentialize" barriers and policies related to gender, ethnicity, and poverty. We hope that this chapter helps to shift the discourse beyond parity and efficiency for minority children to more substantive ideas and practices associated with solidarities and the confrontation of injustice.

# NOTES

1. This manuscript is based on a study "Transition of Ethnic Minority Girls from Primary to Secondary Education" conducted by the Ministry of Education and Training in Viêt Nam and supported financially and technically by UNESCO and UNICEF as an activity of the United Nations Girls' Education Initiative (UNGEI).

We offer special thanks to all the national researchers at the Research Centre for Ethnic Minority Education, Ministry of Education and Training in Viêt Nam. Throughout the research, we benefited from their devotion and commitment to the commissioned study, with preparation, design, data collection, and analysis.

The study benefited considerably from the support of a distinguished teacher, Professor Dang Huynh Mai, former vice minister of the Ministry of Education and Training, and Dr. Bui Thi Ngoc Diep, director of the Research Centre for Ethnic Minority Education, Ministry of Education and Training.

We are grateful to Ms. Noala Skinner of UNICEF and Mr. Eisuke Tajima of UNESCO, who guided the technical design and implementation of the study. Several education officers, Ms. Doan Thi Dung, Mr. Nguyen Anh Ngoc in UNESCO, and Ms. Ngo Kieu Lan, Ms. Le Anh Lan and Ms. Sena Lee in UNICEF, also contributed greatly to the technical and practical implementation of the study.

Ms. Vibeke Jensen, UNESCO representative, and Mr. Jesper Morch, UNICEF representative, provided organizational support to the study. We also thank Suzanne Miric for her contributions to the larger study. Last but not least, we would like to thank all the people who were involved in this study, including girls and boys, parents, teachers, and local authorities who were interviewed and contributed their life experience and viewpoints.

2. More recent data disaggregated by ethnic group are not available in Viêt Nam.

3. The Vietnamese researchers represented mostly the majority Kinh ethnic group; none of the researchers represented the Hmông ethnic group. Hmông educators were involved in the research as cultural informants and translators.

4. In the process of translation information and meanings conveyed by Hmông girls and parents may have been lost. We attempted to clarify meanings in follow-up conversations with the researchers and translators.

5. See Vang (2003) for a discussion on a reduction in families living in poverty and the nuances of what these statistics mean with regard to Hmông families' well-being.

## REFERENCES

Asian Development Bank. (2002). *Country briefing paper: Women in Vietnam.* Manila: Asian Development Bank.

Baulch, B., Chuyen, T. T. K., Haughton, D., and Haughton, J. (2004). Ethnic minority development in Vietnam: A socioeconomic perspective. In P. Glewwe, N. Agrawal, and D. Dollar (Eds), *Economic growth, poverty, and household welfare in Vietnam* (pp. 273–310). World Bank Publications. Washington, DC: World Bank Regional and Sectoral Studies.

Bosher, S. (1997). Language and cultural identity: A study of Hmông students in postsecondary level. *TESOL Quarterly, 31*(3), 593–603.

Buchmann, C., and Hannum, E. (2001). Education and stratification in developing countries: A review of theories and research. *Annual Review of Sociology, 27,* 77–102.

Centre for International Economics. (2002). *Vietnam poverty analysis.* Canberra, Australia: Australian Agency for International Development.

Chan, S. (1994). *Hmông means free: Life of Hmông in Laos and America.* Philadelphia: Temple University Press.

Chantrill, P., Lendon, S., Sit, H. V., and Thanh, T. T. (2002). *Evaluation of basic education project for ethnic minority and other disadvantaged children in Vietnam.* Sydney: UNICEF Australia.

DePouw, C. (2006). *Negotiating race, navigating school: Situating Hmông American university student experiences.* Unpublished doctoral dissertation, University of Illinois, Urbana-Champaign.

Dutcher, N. (2004). *Expanding educational opportunity in linguistically diverse societies.* Washington, DC: Center for Applied Linguistics.

Filmer, D. (2000). *The structure of social disparities in education: Gender and wealth* (Policy Research Working Paper 2268). Washington, DC: World Bank.

Gay, G. (2000). *Culturally responsive teaching: Theory, research, and practice.* New York: Teachers College Press.

Goldstein, B. L. (1985). *Schooling for cultural transitions: Hmông girls and boys in American high schools.* Unpublished doctoral dissertation, University of Wisconsin, Madison.

Hill Collins, P. (1990). *Black feminist theory: Knowledge, consciousness and the politics of empowerment.* Cambridge: Unwin Hyman.

Kane, E. (2004). *Girls' education in Africa: What do we know about strategies that work?* (Africa Region Human Development Working Paper Series No. 73). Washington, DC: World Bank.

Kosonen, K. (2004). *Language in education: Policy and practice in Vietnam.* Hanoi, Việt Nam: UNICEF.

Ladson-Billings, G. (1995). Toward a theory of culturally relevant pedagogy. *American Educational Research Journal, 32*(3), 465–91.

Lee, S. J. (2001). More than model minorities or delinquents: Hmông American high school students. *Harvard Educational Review, 73*(3), 505–28.

Lee, S. J. (2005). *Up against whiteness: Race, schools, and immigrant students.* New York: Teachers College Press.

Lee, S. J. (2007). The truth and myth of the model minority: The case of Hmông Americans. In S. J. Paik and H. J. Walberg (Eds.), *Narrowing the achievement gap: Strategies for educating Latino, Black and Asian students* (pp. 171–84). New York: Springer.

Lewin, K. (2005). Planning post-primary education: Taking targets to task. *International Journal of Educational Development, 25*(4), 408–22.

Lewis, M. A., and Lockheed, M. E. (2006). *Inexcusable absence: Why 60 million girls still aren't in school and what to do about it.* Washington, DC: Center for Global Development.

McBrien, J. L. (2005). Educational needs and barriers for refugee students in the United States: A review of the literature. *Review of Educational Research, 75*(3), 329–64.

Miske, S., Schuh Moore, A., and DeJaeghere, J. (2000). *Beyond access: Improving educational quality in FSSAP schools of Bangladesh.* Washington, DC: World Bank.

Ngo, B. (2002). Contesting "culture": The perspectives of Hmông American female students on early marriage. *Anthropology and Education Quarterly, 33*(2), 163–88.

Ngo, B., and Lee, S. J. (2007). Complicating the image of model minority success: A review of Southeast Asian American education. *Review of Educational Research, 77*(4), 415–53.

Pfeifer, M. E., and Lee, S. L. (2003). Hmông population, demographic, socioeconomic and educational trends in the 2000 census. In *Hmông 2000 Census Publication: Data and Analysis* (pp. 3–11). Washington, DC: Hmông National Development Corporation.

Root, S., Rudawski, A., Taylor, M., and Rochon, R. (2003). Attrition of Hmông students in teacher education programs. *Bilingual Research Journal, 27*(1), 137–48.

Rumbaut, R., and Ima, K. (1988). *The adaptation of Southeast Asian refugee youth: A comparative study.* Washington, DC: U.S. Office of Refugee Resettlement.

Sen, A. K. (1992). *Inequality reexamined.* Cambridge, MA: Harvard University Press.

Sen, A. K. (1999). *Development as freedom.* Oxford: Oxford University Press.

Socialist Republic of Viêt Nam. (2003). *Comprehensive poverty reduction and growth strategy paper.* Washington, DC: International Monetary Fund.

State Committee for Ethnic Minority and Mountainous Area Affairs. (2005). *Socio-economic development programme for extremely difficult communes in ethnic minority and mountainous areas in the period 2006–2010.* (Third Draft). Hanoi, Viêt Nam: State Committee for Ethnic Minority and Mountainous Area Affairs.

Stromquist, N. (2001). What poverty does to girls' education: The intersection of class, gender, and ethnicity in Latin America. *Compare, 31*(1), 39–56.

Stromquist, N., and Monkman, K. (2000). Defining globalization and assessing its implications on knowledge and education. In N. Stromquist and K. Monkman (Eds.), *Globalization and education: Integration and contestation across cultures* (pp. 3–26). Lanham, MD: Rowman & Littlefield.

Subrahmanian, R. (2002). *Gender and education: A review of issues for social policy.* (Social Policy and Development Programme Paper No.9). Geneva, Switzerland: United Nations Research Institute for Social Development.

Sutton, M. (2001). Policy research as ethnographic refusal: The case of women's literacy in Nepal. In M. Sutton and B. A. U. Levinson (Eds.), *Policy as practice: Toward a comparative sociocultural analysis of educational policy* (pp. 77–99). Westport, CT: Ablex Publishing.

Thao, P. (1999). *Mong education at the crossroads.* New York: University Press of America.

Thao, Y. (2003). Empowering Mong students: Home and school factors. *The Urban Review, 35*(1), 25–42.

UNESCO Institute for Statistics. (2000). *UIS Statistics in Brief.* Retrieved October 18, 2008, from UNESCO at stats.uis.unesco.org/unesco.

United Nations Children's Fund. (2004). *A gender desk review in education.* Hanoi, Viêt Nam: United Nations Children's Fund.

United Nations Children's Fund. (2005). *Situation of girls' education in Vietnam—adolescence.* Retrieved July 9, 2005, from www.unicef.org/vietnam/children_273.html.

United Nations Children's Fund. (2008). *Transition to post-primary education with a special focus on girls: Examining medium-term strategies for developing post-primary education in ESAR.* Nairobi: United Nations Children's Fund.

United Nations Development Programme. (2002). *Localizing MDGs for poverty reduction in Vietnam: Promoting ethnic minority development.* Hanoi, Viêt Nam: United Nations Development Programme.

United Nations High Commissioner for Refugees. (2002). *Vietnam: Indigenous minority groups in the central highlands* (WriteNet Paper 05/2001). Geneva, Switzerland: United Nations High Commissioner for Refugees.

United States Agency for International Development. (2006). *Strengthening gender and education programming in the 21st century.* Washington, DC: United States Agency for International Development.

United States Census Bureau. (2000). United States Census 2000. Retrieved February 20, 2008, from www.census.gov/main/www/cen2000.html.

Unterhalter, E. (2007). Global values and gender equality in education: Needs, rights, and capabilities. In S. Fennell and M. Arnot (Eds.), *Gender education and equality in a global context: Conceptual frameworks and policy perspectives* (pp. 19–34). London: Routledge.

Vang, C. Y. (2003). Contested economic growth among Hmông Americans. In *Hmông 2000 census publication: Data and analysis* (pp. 29–31). Washington, DC: Hmông National Development Corporation.

Vavrus, F. (2002). Uncoupling the articulation between girls' education and tradition in Tanzania. *Gender and Education, 14*(4), 367–89.

Viêt Nam Youth Association, Viêt Nam Women's Union, UNICEF, and World Bank. (2006). *Results of youth consultations* (Draft). Hanoi, Viêt Nam: Viêt Nam Youth Association.

Vietnamese Academy of Social Sciences. (2006). *Vietnam poverty update report 2006: Poverty and poverty reduction in Vietnam 1993–2004.* Hanoi, Viêt Nam: Vietnamese Academy of Social Sciences.

Weis, L., and Fine, M. (2004). *Working method: Research and social justice.* New York: Routledge.

Wils, A., Carrol, B., and Barrow, K. (2005). *Educating the world's children: Patterns of growth and inequality.* Washington, DC: Academy for Educational Development, Education Policy and Data Center.

Xiong, B. Z., and Tuicomepee, Z. (2003). Hmông families in America in 2000: Continuity and change. In *Hmông 2000 census publication: Data and analysis* (pp. 12–20). Washington, DC: Hmông National Development Corporation.

Zhang, Y., Kao, G., and Hannum, E. (2007). Do mothers in rural China practice gender equality in educational aspirations for their children? *Comparative Education Review, 51*(2), 131–57.

*Chapter Thirteen*

# Minority Students in Asia: Government Policies, School Practices, and Teacher Responses

## JoAnn Phillion, Yuxiang Wang, and Jungmin Lee

An overarching factor affecting minority students in Asia is the process of globalization with resulting mass movements of peoples around the globe due to economic influences. Asian countries such as China and South Korea in particular are experiencing rapid economic growth. After its accession to the World Trade Organization, China has sped up its globalization process; however, this process is mainly limited to the economy and minimally affects social conditions in the country. At the political level, China has a "one party system" that determines the destiny and affairs of 1.3 billion people (Veek, Pannell, Smith, and Huang, 2007). After Hong Kong returned to China in 1997, its political practices have been overseen by the same one party—the Chinese Communist Party; this has also affected social conditions (Veek et al., 2007).

South Korea, also undergoing rapid economic growth, has experienced dramatic increases in ethnic and racial diversity from international migrations of populations with resulting social and educational change (Korean Ministry of Education and Human Resources Development, 2006b). Because of the focus on the economy and trade, social and educational conditions resulting from globalization—in particular issues pertaining to minority groups' education, language, and other human rights—receive less attention (Bigelow and Peterson, 2002). In addition, many areas of Asia have traditionally viewed themselves as single-ethnicity countries and have not articulated strong agendas around minority rights or human rights.

The purpose of this chapter is to highlight these issues seldom discussed in Asia and in globalization literature on Asia. The disparity between government policies, and experiences of students in schools and educational outcomes, is described based on research conducted by the authors and reviews of relevant literature. We find that in China, Hong Kong, and South Korea, minority groups encounter the following related issues: loss of first languages, neglect of culture in curriculum, low teacher expectations, early drop-out rate, retention in grade, and low attendance in higher education. These issues are discussed using multicultural education theories that allow for a comparison to the situation for minority groups in the United States. We conclude by arguing that multicultural education—a process dedicated to social justice for individuals and communities, regardless of factors such as race, ethnicity, gender, language, sexual orientation, disability, religion, and socioeconomic status—is urgently needed in Asia. Strategies for the successful implementation of multicultural education in Asia in the age of globalization are suggested.

# METHODS: MULTICULTURAL AND CROSS-CULTURAL NARRATIVE INQUIRY

In this study, we use *multicultural and cross-cultural narrative inquiry* (MCNI) (Phillion, 2008) as our research method in examining minority education issues in China, Hong Kong, and South Korea. This inquiry focuses on the untold experience of marginalized groups and individuals enacted in contested cultural, linguistic, and sociopolitical milieus. MCNI is developed as a method to portray the way life is lived out, expressed, and addressed in international contexts as people move from country to country, culture to culture, place to place, and language to language. MCNI evolves in response to the need to portray the shifting dynamics in the experiences of those caught up in, and often lost in the global context, and is being developed in response to the call for research that is more relevant to pressing issues of social justice and to addressing issues of human rights (Ladson-Billings and Tate, 2006).

## Specific Methods Used

Document analysis and elementary textbook analysis (Sleeter and Grant, 1991; Wang, in press) are used in the study in mainland China to examine the effects of language policy and its practice on minority students' language learning, cultural maintenance, and identity construction. In Hong Kong, we focus on understanding the lived experiences of minority students and parents; methods included participant observation in schools, interviews with students, parents, and teachers, and analyses of government documents on policies for mainland Chinese students (Phillion, 2008). In South Korea, an in-depth analysis of the new multicultural policy is presented, interviews with a government official and teachers are reported, and site visits to schools with minority populations are used in order to describe how participants experience and make sense of multicultural phenomena in the country.

# MAINLAND CHINA

## Minority Language Policies

Officially, the Chinese government has enacted laws and policies for purposes of protecting minority groups' language and culture rights. When these laws and policies are interpreted in schools, however, discrepancies between policy and practice are significant (He, 2005; Zhou, 2004). In this section we discuss mainland China's minority language policies and examine discrepancies between policy and practice in terms of minority language rights and minority representation in school textbooks.

There are fifty-six nationalities in mainland China. Han, the dominant nationality, comprises 90 percent of China's population of about 1.3 billion; the other fifty-five nationalities are minorities, representing approximately 130 million people. Han people control most institutions and government agencies. Historically, Han people have been dominant and held government posts except during the Yuan Dynasty (1271–1368 CE) and the Qing Dynasty (1644–1911 CE) when China was governed by the Mongols and the Manchus, respectively (Mackerras, 1994). Almost half of China's territory is occupied by minority nationalities; they inhabit the inner border regions where there are either deserts or mountains, which are poor areas. Tibetans and Uighurs constitute a majority in the Tibet Autonomous Region and Xinjiang province, respectively, in western China. Fifty-three nationalities have their own languages; Manchu and Hui speak Chinese (Zuo, 2007).

To protect minority groups' rights and interests in multiethnic China, the 1982 Constitution of the People's Republic of China (PRC) stipulates that:

> All ethnic groups in the People's Republic of China are equal. The state protects the lawful rights and interests of the minority nationalities and upholds and develops the relationship of equality, unity and mutual assistance among all of China's nationalities.

In the PRC Regional Autonomy Law for Minority Nationalities enacted in 1984, six articles address minority groups' rights and those of language use (Zhou, 2004). Article 37 states: "In schools which mainly recruit students of minority nationalities, textbooks in languages of minority nationalities concerned should be used where conditions exist. Languages for instruction should also be the languages of the minority nationalities concerned."

In practice, language rights are often implemented through bilingual education in minority regions. In 1984, for instance, Qinghai province proposed the use of minority languages and Mandarin Chinese for ethnic elementary and secondary schools. The Guangxi Zhuang Autonomous Region and the Tibet Autonomous Region have also set forth the principle of using their minority languages for basic education, in addition to learning Mandarin Chinese, with the goal of students' achieving fluency in both languages after secondary school graduation (Dai and Dong, 2001).

## Discrepancies between Policy and Practice: Minority Students' Language Rights

Although minority groups are officially guaranteed the use of their native languages in ethnic autonomous regions, Zhou (2004) finds discrepancies between what was stipulated in the constitution by law and what was enacted in governmental practices. Zhou uses the distinction between group rights and state rights to examine whether minority groups have their individual language rights and whether the minority individual has any means of asking the state to fulfill its commitment to minority groups in terms of language rights. Zhou concludes that minority groups' language rights stipulated by law are group rights that empower the state rather than minority individuals; in effect, state rights are weightier than individual minority rights.

In China, national unity and stability are considered top national priorities; individual rights or policies regarded as threats to national unity are abandoned (He, 2005; Mackerras, 1994). In Tibet, for example, in 1987, the Tibet Autonomous Regional People's Congress developed a plan for Tibetan language use and respect for Tibetan culture. Special regulations were made about the exclusive use of the Tibetan language in school textbooks and classroom teaching. This plan, however, "has been abandoned as part of the post-1989 crackdown on "separatism" and almost all subjects are now taught in Chinese" (He, 2005, p. 72). Moreover, what is stipulated by law is undermined by the practices of Han officials, whose stereotypical and discriminatory views have a negative impact on minority culture and language. Nima (2001), for example, finds some Chinese officials in minority regions interpret minority language and culture as "backwardness" and Han language and culture as "civilization."

The dominance of Mandarin Chinese is the paramount negative influence on minority language rights. Starting in 1956, the promotion of Mandarin Chinese in the government at the county and higher levels (Zhou, 1999) meant that Mandarin Chinese would be the official language in China. Article 19 of the 1982 Constitution of the PRC (in contrast with Article 37 of the Minority Nationalities Law mentioned above) stipulates that "The state promotes the nationwide use of Putonghua [Mandarin Chinese] (common speech based on Beijing pronunciation)." In effect, Mandarin Chinese is nationally promoted and minority languages are not (Zhou, 2004). Also, importantly, researchers have found that speaking Mandarin Chinese guarantees not only better employment opportunities but also "the option of entry into the identity of being Chinese" (Nelson, 2005, p. 26). As a result of the globalization process and because of China's strong economic development, Mandarin Chinese has become essential in local, national, and global contexts.

Mandarin Chinese pervades all minority areas and all aspects of public life; for example, Nima (2001) finds that Mandarin Chinese permeates Tibet: from government documents to telegrams, from electrical appliances' instructions to technical concepts used in work environments, from businesses to schools. This massive use of Mandarin Chinese in Tibet has had devastating effects on Tibetan language learning, maintenance, and use; the effect is a loss of the minority heritage language. Many multicultural theorists who focus on language issues have made similar claims in the United States (Cummins, 1989).

Some Tibetans believe that learning Chinese is the only way to improve their life by "getting government jobs after graduation" (Nima, 2001, p. 95). Moreover, Tibetan students who have graduated from all-Chinese language elementary schools more easily find and adapt to education in secondary schools, which are Chinese dominant in both teaching and curriculum (Stites, 1999). As a result, "some Tibetans are actually working against those who advocate Tibetan-language education, punishing lower officials who do so" (Nima, 2001, p. 98) for fear of conflicts between Tibetan officials and Han officials.

Zuo (2007) discusses the extinction of minority languages, such as Tibetan, in China during the last fifty years and suggests that measures should be taken to protect these languages by promoting minority language teacher training, bilingual education, and the learning of minority culture and knowledge. These same measures are advocated by multicultural scholars in the United States and Canada concerned with minority students' loss of heritage languages, cultures, and knowledge (Banks, 2007; Cummins, 1989; Gay, 2000).

## The One-Child Policy and Human Rights Abuse

The Chinese Communist Party values the unity of different peoples and the unification of the nation (He, 2005; Mackerras, 1994). This position affects more than the language rights of minority groups. Those regarded as a threat to Chinese Communist Party values can be detained or imprisoned; any materials perceived as a threat to unity and harmony are banned (He, 2005). Although the Chinese government has taken measures to protect registered religious groups, unregistered groups are not protected (U.S. State Department, 2008). Furthermore, the one-child policy put into effect in January 1979 deprived families of the right to choose the number of children that they wanted to have; this policy engenders conflict for peasant families, who prefer to have a male heir to work in the fields and to keep the family name from generation to generation. Many couples who violated the policy were punished economically and physically. In rural areas, forced sterilizations and abortions are still reported (U.S. State Department, 2008). Minority groups, however, are exempt from the one-child policy (He, 2005). There are two reasons that account for the special treatment. First, most minority groups reside in border regions and mountainous areas where the population is much sparser than in the rest of the country (Veek et al., 2007). Second, the government wants to win the support of minority groups because the border regions are critical when wars arise with neighboring countries; in addition there are rich natural resources in the border regions (Mackerras, 1994; Veek et al., 2007).

Gender biases are also demonstrated in the education received by males and females. A sample survey showed that about 47 percent of all enrolled students in 2003 were females; 41 percent of those enrolled in colleges and universities were women (National Bureau of Statistics, 2004). In rural areas and minority areas, males usually receive more education than females (Veek et al., 2007). Women and men's literacy rates demonstrate that women are discriminated against and do not have rights in education equal to those of men. In 1982, 19 percent of adult males and 45 percent of females in China were reported as illiterate (Veek et al., 2007). Although only 6.12 percent of adult males and 13.85 percent of females were reported as illiterate by 2003 (Veek et al., 2007), it is clear that women are still not equal with men in the field of education in Chinese society. Due to the need for a literate population to increase economic development, the government has made efforts to improve the literacy rate by providing night schools for literacy education. However, women have to look after children and take care of family chores, which has made it more difficult for them to participate in the same literacy education as men (Veek et al., 2007). Gender bias in terms of the devaluing of female children and subsequent educational inequality, coupled with discrimination against minority groups in general, has compounded problems for minority women. Similar issues for minorities have been found in the United States and Canada (Cummins, 1989).

## Minority Languages, Textbooks, and School Knowledge

From grade 3, minority students in autonomous regions are required to use the national uniform curriculum (Zuo, 2007). This mandated curriculum features Han knowledge as the norm and Mandarin Chinese as the official language. Thus the national curriculum makes it possible for the dominant Han group to manipulate school knowledge. Researchers contend that the national curriculum causes minority students to lose access to their minority languages and cultures; this can result in minority students' losing their indigenous identities (Gladney, 2004). Banks (2007) has developed similar theories in multicultural education research in the United States.

In an analysis of elementary textbooks in mainland China, Wang (in press) finds sthat minority knowledge, language, and culture are underrepresented or nonexistent. Since minority students do not encounter minority knowledge and culture in textbooks or curriculum, they do not study material related to their daily life. Many minority parents thus decide to send their children to temples and mosques for education since literacy education is provided in minority languages, and content and knowledge are related to their culture (Bradley, 2001; Hansen, 1999). Wang, building on work done by Apple and Christian-Smith (1991) and Banks (2007), theorizes that the exclusion of minority groups' knowledge, language, and culture from school textbooks conveys the message to both minority and Han students that minority knowledge, language, and culture are not important and not worth learning.

Not only do Han knowledge, language, and culture dominate school textbooks, but minority knowledge, language, and culture—when represented—are constructed solely from the Han perspective. Wang (in press) finds few texts written from minority groups' perspective or languages, few texts that discuss minority experiences or concerns, and none that address struggles with poverty or economic and education inequalities. "Respect for Minority Culture" (2006), an article in a school textbook on moral education, describes one education plan that the Chinese Communist Party provides for Tibetan students. Every year about one thousand Tibetan middle school students are sent to schools outside of Tibet for an education in an exclusively Han Chinese school environment (Development and Cultural Destruction in Tibet, 1995; Postiglione, 1992). They are taught in Chinese; only Han culture and values are instilled in the Tibetan students. They are encouraged to remain at school; for example, Tibetan students would usually spend the New Year with their families, but they are far from their home and do not return. The article in the textbook, however, indicated that Tibetan students were happy, as if they were comfortable with the New Year blessings in Chinese from the Han principal, Han teachers, and Han students (Respect for Minority Culture, 2006).

The former paragraph illustrates how the dominant Han group interprets minority students' feelings and needs from their own point of view rather than from the perspectives of minority students. The article did not discuss how Tibetan students missed their parents at the traditional time of family union or how the students feel about learning Chinese, speaking Chinese, and living in a Han dominant cultural environment. Rather, the text portrayed the Han people as having the responsibility to make Tibetan students happy by providing them with festival foods and decorations and by making them learn Han language, culture, knowledge, and ideology (Gladney, 1999).

Further building on Apple and Christian-Smith's (1991) work and Banks's (2007) work, we contend that the purpose of these educational practices is to take away Tibetan (and other minority groups) students' home language, culture, and identity. Through the selection and construction of knowledge and the teaching of Han dominant knowledge in Chinese, the dominant Han group legitimates Han knowledge and Mandarin Chinese. The dominant ideology, as a result, is reproduced and instilled in minority students. Han knowledge, Han culture, and Mandarin Chinese represent advancement, science, and truth; minority knowledge, culture, and language, on the other hand, are represented as backward, unscientific, and not worthy of learning (Nelson, 2005). Despite provisions in the constitution and laws enacted to protect minority rights, it is the dominant group, the Han, that determines what knowledge, culture, and language to include and what to exclude from school curricula and school knowledge in mainland China; through this determination, hegemonic control is maintained and minority groups' knowledge, language, and culture are subjugated. The treatment received by Tibetans and other minority groups resonates with treatment received by Native Americans in the United States and indigenous people globally: eradication of language and culture; removal of children from homes and placement in dominant culture environments; loss of cultural identity; and, in many cases, the complete eradication of indigenous tribes (Smith, 1999).

## HONG KONG[1]

Similarly to the government of mainland China, the Hong Kong government has enacted laws and educational policies for purposes of protecting minority groups' language and culture rights and guaranteeing minority students an education (Home Affairs Bureau, 2006). These policies have spurred much public discussion about the need for them. Many mainstream residents of Hong Kong believe these policies will destroy the harmony of what they think of as "one people"; minority groups and advocacy groups, however, have found discrimination in terms of housing, employment, and educational opportunities (ATV News and Public Affairs, 2006). In addition, when these laws and policies are implemented in schools and interpreted by teachers, discrepancies between policy and practice and educational goals and outcomes are significant. In this section, we discuss the experiences of mainland Chinese students who enter Hong Kong schools. This is important as there is little research that examines the complexities of schooling for immigrant minority students, such as these students, who are members of the same ethnic group as the majority students in the schools they enter.

Students who have come from mainland China and have been in Hong Kong for fewer than four years are termed "newly arrived children" (NAC); while ethnically the same as Hong Kong students, the newly arrived children often have different religious, cultural, linguistic, and socioeconomic backgrounds. Therefore, "NAC moving to Hong Kong are analogous to immigrants entering a new country" (Chong, 2004,

p. 3) and are often treated as such by their teachers and peers. There are significant numbers of NAC in Hong Kong; from 1998 to 2004, since Hong Kong was returned to China, there were 358,662 new arrivals from mainland China, of which 131,557 were NAC in schools, with a high of 30,171 in 1998 and a low of 11,320 in 2004 (Home Affairs Department and Immigration Department, 2006).

Researchers examining challenges encountered by NAC are finding significant factors affecting the adjustment of children (Chong, 2004; Phillion, 2008; Yuen, 2002): many NAC do not arrive in Hong Kong as part of a family unit due to the way immigration is handled in Hong Kong (individual admission); families are separated and children often live with only one parent or with relatives; arranged marriages are common for NAC families, and many fathers are older than mothers—there is heated discussion in the media about this and the stigma associated with this type of marriage pervades public discourse; many families struggle financially, unemployment is an issue, and an increasing number of these families are on government assistance; many NAC mothers do not speak Cantonese (the primary language in Hong Kong) and have difficulty adjusting to their new environment; many NAC mothers and fathers have received only a few years of public school education and cannot assist their children with schoolwork. These factors directly impact the children.

The following sections describe research done in 2005–2006 with six NAC children in an elementary school in Hong Kong, their mothers, their teachers, the school counselor, and the principal (Phillion, 2008). Triads (child, parent, and teacher) were interviewed and observed. For the purposes of this chapter, the focus is on one student, Fai, a nine-year-old boy, his mother and teacher, and others in contact with him. Fai had been in Hong Kong for three years; his father was unemployed at the time of the research, and the family was on government assistance. Fai's experiences illustrate issues and challenges faced by many NAC children, and by many other children caught up in the forces of globalization and resulting movements from place to place, language to language, culture to culture, school system to school system.

## Language Issues

Fai was born in Shenzhen, a border city of Hong Kong. While he spoke Cantonese fluently, his first language was his parents' village dialect, Helao. Unlike Fai, however, not speaking Cantonese was a problem for many NAC who learned Mandarin Chinese in school in China and spoke dialects with their families. Writing Chinese was an issue for Fai and other NAC as there are different writing systems for mainland China (simplified characters) and Hong Kong (traditional characters). Fai also had a problem with English as most NAC do not begin to learn English in mainland China as early as students do in Hong Kong. He frequently failed English "dictations"; he often missed every word as the vocabulary was taken out of context and little effort was made to assist him. He also could not get help from his parents, both of whom had only a few years of schooling and did not speak English. Fai made efforts to improve his English by attending special classes offered in his school.

Ability in English impacted Fai and other NAC in many ways. It determined the classes in which they were placed; as a result of low scores on tests administered when they first arrived, NAC were often placed in grades with younger students. It determined their success in school and judgments teachers made about their ability and motivation to learn. It also determined whether they could enter colleges and universities. In 2007, English-language programs funded by the Education Bureau for NAC were being cut (Education and Manpower Bureau, 2005); the principal in the research school said that at his school most would end next year. Fai's mother was concerned about her child's ability in English and connected this to worry over future job prospects.

## Teachers and Counselors Views of NAC

Teachers held stereotypical views of NAC children. Miss Lee, Fai's teacher and the teacher of several other NAC, said:

> I do not know who the NAC children are; all children are the same to me. . . . [however] newly arrived Mainland students are rich; they have nice paper and expensive erasers. The government's welfare system supports NAC families; those parents are lazy and do not look for jobs . . . many Mainland Chinese collect unemployment and some NAC do not work hard because they will do the same.

This seemed to be a universal story. Hong Kong born and raised teachers (mainstream teachers) said on one hand that "Mainland students are the same to me as the Hong Kong students"; then they said, "they are welfare cheats and lazy." The counselor in Fai's school also said they were the same; however, she also spoke of poverty, hardship, arranged marriages, health issues, and parents' lack of education. She said:

> If children are motivated, however, no matter the obstacles [such as those listed above], they will succeed . . . in the past NAC were good students and did well in school. Recently the NAC are not good students; they are unmotivated and their parents do not care about their children's education.

Teachers did not question their role in the situation, or suggest other reasons NAC might not do well. These findings resonate with research in the United States; many white (mainstream) teachers hold stereotypical views of minority parents and students similar to those held by Hong Kong teachers (e.g., Ladson-Billings, 1994).

## Challenges Faced by NAC

Mr. Wu, the principal of the research school, had been there for over a decade and had experience working with families of NAC, like Fai's family. He indicated that NAC experienced what he referred to as "challenges." (These challenges are also discussed in Chong, 2004; Phillion, 2008.) He felt the major challenge was *academic*:

> NAC use simplified characters for writing Chinese whereas in Hong Kong they use traditional characters. NAC could read and write well when they were in the mainland, but are confused in Hong Kong. . . . NAC often receive no points at all in "dictations" done on a daily basis and get poor grades in English. In mainland China they usually only learned

the English alphabet in the first few years of school; they are behind their Hong Kong classmates. [Fai was a student like that; he struggled in English class and seemed lost.]

Mr. Wu also felt there were *cultural* challenges:

> The environment is not as safe for them to play outside as it was in mainland China . . . the students want to run around more than they can. This could lead to associations with gangs in the estate [the low-income housing complex near the school where Fai lived] . . . the housing space is much smaller in Hong Kong and this makes for problems.

Finally, he felt there were what he termed, *living* challenges (related to cultural ones):

> Life is very different in Hong Kong. In mainland China, you can survive even though you don't earn too much. But in Hong Kong, it's very materialistic. It has so many attractions to newly arrived immigrated students. There are more material goods and children want more things. This is why some of the NAC steal things from stores. . . . More support for NAC is needed.

Young students such as Fai often do not recognize the challenges they face; Fai indicated:

> In LuFeng [grandparents' village where he spent a lot of time] I play with chickens. I also swim and catch fish in the river. It's very spacious. I am happy in Hong Kong although I miss my school. . . . I feel half mainland Chinese and half Hongkonger. I have good friends [his mother said he spent most of his time watching television].

NAC often do not have friends and, in fact, are not allowed to leave their apartments as parents view the estate as dangerous and having gangs. Phillion (2008) finds that some NAC are bullied by their Hong Kong classmates.

Fai's experiences illustrate many of the challenges that NAC encounter in Hong Kong. *Poverty* is a key issue; in 2004, 70 percent of NAC families made less than $9,000 HK per month (about $1,100 US) and the numbers on government assistance increased to 15 percent (Home Affairs Department and Immigration Department, 2006). *Adaptation* is another key issue, with over 50 percent of newly arrived mainland immigrants indicating that they were having difficulties, particularly in employment and living conditions (Home Affairs Department and Immigration Department, 2006). *Education* is the key issue for NAC. In 2004, about 50 percent of NAC elementary students and over 80 percent of secondary students were placed in grades below their age level. The retention in grade rate in 2004 for NAC elementary students was 40 percent and for secondary students it was over 70 percent. About 40 percent of NAC elementary and over 50 percent of secondary students were termed "weak" in English (a key subject as demonstrated above). However, fewer than 20 percent of all NAC were reported as "weak" in Chinese (Education and Manpower Bureau, 2005).

Although NAC continue to immigrate/migrate to Hong Kong and experience difficulties financially, in adjustment and adaptation, and in academics, the education system no longer views NAC as a priority requiring special attention. Support programs for English language skills and adaptation to life in Hong Kong, such as those offered in the research school, are being cut. Research funds are generally not available for NAC issues, as funds are allocated to other interests (Chong, 2004).

Applying a critical multicultural theoretical framework, we can see that Fai's and other NAC children's situation parallels that of ethnic minorities in the United States. Many mainstream teachers like Miss Lee, Fai's teacher, hold minority students responsible for their failure in school without reflecting on racism within themselves and in society (Sleeter, 2001). Teachers cling to the attitude that they treat all children the same regardless of race or color (Cochran-Smith, 2000), or in the case of Hong Kong, place of origin and socioeconomic status. NAC children's language and cultural background are ignored in school in a one-size-fits-all, sink-or-swim kind of curriculum and pedagogy, and testing that judges them on the basis of criteria they can not meet, such as English language skills (Cummins, 1989). Unquestioned, stereotypical views of parents are held; they are seen as deficient and deviant, as contributing to their children's problems in school (Delpit, 1995).

Teachers see themselves and Hong Kong born students as the norm; NAC and their parents are different and unacceptable. Understanding privilege, based on place of origin, familiarity with the English language, education level, and socioeconomic status is not part of teacher education programs or teacher discourse in Hong Kong. Without this discourse, without a critical examination of the exclusionary practices perpetuated in Hong Kong schools, the situation for Fai and other NAC remains grave. It is also important to note that this situation is not restricted to areas discussed in this chapter; it is a situation that impacts virtually the entire world as forces of globalization cause families to move to seek better economic and educational opportunities for themselves, their children, and future generations.

## SOUTH KOREA

Similarly to mainland China and Hong Kong, South Korea has minority populations for whom it is developing policies. Unlike the other two areas, however, South Korea is developing these policies as "human rights policies." Traditionally thought of as ethnically and racially homogeneous, South Korea recently acknowledged it is a diverse society due to increases in migrant foreign workers and in international marriages. In response to its newly emerging ethnic and racial diversity, the South Korean government has enacted laws, policies, and educational measures, and some schools have implemented educational programs to provide minority groups with a better public education (Korean Ministry of Education and Human Resources Development, 2006b). In this section, we examine South Korean educational policies created in response to the "multicultural challenges" posed by the new ethnic and racial diversity and explore how the policies are interpreted into school practices. The primary focus is on school education for undocumented children of undocumented migrant workers using interview data with two teachers (the larger study on which this chapter is based has additional participants).

Recently, there have been significant increases in foreign migrant workers and in international marriages in South Korea. Foreign migrant workers numbered 6,409 in 1987; in 2005, however, the number was estimated at 345,679, of which 180,792 (52.3 percent) were undocumented (Korean Ministry of Education and Human Resources Development, 2006b). International marriages numbered 43,121 in 2005, representing 13.6 percent of all marriages in South Korea, up tenfold from 1990; this trend is continuing (Korean National Statistical Office, 2006).

With the increase in foreign labor and international marriages, foreign children and interracial children are appearing in South Korean schools. The Korean Ministry of Education and Human Resources Development (2006a) found that the number of foreign children who are school age is 17,287. Among them, 9,374 children attend foreign schools or Korean schools. Children who attend school and have one Korean parent and one foreign parent numbered 7,998 in 2006, an increase of 30.6 percent over the previous year. As the number of international marriages has increased in the past few years, it is expected that the number of interracial children who will enter school will likewise increase.

There are about 120 million "guest workers" (Du, Gregory, and Meng, 2006) in cities in China, who migrated from rural areas to cities. Although they contribute greatly to the prosperity of the cities and the nation, guest workers do not enjoy the same social benefits as city residents. For example, they have no medical insurance, their children cannot receive education in the city schools, and most guest workers live in poverty (Du, Gregory, and Meng, 2006) This situation also exists in Hong Kong in term of minority populations being unable to attain the same access to education, particularly after middle school, and with high poverty rates among minority families (Chong, 2004).

## Government Educational Policies on Minority Students

In 2006, the Korean Ministry of Education and Human Resources Development (2006b) established a comprehensive set of measures to assist children of international marriages and children of migrant workers residing in South Korea in order for these groups to receive a better public education. This measure, titled *Educational Support Plan for Children from Multicultural Families*, was devised to meet three areas of concern: (1) to foster understanding diversity, to improve human rights of minority people, and to strengthen social integration; (2) to ensure educational equity for interracial children and migrant children through educational support; and (3) to educate students with diverse cultural and linguistic characteristics as human resources in a globally competitive world. These government policies include two (sometimes contradictory) conceptions of multicultural education: that all ethnic and immigrant groups should adapt to the commonly shared culture and language for social integration, and that they need to maintain their cultures and languages because groups with diverse cultures and languages will make significant economic and social contributions to Korea.

In mainland China, guest workers are regarded as different from city-born residents (Solinger, 1999). Guest workers have fewer citizenship rights that they can enjoy than city-born residents (Solinger, 1999). Guest workers work longer hours to support themselves and their family because of their low hourly pay. These workers often send their children to their home areas to receive their education because their children do not have similar access to schooling as the city children (Du, Gregory, and Meng, 2006; Solinger, 1999). In Hong Kong the situation for minorities is similar, they often drop out of school before completing high school and are relegated to low-wage jobs with little future advancement (Chong, 2004; Yuen, 2002).

The government policies for interracial children, one of the target groups, focus on Korean language and school support for them and Korean language and social adaptation programs for their immigrant mothers. The ministry's support began with assumptions that interracial children experience difficulties in Korean-language learning, school academic achievement, and school life adaptation because of the lack of home education due to married immigrant mothers who are not fluent in the Korean language and do not know Korean culture, and that they suffer from discrimination that could lead to school dropout.

The key mandate of government policies for undocumented children, the other target group, is to ensure that these children obtain an education. This is an important theme discussed later in the section on school practices. Undocumented children are guaranteed the basic right to receive an education in spite of their legal status. In 2005, it was estimated that about 90 percent of undocumented children of school age in South Korea do not attend school. This low enrollment is caused by their insecure legal status, fear of a government crackdown and possible deportation, and poverty (Korean Ministry of Education and Human Resources Development, 2006a, 2006b). To ensure the educational rights of undocumented children, the Ministry of Education has simplified regulations to enter elementary school; for instance, these students can present a copy of a housing rental contract or a neighbor's written guarantee of their residence (Korean Ministry of Education and Human Resources Development, 2006b). In addition, the ministry announced a policy banning immigration officials and police from chasing undocumented children near schools as a way to catch their parents in order to ensure that these children obtain an education (Korean Ministry of Education and Human Resources Development, 2006c).

## SCHOOL PRACTICES FOR UNDOCUMENTED CHILDREN

Educational support for children from multicultural backgrounds is being implemented into practice in schools in different areas of South Korea. In 2006, two public elementary schools created a special class for children of undocumented migrant workers and recruited these children with financial support and educational measures developed by the Gyeong-gi provincial education office. The two schools are located near industrial complexes where many undocumented foreign migrants work. In order to understand how the multicultural law and its policies were being implemented into practice, interviews with two teachers from the two schools were conducted in 2007.

In these schools, undocumented children learn the Korean language and "academic" subjects with a special class teacher; they study physical education, art, and music in regular classes with Korean classmates. The special class has multiple functions. First, through implementing specific instructional strategies, the class provides foreign students who are learning the Korean language with educational support. Second, it provides a sense of security for students as it functions as a place that protects undocumented children from legal problems. Third, it functions in a systematic way to recruit undocumented children who are left out of school to ensure educational opportunities. However, in these schools most of the Korean students are from low-income families; this privilege given to undocumented children causes "reverse discrimination." Mr. Gi, one of the teacher interviewees, said:

> In our school, students, parents, and teachers often feel reverse discrimination. I understand them because I also did about the special supports for children of undocumented foreign workers before I have these children as my students in my class. The children of undocumented foreign workers go to school without paying tax and receive free lunch and free trips (because of the special financial support provided by the office of education). But many Korean children can not although they are poor and skip meals and cannot take a school excursion because they have no money.

Another key challenge that the schools experience is the language issue. Language issues are also problems in Hong Kong, but the issues differ: since most undocumented children were born in their home country but have been living in Korea for years, they speak in their first language but are not able to read and write in their language. In addition, children who are left out of school have no opportunity to learn Korean. Ms. Song, another teacher, discussed three Pakistanis who wanted to enter the school but did not because the school is far from their homes:

> [To avoid a crackdown on their undocumented status] they kept out of sight during the day but went on the street with Pakistani friends at night. They speak Pakistani but cannot read and write.

She was concerned about the loss of their first language. She indicated it was beyond the school's capacity to teach native languages to twelve foreign students from Mongolia, India, Japan, China, Sri Lanka, Uzbekistan, and Russia.

Ms. Song's school invites foreign cultural exchange volunteers and Korean volunteer interpreters to introduce diverse cultures and languages to Korean students and foreign students. This project is intended to improve students' cultural understanding and tolerance, and mutual respect (Banks, 1990), but Ms. Song felt there is a limit to teaching languages and cultures in school; she indicated she expected parents to teach their children home languages and cultures. Similar issues have been addressed by multicultural theorists who call for preservation of heritage languages and cultures (e.g., Cummins, 1989). In contrast to Ms. Song, however, these theorists indicate that schools must be the place where language and culture are taught and they must be embedded in core curriculum.

## Dilemma between Policy and Practice in Undocumented Children's School Education

Government policy allows undocumented children to receive a public education and protects their education from insecure legal status by banning police from chasing them near school zones. However, in practice, there are serious problems in their education due to their legal status. For example, due to their parents' undocumented status, undocumented children can not be officially enrolled in regular public schools except in the two schools with the special class. Therefore, their educational opportunities are restricted. Ms. Song, a special class teacher, said:

> I heard from teachers in other schools in which undocumented children are not officially enrolled that they often worry about the safety issues of their undocumented children so they ask those children not to join some outside school activities to have them be protected from some insecure legal issues.

There are also serious obstacles preventing undocumented children from going to middle school. To enroll in middle schools, students must prove they spent six years in elementary school either in their own country or in South Korea. However, many undocumented children who have not attended schools for a long time can not meet this attendance requirement. Ms. Song said:

> A few of my students, who can show documentary evidence that the total years they attend elementary schools both in their own country and in South Korea are 6 years, will be able to go to the middle school. However, Gil-dong, who had been left out of school for a long period and then entered this class and is over-aged, has only a 6 month school education period. So he can not go on to middle school. I asked to solve this problem. I heard that this entrance problem is being discussed at the local office of education and at the Ministry of Education.

This is a complex problem; policy and practice are in conflict. Allowing undocumented children who have not received an elementary education to go to middle school could be viewed by some as reverse discrimination. On the other hand, denying them entry to middle school causes them to be left out of school education again. Teachers who teach undocumented children recognize this dilemma. Ms. Song said:

> There were many children who were not able to be promoted to middle school last year. . . . I heard that six students of the other school did not go on to middle schools and they are working at a car wash without documents.

The policies and practices for undocumented children in South Korea incorporate a key multicultural perspective: educational equity aimed at equal educational opportunities for minority groups (Banks, 2006). When the policies are interpreted into school practices, however, practice and policy are in conflict in spite of the same perspective. As discussed above, although government policy ensures basic educational rights for undocumented children, in practice, their education activities and entrance to middle school are restricted due to their insecure legal status, and they experience educational inequity. This dilemma will not be easily resolved; change must involve more than government decrees, it must involve the total educational and social environment (Nieto and Bode, 2008). Much work has been done in the United States and other countries addressing similar issues. In the following section we briefly address the need for multicultural education in South Korea and other Asian countries.

# CONCLUSION: A CRITICAL NEED FOR MULTICULTURAL
# EDUCATION IN THE GLOBALIZATION AGE

Through an examination of official minority language and cultural policies in mainland China, and policies, practices, and teacher responses in Hong Kong and South Korea, we found that the discrepancy between the stated intention of government policies, and the experiences of students in schools and their educational outcomes, is significant in the three areas. While each region has different issues and concerns, and different policies and practices, overall this discrepancy has a negative impact on minority students: home language and culture loss, identity confusion or loss, high drop-out rate, and little chance of higher education.

Mainland China, Hong Kong, and South Korea demonstrate similarities in dealing with minorities. Officially they claim that minority cultures and languages are respected and preserved, and language rights and political rights are guaranteed. In Hong Kong these rights are discussed as educational rights; in South Korea they are discussed as human rights; in mainland China as constitutional rights. In practice, however, large gaps were found; minority students' language and culture were seldom infused in their school life. Instead, unequally distributed wealth, and social and educational resources, have contributed to making minority students' educational attainment and life chances more difficult than ever. This is demonstrated in the three areas by minority students' high drop-out rate and little opportunity of receiving higher education. The poverty of minority groups forms a striking contrast to the fast-growing economies of the three regions in the process of globalization. Globalization should not mean that minority students' home language and culture should be lost, that minority students have no democratic rights, and that minority students should not be heard (Stromquist and Monkman, 2000). Rather, minority students should have the right to enjoy the fruits of democracy and globalization, the right to retain their languages and cultures, and basic human rights.

In the globalization age, the fast-growing economy and trade in Asian countries such as China and South Korea should not overshadow the issues of political democracy, human rights abuse, educational inequality, and minority students' rights. Globalization requires "tolerance for diversity and individual choice" (Walters, 1995, p. 3) and opens a space for educators and researchers to examine these issues, to make minority students' voices heard, and to guarantee democracy and equal rights to all students. Based on our research and reviews of existing literature, it is our contention that to address issues related to minorities and globalization discussed in this chapter, there is a critical need for multicultural education in Asia because multicultural education has shared concerns with issues in the globalization age. While not a panacea, applying established theories of multicultural education derived from the United States and other countries to the Asian context will be beneficial in addressing issues of educational inequity for minority students. As Gay (1992) contends, the major goals of multicultural education apply in all settings, although practices should be appropriately contextualized. Along with the need for multicultural education and the need for specific contextually grounded practices, there is a corresponding need for research that systematically and deeply engages these issues.

With this premise, we believe that many well-developed and well-researched multicultural education principles could be infused in Asian teacher education, school policies, and teacher practices, which will meet the needs of these three regions in Asia in the globalization age. As a starting point, Banks's (2006) five dimensions of multicultural education could be used as a guideline for policymakers, school administrators, and teachers to address Asian issues regarding minority students: (1) content integration (include minority perspectives as well as minority knowledge and languages in curriculum and textbooks); (2) knowledge construction process (infuse a systematic critique of the sources of knowledge and perspectives used into teaching and learning); (3) equity pedagogy (modify teaching to include strategies that will promote diverse student success); (4) prejudice reduction (utilize multicultural textbooks, teaching strategies, and cooperative learning to enable positive intergroup interactions and positive racial attitudes among students); and (5) an empowering school culture and social structure (restructure schools so that minority students experience educational equality and cultural empowerment). These principles could provide an overall framework to develop multicultural education plans in Asia.

Specifically, there is a need for practices such as culturally relevant pedagogy (Ladson-Billings, 1994), pedagogy that brings in the experiences of minority students and focuses on their specific learning styles. There is also a need for culturally responsive teaching (Gay, 2000), teaching that is culturally compatible and congruent with minority students' home cultures and languages. These two approaches have been well-researched and have demonstrated success in working with a variety of minority students in the United States, and could be adapted to the Asian context. These strategies could be used to develop the instructional basis for teacher education programs for preservice teachers working with minority students.

The work of Nieto (Nieto and Bode, 2008) would also provide a useful guide for policymakers and practitioners willing to develop multicultural education in their districts, schools, and classrooms. Nieto sees multicultural education as "a process of comprehensive school reform and basic education for all students" (Nieto, 1992, p. 208). Nieto (1992) sees the process as one that challenges and rejects all forms of discrimination, such as racism in schools and society, while accepting and affirming the pluralism that students and teachers represent in ethnicity, race, language, religion, socioeconomic status, and gender. She argues that the process of multicultural education should permeate the curriculum and instructional strategies such as textbooks and policies used in schools, as well as interactions among teachers, students, and parents.

Nieto's (Nieto and Bode, 2008) comprehensive view of multicultural education, Banks's (2007) key dimensions of multicultural education, and Ladson-Billings's (1994) and Gay's (2000) teaching and instructional strategies for diverse students provide the outline of a multicultural education policy and plan for Asia. Multicultural education, long established in the United States and elsewhere is well-researched, with a proven record of effecting change. Growing interest in multicultural education in mainland China, Hong Kong, and South Korea holds promise as a solution for urgent problems regarding educational equity for minority students in Asia in an increasingly globalized world.

## NOTE

1. This research is based on a project funded by the Hong Kong Institute of Education. The project is described in-depth in Phillion, 2008.

## REFERENCES

Apple, M. W., and Christian-Smith, L. K. (1991). The politics of the textbook. In M. W. Apple and L. K. Christian-Smith (Eds.), *The politics of the textbook* (pp. 1–21). New York: Routledge.

ATV News and Public Affairs (2006, December). *Newsline—Racism in Hong Kong.* Retrieved February 14, 2007, from edvideo.ied.edu.hk/VVM_2summary2.php?callno2titleid=fb15591 001_57&prog=&sid=innopac&searchlang=ENG&list=b15941231.

Banks, J. A. (1990). Citizenship education for a pluralistic democratic society. *The Social Studies, 81*, 210–14.

Banks, J. A. (2006). Democracy, diversity, and social justice: Educating citizens for the public interest in a global age. In G. Ladson-Billings and W. F. Tale (Eds.), *Education research in the public interest* (pp. 141–57). New York: Teachers College.

Banks, J. A. (2007). Approaches to multicultural curriculum reform. In J. A. Banks and C. A. M. Banks (Eds.), *Multicultural education: Issues and perspectives* (sixth ed.) (pp. 247–69). Hoboken, NJ: John Wiley and Sons.

Bigelow, B., and B. Peterson. (2002). *Rethinking globalization: Teaching for justice in an unjust world.* Milwaukee: Rethinking Schools.

Bradley, D. (2001). Language policy for the Yi. In S. Harrell (Ed.), *Perspectives on the Yi of Southwest China* (pp. 194–98). Berkeley: University of California Press.

Chong, S. C. (2004). *A critical perspective of culturally diverse children in the changing school population in Hong Kong.* Unpublished doctoral dissertation, University of Toronto.

Cochran-Smith, M. (2000). Blind vision: Unlearning racism in teacher education. *Harvard Educational Review, 70*(2), 157–90.

Constitution of the People's Republic of China. (1982). Retrieved January 13, 2008, from english.people.com.cn/constitution/constitution.html.

Cummins, J. (1989). *Empowering minority students.* Sacramento: California Association for Bilingual Education.

Dai, Q., and Dong, Y. (2001). The historical evolution of bilingual education for China's ethnic minorities. *Chinese Education & Society, 34*(2), 7–47.

Delpit, L. (1995). *Other people's children: Cultural conflicts in the classroom.* New York: The New Press.

Development and Cultural Destruction in Tibet. (1995). Retrieved January 2, 2007, from www .tibet.org/Why/cultdestruct.html.

Du, Y., Gregory, R., and Meng, X. (2006). *Impact of the guest worker system on poverty and wellbeing of migrant workers in urban China.* Retrieved October 9, 2006, from www.iza .org/conference_files/worldb2006/meng_x1729.pdf.

Education and Manpower Bureau. (2005). *Survey on children from the mainland newly admitted to schools, October 2003–September 2004.* Hong Kong: Education and Manpower Bureau.

Gay, G. (1992). The state of multicultural education in the United States. In K. A. Moodley (Ed.), *Beyond multicultural education: International perspectives* (pp. 41–65). Calgary, Alberta: Detselig Enterprises.

Gay, G. (2000). *Culturally responsive teaching: Theory, research, and practice.* New York: Teachers College Press.

Gladney, D. C. (1999). Making Muslims in China: Education, Islamicization and representation. In G. A. Postiglione (Ed.), *China's national minority education: Culture, schooling, and development* (pp. 55–94). New York: Routledge Falmer.

Gladney, D. C. (2004). *Dislocating China: Reflections on Muslims, minorities, and other subaltern subjects.* Chicago: University of Chicago Press.

Hansen, M. H. (1999). Teaching backwardness of equality: Chinese state education among the Tai in Sipsong Pana. In G. A. Postiglione (Ed.), *China's national minority education: Culture, schooling, and development* (pp. 243–80). New York: Falmer Press.

He, B. (2005). Minority rights with Chinese characteristics. In W. Kymlicka and B. He (Eds.), *Multiculturalism in Asia* (pp. 56–79). Oxford: Oxford University Press.

Home Affairs Bureau. (2006). *Race Discrimination Bill.* Retrieved February 19, 2008, from www.hab.gov.hk/file_manager/en/documents/policy_responsibilities/the_rights_of_the_ individuals/race/RaceDiscriminationBill_e.pdf.

Home Affairs Department and Immigration Department. (2006). *Statistics on the new arrivals from the Mainland (Third Quarter of 2005).* Retrieved January 24, 2006, from www.had. gov.hk/file_manager/en/documents/about_us/organization/responsibilities/report_2005q3 .pdf.

Korean Ministry of Education and Human Resources Development. (2006a). *The announcement of educational supports for the children from multicultural families.* Retrieved May 1, 2006, from news.naver.com/news/read.php?mode=LSD&office_id=098&article_ id=0000131084&section_id=117&menu_id=117.

Korean Ministry of Education and Human Resources Development. (2006b). *Educational Support for Children from Multi-cultural Backgrounds.* Retrieved June 14, 2006, from english .moe.go.kr/main.jsp?idx=030101&brd_mainno=253&mode=v.

Korean Ministry of Education and Human Resources Development. (2006c). *The children of undocumented workers can go to school without fear.* Retrieved July 1, 2006, from news. naver.com/news/read.php?mode=LSD&office_id=165&article_id=0000000071&section_ id=117&menu_id=117.

Korean National Statistical Office. (2006). *Statistics on international marriage.* Retrieved July 20, 2006, from kosis.nso.go.kr.

Ladson-Billings, G. (1994). *The dreamkeepers: Successful teachers of African American children.* San Francisco: Jossey-Bass.

Ladson-Billings, G., and Tate, W. (Eds.). (2006). *Education research in the public interest: Social justice, action, and policy.* New York: Teachers College Press.

Mackerras, C. (1994). China's minorities: Integration and modernization in the twentieth *century.* Hong Kong: Oxford University Press.

National Bureau of Statistics. (2004). *Zhongguo tongji nianjian 2004* [China statistical yearbook 2004]. Beijing: China Statistics Press.

Nelson, K. (2005). *Language policies and minority resistance in China.* Retrieved November 7, 2007, from www.tc.edu/students/sie/LCEjr05/pdfs/Nelson.pdf.

Nieto, S. (1992). *Affirming diversity: The sociopolitical context of multicultural education.* New York: Longman.

Nieto, S., and Bode, P. (2008). *Affirming diversity: The sociopolitical context of multicultural education* (fifth ed.). Boston: Allyn and Bacon.

Nima, B. (2001). Problems related to bilingual education in Tibet. *Chinese Education and Society, 34*(2), 91–102.

Phillion, J. (2008). Multicultural and cross-cultural narrative inquiry into understanding immigrant students' educational experience in Hong Kong. *Compare: A Journal of Comparative Education, 38* (3), 281–93.

Postiglione, G. A. (1992). The implications of modernization for the education of China's national minorities. In R. Hayhoe (Ed.), *Education and modernization: The Chinese experience* (pp. 307–36). Oxford: Pergamon.

Respect for minority culture. (2006). In *Si xiang pin de* [Moral education] (no. 7) (pp. 15–17). Hefei, Anhui, China: Anhui Educational Publishing House.

Sleeter, C. (2001). Epistemological diversity in research on preservice teachers' preparation for historically underserved children. *Review of Research in Education, 25,* 209–50. Washington, DC: American Educational Research Association.

Sleeter, C. E., and Grant, C. (1991). Race, class, gender and disability in current textbooks. In M. W. Apple and L. K. Christian-Smith (Eds.), *The politics of the textbook* (pp. 78–110). New York: Routledge.

Smith, L. T. (1999). *Decolonizing Methodologies: Research and Indigenous Peoples.* New York: St. Martin's.

Solinger, D. J. (1999). Human rights issues in China internal migration: Insights from comparisons with Germany and Japan. In O. R. Bauer and D. A. Bell (Eds.), *The East Asian challenge for human rights* (pp. 285–312). New York: Cambridge University Press.

Stites, R. (1999). Writing cultural boundaries: National minority language policy, literacy planning, and bilingual education. In G. A. Postiglione (Ed.), *China's national minority education: Culture, schooling, and development* (pp. 95–130). New York: RoutledgeFalmer.

Stromquist, N. P., and Monkman, K. (2000). Defining globalization and assessing its implications on knowledge and education. In N. P. Stromquist and K. Monkman (Eds.), *Globalization and education: Integration and contestation across cultures* (pp. 3–25). Lanham, MD: Rowman & Littlefield.

U.S. State Department. (2008). China is abusing human rights. In J. Langwith (Ed.), *Human rights* (pp. 88–100). Detroit: Thomson Gale.

Veek, G., C. W. Pannell, C. J. Smith, and Y. Huang. (2007). *China's geography: Globalization and the dynamics of political, economic, and social change.* Lanham, MD: Rowman & Littlefield.

Walters, M. (1995). *Globalization.* London: Routledge.

Wang, Y. (in press). Whose knowledge is valued? A critical study of knowledge in elementary school textbooks in China. *Transnational Curriculum Inquiry.*

Yuen, Y. M. (2002). Education for new arrivals and multicultural teacher education in Hong Kong. *New Horizon in Education, 45,* 12–21.

Zhou, M. (1999). The official national language and language attitudes of three ethnic minority groups in China. *Language Problems and Language Planning, 23*(2), 157–74.

Zhou, M. (2004). Minority language policy in China: Equality in theory and inequality in practice. In M. Zhou and H. Sun (Eds.), *Language policy in the People's Republic of China: Theory and practice since 1949* (pp. 71–95). Boston: Kluwer.

Zuo, X. (2007). China's policy towards minority languages in a globalizing age. *Transnational Curriculum Inquiry, 4*(1), 80–91. Retrieved November 5, 2007, from nitinat.library.ubc.ca/ojs/index.php/tci.

## Chapter Fourteen

# Schooling Minorities: An Examination of Dowa and *Minzokugakkyu* Educational Models in Japan

## Ruth Ahn

"Obachan Nanijin? Watashiwa Kankokujin!
(What nationality are you, ma'am? I'm Korean!)"

> From my childhood memory when I was five years old.

## THE MINORITY EXPERIENCE

My name was Ohara Megumi. In my distant memory, I remember writing "Ohara" on my notebooks and textbooks in early grades. Before attending school, I remember proudly telling others about my Korean heritage, just as my parents taught me at home. My parents were originally from Taegoo, South Korea, and they migrated to Japan in 1939. After I started attending school, however, my sense of pride in being Korean disappeared. A life-changing event happened when I started third grade and my father decided to change our last name from our Japanese name "Ohara" to our Korean name "Ahn." My father wanted us to take pride in our Korean heritage and live openly as Koreans in Japan. In the late 1960s and early 1970s, this was considered quite daring, since most, if not all, Koreans hid their ethnicity for fear of discrimination.

Switching our last name from "Ohara" to "Ahn" took a toll on the lives of my father's four children. My three siblings and I began to experience open discrimination with verbal and sometimes physical attacks by Japanese schoolmates. My older sister, who excelled in both academics and sports, shared her experience with discrimination from her fourth grade teacher when her last name was switched to Korean. She recalled that her teacher encouraged and promoted another female student to be a leader of the class when my sister was equally or more capable. Even though the teacher never verbally told my sister why she was not selected for a leadership position, she still remembers her feelings of being discriminated against because of her Korean last name. Her negative experience in fourth grade thus resulted in lower grades and decreased her sense of self-efficacy. During her fifth and sixth grades, she met a teacher who was understanding of her ethnicity and encouraged her to do well in class. Even after thirty-five years, my sister still smiles and gets excited about what her fifth and sixth grade teachers did, giving her many large star stickers that said "Excellent!" or "Good job!" on her homework and tests, which motivated her to rise to the top of her class. This resulted in her being selected as the class president the following year in seventh grade and ranking within the top fifteen in the entire junior high school.

My younger brother also encountered discrimination when he was in fourth grade. He had a fight because his classmates teased him and called him "Chosenjin," a malicious and derogatory term for Koreans in Japan. My mother recalls that when my brother returned home from school that day his face was full of dirt and stains of tears and sweat. She asked him what happened, and he told her, as he wiped his tears, that he fought with his classmates who picked on his Korean last name.

I grew up feeling fearful and guilty about my identity as a Korean in Japan. One day after school in fifth grade, I visited a classmate's home. Her mother, not knowing that I was Korean, began telling her daughter not to associate with Koreans since they are "scary people and not to be trusted." I froze and could not move. At the same time, however, I felt a sense of relief knowing that they did not recognize I was Korean. This same feeling continued into junior high school when my family moved from Osaka to Tokyo. We continued to use our Korean last name "Ahn," and I was always afraid that my classmates or teachers would know that I was Korean. Even at the slightest mention of things Korean, I would panic, unsure if such comments were aimed at me. For example, every time a male classmate would say "Soul (music) is cool," I would freeze at the word "soul," which sounded identical to Korea's capital "Seoul." Another male classmate who knew I was Korean would always kick the desk and chairs at me, hurling insults like "Chosenjin!" My fear and guilt about being Korean continued even after immigrating to the United States in 1978.

Adult Koreans in Japan generally experience limited access to resources. Except for very few, the Koreans that I knew as a child were all poor and uneducated. Some tried to naturalize as Japanese, but the process was often very difficult and scrutinizing, and even one traffic ticket would prevent them from becoming a citizen. One of the brightest Korean youths that my relatives frequently talked about was my older cousin who advanced to a famous university in Nagoya and majored in business. Upon graduation, however, unlike his Japanese classmates who were hired by large Japanese corporations, my cousin could not find attractive employment because he was Korean. After many months, he finally found a job at a small hotel in Nagoya as a front desk clerk. Subsequently, he switched jobs multiple times, going from one small company to another. The last time I heard he was a taxi driver getting ready to retire.

## JAPAN: A MULTICULTURAL SOCIETY

While Japan is widely believed by many to be a homogeneous country with one language and one culture, Weiner (1997) notes that there are approximately three million minorities in Japan. They include: (a) the Ainu: the indigenous people of northern Japan; (b) the Buraku: the social outcasts that originated in the 1700s; (c) the Chinese: the only minority that is considered a "model" and successful; (d) the Okinawans/Ryukyuans: the proud people of the vanished Ryukyu kingdom; and (e) Koreans:

the largest ethnic minority in Japan, to name a few (Weiner, 1997). In addition, since the late 1970s, an influx of "newcomers" started to immigrate into Japan for various social, economic, and political reasons (Shimizu and Shimizu, 2001). Beginning with women workers from the Philippines and Thailand, these newcomers include Indo-China refugees from Vietnam, Cambodia, and Laos, returnees from northeastern China, and business people from the United States and Europe. Furthermore, from the late 1980s, illegal workers from South Asia, the Middle East, the Nikkeijin from Latin America, and those who ended up staying in Japan due to marrying Japanese spouses have added to the population of newcomers in Japan (Shimizu and Shimizu, 2001).

## EDUCATING JAPAN'S MINORITIES: THE BURAKU AND KOREAN CASES

Due to the significant numbers of Japan's old and new minorities, schools are faced with similar problems as the United States in their attempts to educate racial and ethnic minorities who experience social, economic, and academic discrimination. Perhaps, the two most stigmatized and largest minority groups in Japan are Buraku and Koreans. By Koreans, I am referring to both North and South Koreans living in Japan. It is the ethnicity as Korean, rather than the political ideology of North versus South Korea that brings about discrimination in Japan. Most Koreans have similar physical features to Japanese, and they can often pass as such if they change their names and suppress their accents. Similarly, it is nearly impossible to identify Buraku from the majority Japanese population based on their physical features or speech patterns since Buraku are ethnically Japanese. Therefore, Buraku and Koreans are considered Japan's "invisible" and "untouchable" minorities, since many of them have successfully assimilated into Japanese society. Not surprisingly, many of these students have lower academic performance than majority Japanese students. For example, Rohlen (1981) shows the discrepancy in the rate of advancing to high school between minority students and Japanese students. In Hyogo in the western region of Japan, 88.8 percent and 88.2 percent of the Buraku and Korean junior high school students respectively entered high school; while 93.7 percent of Japanese students entered high school. (High school education is not compulsory in Japan.) The gap widens for Buraku and Korean high school students advancing to higher education: 32.1 percent and 26.3 percent of Buraku and Korean high school students respectively advanced to higher education, compared to 45.8 percent prefecture-wide [statewide] (Rohlen, 1981). Similarly, in Osaka, 81.6 percent of Buraku students and 76.5 percent of Korean students advanced to high school compared to 90.7 percent for the total junior high school students in 2001 (Osakafu Jinken Kyoiku Kenkyu Kyogikai, 2002).

In addition, in Kyoto adjacent to Osaka, a study of Korean students conducted by the Kyoto City Board of Education found that while 89.7 percent of Korean students entered high school in 1990, 95.3 percent of the total junior high school students in Kyoto City entered high school (Kyotoshi Kyooiku Iinkai, 1992). It is important to remember that these numbers only reflect those students who were identified by the local city governments based on voluntary responses. Thus, considering minorities' inclination to hide their ethnic origin (Kim, 2005; Kyo, 1990; Nabeshima, 2003), the academic achievement discrepancies are possibly wider.

Similarly, an examination of the academic achievement of U.S. students based on race and ethnicity reveals an alarming lack of educational achievement among underrepresented students in U.S. schools. For example, according to 2007 reading assessment data from the National Association for Educational Progress (NAEP), 42 percent of white fourth-graders scored at or above the proficient level, whereas only 14 percent of African Americans, 17 percent of Hispanics, and 20 percent of Native American students scored at the same level (NCES, 2007b). In addition, the NAEP mathematics measure showed similar results: 51 percent of white fourth-graders scored at or above the proficient level, but only 15 percent of African Americans, 22 percent of Hispanics, and 26 percent of Native American students reached such level (NCES, 2007a). Despite some gains in 2007 from 2005 across most racial and ethnic groups, the clear academic disparity among these students has been consistent since 1971 with some year-to-year fluctuations. Overall, these findings suggest that there is low school achievement across these three racial and ethnic groups and in the broader U.S. school population, where although white students generally receive a better quality education than minority students, only 42 percent of them were proficient in reading and 51 percent in math. The achievement challenges are even more despairing for minority students because they commonly receive the lowest quality education. Thus, the academic achievement difference between the white majority and minority students is evident in the United States and can be understood largely as a structural inequality issue.

In the Japanese scenario, and in response to its achievement problems and concerns with social and cultural exclusion of minority students, several intervention programs are implemented. Concepts such as culturally relevant and culturally responsive instruction have become a common part of the broader multicultural education vocabulary, all in an attempt to expand educational opportunities to all citizens. In the following sections, I describe the Dowa and *Minzokugakkyu* educational models that aim to promote Buraku and Korean students' schooling experiences in Japan. The social context of this work is supported by observations, interviews, and interactions with administrators, teachers, students, and community members. Finally, I discuss implications for the Dowa and *Minzokugakkyu* educational models in a global context.


## METHOD

Being born and raised in Japan as a third-generation Korean Japanese, I have witnessed and experienced countless injustices against Koreans and other minorities in Japan. Revisiting Japan more than three decades later for my dissertation project in 2006, with a follow-up visit in 2007, I hoped to illustrate minority student experiences in Japan from the perspective of a Korean Japanese and now as a Korean American. How might minority student experiences in Japan differ from my experiences in the 1970s? I chose to visit two junior high schools that have high Buraku and high Korean populations, characterized by special programs called *Dowa Kyoiku* or Dowa education and *Minzokugakkyu* respectively. These programs are typically offered in schools that have a high minority population and were not available in my school when I was a child.

I conducted interviews and observations during the period of February of 2006 and May and June of 2007 in Osaka in western Japan. At Shiki Junior High School,[1] which is well known in Japan for its innovative Dowa education program, nearly 50 percent of their student population is of Buraku origin. Similarly, more than 50 percent of the student population has Korean heritage at Nishi Junior High School. These two junior high schools have consistently experienced and struggled with low academic performance and classroom behavioral issues, appropriately expressed by their teachers as the *shindoi* syndrome. While no direct translation is available for *shindoi*, its closest meaning would be "hard" or "struggling." During the entire time I was there, both schools continued to describe their experiences as *shindoi* schools, *shindoi* students, *shindoi* class, and so forth. Despite their situations, the administrators, teachers, and students all welcomed me warmly and curiously, giving me opportunities to interact with them and speaking to the students about my background as a Korean-Japanese-American, living in the United States.

My primary questions when I visited the sites were: What are the Korean and Buraku students' academic and social experiences in their schools and how do the schools provide support for these students to meet their academic and social needs? Based on documents, observations, and interviews, I will portray the two educational models and the students' experiences in each context.

## THE BURAKU AND DOWA EDUCATION

Buraku people or Burakumin are ethnically Japanese but historically have been marginalized in the Japanese society due to their lineage. Many believe that Buraku originated in the Tokugawa era, dated between 1603 and 1868, but in recent years, some research suggests that they can be traced back as early as the eleventh century (Uesugi, 1990). The Tokugawa government created four social classes: samurai, peasant, artisans, and merchants. However, in order to satisfy the peasants, artisans, and merchants, the government further created a lower group called Eta-Hinin. They were regarded as "untouchables" or "polluting" because of their assigned roles as animal slaughterers, sewage removers, and prison guards (Ogbu, 1978; Shimahara, 1991; Tokyo Shoseki, 1996). The influences of Buddhism and Shintoism, which viewed killing animals or handling their carcasses as "polluting" (Ogbu, 1978; Shimahara, 1991), contributed to the stigmatized status of the Buraku today. Ogbu (1978) adds that they rank lower than the Koreans who are immigrant minorities in Japan. According to Alldritt (2000), there are 4,603 Buraku districts with a total population of 1,166,733 in 1987. However, considering that these figures only come from the designated areas for Buraku people, actual figures may exceed three million Burakus in all of Japan.

In an effort to address the historical and social problems that have resulted in economic hardships and academic underachievement among Burakus, the Japanese national government established Dowa education as a part of their Dowa policies from 1969 to 2002 (Hawkins, 1983). This is largely due to the work of the Buraku Liberation League (BLL), which is a powerful community organization for Burakus and, by extension, for all people including the poor, physically disabled, minorities, and foreigners (Hawkins, 1983). According to Hawkins (1983), there are general purposes of Dowa education: (1) to improve the overall educational environment through financial subsidies; (2) to introduce educational programs to increase the social consciousness of both Buraku and the general population; and (3) to improve the occupational opportunities for Buraku in general (p. 217). Based on these purposes, Dowa education's two primary foci are to teach human rights to all students and to provide equal access to Buraku students, such as reducing class size and providing study materials, extra teachers, and scholarship.

Buraku community intervention in school affairs has been shown to contribute greatly to the fundamental transformation of school practices. While I was observing different classes at Shiki Junior High School, I noticed that the class size was considerably smaller than Nishi Junior High School. For example, at Shiki High School, eighth and ninth grade math classes I visited had twenty-five and twenty-one students respectively, whereas there were thirty-three and thirty-seven students in eighth and ninth grade math classes at Nishi Junior High School. In addition, one of the most remarkable teaching practices I witnessed the entire time I was at Shiki Junior High School was the active involvement of the teachers. Unlike the United States, teachers in Japan have a varied teaching schedule Monday through Friday. Many teachers at Shiki Junior High School teach three classes a day on the average, in addition to providing student guidance, overseeing clubs after school, and attending faculty meetings, workshops, and other community events, which means that many of them leave work after 8 o'clock every night. Despite the teachers' overwhelming workload, when they are not teaching, they identify the classes and students in need and go into other teachers' classrooms, jumping in to provide support for struggling students and teachers. Oftentimes I saw teachers during their nonteaching periods poking their heads through windows and doors, and providing support to each other. On one occasion, I saw team teaching in which two math teachers were teaching together in the same classroom. When one teaches, the other roams the classroom to ensure student understanding. I witnessed as many as three teachers in one classroom helping to support student learning. When I asked Mr. Tada, who is in charge of the Human Rights Education at the school, whether the teachers are required to do this, he said no. He explained that these teachers voluntarily jump in to support teaching because they love their school and their *shindoi* students, many of whom have Buraku backgrounds. It is the teachers' commitment to Dowa education that drives them to work to this extent.

In addition to observing their daily teaching, I was invited to take a field trip to a Buraku Liberation League (BLL) community center with a class of seventh graders. The BLL community center provides Buraku students with a place where they can receive social support and help with their academics. It also provides training in issues of human rights. I accompanied the students to interview Mr. Ikeda, who is a graduate of Shiki Junior High School and now works as a community organizer. Mr. Ikeda works at the community center, which is provided as a place for those Buraku students who wish to learn and to support human rights. While the students took notes, Mr. Ikeda shared his own story of transformation. He used to fail his tests in junior high school, but after advancing to high school he was able to improve his academic achievement because of the support he received from BLL. In this particular area of Osaka, about three to four decades ago (1960s–1970s), people used to throw stones at the Buraku people. When they went to a public bathhouse, they were told to leave. Grocery storeowners used baskets to receive payments for purchases from Buraku people whom they considered filthy. Mr. Ikeda continued that because of Buraku people's struggles with discrimination and the parents' desire for their children to succeed academically, the community center was created to support children through academic and social programs. He explained that he himself came to the center twice a week after school to study academic subjects and once a week to study about human rights. He added that the community centers still provide similar activities. Mr. Ikeda concluded his story by encouraging all of the students, Buraku and non-Buraku alike, to participate in the center's programs. The seventh graders then asked questions about Mr. Ikeda's work and human rights, and they wrote about this experience once they returned to their school.

In addition to these small-scale fieldtrips to nearby community centers, the students take longer field trips. For example, at Shiki Junior High School, they take an annual field trip to Nara, the birthplace of the BLL. Mr. Tada described a one-night and two-day field trip involving eighth graders where they interview community members who are largely of Buraku origin. The students also take notes based on what they see and hear. At night, they share with their teachers and classmates their findings, personal feelings, and experiences with discrimination and human rights. Mr. Tada noted that this is one of the most powerful experiences for his students because Buraku and non-Buraku alike all come together to support each other. Oftentimes the sharing time extends for hours, as they listen to testimony after testimony about each other's pains and they develop deeper understandings and relationships with each other. After students go back to school, they prepare a journal about what they learned from their experience.

Dowa education is thus closely connected with the Buraku community and it aims to provide academic, social, and cultural support, which is vital to self-growth and social awareness. Hearing the ancestral voices of Buraku community members, recounting their experiences and struggles for human rights is a powerful component of Dowa education. In addition, taking fieldtrips to historical and community sites strengthens Dowa education and reaches out to both Buraku and non-Buraku students, which is one of the primary purposes of Dowa education.

## KOREANS AND *MINZOKUGAKKYU*

Among the many Koreans spread across the Diaspora, such as those in Kazakhstan and Yanbian in northeastern China, Koreans in Japan make up one of the largest Korean communities outside Korea: Over 610,000 ethnic Koreans are living in Japan today, an equivalent of 32 percent of all foreigners registered in Japan, which makes Koreans the largest ethnic minority in the country (Taminzoku Kyoosei Jinken Kenkyuu Shuukai Jikkoo Iinkai, 2004). This figure includes diverse groups of Koreans that currently live in Japan: descendants of those Koreans who were solicited or forced to migrate from Korea; those who have been in Japan for multiple generations and those that have recently arrived from Korea by business or academic route on a temporarily basis; and others who found venues to enter Japan, some of whom married to Japanese or Koreans (Harajiri, 1998).

Since their first arrival in the early 1900s, Koreans in Japan have been discriminated against in many areas including education, employment, marriage, and legal rights (Hicks, 1997; Kirihata, 2000; Lee and De Vos, 1981; Osakashi Shiminkyoku Jinkenbu Kikaku Suishinka, 2005; Tanaka, 2004). At that time, most Koreans who chose to migrate to Japan were poor farmers without education, thus they suffered from extreme poverty under the Japanese regime. During the period of 1939 and 1945, large influxes of Koreans were involuntarily brought to Japan to help address a shortage of labor (Lee and De Vos, 1981). The high illiteracy rate among Korean adults and their children was not surprising considering their low socioeconomic status and a lack of organized policy to educate Korean children by the Japanese government. Today, many Koreans in Japan have blue-collar jobs and very few of them have professions as lawyers, professors, and teachers, due to both open and hidden employment discrimination practices (Harajiri, 1989; Hicks, 1997; Kim, 1999; Kirihata, 2000; Tanaka, 2004). This history of discrimination affects the self-esteem of young Korean students in Japan in many ways, including their academic achievement (Kanai, 2004; Kirihata, 2000; Rohlen, 1981).

For those Korean children attending Japanese public schools,[2] one of the schools' efforts to meet the educational needs of Koreans is providing cultural support, commonly known as *Minzokugakkyu*, which literally means "ethnic class." Many elementary and junior high schools in Osaka and its surrounding vicinities with high percentages of Korean students, offer *Minzokugakkyu*. According to Seka, the director of the Osaka Foreigners Education Consortium, there are currently over two hundred *Minzokugakkyus* in elementary and junior high schools in Osaka, 105 of which are located within Osaka City. To establish and keep these programs going, schools work closely with the Korean community groups. One Korean parent, Mrs. Park, who is involved in the Parent Teacher Association (PTA) at her child's school, shared how the *Mindan* has played a supportive role in founding a special committee for Korean and other minority students in a junior high school. The *Mindan*, the Korean Resident Association in Japan, is a political community organization established in 1946 to protect the rights of Koreans in Japan, among some of their goals (Lee and De Vos, 1981). Mrs. Park described its influence in the community this way:

> To tell you the truth, there was a committee that a Korean parent, who was a member of the Foreigner Education Committee, was serving in a junior high school. Actually I have been serving there for several years, and I have been watching their activities. You know the organization for Koreans called the *Mindan*, right? It's kind of funny that we borrowed their power, but when that committee was founded, I heard, of course, [the *Mindan*] exercised a lot of influence. I heard the committee has a long history, well, how many decades did they say? And that committee has been continuing for a long time. But in order to continue functioning, of course they need a budget and it comes from the Board of Education all the time. Although it is a limited amount, I heard that we Korean parents have been trying hard not to lose it. That [kind of effort] has been continuing for

several decades, and the other day, we called people from the *Mindan* and other consultants that have helped us and played games and gave them a welcoming party by the PTA committee.

Mrs. Park emphasized the importance of the *Mindan* and its influence, which has greatly benefited Korean students, parents, and the community to gain additional support and visibility, resulting in the creation and maintenance of *Minzokugakkyu*.

According to Hester (2000), *Minzokugakkyu* is offered in order to build a Korean ethnic identity among Korean students who attend Japanese public schools. He explains the ethnic education, under which *Minzokugakkyu* serves three purposes. The first purpose is "raising the ethnic self-awareness of foreign students and to instill in them pride in their ethnic heritage." The second purpose is "cultivation of a respect for human rights and international understanding." The final purpose is in "fostering solidarity between Japanese and foreign children based on mutual respect" (Hester, 2000, p.181–82).

In my 2007 trip, I observed a *Minzokugakkyu* classroom in an elementary school in Osaka. In this elementary school, the *Minzokugakkyu* typically meets during the sixth period each Wednesday where Korean students learn about their cultural and linguistic heritage. It is usually taught by a Korean guest instructor from the Korean community. During this hour, Japanese children are excused early to go home.[3] The day I visited happened to be the official opening ceremony of the *Minzokugakkyu*, attended by over twenty-four Korean students, first through sixth grade, and their parents, teachers, principal, and community members. At this particular event, led by their veteran Korean instructor from the Korean community, the twenty-four students introduced their Korean names in Korean and played Korean drums called *chango* with the Korean background music, all dressed in Korean attire. The parents supported their children's performance by standing around them, taking pictures, and applauding.

These children, upon advancing to junior high school, have the option of continuing to be involved with the *Minzokugakkyu*. For example, at Nishi Junior High School where more than 50 percent of the students are said to have Korean roots, the *Minzokugakkyu* meets every Thursdays at 2:20 p.m. after school as a club. Clubs, in Japanese junior high schools, include cultural interest groups as well as sports such as baseball, tennis, and soccer. While Korean students meet in their *Minzokugakkyu*, other students are not allowed to participate in any other club activities from 2:20 p.m. to 3:00 p.m. According to the principal, this is to ensure that those Korean students who are athletes are not forced to make decisions about whether to attend the *Minzokugakkyu* or practice. During the *Minzokugakkyu*, which supposedly lasts for forty minutes but often goes over one hour, the students normally learn the Korean language, history, and culture, taught by a Korean instructor who is a third-generation Korean. On the day I visited, there were over twenty students ranging from seventh through ninth grade. This amounts to approximately 10 percent of the students who have Korean roots in the school. Two Japanese teachers as well as the principal attended the club meeting, standing and observing in the back.

After I was invited to speak to the students for twenty minutes at the beginning of the club meeting, the instructor taught them various Korean words pertaining to their schools. Then they were given time to practice their favorite subjects with each other in Korean. During the conversational activities, the students practiced using Korean words among themselves and with the adults who were in the classroom. They asked such questions as "How do you say 'baseball' in Korean?" and "How do you say 'music' in Korean?" as they tried to tell others "My favorite sport is baseball" and "My favorite subject is music." The instructor responded to their questions by writing the equivalent Korean vocabulary on the board and helping the students pronounce the words correctly by writing the pronunciation symbols in Japanese next to the Korean word.

The benefit of this type of cultural support is documented in the interviews conducted in my previous trip from 2006 when I visited the *Minzokugakkyu* at the same junior high school in Osaka. I found that Korean students experienced less discrimination when schools provided cultural support such as *Minzokugakkyu*, and encouraged socialization and cultural maintenance for Korean students. One female Korean student, Ito, shared her own experience of attending the *Minzokugakkyu* when she was in elementary school. When asked whether the experience was enjoyable, she responded "yes." She then explained, "Every year there's a presentation. First graders sing Korean songs. They dance and play (hit) instruments. It's kind of fun doing different things." Similarly, another female Korean student, Kimura, described her participation in the *Minzokugakkyu* at her junior high school this way when asked when she felt proud of being Korean:

> Well, [I feel proud as Korean] in a time like this when I get together with everyone at a Korean club and play "*chango*" (Korean drums) and learn [Korean] words, I feel it is fun from the bottom of my heart. . . . I've never been to Korea, but when I come here, I think I can feel my country.

Another student, Kaneda, who is an active member of the *Minzokugakkyu*, revealed his complex feelings about his Korean identity. He repeatedly stated that he did not like his Korean name or for the school to display his Korean name in public. However, despite his reluctance to use his Korean name and his wish to be Japanese, he still was an active member of the *Minzokugakkyu* at his school and regularly attended a Korean community event hosted in Osaka several times a year. Initially, Kaneda said he did not like to be involved in Korean activities, but as he attended these events he became fond of them and even made Korean friends. He expressed that he wished to continue his involvement with the Korean community.

These Korean students' voices point to an important role *Minzokugakkyu* plays in providing a context for socialization among Korean students, and in presenting a space for them to learn about—and to share their Korean culture. Although some of the Korean students who attended the *Minzokugakkyu* did not wish to be known as Koreans publicly, they still came to seek support from their Korean peers, and from teachers who affirmed their Korean identity.

## DISCUSSION

Japan has come a long way in dealing with issues of diversity. In the last ten years, I have met many dedicated teachers and community organization leaders who tirelessly pour out their hearts and time to fight for human rights and equal access for Buraku, Korean, and other underserved students in Japan. On many occasions, these leaders invited me to attend various human rights workshops, conferences, and club meetings that were attended by many teachers and community members to discuss pressing social issues regarding discrimination and *shindoi* experiences. The dedication of these social activists is the reason why I continue to visit these sites. I am truly envious that these minority students have so much more access and support from their schools, teachers, and community organizations than when I was a child. Yet in the midst of these positive forces, I realize that the same comment I heard more than three decades ago still persists today: "Be careful with Koreans. They are scary people." Not knowing I was Korean, my Japanese host family made a casual comment when I asked them about their perceptions of Koreans during my 2002 visit to Japan as a part of a sister city exchange program. I was struck by the reality that when the world has supposedly become more globalized, generally, Japanese's perceptions of Koreans are slowly changing.

The negative ethnic perceptions of Koreans in Japan resonate with the minority school experience in the United States. Lewis (2003) illustrates in her ethnographic study that racism is still rampant in daily interactions in classrooms and even in the schoolyard. She describes how race is present in the hidden curriculum, in historical lessons, in discipline practices, and in interpersonal relations at school (Lewis, 2003). These often disempowering experiences that minority children encounter daily at schools—not only affect their perceptions of their own ethnic identity, but also have consequences for their academic achievement (Cummins, 1996). However, minority students who are empowered by their schools tend to "develop the ability, confidence, and motivation to succeed academically" (Cummins, 1986, p. 23).

Dowa education and *Minzokugakkyu* precisely address this aspect of minority students' schooling experiences, providing support that affirms their unique cultural and historical backgrounds and their identity. Although there are differences in their approaches and goals, these two educational models offer the kind of support that is urgently needed for Buraku, Korean, and other minority populations to succeed in schools. When examining these two educational models in a global context, they offer insights for educators and policymakers in the United States and other countries. Community organizations such as BLL and *Mindan* can play a powerful role in offering support for minority students' schooling experiences. As BLL and the *Mindan* continue to work with the national, municipal, and local governments and school districts, they exert influence and work as watchdog groups to ensure schools provide access to Buraku, Koreans, and other minority students. Witnessing and experiencing cultural crafts-making, dancing, field trips, and intergenerational intermingling supported by the community organizations, help to bring immeasurable benefits to minority students, as evidenced in their interview responses.

Another insight that can be gained from these two educational models is the importance of teachers' commitment to supporting minority students during instruction and noninstruction activities throughout the school day. Teachers and other adults can show keen sensitivity and effort in their instruction, curriculum, and after-school club activities to provide continuous and genuine care for minority students. Those scenes I often encountered at Shiki Junior High School where teachers voluntarily support other teachers and students during their nonteaching periods, are prime examples of the commitment to minority education. At Nishi Junior High School, *Minzokugakkyu* was attended and supported by the principal, teachers, and a Korean teacher from the community. The teachers, administrators, and community members are aware of the extraordinary challenges they face when they come to *shindoi* schools. As Mr. Tada noted, they need teachers who truly care about their student populations and their needs. He shared his concern about those elite teachers who cannot see from the students' perspectives, resulting in student academic disengagement. His sentiment echoes the problem in the United States where high minority schools lack quality teachers and a "culturally relevant education" (Ladson-Billings, 1994). The Dowa and *Minzokugakkyu* education models seek to provide a culturally relevant classroom for Buraku and Korean students.

As a minority member, one of the most alarming phenomena that I witnessed during my visits to the schools was that an increasing number of Koreans had completely abandoned their Korean identities. Many of these students had entirely assimilated into a Japanese identity, hiding their Korean names and sometimes naturalizing into Japanese in order to live as accepted and equal members of the society. Some teachers expressed that when they visited their students' homes, that was when they found out about the students' ethnic background from their grandparents' heavy accents, family pictures, and other household decorations. On one such visit, a Korean mother told the teacher to leave them alone when she encouraged the mother to take pride in her Korean roots. These struggles and frustrations experienced by teachers in Japan point to the social tension that minorities face both in schools and in the larger society. Even at Nishi Junior High School where one out of two students have Korean roots, the teachers and administrators share the same concern of seeing increasing numbers of Korean students becoming assimilated into Japanese culture and hiding their Korean ethnicity.

Thus, in the age of globalization and transnational migrations of people, cultures, and languages, it is important to improve understandings of various distant social groups and communities, because through each generation the hope of creating a more democratic and civil society is made a more sensible reality. In Japan, a country that has its own history of domination and minority oppression, the experiences of minority populations have become a public issue in the broader society and also in schools. The Dowa and *Minzokugakkyu* educational models in Japan present hope for building social awareness and improving the educational outcomes of underserved groups. The prospect for the Dowa and *Minzokugakkyu* models may have even wider implications for educators and policymakers in other countries, who are interested in improving social relations and minority students' success.

## NOTES

The author wishes to thank Dr. Arlene Hijara from the Massachusetts Department of Education for her generous feedback and assistance in the preparation of the manuscript.

1. All of the names of the schools, teachers, parents, and students that appear in this manuscript are pseudonyms.

2. According to Lee (1999), of all the Korean children in Osaka, approximately 83 percent of them attend Japanese public schools while 17 percent of them attend ethnic schools run either by *Ch'ongnyon*, the organization controlled by the Democratic People's Republic of Korea (DPRK) or *Mindan*, supported by the Republic of Korea (ROK). These ethnic schools were created "in order to claim back their stolen ethnic culture" (Lee, 1999, p. 139). Currently, there are over 150 such Korean ethnic schools in Japan (Harajiri, 1998). However, due to government anti-ethnic school policies and stigma attached to such schools, an overwhelming number of Korean children choose to attend Japanese public schools rather than ethnic schools (Lee, 1999). In some public schools in Osaka, Korean students constitute more than 50 percent or as high as 80 percent of the school population. In extreme cases, 100 percent of the public school population is comprised of Korean and Buraku students.

3. *Minzokugakkyu* is normally offered as an extracurricular activity in public schools with a large number of Korean students in western Japan. Unlike Dowa education, the *Minzokugakkyu* model is extracurricular since under the current Japanese law, any students who are non-Japanese nationals are exempt from mandatory public school education (Ministry of Education, Science, Sports, and Culture, 2008). The essential difference between the Dowa and *Minzokugakkyu* models lies in the Japanese primary focus on providing education to Japanese nationals, not those of foreign origin. Thus, although both Buraku and Korean students' experience consistent academic underachievement, the former benefits from the Dowa educational model that is included in the curriculum, while the latter benefits from the *Minzokugakkyu* model that only exists as extracurricular.

## REFERENCES

Alldritt, L. (2000). The Burakumin: The complicity of Japanese buddhism in oppression and an opportunity for liberation. Retrieved October 17, 2008, from www.buddhistethics.org/7/alldritt001.html.

Cummins, J. (1986). Empowering minority students: A framework for intervention. *Harvard Educational Review, 56*(1), 18–36.

Cummins, J. (1996). *Negotiating identities: Education for empowerment in a diverse society.* Ontario, CA: California Association for Bilingual Education.

Harajiri, H. (1989). *Zainichi choosenjin no seikatsu sekai* (The living world of Koreans in Japan). Tokyo: Koobundo.

Harajiri, H. (1998). *Zainichitoshiteno Korean* (Koreans as "Zainichi"). Tokyo: Koodansha.

Hawkins, J. H. (1983). Educational demands and institutional response: Dowa education in Japan. *Comparative Education Review, 27*(2), 204–26.

Hester, J. (2000). Kids between nations: Ethnic classes in the construction of Korean identities in Japanese public schools. In S. Ryang (Ed.), *Koreans in Japan: Critical voices from the margin* (pp. 175–96). London: Routledge.

Hicks, G. (1997). *Japan's hidden apartheid: The Korean minority and the Japanese.* Aldershot, UK: Ashgate.

Kanai, K. (2004, March). *Nihonni okeru minority no gakugyo fushin wo meguru giron* (Debates concerning academic underachievement of minorities in Japan). Retrieved March 31, 2006, from www.p.u-tokyo.ac.jp/coe/workingpaper/vol.10.pdf.

Kim, C. (1999). Zainichi chosenjin no keizai mondai (Economic problems of Koreans in Japan). In C. Park (Ed.), *Zainichi Chosenjin* (Koreans in Japan) (second ed.) (pp. 101–34). Tokyo: Akashi Shoten.

Kim, K. (2005). *Zainichi Korean no identity to hooteki chii* (Identity and legal status of Koreans in Japan) (second ed.). Tokyo: Akashi Shoten.

Kirihata, Z. (2000). C sha shuushoku sabetsu jiken ni torikunde (Dealing with a case of employment discrimination with Company C). *Asuwo Hiraku, 32,* 5–26.

Kyo, N. (1990). *Goku hutsuuno zainichi kankokujin* (An ordinary Korean in Japan). Tokyo: Asahi Bunko.

Kyotoshi Kyooiku Iinkai. (1992). *Kyotoshiritsu gakkoo gaikokujin kyooiku hooshin: shutoshite zainichi kankoku choosenjinni taisuru minzoku sabetsuwo nakusu kyooikuno suishinni tsuite* (Kyoto city school foreign education policy: Recommending education to get rid of racism against Koreans in Japan). Kyoto: Kyotoshi Kyooiku Iinkai.

Ladson-Billings, G. (1994). *The dreamkeepers: Successful teachers of African American children.* San Francisco: Jossey-Bass.

Lee, C., and De Vos, G. (1981). *Koreans in Japan.* Berkeley: University of California Press.

Lee, W. (1999). Zainichi chosenjin no minzokukyoiku (Ethnic education of Koreans in Japan). In C. Park (Ed.), *Zainichi Chosenjin* (Koreans in Japan) (second ed.) (pp. 135–73). Tokyo: Akashi Shoten.

Lewis, A. (2003). *Race in the schoolyard: Negotiating the color line in classrooms and communities.* New Brunswick, NJ: Rutgers University Press.

Ministry of Education, Science, Sports, and Culture. (2008, February). *Gaikokujin jidooseito shuugaku sokushin plan onbu* (Policy concerning education for foreign children). Retrieved February 9, 2008, from www.mext.go.jp/a_menu/hyouka/kekka/05090202/014.pdf.

Nabeshima, Y. (2003). *Miezaru kaisooteki hubyoodoo* (Inequality of the invisible caste). Osaka: Kaihoo Shuppan Sha.

National Center for Education Statistics. (2007a). *The nation's report card mathematics 2007.* Washington, DC: Institute of Education Sciences, U.S. Department of Education.

National Center for Education Statistics. (2007b). *The nation's report card reading 2007.* Washington, DC: Institute of Education Sciences, U.S. Department of Education.

Ogbu, J. (1978). *Minority education and caste.* New York: Academic Press.

Osakafu Jinken Kyooiku Kenkyuu Kyoogikai (2002). *Osaka no kodomotachi: Kodomo no seikatsu hakusho* (Children in Osaka: White paper on children's living). Osaka: Osakafu Jinken Kyooiku Kenkyuu Kyoogikai.

Osakashi Shiminkyoku Jinkenbu Kikaku Suishinka. (2005). *Osakashi gaikokuseki juumin shisaku kihon shishin* (A basic policy guide to Osaka residents with foreign nationality). Osaka: Osakashi Shiminkyoku Jinkenbu Kikaku Suishinka.

Rohlen, T. (1981). Education: policies and prospects. In C. Lee, and G. De Vos (Eds.), *Koreans in Japan* (pp. 182–222). Berkeley: University of California Press.

Shimahara, N. (1991). Social mobility and education: Burakumin in Japan. In M. Gibson and J. Ogbu (Eds.), *Minority status and schooling: A comparative study of immigrant and involuntary minorities* (pp. 327–53). New York: Garland.

Shimizu, K., and Shimizu, M. (2001). *Newcomerto kyoiku (Newcomer and education).* Tokyo: Akashi Shoten.

Taminzoku Kyoosei Jinken Kenkyuu Shuukai Jikkoo Iinkai. (2004). *Taminzoku kyoosei jinken kenkyu shukai, 2004 (Multiracial coexistence human rights consortium).* Osaka: Taminzoku Kyoosei Jinken Kenkyuu Shuukai Jikkoo Iinkai.

Tanaka, H. (2004). Jikokumin chuushin shugi karano dakkyakuwo (Escaping from nationalistic ideology). *Taminzoku kyosei jinken kenkyu shukai,* 6–33.

Tokyo Shoseki. (1996). *Atarashii shakai: Rekishi* (New social studies: History). Tokyo: Tokyo Shoseki.

Uesugi, S. (1990). *Tennoseito buraku sabetsu: Buraku sabetsuwa ima naze arunoka?* (The Imperial system and Buraku discrimination: Why is there Buraku discrimination now?). Tokyo: San-ichi.

Weiner, M. (1997). *Japan's minorities: The illusion of homogeneity.* London: Routledge.

*Chapter Fifteen*

# Japanese Mathematics Achievement and Global Factors of Diversity

Linda H. L. Furuto

## MODERNIZATION AND EDUCATIONAL DEVELOPMENT

Education has often been referred to as the catalyst that shaped Japan's modernization and economic development (Rohlen and LeTendre, 1996; Rosenbaum and Kariya, 1989). Japan's virtually universal literacy, high levels of school attendance from elementary school through university, and capacity to impart great quantities of information through formal education, particularly in fields such as mathematics, are world-renowned (Duke, 1989). The performance of Japanese students on international tests of mathematics achievement is among the highest in the world. Over 99 percent of Japan's students' complete compulsory education through grades nine successfully, and almost 95 percent go on to complete the three years of noncompulsory upper-secondary school. Moreover, even though it has a significantly smaller population than the United States, Japan still produces twice as many engineer graduates (Sōmuchō Tōkeikyoku, 2006; U.S. Department of Education, 2007).

The ready acceptance of such an optimistic understanding of schooling has in part been due to the economic prosperity, academic achievement, and relative social stability that the Japanese public has enjoyed over the past five decades (Baker, 2001; Fuller and Rubinson, 1992; Ishida, 1993; Sasagawa, 1993; Torney-Purta, 1987). While it is acknowledged that there has been progress, the general success of the Japanese schooling system undermines individual differences that are consumed by the focus on homogeneity.

The study of achievement in conditions of social change is illuminating, not only because it highlights the relationship between the priorities of policy and how these work themselves out in practice, but also because it frequently comments on the appropriateness of educational priorities that have become inscribed in policy agendas worldwide (Amano, 1990; Hawkins, 1983; Rohlen and LeTendre, 1996; Rosenbaum and Kariya, 1989). Japanese Ministry of Education, Culture, Sports, Science, and Technology (MEXT) officials have claimed that schools effectively socialize and acculturate the young, transmit modern skills and knowledge, and raise the population's academic achievement based on recent international mathematics and science scores (Monbukagakushō, 1997; NCES, 2003; Sōmuchō Tōkeikyoku, 2006).

This picture is not invalid, but it is incomplete and the assumption of equal opportunity in education merits reexamination (Buraku Kaihō Kenkyūsho, 1983; Okano, 1995). It is not surprising that issues of diversity and equity center around education in Japan. It was expected that following the U.S. occupation and World War II, education would expand and embody a meritocratic principle promoting opportunity in society. The underlying reason is expressed as follows, "Industrialization and economic development result in change of the occupational structure, increasing demand for various types of wage earners and for more highly educated workers and making the intergenerational transmission of skills and occupation statuses difficult and insufficient" (Fujita, 1978, p. 2). In such a situation, school education expands its selective function, as well as its socialization function, to create demands that are efficiency-oriented and meritocratic in nature. Furthermore, since school education should be concerned with the capacity to educate individuals, we would expect it to promote diversity.

While the post–World War II system of Japanese schooling has provided valuable ingredients for economic success and social stability, these have been accompanied by unfavorable developments. Examples include excessively competitive examinations for entry into education, uniformity that some claim stifles individual development, and monocultural orientations, which assume that all students are from a single, Japanese ethnic group (Beauchamp, 1991, 2003; Lynn, 1988). In this manner, the practice of schooling continues to reproduce, rather than eliminate, systemic disadvantages.

## HISTORICAL PERIODS OF JAPANESE EDUCATION

In order to provide social context, major periods of Japanese education are highlighted. Japan's rise during the past century and a half from being an isolated, feudal nation to being one of the greatest world industrial powers is one of the most significant historical developments of modern times. Education is among the reasons for this incredible accomplishment (Hawkins and Cummings, 2000; Sato, 1992; Tsuchimochi, 1993), of which there are three main periods of transformation: (1) Meiji Era (1868–1912), (2) post–World War II (1945–1952), and (3) 1978 to the present. In the first instance, the reform movement was initiated by the new Meiji government as a means of building a modern state as quickly as possible. In the second case, public policy reforms were imposed by U.S. occupation forces, intending to restructure Japan into a democratic society. Finally, in the third period, Japanese policymakers, educators, and ministry officials have begun to focus on equity and accessibility in the quality of education (Amano, 1990; Reich, 1992). For the purposes of this study, I begin with post–World War II, and then proceed to 1978 to the present.

### Occupation of Japan, 1945–1952

When Japan surrendered to the Allies in August 1945, the United States was charged with assisting in the development of a new educational system (Beauchamp and Vardaman, 1994). Since the Meiji Restoration of 1868, Japan's political leaders had consciously used education as an instrument to advance the ends of the state, which included economic development, national integration, and military power and conquest. When Japan surrendered aboard the U.S.S. *Missouri* on September 2, 1945, its educational system was in shambles. The aftermath of World War II left eighteen million students idle, four thousand schools destroyed, and only 20 percent of the necessary textbooks were available (Beauchamp and Vardaman, 1994). More than one out of every three institutions of higher education were in ruins; thousands of teachers were homeless, hungry, dispirited, and many of their pupils had been moved to safer areas. In short, a functioning education system was virtually nonexistent (Horio, 1994).

The main goals of the occupation of Japan were the democratization, demilitarization, and decentralization of Japanese society. The United States recognized that reorienting the educational system was an indispensable element in achieving these objectives, especially that of remaking Japan into a functioning democracy. Educational reforms were designed to mold Japanese education along the lines of a U.S. model, which meant that the occupation authorities would have to transform the prewar orientation of the Japanese people. This was characterized by an emphasis on filial piety, the perfection of moral powers, group cohesion and harmony, and loyalty and obedience to the emperor and the nation. The U.S. reformers suggested dismantling the highly differentiated multitrack system of prewar days in favor of a nine-year compulsory single track as part of a U.S.-style 6–3–3 (elementary–middle–high school) ladder, along with steps designated to foster greater individuality, freedom of inquiry, the development of the whole child, coeducation, greater flexibility in the curriculum, and a reform of Japan's written language (Beauchamp, 1991).

As research has shown, both Japanese and United States, many of these reforms, such as coeducation, comprehensive schools, and local control, were deeply rooted in the U.S. democratic model but were dysfunctional when transported to the Japanese context (Beauchamp, 1991). The Japanese educational authorities, however, had little choice but to officially accept the recommendations of the mission's report. These recommendations became the basis for a series of important educational laws implemented between 1947 and 1949. The most important of these were the Fundamental Law of Education (Law No. 25, 1947) and the School Education Law (Law No. 26, 1947), both enacted in 1947. The former represented a 180-degree change from the 1890 Imperial Rescript, declaring that "education shall aim at the full development of personality, striving for the rearing of the people sound in mind and body, who shall love truth and justice, esteem individual value, respect labor and have a deep sense of responsibility, and be imbued with the independent spirit, as builders of a peaceful state and society" (Beauchamp, 1991, p. 102). It also established the important principle that all major educational regulations would be made by parliamentary procedure. The School Education Law, in part, established a new educational structure in which a 6–3–3 school ladder was created, the age at which one could leave school was raised to fifteen years, and coeducation was legitimatized. These two basic pieces of legislation are still the legal underpinnings of Japanese education today.

This committee eventually evolved into the Japanese Ministry of Education's powerful Central Council on Education. One of the first contributions of the committee was to shape A Guide to the New Education, disseminated by the Ministry of Education on June 30, 1946. It laid down "the task of educators in Japan to take it upon themselves to promote, through reeducation of the people, the construction of a new Japan which is democratic, peace-loving, and civilized" (Beauchamp, 1991, p. 15). By 1949, the major accomplishments of the occupation were completed. With the end of the occupation in spring 1952, U.S. reformers had been successful in providing Japanese educators with new curricula, textbooks, and ways of thinking.

In August 1950, the Japanese Minister of Education described U.S. efforts as follows, "the reforms initiated after World War II were unprecedented in depth and scope." The official went on to say that "they are unprecedented because there has been a complete revolution in the fundamental concepts that support the education system" (Beauchamp, 1991). Whatever the reality of the U.S. influences from 1945 to 1952, there is agreement that it has played a guiding role in Japan's emergence as a world economic power.

## Current Reform Period, 1978 to the Present

From the 1950s to the early 1970s, Japan experienced a period of building capacity, without any major deviations from the one set up during the U.S. occupation in the post–World War II era. This began to change in the late 1970s and early 1980s, which served as a precursor period to Japan's current reform movement toward quality education (Sasagawa, 1993; Vogel, 1979).

In the early 1970s, several important reports calling for educational reforms stirred widespread discussion among the Japanese. The Central Council for Education's report addressed both conservative proponents of the existing system and the radical Japan Teacher's Union when it warned, "Education is rapidly falling behind the times because vested interests protect the status quo, because idealists oppose reforms which have no possibility of being implemented" (Beauchamp, 1991, p. 50). The report advocated:

> Long-range fundamental policies and measures for developing the educational system, basing these proposals on examination of the educational system's achievements over the past 20 years and on its understanding of the system of education appropriate for the years to come in which rapid technological innovations and national and international changes are anticipated. (Central Council for Education, 1972, p. 56)

The minister of education at the time, Sakata Michita, was sufficiently impressed by this analysis and referred to it as a "plan for the third major educational reform in Japan's history" (*Mainichi Daily News*, 1984, p. 1).

Its proposals, all of which required much financial support, included extending free public education to four- and five-year-olds, providing teachers with large salary increases, allowing teachers more time to teach by shifting paperwork to an expanded clerical staff, expanding special education programs, and increasing subsidies to private universities. This report recognized that there was now a need to move toward improving the quality of education.

Although Japan's commitment to education is still very high, cracks are beginning to appear in the surface of that commitment. Amano Ikuo of Tōkyō University presents a persuasive argument in which he refers to a "crisis of structuration" (Amano,

1990). Amano argues that postwar Japan was successful in creating a society that was egalitarian and mobile, but since the slowdown of the economy after the oil crisis of 1973, opportunities for mobility have been significantly reduced. He believes that a stable hierarchy of high schools, dominated by the relative few serving as feeder schools to the top universities, has emerged. Graduates of these top universities tend to secure jobs leading to the elite positions in society. In the earlier stage of rapid expansion of secondary and higher education, Amano contends, there existed healthy competition. However, as a result of the changes described above, the number of places in elite universities has decreased and there are fewer desirable jobs available upon graduation. This crisis of structuration is first noticeable within the upper levels of elementary school (Amano, 1984). The most significant policy issues include the examination system, the role of education in fostering economic development, and reforming Japanese education to meet the challenges of the twenty-first century while at the same time ensuring that reforms are harmonious with Japanese values.

There is no doubt that the socioeconomic, cultural, and social environment of contemporary Japan is very different from the past. Children today are growing up amid an affluence that is in stark contrast to the economic reality of previous generations. The consumer orientation of today's young people is a far cry from their counterparts of the postwar era. Whereas politically active students a quarter century ago tended to be committed to idealistic goals and were intensely interested in building what they perceived to be an economically prosperous society, today's children have an orientation grounded in individual advancement (Cummings, Tatto, and Hawkins, 2001). If the two previous major reforms in early Meiji and following World War II are any guide, it is expected that reforms of a rather sweeping nature will be made, followed shortly by a period of reflection in which modifications of the original reforms are brought closer to conformity with Japanese life (Amano 1990; Beauchamp, 2003).

Whether English, French, German, or American, there were previously models with which the Japanese were reasonably satisfied in borrowing. One of the most conspicuous differences between the third major transformation and the two earlier reform experiences is that in both the Meiji and the occupation periods, there were foreign models that were worthy of international emulation. Virtually all of the countries to which Japan has traditionally looked for ideas are themselves engaged in reform efforts to address inadequate educational systems. In many ways, the upper levels of elementary school experience function as the rite of passage into adolescence and adulthood. Understanding how children balance culture, peers, academics, and other social processes, offers a valuable opportunity to examine the impact of social institutions on educational achievement.

## RESEARCH OVERVIEW

In this study, contemporary social conditions of upper-elementary school (fifth and sixth grade) mathematics achievement are examined in Japan. The overall research question is summarized as follows, what factors of diversity affect mathematics achievement as observed in upper-level Japanese elementary schools? Relationships are discussed from a range of mathematics instruction, socioeconomic background, sociocultural identity, family/community involvement, geographical location, and gender perspectives in elementary schools.

Upper-elementary school students were selected because of the major shift in educational paradigms that occurs during the schooling of preadolescents (ten- to twelve-year-olds). The tensions and conflicts around early youth development mirror wider conflicts in Japanese society (e.g., between the ideal of learning as an exploration and learning as examination preparation). In upper-elementary school, students experience dramatic shifts in the type of instruction received, become aware of the expectations adults have for them, and undergo psychological and physiological changes. Japanese students are also subjected to powerful social pressures from peers and the media. How they cope with these pressures, and the support they receive from various institutions, illuminates how diversity impacts Japanese society. The complexity of educational concerns at this juncture makes change difficult, and the experiences of Japanese students provide valuable information.

This research comes at an opportune moment for Japanese and U.S. educators, policymakers, and researchers. Standards-based reform has consumed discussions of academic achievement in both societies, especially over the past ten years. U.S. schoolchildren continue to lag behind international standards in most areas of academics in terms of achievement tests. However, even though almost every state in the country is working to develop higher standards for what students should be learning, along with the means for assessing their progress, the quick-fix solutions implemented so far have not had a noticeable impact.

The Trends in International Mathematics and Science Study (TIMSS) 2003 resulted from the need for reliable and timely data on the mathematics and science achievement of U.S. students compared to that of students in other countries. TIMSS is the most comprehensive and rigorous assessment of its kind ever undertaken with a total of forty-one participating countries. Director of TIMSS, James Stigler, concludes that socioeconomic background, cultural identity, and gender are leading indicators of achievement in both Japan and the United States (National Center for Education Statistics, 2003; OERI, 1988). However, in spite of this, very little work has been done in the fields of diversity, equity, and mathematics achievement.

## METHOD

Research was conducted at Wakabadai Elementary School, Inagi Daiichi Elementary School, Takashima Daigo Elementary School, and Nichinōken *Juku* Cram School, with permission to use data granted by the respective schools and districts. Throughout quantitative and qualitative data collection, concurrent enrollment as a Visiting Scholar at the University of Tōkyō, and maintaining connections with the four research sites provided complementary macroperspective analysis and access to databases at the national level, as well as hands-on learning within the classroom environment. This research is a cooperative project, supported by the University of Tōkyō, Waseda University, Ōbirin University, University of California, Los Angeles, and the MEXT.

## School Sites

Wakabadai Elementary School is located in the suburbs of Inagi City, about 1.5 hours from Shinjuku. When Wakabadai Elementary School was founded seven years ago, the student enrollment was 139. Today, due to the desirable location and marketing to residents of higher socioeconomic background, the number has increased to 973. The brand new school buildings are beautifully kept and the swimming pool was recently enlarged to accommodate the influx in student numbers. Students live within a one-mile radius from school, and most are within fifteen-minute walking distance. Approximately 20–25 percent of fifth and sixth grade students attend academic *juku* (cram school). Japan has long been known as an academically oriented society (*gakureki shakai*), and students at Wakabadai Elementary School are at the forefront of this model.

Inagi Daiichi Elementary School is one of the oldest schools in Tōkyō, and was founded over 130 years ago. The mission of the school is to "nurture confident, open-minded, independently thinking, well-balanced inquirers for responsibility" (Inagi Daiichi Elementary School pamphlet, 2005). There are thirty full-time teachers, two school nurses, four office staff, one groundskeeper, and 860 students. Similar to Wakabadai Elementary School, there is a music room, arts and crafts room, swimming pool, gymnasium, chicken coop, and home economics room, in addition to academic classrooms. Students tend to live within a twenty-minute walking commute of the school. The school is well supported by families and the surrounding community.

Takashima Daigo Elementary School is located in the city of Takashimadaira. It was built during the baby boom of the 1970s, and is surrounded on all sides by inexpensive, public housing complexes. Takashima Daigo Elementary School is located in a lower socioeconomic residential community, and there are not many urban or shopping areas nearby. Enrollment decreased from 671 students in 1973 to 256 students in 2006, and maintaining enrollment is one of the challenges the school faces. Classes are held in a four-story building, with one-third of the classrooms unused.

Nichinōken *Juku* is among the most prestigious cram schools in all of Japan. There are 37,500 fourth through sixth grade students enrolled in Nichinōken *Juku* throughout the country. Of that figure, twenty-nine thousand of the total students reside in the Tōkyō area. Each year, Nichinōken *Juku* provides 33.5 percent of the students to the top ten private junior high schools in the Tōkyō area (Gonzales, Calsyn, Jocelyn, Mak, Kastberg, Arafeh, Williams, and Tsen, 2001). This is by far the highest and most distinguished figure among *juku* institutions. Research occurred with the general manager of the Nichinōken *Juku* in Shibuya. Students generally attend Nichinōken *Juku* three times per week (Monday, Wednesday, Friday) from 16:50–20:45. The subject content mainly focuses on mathematics, social studies, science, and Japanese language.

## Quantitative Survey

Survey analysis was the first methodological strategy used to answer the underlying research question, what factors of diversity affect mathematics achievement as observed in upper-level Japanese elementary schools? The quantitative survey took approximately thirty minutes to complete, and was based on the work of Helen Astin (2000), Alexander Astin and contributors (1987, 2000), William Korn (1987), and Derek Bok (1996). The survey included demographic, attitudinal, family/community-related, and future-oriented objective questions. Part of the survey was drawn from the existing Higher Education Research Institute (HERI) Freshmen Survey housed at the University of California, Los Angeles, with sections altered to the targeted population.

Data analysis of ordered logistic regression focused on the logit and probit versions of the ordered regression model, in terms of an underlying latent variable, selected to fit the types of data and variables under consideration. Table 15.1 provides a description of the major variables and measurements.

## Qualitative Focus Group Interviews

Features of Japanese schooling were investigated secondarily with qualitative techniques. The focus groups were semistructured, open-ended interviews, involving four to five participants. They were complementary to the quantitative methods, providing further understanding of the organizational history and structure of schools, issues in planning and organizing, assessment, changes in organization, and their influences on issues of diversity (Fetterman, 1998; Bickman et al., 1993; Rog and Bickman, 1998). Focus group interviews were conducted with twenty-five fifth and sixth grade students and twenty-five teachers/administrators at the four research sites, for a total of five student focus groups and five teacher/administrator focus groups. To analyze the qualitative data portion, Richard Boyatzis's method of coding was implemented based on themes emerging from the text (1998).

## MAJOR FINDINGS

### Descriptive Analysis

Descriptive analysis illustrates general characteristics of the sample population of 278 fifth and sixth grade students at four schools. There was no missing data for any of the variables in the regression analyses. Table 15.2 is a contingency table of grade level (q01) by school (q00). The chi-square test is not statistically significant, indicating there is no association between grade level and school attended. There is a fairly even representation of fifth and sixth graders across all four schools. Overall, 52.52 percent of the population is in the fifth grade (146 students) and 47.48 percent is in the sixth grade (132 students). Wakabadai Elementary is coded as school 1, Inagi Daiichi Elementary is school 2, Takashima Daigo Elementary is school 3, and Nichinōken *Juku* is school 4. 24.82 percent of the sample is from Wakabadai Elementary School (69 students), 30.58 percent is from Inagi Daiichi Elementary School (85 students), 28.42 percent is from Takashima Daigo Elementary School (79 students), and 16.19 percent is from Nichinōken *Juku* (45 students).

Contingency tables of gender by school and age by school indicate that gender and age composition are relatively homogeneous across schools. Approximately half of the

**Table 15.1.   Description of Major Variables and Measurements**

| Variable Name | Description | Measurement |
|---|---|---|
| q00 | School | 1 = Wakabadai Elementary<br>2 = Inagi Daiichi Elementary<br>3 = Takashima Daigo Elementary<br>4 = Nichinōken *Juku* |
| q01 | Grade Level | 1 = Fifth Grade<br>2 = Sixth Grade<br>3 = Other |
| q02 | Gender | 1 = Male<br>2 = Female |
| q03 | Age | 1 = < 9 Years<br>2 = 9 Years<br>3 = 10 Years<br>4 = 11 Years<br>5 = 12 Years<br>6 = > 12 Years |
| q04 | Anticipated Highest Academic Degree | 1 = Junior College<br>2 = University<br>3 = Graduate/Professional School<br>4 = Other |
| q05 | School-related Experiences | 1 = Frequently<br>2 = Occasionally<br>3 = Never |
| q06 | Future Occupation | 1 = Scientific researcher<br>2 = Architect or urban planner<br>3 = Engineer<br>4 = Computer programmer<br>5 = Dentist<br>6 = Doctor<br>7 = Lawyer or judge<br>8 = Schoolteacher<br>9 = School principal or superintendent<br>10 = Clergyman (monk)<br>11 = Reporter or journalist<br>12 = Artist<br>13 = Actor or entertainer<br>14 = Government employee<br>15 = Home helper<br>16 = Military<br>17 = Police officer<br>18 = Firefighter<br>19 = Other<br>20 = Haven't Decided |
| q07 | Hours Spent Doing Weekly Activities:<br>q07_01  School classes<br>q07_02  Studying/homework<br>q07_03  Math studying/homework<br>q07_04  *Juku* classes<br>q07_05  *Juku* mathematics classes<br>q07_06  Traveling to school<br>q07_07  Traveling to juku<br>q07_08  Playing with friends | 1 = None<br>2 = 1-2 Hours<br>3 = 3-5 Hours<br>4 = 6-10 Hours<br>5 = 11-15 Hours<br>6 = 16-20 Hours<br>7 = 20+ Hours |

*(continued)*

**Table 15.1.** (*Continued*)

| Variable Name | Description | Measurement |
|---|---|---|
| | q07_09 Exercise or sports | |
| | q07_10 Volunteer work | |
| | q07_11 Watching TV | |
| | q07_12 Household duties | |
| | q07_13 Reading for pleasure | |
| | q07_14 Using the internet | |
| | q07_15 Playing video games | |
| q08 | Personal Importance of Values/Goals: | 1 = Essential |
| | q08_01 Becoming accomplished in one of the performing arts | 2 = Somewhat Important |
| | | 3 = Not Important |
| | q08_02 Becoming an authority in my field | |
| | q08_03 Raising a family | |
| | q08_04 Succeeding in a company | |
| | q08_05 Being well off financially | |
| | q08_06 Helping others who are in difficulty | |
| | q08_07 Making a contribution to science or mathematics | |
| | q08_08 Becoming involved in programs to clean up the environment | |
| | q08_09 Keeping up to date with political affairs | |
| | q08_10 Becoming a community leader | |
| | q08_11 Deepening my relationships with friends | |
| | q08_12 Living the life I would like to lead | |
| q09 | Items Possessed by Respondent | 1 = Television |
| | | 2 = Study desk |
| | | 3 = Radio-cassette player |
| | | 4 = DVD player |
| | | 5 = Walkman/iPod |
| | | 6 = Digital camera |
| | | 7 = Personal computer |
| | | 8 = Musical instrument |
| | | 9 = Piano |
| | | 10 = Bike |
| | | 11 = Car |
| | | 12 = Cellular phone |
| q10 | Rating of Respondent's Characteristics/Traits: | 1 = Upper 10% |
| | q10_01 Scholastic/academic ability | 2 = Above Average |
| | q10_02 Artistic ability | 3 = Average |
| | q10_03 Computer skills | 4 = Below Average |
| | q10_04 Competitiveness | 5 = Lower 10% |
| | q10_05 Cooperativeness | |
| | q10_06 Creativity | |
| | q10_07 Drive/motivation to achieve | |
| | q10_08 Emotional stability/health | |
| | q10_09 Leadership ability | |

| Variable Name | Description | Measurement |
|---|---|---|
| | q10_10  Mathematical ability | |
| | q10_11  Physical health | |
| | q10_12  Popularity | |
| | q10_13  Public speaking ability | |
| q11 | Elementary School Mathematics Grades | 1= High |
| | | 2 = Upper Middle |
| | | 3 = Middle |
| | | 4 = Lower Middle |
| | | 5 = Lower |
| | | 6 = Don't Know, Can't Remember |
| q12 | Teacher Expectations and Views: | 1 = Frequently |
| | q12_01  Heartfelt support and encouragement | 2 = Occasionally |
| | | 3 = Never |
| | q12_02  Help in order to improve learning ability | |
| | q12_03  Intellectually interesting topics/encouragement | |
| | q12_04  Opportunities to discuss courses outside of class | |
| | q12_05  Opportunities to apply studies from class | |
| q13 | Number of Years Attending *Juku* | 1 = < 1 Year |
| | | 2 = 1 Year |
| | | 3 = 2-3 Years |
| | | 4 = 4-5 Years |
| | | 5 = 6-7 Years |
| | | 6 = > 7 Years |
| q14 | Grade Level Began Attending *Juku* | 1 = First Grade |
| | | 2 = Second Grade |
| | | 3 = Third Grade |
| | | 4 = Fourth Grade |
| | | 5 = Fifth Grade |
| | | 6 = Sixth Grade |

**Table 15.2.  Contingency Table of Grade Level (q01) by School (q00)**

| Grade Level | School | | | | Total |
|---|---|---|---|---|---|
| | 1 | 2 | 3 | 4 | |
| Grade 5 | 38 | 42 | 42 | 24 | |
| | 55.07 | 49.41 | 53.16 | 53.33 | 52.52 |
| Grade 6 | 31 | 43 | 37 | 21 | 132 |
| | 44.93 | 50.59 | 46.84 | 46.67 | 47.48 |
| Total | 69 | 85 | 79 | 45 | 278 |
| | 100.00 | 100.00 | 100.00 | 100.00 | 100.00 |

Pearson chi2(3) =  0.5347  Pr =

population sample is male (48.56 percent, 135 students), and the other half is female (51.44 percent, 143 students). Interestingly, there is a noticeable difference between male and female numbers at Nichinōken *Juku*, where 57.78 percent of the students are male and 42.22 percent are female. The majority of students are eleven to twelve years of age (97.84 percent), with a few ten- and thirteen-year-olds. The ages are generally evenly spread across school. There tend to be slightly more eleven-year-olds (53.60 percent, 149 students) than twelve-year-olds (44.24 percent, 123 students).

The intraclass correlation of mathematics achievement (acadachvt) by school (q00) also provides useful information. The intraclass correlation (0.55762) is substantial and shows that schools are significantly different across populations and fairly homogeneous within, as expected. Table 15.3 is a contingency table of cross-tabulation and chi-square of mathematics achievement (acadachvt) by school (q00) that support intraclass correlation findings. The chi-square test is statistically significant at the 0.001 α-level (p = 0.000), indicating there is a strong association between mathematics achievement and school attended.

Figure 15.1 shows a graphical representation of intraclass correlation. It is revealing about the relationships between socioeconomic status and mathematics achievement between schools (q00). In order of highest to lowest socioeconomic class, the schools are as follows: Nichinōken *Juku*, Wakabadai Elementary School, Inagi Daiichi Elementary School, and Takashima Daigo School. The four schools are mutually exclusive, and there is no duplicate sampling. There is a distinct linear pattern and positive relationship between school and mathematics achievement. Mathematics achievement is on a three-point scale from 1 (low) to 3 (high). As socioeconomic class increases, mathematics achievement follows a similar pattern.

According to qualitative and quantitative findings at Wakabadai Elementary School, Inagi Daiichi Elementary School, Takashima Daigo Elementary School, and Nichinōken *Juku*, the following emerged as overarching themes: mathematics instruction, socioeconomic background, sociocultural identity, family/community involvement, geographical location, gender, and other research factors. In order to best assess the variables' overall predictive power on mathematics achievement, the six themed scales were combined.

**Table 15.3. Contingency Table of Mathematics Achievement (acadachvt) by School (q00)**

| Acadachvt | School | | | | Total |
|---|---|---|---|---|---|
| | *1* | *2* | *3* | *4* | |
| 1 | 3 | 3 | 35 | 0 | 41 |
| | 4.62 | 3.90 | 52.24 | 0.00 | 16.27 |
| 2 | 19 | 55 | 29 | 3 | 106 |
| | 29.23 | 71.43 | 43.28 | 6.98 | 42.06 |
| 3 | 43 | 19 | 3 | 40 | 105 |
| | 66.15 | 24.68 | 4.48 | 93.02 | 41.67 |
| Total | 65 | 77 | 67 | 43 | 252 |
| | 100.00 | 100.00 | 100.00 | 100.00 | 100.00 |

Pearson chi2(6) = 168.0325  Pr = 0.000

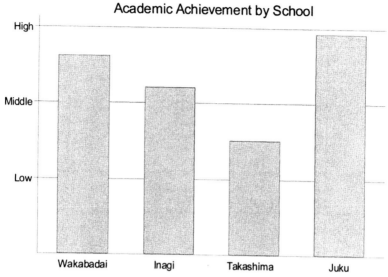

**Figure 15.1. Histogram of Mathematics Achievement**

## Ordered Logistic Regression Combined Scales Model

The ordered logistic regression combined scales model is first presented, followed by qualitative and quantitative analyses of each of the statistically significant factors of diversity in relation to mathematics achievement. Mathematics achievement is measured by student grades, participant observations, and a national database accessed through the University of Tōkyō.

The collapsing of variables into more generalized scales increases the reliability of statistical results. Prior to quantitative analysis, bivariate scatterplots were examined to justify collapsing and recoding variables. The linearly increasing relationships between the generated locally fitted weighted regression lines and trends in the fitted values provided positive confirmation. The null hypothesis was that there was a relationship between mathematics instruction (mathinst), socioeconomic background (finance), sociocultural identity (sociocult), family/community involvement (famcomm), geographical location (location), and gender (gender), and mathematics achievement.

Table 15.4 shows the result of adding the six-predictor scales into the ordered logistic regression model, clustered by school. In this case, the pseudo R-square value is 0.144, meaning that the overall combined scales model accounts for approximately 14.4 percent of the variation in mathematics achievement, which is a fairly good indicator of how well the model fits the data.

Ultimately, three of the six scales had high predictive values. The mathematics instruction and socioeconomic background scales were statistically significant at the 0.001 α-level (p = 0.000 and p = 0.001, respectively). The sociocultural identity (sociocult) scale was statistically significant at the 0.05 α-level (p = 0.028).

A comparison of the means for each of the six scales by mathematics achievement yields the chart in figure 15.2. The lines represent the three mean levels of mathematics

**Table 15.4.** Combined Scales Model of Mathematics Instruction (mathinst), Socioeconomic Background (finance), Sociocultural Identity (sociocult), Family/Community Involvement (famcomm), Geographical Location (location), and Gender (gender)

| Acadachvt | Robust Coefficient | Std. Err. | z | P>\|z\| | [95% Confidence Interval] | |
|---|---|---|---|---|---|---|
| Mathinst | .6971121 | .1131994 | 6.16 | 0.000 | .4752453 | .9189789 |
| Finance | .2798443 | .0826604 | 3.39 | 0.001 | .1178329 | .4418558 |
| Sociocult | .1206075 | .0548248 | 2.20 | 0.028 | .0131529 | .2280621 |
| Famcomm | -.0414052 | .0613317 | -0.68 | 0.500 | -.1616132 | .0788028 |
| Location | 1.822916 | 1.100357 | 1.66 | 0.098 | -.3337438 | 3.979577 |
| Gender | .3035284 | .3808466 | 0.80 | 0.425 | -.4429173 | 1.049974 |
| _cut1 \| | 5.994798 | 2.175282 | (Ancillary parameters) | | | |
| _cut2 \| | 8.392183 | 2.699344 | | | | |

Ordered logit estimates

Log pseudolikelihood = -225.35465
(standard errors adjusted for clustering)

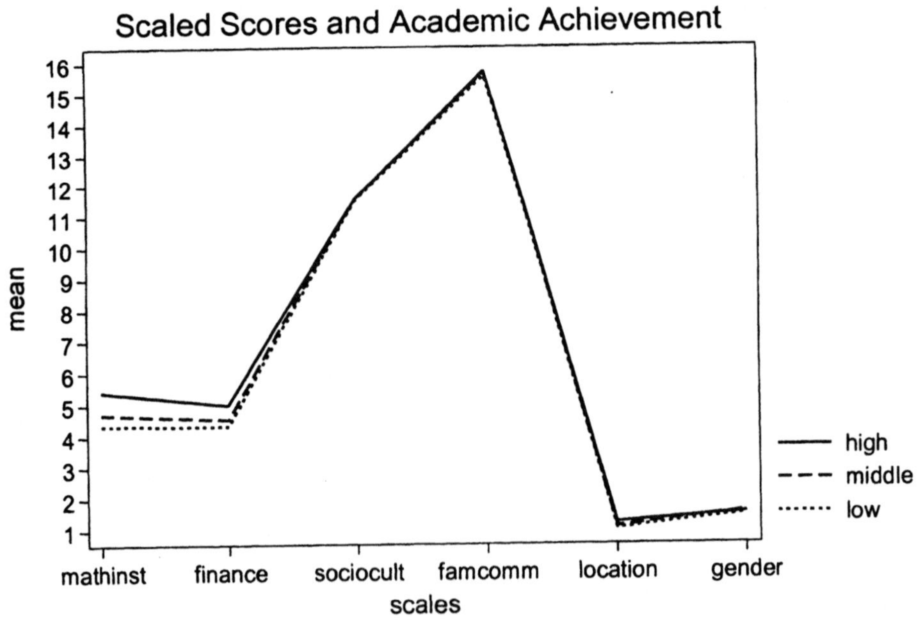

| | | |
|---|---|---|
| Number of obs | = | 251 |
| Wald chi2(1) | = | . |
| Prob > chi2 | = | . |
| Pseudo R2 | = | 0.1241 |

**Figure 15.2.** Means of the Scaled Scores by Mathematics Achievement

achievement (low, middle, high). The greatest difference in means indicates points where the scale is a strong predictor of mathematics achievement. This is particularly the case in mathematics instruction, socioeconomic background, and sociocultural identity, which aligns with the major findings. These three factors are explored further.

## Mathematics Instruction

In general, Japanese teachers are able to deliver effective mathematics instruction because they have a solid understanding of the topics taught and are knowledgeable of mathematical goals based on collaborations across national, municipal, district, and local levels. Focus group interviews show that although the tide begins to turn in junior high and particularly high school, critical thinking strategies are a built-in component of classroom learning at the elementary school level. Moreover, Japanese textbooks prepare teachers to think about teaching in broad and specific contexts, from clearly understanding the unit goal to engaging students in a particular activity in a lesson.

Statistical analyses confirmed the impact of mathematics instruction on mathematics achievement. The variables comprising the mathematics instruction scale in the quantitative analysis included time spent on mathematics studying/homework per week, personally making a contribution to science or mathematics, and rating of mathematics ability level compared to other students. Ordered logistic regression of the mathematics instruction scale, clustered by school, showed that mathematics instruction is a statistically significant predictor of mathematics achievement at the 0.001 $\alpha$-level (p = 0.000). The odds ratio provided further information to determine the effect of mathematics instruction on mathematics achievement. The logistical odds of a student with well-rounded mathematics instruction receiving a high mathematics achievement score are 92.7 percent greater than a student who does not have a one point increase in mathematics instruction. This was the largest increase found within the six scales.

## Socioeconomic Background

Second, Japanese education is guided by a filtering process based on socioeconomic class. While few studies have been done in this area, qualitative data collection shows the pressing need for such research. Striking effects in socioeconomic background were observed through examples of wealth capital, holiday and leisure activities, and other financial indicators. In affluent neighborhoods, students were more likely to attend *juku* (cram school), participate in extracurricular activities, travel domestically and internationally, and have access to additional financial resources. According to an analysis by Thomas Rohlen, there is "a trend toward a greater role for family factors in educational outcomes." A major reason for this is the rising significance of privately purchased advantages in the preparation process—namely, elite private elementary and *juku* (Rohlen and LeTendre, 1996, pp. 23–24).

Socioeconomic class plays a role in academic success because the combination of these kinds of experiences increase students' chances of passing entrance examinations into top-tier Japanese universities and secure employment. Even elementary schools and nursery schools have their place in this status hierarchy. According to an interview with a parent at Takashima Daigo Elementary School, this parent's child was denied admission to nursery school because she did not have the aforementioned "proper credentials" (Suzuki, K., personal communication, February 1, 2006). The parent's concerns are resonated by the Organization for Economic Co-operation and Development (OECD) Examiners' report (1972) on Japanese education. OECD finds that:

> Parents make strategic plans for launching their children on "escalators" leading to the most prestigious career lines by moving into districts with the high schools enjoying a reputation as recruitment grounds for elite universities, and they try to get their children into elementary schools leading to such secondary schools and into kindergartens leading to such elementary schools, some of them attached to universities. There are proverbial stories in Japan of the educational mothers, the *kyōku mama*, who even register under false addresses in order to launch their children into the Bancho Elementary School leading to Hibiya High School or the private Azabu Junior High School. The pressure on the individual student becomes so great that it probably is even reflected in the suicide curve, which has a life-cycle maximum for both sexes at the age of university examinations and an annual maximum for boys in the month the results of the examinations are known. (pp. 2–3)

Similarly, the importance of family effects is addressed in the present study. The quantitative variables comprising the socioeconomic background scale included importance of being financially stable, highest academic degree anticipated, and future occupation. Despite the young age of the students, there was an emerging pattern and relationship between those who had decided on a future occupation and high mathematics achievement. Of the 278 students in the sample population, 73.02 percent had already chosen a career path with the greatest proportion of these students enrolled at Wakabadai Elementary School and Nichinōken *Juku*, the schools with the two highest socioeconomic levels. Ordered logistic regression of socioeconomic background scale, clustered by school, showed that socioeconomic background is a statistically significant predictor of mathematics achievement at the 0.001 $\alpha$-level ($p = 0.000$). The logistical odds of a student with supportive socioeconomic background receiving a high mathematics achievement score is 45.5 percent greater than a student who does not have a one point increase in socioeconomic background. Similar to mathematics instruction, ordered logistic regression showed that a one unit change in the socioeconomic background scale leads to a significant difference on the outcome of mathematics achievement. The predicted probability of high mathematics achievement (outcome 3) is 0.6281 or 62.81 percent. Predicted probabilities illustrate a strong, positive relationship between high socioeconomic background scores and high mathematics achievement scores.

## Sociocultural Identity

Third, sociocultural identity is founded upon complex systems created by interactions of cultural, historical, religious, and linguistic influences on the lives of students.

Examples of sociocultural identity were provided through participant observations in the areas of civic education and transmission of culture through major school events. Through civic education, schools transmit deeply rooted national culture and traditions. For example, according to a student at Takashima Daigo Elementary School:

> Every day after lunch we clean the classroom. Each of us has a responsibility, whether it is wiping the floor, holding the dustpan, sweeping with a broom, cleaning the chalkboard, writing the next day's schedule . . . the responsibilities are rotated and I think our teacher wants us to learn how to take care of the space we're in. (Personal communication, January 20, 2006)

Major school events such as performance days (*gakushū happyōkai*), sports festivals (*undōkai*), and children's festivals (*kodomo matsuri*) that occur regularly over the course of the academic year help build relationships amongst students, teachers, and the community. Teacher/administrator focus group participants agreed that sociocultural identity directs the lives of elementary school students on their path toward adolescence and adulthood because teaching and learning in these environments provide central values inculcated by the educational system.

Quantitative data analysis complemented qualitative focus group findings. Six variables were selected for the sociocultural identity scale, including how often students studied together, participated in sports, participated in cultural activities, played with friends, volunteered, and how important it was to develop relationships with others. In general, the more students interacted with others and collaborated in relationship-based activities, the more inclined they were to perform well academically. While sociocultural identity was not a statistically significant predictor of mathematics achievement in the individual ordered logistic regression, it was a statistically significant predictor of mathematics achievement in the combined scales model at the 0.05 $\alpha$-level ($p = 0.028$).

Following the ordered logistic regressions for the aforementioned factors of diversity, each individual scale was tested for the assumption of parallel regression/proportional odds. Tests of parallel regression/proportional odds were used to examine the generalizability and reliability of the model across datasets. None of the values were significant, indicating that the parallel regression/proportional odds assumption had not been violated.

## CONCLUSIONS AND IMPLICATIONS FOR U.S. PRACTICE

Upper-elementary school students proved to be a critical population to study because the experiences of Japanese students provide unique perspectives on the complexity of support, social pressures, and expectations in educational paradigms. With a sample population of 278 fifth and sixth grade students at Wakabadai Elementary School, Inagi Daiichi Elementary School, Takashima Daigo Elementary School, and Nichinōken *Juku*, descriptive analyses and intraclass correlation illustrated general characteristics and an overview of the dataset. There were fourteen questions and six scales in the ordered logistic regression analysis. Based upon content, variables were combined into the following six-predictor scales: mathematics instruction, socioeconomic background, sociocultural identity, family/community involvement, geographical location, and gender.

Collapsing variables into a combined scales model increased the reliability of statistical results, and allowed better assessment of the variables' overall predictive power on mathematics achievement. Ordered logistic regression on the combined scales model, clustered by school, produced an R-square value of 0.144, which is conventionally a fairly good indicator in the social sciences. Ultimately, three of the six scales had high predictive values. The mathematics instruction and socioeconomic background scales were statistically significant at the 0.001 $\alpha$-level, and sociocultural identity scale was statistically significant at the 0.05 $\alpha$-level. These findings were supported by qualitative data in the form of participant observations and focus group interviews.

Although it is difficult to isolate all the conditions that have made it possible for the Japanese educational system to take root, it is recommended that future research focus on mathematics instruction and curriculum as a means to highlight issues of socioeconomic class and sociocultural identity. These studies may be used as points of reference to further examine Japanese and other global educational systems, particularly the United States. For example, collaboration is routine for Japanese teachers, and even without research lessons, teachers would not be isolated from one another as they commonly are in the United States.

Japanese teachers plan lessons together and spend thirty or more days per year on schoolwide activities. They work together on numerous school-wide committees, including performance day (*gakushū happyōkai*), sports festival (*undōkai*), and children's festival (*kodomo matsuri*). Accounts of Japanese elementary school life suggest that competition is avoided (Lewis and Tsuchida, 1988). Electing a teacher of the year is, for example, a practice that surprises many Japanese teachers who visit the United States. Japanese attribute success to hard work rather than ability, and teachers see collaborative lessons as an important way of working toward this goal (Stevenson, Azuma, and Hakuta, 1986; Stigler and Hiebert, 1988). Shared planning of mathematics instruction and lessons means that criticism is generally appreciated amongst colleagues, which is a good place to delve into more sensitive issues such as socioeconomic class and sociocultural identity.

By U.S. and global standards, the Japanese mathematics curriculum is very sparse. As the 1999 Trends in International Mathematics and Science Study researchers found, Japanese mathematics textbooks cover just eight topics compared to an average of more than sixty-five for the U.S. textbooks (LeTendre, Baker, Akiba, Goesling, and Wiseman, 2001; Stigler and Hiebert, 1999). Japanese textbooks tend to be brief, so there is substantial time to cover each of the small number of topics they study. For example, Japanese fifth graders are expected to spend twelve mathematics periods studying levers, although there are just a few pieces of knowledge that they are expected to take away. This allows plenty of time for hands-on exploration of how the force needed to lift an object differs depending on where the fulcrum is placed. Since Japanese teachers have a proportionately large number of class periods to help students master a relatively small amount of curriculum, teachers can devote time to studying the most effective ways to present it, rather than wading through massive textbooks to figure out what is really important to teach (Lewis and Tsuchida, 1988; Stigler and Hiebert, 1999). The education standards, which are being developed in most states, could make U.S. curricula more cohesive and uniform if the educational system is viewed as a whole rather than in parts.

Although the Japanese educational system has a rigid structure, a soft middle level tends to allow for modifications to take place in policymaking and implementation, especially through the work of prefectural and municipal curriculum specialists (De-Coker, 2002). Japanese teachers have an important voice in policymaking, standards setting, and textbook writing, and many of Japan's top-down reforms undergo a transformation in the gradual process of implementation. As a result, Japan's educational system, from the policy level to the classroom, involves substantial collaboration in the creation and implementation of MEXT standards.

## FURTHER DISCUSSION

Although global education is often resistant to modification (Shimahara and Sakai, 1995), it should be mentioned that overall stability of the Japanese system makes it easier to concentrate on the policy changes that do occur. The comments of a MEXT official (2006) suggest a surprisingly long timetable for alteration:

> We change the *Course of Study* about every ten years. But the truth is that ten years is too short a time to change classroom education. If we greatly changed the *Course of Study* every ten years, teachers would be turning their heads this way and that so often that their necks would break. So we make major changes in the *Course of Study* only every twenty years or so, and in between it's just fine-tuning. (pp. 10–11)

This feature suggests that caution should be placed when adopting Japanese mathematics pedagogy, curriculum, and practices. Educational borrowing should always occur with an understanding of the social, economic, political, cultural, and other conditions that form the undercurrent of the Japanese and global systems in the wider context.

Studies of shared mathematics curriculum and instruction collaboration among teachers provide valuable insight and direction for further research on issues of cross-national comparisons. Examining factors of diversity requires the establishment of structural change in planned, cooperative steps. Progress may not necessarily occur quickly; however, each step contributes in the process of continuous, long-lasting impact.

## REFERENCES

Amano, I. (1984). *Striving toward a society of learning*. Tōkyō: Nihon Keizai Shinbunsha.

Amano, I. (1990). *Education and examination in modern Japan*. Tōkyō: Tōkyō University Press.

Astin, A., and Astin, H. (2000). *Leadership reconsidered: Engaging higher education in social change*. Battle Creek, MI: W. K. Kellogg Foundation.

Astin, A., Green, K., and Korn, W. (1987). *The American freshman: Twenty year trends, 1966–1985*. Los Angeles: Higher Education Research Institute, University of California, Los Angeles.

Baker, D. (2001). TIMSS-R: Innovation in international information for American educators. *Education Statistics Quarterly, 3*(1), 17–19. Washington, DC: National Center for Education Statistics.

Beauchamp, E. (Ed.). (1991). *Windows on Japanese education*. Westport, CT: Greenwood Press.

Beauchamp, E. (2003). *Comparative Education Reader*. New York: Routledge.

Beauchamp, E., and Vardaman, J. (1994). *Japanese education since 1945: A documentary study*. Armonk, NY: M. E. Sharpe.

Bickman, L., Hedrick, T., and Rog, D. (1993). *Applied research design: A practical guide*. Thousand Oaks, CA: Sage.

Bok, D. (1996). *The state of the nation: Government and the quest for a better society*. Cambridge, MA: Harvard University Press.

Boyatzis, R. (1998). *Transforming qualitative information: Thematic analysis and code development*. Thousand Oaks, CA: Sage.

Buraku Kaihō Kenkyūsho (Ed.). (1983). *The road to a discrimination-free future*. Ōsaka: Buraku Liberation Research Institute.

Central Council on Education. (1972). *Basic guidelines for the reform of education*. Tōkyō: Ministry of Education.

Cummings, W., Tatto, M., and Hawkins, J. (2001). *Values education for dynamic societies: Individualism or collectivism*. Hong Kong: University of Hong Kong, Comparative Education Research Centre.

DeCoker, G. (2002). *National standards and school reform in Japan and the United States*. New York: Teachers College Press.

Duke, B. (1989). *The great educators of modern Japan*. Tōkyō: Tōkyō University Press.

Fetterman, D. (1998). *Qualitative approaches to evaluation in education: The silent scientific revolution*. New York: Praeger.

Fujita, H. (1978). *Educational status attainment in modern Japan*. PhD dissertation, Stanford University.

Fuller, B., and Rubinson, R. (1992). *The political construction of education: The state, school expansion, and economic change*. New York: Praeger.

Gonzales, P., Calsyn, C., Jocelyn, L., Mak, K., Kastberg, D., Arafeh, S., Williams, T., and Tsen, W. (2001). Pursuing excellence: Comparisons of international eighth-grade mathematics and science achievement from a U.S. perspective: 1995 and 1999. *Education Statistics Quarterly, 3*(1), 13–16. Washington, DC: National Center for Education Statistics.

Hawkins, J. (1983). Educational demands and institutional response: Dowa education in Japan. *Comparative Education Review, 27*(2), 204–26.

Hawkins, J., and Cummings, W. (2000). *Transnational competence: Rethinking the U.S.-Japan educational relationship*. Albany: State University of New York Press.

Horio, T. (1994). *Education in modern Japanese*. Tōkyō: Tōkyō University Press.

Ishida, H. (1993). *Social mobility in contemporary Japan: Educational credentials, class and the labour market in a cross-cultural perspective*. London: Macmillan.

LeTendre, G., Baker, D., Akiba, M., Goesling, B., and Wiseman, A. (2001). Teacher's work: Institutional isomorphism and cultural variation in the U.S., Germany, and Japan. *Educational Researcher, 30*(6), 3–15.

Lewis, C., and Tsuchida, I. (1988). Teaching is Cultural. *American Educator, 22*(4), 12–17.

Lynn, R. (1988). *Educational achievement in Japan: Lessons for the west.* London: Macmillan.

*Mainichi Daily News.* (1984, September 13). U.S. education secretary envies *Juku.* Tōkyō.

Ministry of Education, Culture, Sports, Science, and Technology (MEXT). (2006). *Ministry of Education, Culture, Sports, Science, and Technology statistical portrait.* Tōkyō: Ministry of Education.

Monbukagakushō. (1997). *Gakkō Kyōin Tōkei Chōsa Hōkokusho Heisei 7 Nendo.* Tōkyō: Monbushō.

National Assessment for Educational Progress (NAEP). (2001). *The nation's report card mathematics 2000.* Washington, DC: U.S. Department of Education.

National Center for Education Statistics (NCES). (1999). *Teaching mathematics in seven countries: Results from the TIMSS 1999 video study.* Washington, DC: U.S. Department of Education.

National Center for Education Statistics (NCES). (2003). *Teaching mathematics in seven countries: Results from the TIMSS study.* Washington, DC: U.S. Department of Education.

Office of Educational Research and Improvement (OERI). (1988). *The educational system in Japan: Case study findings.* Washington, DC: U.S. Department of Education.

Organization for Economic Co-operation and Development (OECD). (1972). *Reviews of national policies for education: Japan.* Paris: Organization for Economic Cooperation and Development.

Okano, K. (1995). Habitus and intraclass differentiation. *International Journal of Qualitative Studies in Education, 8*(4), pp. 357–69.

Reich, R. (1992). *The work of nations. Preparing ourselves for twenty-first century capitalism.* New York: Vintage Books.

Rog, D., and Bickman, L. (1998). *Handbook of applied social research methods.* Thousand Oaks, CA: Sage Publications.

Rohlen, T., and LeTendre, G. (Eds.). (1996). *Teaching and learning in Japan.* London: Cambridge University Press.

Rosenbaum, J., and Kariya, T. (1989). From high school to work: Market and institutional mechanisms in Japan. *American Journal of Sociology, 16*(1), 134–65.

Sasagawa, K. (1993). Gaikokujin no gakushūken mondai to "posutokokuminkyōiku-jidai" no kyōiku-gaku. *Kyōiku, 43*(2), 16–27.

Sato, M. (1992). Japan. In H. Leavitt (Ed.), *Issues and problems of teacher education: An international handbook* (pp.155–68). Westport, CT: Greenwood Press.

Shimahara, N., and Sakai, A. (1995). *Learning to teach in two cultures.* New York: Garland.

Sōmuchō Tōkeikyoku. (2006). *Japan statistical yearbook 2005/2006.* Tōkyō: Sōmuchō.

Stevenson, H., Azuma, H., and Hakuta, K. (1986). *Child development and education in Japan.* Tōkyō: Shibundō.

Stigler, J., and Hiebert, J. (1988). Teaching is cultural. *American Educator, 22*(4), 4–11.

Stigler, J., and Hiebert, J. (1999). *The teaching gap: Best ideas from the world's teachers for improving education in the classroom.* New York: Free Press.

Torney-Purta, J. (1987). The role of comparative education in the debate on excellence. In R. Lawson, V. Rust, and S. Shafer (Eds.), *Education and social concern: An approach to social foundations* (pp. 16–23). Ann Arbor, MI: Prakken Publications.

Tsuchimochi, G. (1993). *Education reform in postwar Japan.* Tōkyō: Tōkyō University Press.

U.S. Department of Education. (2007). *International comparisons of entrance and exit examinations.* Washington, DC: Office of Educational Research and Improvement.

Vogel, E. (1979). *Japan as number one: Lessons for America.* Cambridge, MA: Harvard University Press.

## Chapter 16

# Inclusive Education in the Global Context: The Impact on the Government and Teachers in a Developing Country— Trinidad and Tobago

### Alicia Trotman and Greg Wiggan

Since the United Nations Educational Scientific and Cultural Organization (UNESCO) publicized its educational goals through its vision of Education for All, education in developing countries has become more globally focused (UNESCO, 2000). After the signature of the Dakar Framework for Action in Dakar, Senegal, in 2000, the vision of Education for All was made a top priority in developing countries like Trinidad and Tobago (T&T). T&T's Ministry of Education's (MOE) commitment to providing education for all is generated through the global context of the United Nations and other international governance institutions. With the emphasis on improving education, many of the educational structures and practices that were imported from advanced industrial societies influenced the educational system in T&T in terms of what is taught in schools, where British ethos are privileged (Barrow and Reddock, 2001). Given the country's resource limitations and urban-rural infrastructure challenges, T&T's government has been struggling to make education for all a reality. However, a more central concern is whether education for all is realistic for T&T given its history and its social class system, and if so, what structural changes are needed to make this happen? This chapter explores these questions. It begins with a discussion on the historical and social context of T&T and its educational system, and connects this to the emergence of education for all discourses. The findings and recommendations are presented with implications for educational policy reform.

## THE HISTORY OF COLONIZATION IN TRINIDAD AND TOBAGO

Trinidad and Tobago was a British colonial society, and it gained independence in August 1962. As a result of being under colonialism for four centuries (Trinidad was a Spanish and then British colony, while Tobago was a Dutch and then French colony, and was later united with Trinidad under British colonialism), many of the colonial structures remained in terms of commerce, education, and social promotion. Eric Eustace Williams, who was a scholar and first prime minister of T&T in 1962, acknowledged that the colonization of the Caribbean was aimed at addressing Britain and other European nations' need for free labor and natural resources, and consequently was an extension of European domination (Palmer, 2006, pp. 27–29). As a result, similar stereotypes that existed between the privileged and poorer classes in Britain were reproduced in T&T. In T&T the privileged classes were the colonials (the slave masters or those of British ancestry) and the poorer classes were the colonized (the slaves or those of African ancestry). The slaves brought to T&T came principally from West Africa and, to a lesser extent, indentured servants came from other places such as India and China. Joanne Kilgour Dowdy's story "Ovuh Dyuh" in *The Skin We Speak* captures life in T&T's colonial society. She states:

> In order for a Trinidadian to make progress on the ladder of success, she has to embrace the English language. . . . Your job, as a survivor of the twenty-odd generations of slaves and indentured workers and overseers, is to be best at the language that was used to enslave you and your forebears. (Delpit and Kilgour Dowdy, 2002, p. 7)

As the author notes, in order to compete for opportunities in T&T, one had to adopt the culture deemed acceptable by the privileged. Assimilation into British cultural ethos was important for social mobility so many people wore a British mask while being of African and or East Indian descent. This mask was important for social inclusion and to mediate racial and ethnic prejudice and it paralleled racial patterns of discrimination against blacks and browns (other nonwhites) in the United States. Today, a similar mask is evident in the education for all discourse in T&T, which represents an ideal image that all are being educated when in reality the language and culture of those who have been promised education are being excluded. By discourse we mean language as a continuous text of speech that entails systems of representation and power relations. Education for all suggests that all those who are being educated are included in the process of education. This is referred to in the guiding principle for inclusion in the Salamanca Statement published by UNESCO (2000):

> schools should accommodate all children regardless of their physical, intellectual, social, emotional, linguistic or other conditions. This should include disabled and gifted children, street and working children, children from remote or nomadic populations, children from linguistic, ethnic or cultural minorities and children from other disadvantaged or marginalized areas or groups. (p. 6)

In harmony with the UNESCO education agenda, one of the aims of T&T's government is to become "globalized" through its mission toward education for all or inclusive education. However, the glitter of inclusive education appears to be another adornment much like the mask of globalization, where globalization is often espoused as improving opportunities in developing economies through the increased presence of multinational corporations, while failing to unmask the unfair wage structures that transnationals create and how they monopolize local markets and promote environmental degradation in less-developed countries. A similar mask is present in T&T's inclusive education discourse, regarding how equality and access to education are espoused, but the disparities between the privileged and poorer classes are never systematically addressed, and where public policy only includes those who have power and resources. We attempt to illuminate the processes that hinder a truly inclusive education in T&T.

## METHOD OF ANALYSIS

Using critical discourse analysis (CDA), we illustrate the gaps between the discourses of the government and the power elites, versus teachers and the lower class of T&T. This study includes data from a focus group conducted in 2007 with secondary school teachers from the Needs Assessment Study. Due to the study's focus on examining the relationship between education for all and special education in T&T, secondary school teachers were the target group because they had more experience working with special needs students (Miske Witt and Associates, 2008). Thus, their input was necessary for information about challenges that students with disabilities might face at the secondary school level.

Critical discourse analysis was used because it provides a critical examination of the social world and the relationships between groups. As we analyze the discourses of T&T's government and the power elites, versus teachers and the lower class, we highlight instances of what is said within the two groups and in relation to the other group. For this project, the discourses that are analyzed are principally MOE written documents and teacher responses (Rogers, 2004).

## THE HISTORY OF EDUCATION IN TRINIDAD AND TOBAGO

In T&T, there are approximately 636 schools, and of this amount approximately 156 are secondary schools and the remaining 480 are primary schools. The schools are divided into eight districts—namely, Port-of-Spain and Environs (St. George West), St. George East, St. Patrick, Victoria, Caroni, North East (St. David and St. Andrew), South East (Nariva and Mayaro), and Tobago. Today schools are divided into four categories: composite, secondary/senior comprehensive, government secondary, and assisted secondary schools. Junior secondary schools (three-year schools) have transitioned to government secondary schools (five-year schools) as part of the Seamless Education System Project. However, prior to 2008, the secondary schools were divided into five types of schools, which were junior secondary,[1] composite, senior secondary/comprehensive, government secondary, and assisted secondary school. These five school types are explained below.

During colonial times, only students of privilege were allowed to attend school. When the colony gained independence in 1962, the administration formed from the political party called the People's National Movement (PNM), attempted to draft a plan to ensure that all children leaving primary school attended a secondary school. In the period between 1968 to 1983, twenty-one junior secondary schools were built to accommodate primary school children (Alleyne, 1995, p. 88). These schools used a double-shift system with forms from 1 to 3 (grades 8–10) to handle the growing number of students attending schools. Composite schools were also created and they provided a primary and secondary school education. Senior secondary schools were established to provide secondary education for those who graduated from the junior secondary and composite schools. These three types of schools mostly focused on curricula that were technical or vocational in nature. Senior comprehensive schools were five-year (form 1–5) or six-year (form 1–6) schools that provided academic (liberal arts) curricula. During the 1960s and 1970s, special needs students were not considered, and they were educated in separate outmoded school buildings.

Assisted secondary schools were the first secondary schools established in T&T. As a result, only the privileged (children of colonizers) were allowed to attend those schools. They held a reputation that enjoyed a status that surpassed the four types of schools previously mentioned. The assisted schools were six-year schools that only offered an academic curriculum. This type of school presented five years of secondary education and an additional year (sixth form) that was used to prepare students for entry into European universities. Assisted secondary schools were also called the denominational or "prestige" schools because they were partially owned by boards of different religious groups (for example, the Anglican, Hindu, Muslim, Presbyterian, or Roman Catholic boards).

The boards helped the schools obtain easier access to financial and academic resources. As a result, they were far better managed and equipped than government schools. Another difference between assisted schools and government schools was postsecondary employment preparation. There was a sense that the assisted schools prepared students for white-collar jobs, while the government schools prepared students for blue-collar jobs. Thus, an academic structure was already in place to separate the privileged classes from the poorer classes, and this connected to the social landscape of T&T.

Even though the five-year and three-year government secondary schools were created to meet the needs of the large number of students entering public schools, they were met with some critical responses from citizens of T&T. This stemmed from the absence of sixth form classes, which indicated that the students who may have qualified for these schools were not accomplished enough to be university candidates. Thus, the schools may have carried a stigma of inferiority that was felt by teachers and students (Alleyne, 1995). The quality of education was considered to be less than optimal, and the students in the government's schools were believed to be second-rate. These differences among the schools generated a system of inequality despite "the freeness" and "universality" of education which the government claimed to embrace. Furthermore, middle and upper class parents had the resources to pay for extra lessons so their children could prepare for the secondary entrance exams, which were needed for university admittance.

Today, class inequalities persist in T&T and the disparities in school quality are exacerbated by the segregation of wealth. Furthermore, most of T&T's less powerful lower class can discernibly be identified as people of African descent. Even so, T&T's population comprises different racial, ethnic (East Indian 40.0 percent, African 37.5 percent, mixed 20.5 percent, European 0.6 percent, Chinese 0.3 percent, other/not stated 1.1 percent), and socioeconomic groups, and historically schools were created to maintain a hierarchy with the premise of "fair" and "rich" being better than "dark" and "poor." In his sociological study of T&T, Lloyd Braithwaite concludes that "race and colour . . . seemed to have erected a caste-like society with little mobility across caste/class lines" (as cited in Campbell, 1997, p. 13). Although constrained, some mobility existed for fair-skinned females who were able to promote themselves through marriage. Dark-skinned Africans and Indians also had the opportunity for mobility through education, but discriminatory employment practices impeded their outcomes. The upper class was restricted to whites and fair-skinned colonialists (Campbell, 1997). But even as T&T became a more stratified society,

> [e]ducation moved the society away from the paramountcy of articularistic-ascriptive values characteristic of slave societies toward the greater, but imperfect, acceptance of universalistic-achievement values, but still racist society. This was a modernising function of education; it had the effect of modifying the plural society. (Braithwaite as cited in Campbell, 1997, p. 14)

Even after slavery, T&T remained a highly unequal society with race and color being very much determinants of social status, and an approximation to the Caucasoid phenotype and attributes associated with wealth and prestige. Since these structures are still in place, it would be remiss to think that it would not affect any changes that occur in education. These social problems do not merely exist in the area of the social class system, but also in student ability grouping. In T&T, special needs students who are poor are forced to enroll in public secondary schools where they suffer similar discrimination and stigma as their more able peers, who are also poor and often dark skinned, and who attend public schools. Since students with disabilities often need more assistance in schools, their teachers regularly lack the resources and training needed to work with them.

When the first secondary schools were created in T&T, there was little consideration given to the fact that special needs children, and children of the lower class could benefit from a high-quality education. Instead, the focus was on providing children of the gentry with education for leadership, and the lower class for servitude. Today, in the twenty-first century, the national perception is that all children need to be educated. However, is education for all possible given the inequalities that are already inherent in T&T? It is evident that teachers and T&T's government have very different perceptions of inclusive education. As T&T seeks to become global ready, it will need a high-quality education system. Inclusive education can work in T&T, but it should not simply mean that all students are included in the process of education; it should also mean that all levels of the hierarchy (privileged and poor) are *included in its policies.*

## EARLY ROOTS OF EDUCATION FOR ALL IN T&T

The initiative for education for all in T&T began in the early 1990s with a policy document called the White Paper. During the inception of the White Paper, the head of the government was the late Noor Hassanali (1987–1997). By the time the White Paper was formalized, the president was Arthur N. R. Robinson (1997–2003) and the head of the MOE was Kamla Persad-Bissessar (1999–2001). The White Paper documented educational strategies (1993-2003) and addressed the shortcomings and challenges of T&T's educational system (Mortley, 2005, pp. 4, 5). The MOE attempted to merge the educational goals of the country with that of the global context. This was further articulated in another document, the Green Paper, which identified draft quality standards for the education system (Mortley, 2005). For the Green Paper, the president was Dr. George Maxwell Richards (2003–present) and the Minister of Education was Mrs. Hazel Manning (2001–2007).

The standards in the Green Paper were organized around five central areas that focused on improving education for all students. These areas were the instructional environment (particularly school-based management), the school/community environment (particularly the school boards), the administrative environment (T&T's eight districts—Caroni, Tobago, St. Patrick, South East, North East, Victoria, St. George East, and Port-of-Spain and Environs), the regulatory environment (particularly the MOE), and the macrosocioeconomic environment (the societal and global contextual aspects that directly impact T&T's educational process). Each environment produced insights about improving education for all students, and connected to the broader mission of becoming globally ready. This analysis of the Green Paper is revisited later in the discussion.

Similarly, in 2003, at a ministerial roundtable on quality education in which the MOE participated, the meeting highlighted issues surrounding quality of education and student needs (Pigozzi, 2004). One of the major positions taken from this meeting was that

> quality education requires us [MOE] to redefine the perimeters of education to encompass certain basic knowledge, values, competencies and behaviors that are specifically attuned to globalization, but reflect the beauty and richness of our diversity expressed in different forms of belief, spirituality, culture and language. (Mortley, 2005, p. 15)

Through Vision 2020, the government of T&T (GoTT) began to adhere to these standards. Vision 2020 is a national plan for T&T that was created to respond to the global developments in economics, infrastructure, and information and communication technologies. It stressed a vision aimed at improving the educational outcomes for all citizens, so that the nation could compete globally in scientific, social, and technological areas (Lok Jak, 2006). This vision contained initiatives that were aligned with those aims outlined in the Dakar Framework, which were created at the World Education Forum. It included goals to provide education for all and included an agreement to have UNESCO as the lead partner in mobilizing and coordinating the efforts of all participating countries in achieving those goals (UNESCO, 2000). The GoTT sought to execute its aims outlined in the educational component of Vision 2020, by establishing the Seamless Education System Project with the monetary and supervisory assistance of the Inter-American Development Bank (IDB) (Manning, 2007b). This project reinforced the government's educational goals and addressed school processes for inclusive education.

## SPECIAL EDUCATION IN T&T

One of the goals of T&T's government was to address the educational needs of students with disabilities. As the ministry stated, "the opportunity for persons with special education needs to participate fully in all of the educational, employment, consumer, recreational, community and domestic activities that typify everyday society" (Ministry of Education Student Support Services Division Discussion Paper on "Inclusive Education," August 2004, p. 5).

This was not the first time that the GoTT created policies that were designed to meet the educational requirements of persons with special education needs.[2] Special education was defined as children who may need extra or different kinds of assistance because they have learning difficulties or disabilities that make it harder for them to learn than most children of the same age (Mortley, 2005, p. 11). In the early 1980s, the MOE created a special education unit that supervised special education (Pedro and Conrad, 2006, p. 2). However, teachers were not trained to work with special education students. The country was still a fledgling nation trying to develop appropriate social services, and special education may not have been a priority. In the past these students were educated in separate schools and were more or less in contained classrooms. Teachers took it upon themselves to learn about special education. However, training for teachers still did not take place under the stewardship of the MOE. Later, in the first phase of the special education unit, when more than three hundred teachers became certified in special education,[3] they still lacked the resources and continued support from the MOE.

Teachers made the first step to be educated in special education, but the GoTT could not provide full support for them because of its own financial limitations. Today, the GoTT now recognizes the need for special education as part of its initiative for inclusive education. However, the resources and the expertise needed to make this work are still lacking. Furthermore, the idea of inclusion must do more than provide political participation for the elite.

Although the GoTT has more power than teachers, it must recognize the importance of having input from teachers and the broader T&T society, particularly the poor. The GoTT is a legacy of the colonial system and it may have inherited traditions based on racial and class discrimination. In the same way that slave masters ignored their slaves or considered them to be less intelligent, the government ministers make broad statements that allude to goals that are achievable from their perspective, but would be quite difficult or nearly impossible for laborers such as teachers to attain. Inclusive education calls for educational change, so it cannot be achieved if the status quo remains, not only for T&T but the global community.

The impact of globalization on inclusive education can be seen in the responses of secondary school teachers in recent studies in T&T. Miske Witt and Associates[4] (2008) were contracted by the T&T government and the International Development Bank as part of the Seamless Education System Project, to conduct a Needs Assessment Study[5] for Inclusive Education from Early Childhood Care to Secondary Education, aimed at meeting the goal of becoming globally competitive. Once the study was completed, the findings concluded that T&T's education system is in dire need of reform. The results indicated that there is a lack of coordination among stakeholders to facilitate the holistic upbringing of all children in terms of education, health, civic duty, culture, and vocation (Witt and Associates, 2008). This is evidenced by teachers' feelings of apprehension regarding fully supporting the initiative for inclusive education.

## ANALYSIS OF THE GOVERNMENTAL DISCOURSE

As mentioned, the government's Green Paper is an important MOE document explaining education for all and outlining its discourse on the topic (Mortley, 2005). This document articulates the educational improvements that are needed in T&T, and it addresses improving inclusion in the area of special education. For the purposes of our examination and analysis, the content targeted in the Green Paper is language that contains "special education," and/or "disabilities," and/or "special needs." In the document, the GoTT used special educational needs (SEN) and/or special needs to refer to students with disabilities. In the past, the government had a policy of educating special needs students in separate schools, but in more recent times it has been including these students in general education.

There were five environments listed as areas of educational focus in the Green Paper. First, the macro-socioeconomic environment[6] dealt with providing social and economic stability for learners, and second, the regulatory environment[7] focused on programs that would be provided for students with disabilities. Regarding the regulatory environment, the Green Paper stated:

> Special or extraordinary needs are identified as soon as possible and pro-active measures must be taken. To the extent that learners who are assessed as having special needs are provided with Individualized Programmes. . . . Special needs include learners with physical or emotional handicaps and those who are socially or economically disadvantaged.
>
> Individual Programmes comprised of specially tailored and delivered curricula, supporting services delivered in an integrated way and coordinated manner, and the provision of resources and materials, as necessary. (Mortley, 2005, p. 31)

In the above paragraph, there is no statement about the persons responsible for identifying special needs and how proactive measures should be taken. There is also no mention of whether the individualized programs differ for students with different disabilities, and who may come from different social and economic backgrounds. The proactive measures were listed as timely intervention, provision of support, and dissemination of information; but it was not clear who in the MOE was responsible for administering the measures (Mortley, 2005). There was also language about facilitating linkages with other government ministries but those ministries were not listed.

The third area the government addressed was the administrative environment,[8] which focused on the design and infrastructure of schools. The document explained the school designs that were "accommodative to advances in technology, and provide access to persons with disabilities" (Mortley, 2005, p. 57). However, it lacked additional elaboration regarding the types of technology that were needed or the regulations that would be adhered to. The document focused on providing "comprehensive services for learners with disabilities, including fair access to the general curriculum, related services, assistive technology . . . as needed" (Mortley, 2005, p. 62). It was not apparent who in administration was responsible for these services or how the resources would be allocated.

In the fourth area of the Green Paper, school/community environment,[9] the document mentioned but did not explain the role of the community in helping students with disabilities. This was the environment that was closest to students besides the instructional environment; in terms of support, it was crucial to the successful implementation of services for students with disabilities. The fifth and final area, the instructional environment,[10] addressed how students with disabilities were to be educated. There is only one reference to special needs in this section, where it states, "Maintain effective modern facilities and amenities to accommodate students with special needs" (Mortley, 2005, p. 81). Again, there is no indication about the characteristics, providers, or repairers of the modern facilities and student services.

The GoTT's policies are written attempts to make clear what *needs* to take place in education, but it is ambiguous on *how* it is to happen. The discourse is syntactical where there is a heavy focus on language that describes the future, but little attention given to specific processes aimed at meeting the educational goals. This is rather dubious because it fails to place policy in a framework of action. When addressing policy and change, Fulcher (1989) argues:

> We need to conceptualize policy broadly: first, as a form of practice, that is, as an instance of the social practices which we carry out all the time and which constitute social life. In each of our social practices we seek to attain our objectives and we deploy discourse, as both our theory of how that bit of the world in which we want to achieve our objective works, and as tactic, that is, as a means of attaining our objective. Second, more specifically, policy is the outcome of political states of play in policy arenas: in the case of education these arenas occur at all levels: they are exemplified by teacher-parent encounters, school meetings, teacher union meetings, bureaucratic arenas and so on, wherever there is debate and decisions are made. (pp. 15–16)

GoTT listed five areas for supporting students with disabilities, yet there was very little input from current teachers.

Since there were no clear descriptions and explanations regarding how special needs students were to be educated, much was left to be desired from the government. While there was no explicit discussion on inclusive education in the Green Paper, there were many references to "all learners" and "all students," which indicates that the GoTT was moving toward a paradigm of inclusion.

In the Green Paper, the GoTT set forth its policy on education, and the language could be described as a grand narrative because it represented the voice of the government and not teacher practitioners. In other words, it bears the mask of authority that hides the reality of those who have been excluded (teachers). And those who have been barred from school reform discussions are expected to conform despite being excluded.

## TEACHER DISCOURSE

An examination of teachers' viewpoints about special education illustrates that special needs is not a universal theme that holds the same meaning or has the same implications as the government embraced, where the government saw special needs students more as a challenge (this may explain why they were not prioritized), while teachers were trying to understand and meet the students' needs (Rogers, 2004).

The responses from secondary school teachers reveal that they were open to meeting inclusive education goals, but without resources or support, it could prove extremely difficult or impossible. The teachers' reflections are taken from seven secondary school visits. The teachers' viewpoints are summarized below.

Teachers for the most part felt empowered within their schools but experienced tensions with other groups. These groups included the GoTT, parents, and sometimes students. The challenges that the teachers experienced were considerable, which played into their perception of inclusive education. In terms of the challenges of inclusive education, some responses were:

- There is insufficient time for individual instruction.
- What about maturity of pupils, you might have twenty-year-olds with fifteen-year-olds?
- How can a teacher work with pupils of different abilities in one class? Inclusion gives teachers extra work and he/she would need extra time to work with pupils. Is it the right thing for the child? Why not group disabled children and have one person assigned to teach them?
- There is a security problem at this school. If we need to show a movie in the classroom, we have to go to the office to rent the television and CD player. Also, we teachers do not have technical competence with the media. We need someone to help us hook up these media devices.

Given the teachers' concerns, there was apprehension and distrust regarding implementation of inclusive education since there were a number of lingering issues. One teacher said it clearly when she said, "too many visits by the authorities and no action." In addition, teachers were fully aware that they needed more resources to continue their professional development. The GoTT tried to meet this need with the inception of the University of Trinidad and Tobago, which was founded in 2004, and aimed to triple postsecondary enrollment and help produce quality teachers for public schools (Manning, 2007b). This move was praised, but it was also met with some concern among current teachers, as well as T&T's Unified Teachers' Association (TTUTA), since consultation with these groups about programs and services to be offered at the institution was minimal (Permell, 2007).

It appeared that teachers' perspectives about how the GoTT was attempting to improve education were not being addressed. The GoTT was clearly moving at a hastened pace to improve education as it tried to change the system in the swiftest way and with minimal input from teachers. Even though the Green Paper was open to public comment, it would have been difficult for teachers to concede to a document that had drastic implications for their profession, yet it excluded their viewpoints. The different views between the GoTT and teachers showed there was a gap between the two contexts: the local context and the institutional context. These sentiments are similar to how most U.S. teachers may feel powerless to the imposition of No Child Left Behind mandates, which constitute a policy framework that is prescribed by the government and is punitive against teachers, while it provides very little space for teacher input.

T&T teachers spoke about "curricular reform" and "lack of resources." They also had concerns that there were no clear explanations about how to handle special education. Since the teachers had very little experience with students with disabilities, they were not aware of what was needed or what to expect. It appears that since the teachers were less powerful than the GoTT, they may not have been seen as important to the decision-making processes. Most of the input the government received came from high-level administrators.

The teachers generally had to express their concerns to the media. It also appeared that they expressed their experiences repeatedly but there was no follow-up to what they were going through at their respective schools. Teachers' viewpoints were not adopted into the discourse that was taking place at the GoTT's level. It is possible that if the teachers' perspectives were included in the discussion prior to the making of policy documents, the challenges with implementation would have been addressed more effectively.

## A POSSIBLE WAY FORWARD

Since the teachers and the GoTT (mainly politicians) operate in different spheres, it is often difficult to have a meeting of the minds. One solution is to create a space where all the groups can meet and express their concerns, and develop a shared meaning about what *Education for All* entails. Fulcher (1989) poses that "we need to conceptualize policy clearly and then theorize it adequately, meaning we need to put it in a wider theory of social relations, rather than treat it as something different from other actions" (p. 15). Thus, when the GoTT created a mandate for inclusive education, it needed to meet with other groups (for example, teachers, parents, and community members and leaders) to inquire about how they would be connected to this new initiative. Like many other nations, T&T is a developing country, struggling to recover from four hundred years of colonialism, while attempting to modernize its social and educational systems. As T&T attempts to respond to the needs of the twenty-first century, going forward, the mantra should be shifted from *Education for All* to *Education for All by All*—that is, the inclusive education that is needed in T&T.

## ACKNOWLEDGMENTS

Alicia Trotman wishes to acknowledge Dr. Susan Peters and Patrick N. Leahy for their support.

## NOTES

1. The junior secondary schools have been changed into government secondary schools as part of the Seamless Education System Project (Manning, 2007a).

2. Throughout this paper, persons with special educational needs or students or persons with disabilities or special education students refer to the same population.

3. Dennis Conrad was both the president of the Special Education Association (TASETT) and the chair of the special education committee in the teachers' association (TTUTA), and both associations, in joint partnership with the University of Sheffield, introduced a distance education certification program in special education for local teachers.

4. Alicia Trotman, a doctoral student of Michigan State University College of Education, was the only member who was a citizen of T&T.

5. The study was organized in two phases—May and October 2007 and was administered across the eight districts in T&T. Data were collected from (i) focus groups with teachers, principals, parents, and students respectively; (ii) interviews with principals, general education and special education teachers, school psychologists, guidance counselors, social workers, ministry officials, and NGO representatives; (iii) survey data of students' diagnosed, as well as those who were yet to be diagnosed as having disabilities; (iv) observations from school visits; and (v) interviews with teachers and college and university representatives, and union and curriculum officers. The schools visited were government primary and secondary schools, government assisted primary and secondary schools, and private and public special education schools.

6. The macro-socioeconomic environment refers to all the factors that have a direct bearing on the type and quality of education that is delivered. It reflects the nexus between the education system, the national development agenda, and the international arena (Mortley, 2005).

7. The regulatory environment (for the most part) represents or is represented by the government of T&T, particularly the Ministry of Education (Mortley, 2005).

8. For the most part, the administrative environment is comprised of the eight school districts that provide support for their respective schools as they assume greater management of and responsibility for their operations (Mortley, 2005).

9. The school/community environment includes the entrepreneurs, businesses, professionals, agencies, organizations, and others who either directly or indirectly impact or are impacted by the education process (Mortley, 2005).

10. The instructional environment is principally focused on the school, but relates to all the elements that affect student instruction. This includes the school climate, leadership, management, educators, instructional design and practices, access to resources and materials, community participation, supporting and supplemental programs, and student instruction and services (Mortley, 2005).

# REFERENCES

Alleyne, M. H. M. (1995). *Nationhood from the schoolbag—A historical analysis of the development of secondary education in Trinidad and Tobago.* Washington, DC: Multinational Project for Secondary and Higher Education (PROMESUP)—PREDE/OAS.

Barrow, C., and Reddock, R. (Eds.). (2001). *Caribbean sociology: Introductory readings.* Princeton, NJ: Markus Wiener Publishers.

Campbell, C. C. (1997). *Endless education: Main currents in the education system of modern Trinidad and Tobago.* Kingston, Jamaica: University Press of the West Indies.

Delpit, L., and Kilgour Dowdy, J. (Eds.). (2002). *The skin that we speak—Thoughts on language and culture in the classroom.* New York: The New Press.

Fulcher, G. (1989). *Disabling policies? A comparative approach to education, policy, and disability.* New York: Falmer Press.

Lok Jak, A. (2006). *Vision 2020 Draft national strategic plan.* Retrieved March 30, 2008, from www.vision2020.info.tt/plans/National_Plan.pdf.

Manning, H. (2007a). *Presentation of the mid-term report to inform the design of the early childhood care and education component of a seamless education system project for Trinidad and Tobago.* Port-of-Spain, Trinidad and Tobago: Ministry of Education of Trinidad and Tobago.

Manning, H. (2007b). *A seamless education system project for Trinidad and Tobago.* Port-of-Spain, Trinidad and Tobago: Ministry of Education of Trinidad and Tobago.

Ministry of Education (Trinidad and Tobago). (2004). *National policy on student support services system.* Port of Spain: Trinidad and Tobago Ministry of Education.

Miske Witt and Associates, I. (2008). *Achieving inclusion: Transforming the education system of Trinidad and Tobago—Final report: Inclusive education component of the seamless education project.* Port-of-Spain, Trinidad and Tobago: For the Ministry of Education of Trinidad and Tobago.

Mortley, B. (2005). *Green paper for public comment: Draft quality standards for education in Trinidad and Tobago.* Port-of-Spain, Trinidad and Tobago: The Ministry of Education.

Palmer, C. A. (2006). *Eric Williams and the making of the modern Caribbean.* Kingston, Jamaica: Ian Randle Publishers.

Pedro, J., and Conrad, D. (2006). Special education in Trinidad and Tobago: Educational vision and change. *Childhood Education, 82*(6), 324.

Permell, C. (2007). Speech at TTUTA's 28th Anniversary Celebrations [Electronic Version]. Retrieved May 6, 2007, from www.caribbeanteachers.com/index.php?module=News&func=display&sid=69.

Pigozzi, M. J. (2004). The ministerial viewpoint on "Quality Education." *Prospects, 34*(2), 141–49.

Rogers, R. (Ed.). (2004). *An introduction to critical discourse analysis in education.* Mahwah, NJ, and London: Lawrence Erlbaum.

UNESCO. (2000). *Education for all: Meeting our collective commitments.* Dakar, Senegal: UNESCO, France.

## Chapter Seventeen

# In the Diaspora, Black Caribbean Canadian Culture Matters: Perspectives on Education "Back Home"

### Jean Walrond

According to the 2006 Canadian census, 489,645 respondents claimed that their ethnic origin was wholly or partially Caribbean. Those who claimed a single ethnic origin totaled 243,855, while those reporting multiple origins totaled 245,785 (Statistics Canada, 2008a). Similarly, 12,310 Albertans claimed multiple ethnic origins, one of which was Caribbean, while 7,470 Albertans stated that their identity was solely Caribbean (Statistics Canada, 2008b). Many Caribbean heritage students struggle to fit into Canada's education system, and their parents find that public education is a heavily contested area and that it fails to meet the needs of their children (James and Brathwaite, 1996). In 1996, about 60 percent of black[1] Caribbean Canadian youths failed to graduate from high school (Foster, 1996, p. 131); in 2008 the figure quoted was 40 percent (*Macleans*, February 1, 2008; Toronto Board of Education, 2008).

Many people of Caribbean heritage take pride in being part of the black Diaspora. We have brought aspects of our Carnival culture to our new homes in other countries, and are happy to claim it as part of our cultural identity (Walrond-Patterson, 1999). Yet in many instances our children who have been raised in countries such as the United States, Canada, and England, seldom embrace the countries "back home" and are not motivated to lend a hand to those who are less fortunate in the Caribbean. This is especially obvious in environmental disasters such as hurricanes or in social justice issues in the areas of poverty or health. Our children know very little about the history, social, or economic realities of the Caribbean. Dei (2008) writes: "all too often there is the teaching of African history as simply episodic events and not as contributions of language, culture, arts, [and] technology" (p. xv).

In this chapter, I explore the difficulties some Caribbean heritage parents experience as they seek to educate their children. I contend that lack of recognition and representation of Caribbean identity are in part reasons why our children are not getting the education that allows them to be national and global citizens. The terms Caribbean Canadian and black Caribbean Canadian are used interchangeably throughout this chapter. Five families of Caribbean heritage, consisting of two single-parents and three couples, participated in the research. All participants had children who were in the final two years of high school or had completed high school within the last five years. I draw on discourse in critical thought and cultural studies to frame my research—ethnic and inclusive practices, parent and student freedom, social justice, and the importance of linking history to culture and the politics of change in education.

## LACK OF REPRESENTATION
## AND RECOGNITION AS SOCIAL JUSTICE ISSUES

On Saturday, April 22, 2006, my daughter, Michelle, was involved in a traffic accident as a pedestrian. Although she was in a fight for her life, she was sent off to the hospital by the Edmonton police as a Jane Doe, while her purse with all her identification lay on the street in plain view. As she is a sickle cell anemia patient who frequently attends the University of Alberta hospital, she was immediately identified by their emergency department's staff and received their protocol for sickle cell anemia patients. I credit the staff's recognition of my daughter, at a time when she was unable to identify herself, for her survival. Kallen (2003) observes: "The major trust of international human rights instruments has been to endorse the principle of the global unity of humankind and to afford protection for the fundamental rights and freedoms of individuals" (p. 21). The politics of recognition is inextricably linked to self-actualization, and indeed has the potential to scuttle one's efforts for its development.

How a person is recognized in a society determines how that person achieves self-actualization and this precludes Maslow's paradigm. One's self-actualization on a human scale also addresses how people are seen and perceived when they are least able to articulate to others who they are. The following vignette suggests the "politics of recognition" is an important construct of black Caribbean "way of knowing."

In 1988, the maternal side of my family held a reunion in Trinidad to celebrate the passing of our grandmother who died in April. In August of the same year, my brothers, my sister, and I, along with our children, travelled from New Jersey, New York, Canada, and Barbados for this celebration. During our stay in Trinidad we decided to go to Barbados where our sister resides, as it is the ancestral home of my father. While on the island, we visited the Barbados Museum, which my sister described as the best place she had seen Caribbean plantation life historically documented.

Established in 1933, the Barbados Museum collects, preserves, and publishes "matters relating to the history and antiquities of Barbados" with a mandate of promoting the culture of the island (The Barbados Museum and Historical Society, n.d.). The museum is housed in a former British army garrison that was built between 1790 and 1853. The area of the museum that aroused my interest was the plantation house and its period rooms (these are rooms that authenticate original plantation rooms). One room was decorated with a secretary bookcase,[2] chair, table, and bookkeeper's ledger. My eyes travelled through the glassed window to rest on the table with the opened ledger. Amazed, and with wonderment, I noticed that the ledger's hand-printed pages listed the plantation's holdings or assets. Among the assets were horses, other animals, farming implements, tools, and enslaved Africans. I peered at the pages hoping or longing to notice a name, African or otherwise, which would identify these enslaved Africans. However, sadly, this was not to be found. When I entered the map room next door, I observed many interesting maps but focused on an eighteenth century map of Barbados[3] with many names inscribed on it. I realized the names were those of the plantation families who inhabited the island at that time. I decided to see if my family name was on the map and sure enough I saw the name "Walrond"[4] in six-point font. I called my family over to see what I had discovered, and as I stared at the map I continued to see even more Walronds.

What was even more interesting was that there was either a bundle of sugar cane or a windmill next to the name. These insignia denoted the occupation of the landowner. Make no mistake though, I knew then what I had discovered were names of those who had enslaved my ancestors. This profound realization of the chasm that existed between those two adjacent rooms struck me emphatically: I could trace my paternal lineage back to Barbados but not beyond.

The preceding narrative details a pivotal, personal encounter with rupture. Brand (2001), who writes of a similar experience, describes it in terms of "a rupture in the quality of being" (p. 5). In both senses rupture is a contextual dislocation created as a result of a group of people being torn away from one place and deposited into another space to recreate their experiences and their sense of place. Here, the experience connotes the loss of voice, heritage, language, place, geography, history, identity, ethnicity, culture, representation, and humanness, all of which are essential in defining a human being.

**Figure 17.1.  Map of Barbados (from the Collections of The Barbados Museum and Historical Society)**

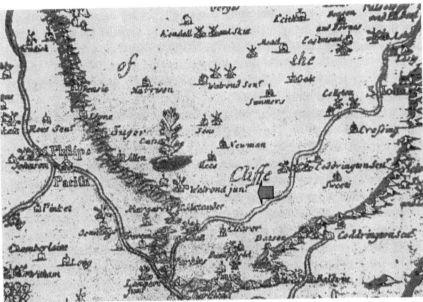

**Figure 17.2.    A Section of the Map of Barbados Showing the Name "Walrond" (from the Collections of The Barbados Museum and Historical Society)**

This experience of rupture is common to the majority of blacks in the Caribbean and the Western world as their history includes post-Columbus enslavement. The ensuing reality of this denial of humanness has caused me to constantly investigate if and how I am represented or recognized in established structures and social institutions.

## OUR HISTORICAL VIEW OF EDUCATION: INFORMAL EDUCATION AT THE DAWN OF INDEPENDENCE—"MASSA DAY DONE"

As a discussion about "border crossing" (Giroux, 2005) is an important aspect of Caribbean life, I will start this section with my own recollections of this phenomenon. Trinidad and Tobago became independent on August 31, 1962, crossing the border from being a colony to becoming an independent country. I remember staying up to watch our prime minister, Dr. Eric Williams, lower the Union Jack and raise the national flag of Trinidad and Tobago aloft in Woodford Square. Colonial states such as India and countries in Africa gained their independence from Britain after protracted struggles, but British Caribbean countries got their individual independence with a "nationalist expression [that] was more genteel, more muted, less confrontational, and less vituperative" (Palmer, 2006, p. 19). Nonetheless, it was a very memorable day for all the people and of course, the school children. Our new motto was "Discipline, tolerance and production." Our political leaders and scholars spoke and wrote about the sense of accomplishment we were experiencing as we were to control our own national destiny, and the English-speaking islands in the Caribbean were no longer

British colonies. Jamaica became independent on August 6, 1962, and, four years later in November 1966, Barbados became the third British West Indian island to become independent. This movement toward independence or republic status continued in the late twentieth century and today most countries in the Caribbean can claim this achievement.

As part of our political education, our parents emphasized that we listen to the parliamentary debates during the preindependence period. This emphasis was possible because of the public pedagogical work Eric Williams and his People's National Movement (PNM) did to educate the citizens of Trinidad and Tobago (Palmer, 2006). The PNM was the first national political party in Trinidad and Tobago, its members educated citizens through meetings in town squares throughout the country. Eric Williams recalls in his 1962 writings: "The People's National Movement made the first plank in its platform the political education of the people" (p. 244). This was an educational position taken by the PNM, which my research participants and I experienced growing up in the Caribbean in the 1950s and 1960s.

The Caribbean region's history includes socioeconomic relationships between a colonizing Eurocentric plantation society and a colonized group consisting of enslaved Africans, indentured South Asians, and Asians, and the few groups of indigenous Amerindians that are now dispersed throughout the area. The latter occupied the Caribbean area copiously and liberally during the pre-Columbian epoch. In the context of the history of the black Caribbean region, education and development are two nuanced and complex concepts. Beckford (1976), whose thesis contributes to the sociology of Caribbean education, writes that "modern Caribbean society displays structural forms that are a direct legacy of the slave plantation system [and that] this legacy provides the single most important clue for an understanding of contemporary Caribbean society" (p. 30).

The cultural framework of this type of society is based on cultural pluralism and acculturation toward that of the dominant white society (Beckford, 1976). He further contends that "during slavery educational opportunities were restricted" (p. 37), and after emancipation even though educational opportunities improved they were geared toward skills useful to the plantation. Blacks shunned this activity and sought social mobility, aspiring instead to a European lifestyle (Miller, 1976). Education was therefore one of the factors which differentiated those individuals "who had 'made it' from those who had not" (Beckford, 1976, p. 38). Within this highly socially stratified society, education is seen as a means of social mobility. As Miller (1976) writes:

> [The lower strata] have always been interested in education and participate in it for social mobility reasons: "To amount to somebody in life," "To become somebody important," "To be able to get a good job and be respected." They have never been interested in education in order to keep the economy on an even keel or to become efficient farmers. (p. 62)

However, the enslavers/colonizers' views of education were totally different. A quote from Nyerere (1968) sums up the purpose of education after slavery and during colonialism. He states: [Education] was motivated by a desire to inculcate the values of the colonial society and to train individuals for the service of the colonial state"

(p. 269). The historical purpose of education for people of the Caribbean is challenged by decolonization efforts. Friboulet (2005) provides a modern definition of education as a learning process that enables societal, interpersonal, and psychological empowerment, participation in development, and lifelong learning. After emancipation the slave owners viewed vocational training as a requirement for economic development and not as a means to building individual or collective identities. However, blacks in the Caribbean viewed education as a means for constructing social and cultural identities.

Thus, my intention for this research was to investigate whether parents of Caribbean heritage, living in Edmonton, shared similar educational aspirations and experiences. In this chapter I unfold the layers of educational discourses within the context of the Caribbean experience, cultural identity, and development.

## EDUCATION LANDSCAPE

Like the majority of Canadian parents, Caribbean Canadian parents are very concerned about the type of education their children receive. While the majority of Canadians are anxious about the level of funding education receives and the cost-benefit ratio of education, there are additional concerns. First, educators are challenged to adapt their curriculum and pedagogical practices to meet the educational needs of a diverse student body (James, 2003; McLaren, 2003; Thomas, 2000). Second, some theorists and many parents are concerned that the present education system, in an effort to fulfill a capitalist agenda, streams or attempts to stream many children into low-paying or low-status jobs (Carby, 1999; Giroux, 2003; James, 2001; McLaren, 2003). Third, there are concerns that the classroom is not a welcoming and accommodating environment where children of Caribbean heritage and other marginalized groups can discuss their life experiences (Foster, 1996; McLaren, 2003; Walrond-Patterson, 1999; Walrond-Patterson, Crown, and Langford, 1998). Fourth, the community and parents are concerned that schools, with their hidden curricula, function to make their children unwitting and unwilling accomplices and participants in a form of social reproduction that undermines their children's opportunities for self-actualization (Bannerji, 2000; Brathwaite, 1996; James, 2001).

In addition, there continues to be a concern that the multidisciplinary views of many black theorists, including James and Brathwaite (1996), Solomon (1992), and Walcott (1996), are perhaps read by scholars, but rarely cited or included in the dominant social or education discourses (Codjoe, 1997; Gilroy, 1991). One cause of this "is the power of Western Civilization as valorised through the fabrication of Whiteness and the racial boundary policing that comes with the engagement of space" (Dei, 2008, p. 49). He continues:

> [T]his fabrication also exacted and continues to exact heavy material, physical, psychological and emotional tolls on racialized subjects via spirit injury and the emotional harm of racism through the "acceptable" ways of producing and validating knowledge via the Eurocentric gaze. (Dei, 2008, p. 49)

By failing to include these theorists' views in the wider educational discourse, educational policy analysts exclude crucial information that should contribute to educational policy debates. Moreover, when the works of black writers or those of other nonmainstream groups are not readily visible because of strategic and systemic silencing, it not only "masks their . . . hidden history" (Gilroy, 1991, p. 12), but, more importantly, it also connotes that the work of nonmainstream people may not be valued as a way to enhance history, heritage, and lived experiences in formal education (Codjoe, 1997; Codjoe, 2001; Dei, 1996; Kallen, 2003; Walrond-Patterson, 1999; Walrond-Patterson, Crown, and Langford, 1998).

I have reflected on the educational experiences of many Caribbean Canadian children but, as Clandinin and Connelly (1995) and Greene (1978) point out, there is a larger story. School narratives are often dominated by the storied lives of school board officials, administrators, teachers, and students. Sleeter (2004), who identifies herself as a white teacher educator, conducted research with white teachers to determine the inherent ill effects of the education system. She was able to conclude that these effects are associatively linked to those in society. She positions the white discourse of nonwhite students' educative potentials squarely on a hegemonic society. She argues that white teachers cannot be expected to be nonracist because they are products of and beneficiaries of a society that is inherently and structurally racist. Further, she contends that "a structural analysis of racism suggests that education will not produce less racist institutions as long as white people control it" (p. 164). As well, a "cultural-deficiency perspective" (Sleeter, 2004, p. 166) is adopted where parental attitudes toward schooling, lack of language skills, and gang influences contribute to a power remissive discourse used to frame the school failure of children of Caribbean and others of nonwhite heritage.

King (2004), another teacher educator, documents the white student teacher experience with the visible minority student through their "dysconscious racism" (p. 72) lenses. She defines dysconsciousness as "an uncritical habit of mind that justifies inequity and exploitation by accepting the existing order of things as given" (p. 73). She conceptualizes dysconscious racism as "limited and distorted understandings about inequality and cultural diversity," which underscores the salience of and hence makes philosophically problematic any praxis toward "truly equitable education" (p. 72). During the course of conducting multicultural seminars for white teachers, Howard (2006), a self-identified white educator, said white teachers were tired of hearing about the white dominance discourse including the reminders of the past sins that whites committed against blacks, and they dismissed the whole notion that improvements in school quality can benefit minority students' school achievement. For these educators, keeping the existing curriculum and pedagogy makes sense, and adding on some cultural minority "stuff" is the way to go, a reflexive practice aimed at keeping the minority quiet.

## CULTURE AND EDUCATION

When culture is defined in disciplines such as anthropology and cultural studies, the consistent analogue with these definitions or understandings of culture is that the phenomenon appears to be embedded within the individual. Similarly, core cultural values are viewed as being harder to eliminate and, in due course, serve as one's heritage. On the other hand, material culture incorporates popular culture and when different cultures come together, cultural layering occurs. Although culture is socially constructed, its uniqueness, individuality, and habitude suggest the difficulty that may be encountered when it is ignored and suppressed in the classroom. This elucidation of the concept "culture" is necessary as it grounds my discussion on the terms diaspora and multiculturalism and their implications for education.

British Caribbean identities are understood to be Métisages, or a mixture of the many cultures that are present on the islands (Alleyne, 2002). Insufficient thought has been given to this form of cultural alliance (Maingot, 1996; Mintz, 1996; Stewart, 1986; Waters, 1999). With the exception of the few local Aboriginal people, we, Caribbean people, all claim a heritage that was foreign to the Caribbean. The "borderlines of the 'present'" arrangement that Bhabha (1994) references is synonymous with the Caribbean cultural identity experience. So we had a mixture of French, Spanish, Syrians, Chinese, East Indians, and African influences all subsumed by an overarching British colonial experience (Alleyne, 2002; Mintz, 1996). Within that fluidity of experiences we learned to be quite adaptable at school. None of these different cultural strands of knowledge were recognized and most of our formal learning was based on the British system.

These historical experiences have equipped us with a particular worldview and lenses to construct a cultural identity that is unique to people of Caribbean heritage today (Alleyne, 2002). How one identifies oneself culturally determines the extent to which one engages with cultural structures. Thus even within Caribbean heritage communities, essentialism statements cannot be made about the group's approach to education. Evidently those who identify themselves as of African heritage and having lost their identity markers may have more reason to distrust dominant systems. On the other hand, those who did not have to involuntarily give up such identity markers as language and worldview may have a more collective approach to development, and could draw on historical identity constructs to interpret goals for self-development.

## THEORETICAL FRAMEWORK

I used Ogbu's (1992) thesis regarding society and schooling as a model to collect my data. He states:

> [A]n essential key to understanding the differences in the school adjustment and academic performance of minority groups is understanding of (a) the *cultural models*[5] a minority group has with regard to the U.S. society and schooling, (b) the *cultural and language frame of reference* of a minority group, (c) the *degree of trust or acquiescence* the minorities have for White Americans and the societal institutions they control and (d) the *educational strategies* that result from the above elements. These factors are dependent in part on the group's history, its present situation and its future expectations. (p. 289)

As I analyzed my data using NUD*IST Version 6 software (QSR International Pty Ltd., 2004), emerging themes indicated that my research participants were identifying themselves as having cultural identities constructed from a multiplicity of cultures. I thus conceptualized my theoretical framework defined as the cultural identity model (figure 17.3) based on a human ecology system (Westney, Brabble, and Edwards, 1988) integrated with a social ecology model (Berry, 1995; Bronfenbrenner, 1979). This modified human or social ecology model consists of seven nested concentric circles with the individual situated in the centre; family, clothing, and the home in the second most inner circle; sectored community structures in the third most inner circle; sectored societal structures in the fourth circle; and sectored world structures in the fifth. The sixth realm ($N_n$) is undefined as this consists of entities that are unknown or unnamed at the present time. As cultural attributes subsume all sectors of these concentric circles, it is placed within the seventh and outermost circle. As the individual draws cultural attributes from all sectors of these concentric circles to varying degrees, the individual can be described as having several cultures. In other words, I visualized

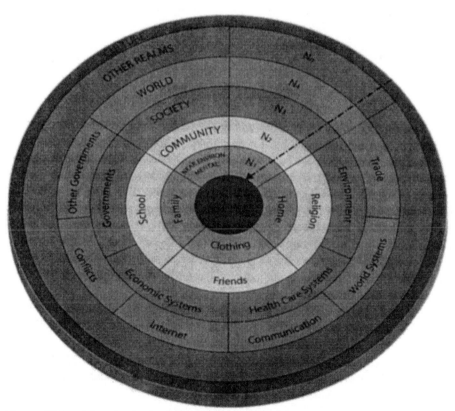

**Figure 17.3. Cultural Identity Model Modified from the Human and Social Ecology Models**

culture as a component of each of these sectors, contributing to the overall cultural identity of the individual, thus accounting for the notion of a multiplicity of cultures.

This emerging framework helps me to define culture within the context of a multi-cultural country such as Canada, and it can be used to interpret Ogbu's (1992) student achievement model. The assumptions I make about cultural identity are:

1. An individual has a collective of cultures not just a culture.
2. Cultural identity may be static in moments or instants, but it is dynamic or fluid (Appadurai, 2003; Hall, 1999) across time and space.
3. Cultural attributes are transmitted through semipermeable boundaries, where the actors' "internalized social attitudes and expectations" (Barakett and Cleghorn, 2000, p. 134) and determine the level of cultural transmission.
4. Cultural homeostasis exists in this environment. Cultural homeostasis is defined as the state of equilibrium that occurs when an individual is at the point of cultural harmony with and in his or her environment.

My study discusses these "edu-cultural" concepts under the rubric of the group's culture. Since my research questions what Caribbean immigrant families wish educators to know about them, I thought that this was the appropriate framework for conceptualizing my investigation in Canada.

## RESEARCH DESIGN

This investigation uses qualitative research methodologies: ethnography, group discussions, and autoethnography. Leaders in the Edmonton Caribbean community identified prospective families for interviews. The interviews were conducted in 2004. These families either had children who were recent high school graduates or were just about to graduate from high school, and the parents attended schools in the Caribbean between the 1960s and 1970s. Interviews were conducted with five families of Caribbean heritage, two were single parents and three were couples. During my initial contact I explained my research and invited them to participate. In the case of the couples I decided to interview the females first, followed by the males, and then both as a couple. Once all individual and couple interviews were completed, a focus group conversation was performed.

Denzin and Lincoln (2000) define qualitative research as, "a situated activity that locates the observer in the world" (p. 3) of the phenomenon under investigation. During this process the researcher transforms the participant's world into a series of "field notes, interviews, conversations, photographs, recordings" (p. 3), memos, and self-reflective diary entries. Because of its ethnographic focus and community base, qualitative research was best suited for this project (Fine, Weis, Weseen, and Wong, 2000). Using two or more interpretive frameworks in research design has particular advantages. First, a multimethod approach makes the research more rigorous because different methods check for plausibility, authenticity, credibility, and relevance (Denzin and Lincoln, 1998, 2000). Second, it helps make the research more holistic because different methods produce different types of data (Fine et al., 2000; Lather and Smithies, 1997). Such a research practice yields optimum results in racialized and minority communities because it helps document the voice of those who were silenced previously and tells the stories that are stored in "safe places" (Fine et al., 2000; Ladson-Billings, 2000). Fine et al. (2000) argues that qualitative research methods acknowledge "up front" the researcher's role in the study. This is important because the "situated researcher approaches the world with a set of ideas, a framework (theory, ontology) that specifies a set of questions (epistemology) that he or she then examines in specific ways (methodology, analysis)" (Denzin and Lincoln, 2000, p. 18).

To obtain a deeper meaning of their education experiences in both the Caribbean and Edmonton, I asked the participants to prepare a reflective exercise for the group discussion, which I facilitated. Each research participant was asked to reflect on his or her experiences and prepare a literary work for the focus group discussion. Pictures, newspaper clippings, or certificates were also used to convey their thoughts on the research topic.

## FINDINGS

### Educational Structure in the Caribbean

Errol (pseudonym) is one of the parents I interviewed. He has two girls who completed high school in Edmonton, Canada. The following is his recollection of schooling in the Caribbean.

> Well in the Caribbean we go from Standard One to Class [Standard] Six and when you get to Class Six it allows you to do an exam and when you pass it then you can go on to teaching. It allows you to be a teacher so you reach to Class Six. They allow [you to write the exam] and then they accept you into Teacher Training College and then you go through one, two, or three and then you go ahead, but when I reached [Form] Five at a secondary College in Georgetown, I went to Bishops College to do [the] advance [level Certificate exam]. . . . Most people would . . . have passed an entrance exam and if you got a junior scholarship and you passed, you got in. (Errol, personal communication, June 30, 2004)

When many of my research participants and I attended school in the Caribbean, the educational structure was modeled after the British system. Most children started school by attending kindergarten at about age five. Although the system varied slightly from one country to another, the basic structure was very similar to the one Miller (1976) describes of the Jamaican school system, which consisted of four stages. These were "early childhood, primary, secondary and further" (p. 49). The primary schooling starts after kindergarten and continues until age twelve when students write the Common Entrance Exam. Those who pass this exam earn a place in Form 1 at a grammar school, which was considered an academic stream.

With a successful completion of schooling in Form 6 in the academic stream, the graduate could pursue a university degree (Miller, 1976). Students who were not successful with the exhibition exam in Standard Five went on to Standard Six and

Standard Seven, at which time they would write the school exiting exam at about age fourteen, and at that time be eligible to leave school. Thus one could potentially leave school at age fourteen with a School Leaving Certificate, which would be the lowest level credential with which one would want to leave school. As research participant Errol described, in the schooling stream that went to Standard 6A and 6B, students wrote an island-wide School Leaving Certificate exam (Miller, 1976). Those who qualified had the option to attend teacher training college, technical college, or theological college for another three years. At this stage females would probably attend beautician or secretarial schools to get those skills, while males would learn a trade. In other schools, these skills were included in the school system.

In an interview, I detected a hesitation in Errol's voice when he described the exam system: "Most people would . . . would have passed an entrance exam." This hesitation indicates his understanding that not everyone who went to schools would pass their exams. As many West Indian education historians and theorists point out, a percentage of places in the elite schools were left for those with more social and cultural capital than others (James, 1963/2002; Miller, 1976; Williams, 1962). Hence they did not have to go through the rigorous selection process Errol would have had to go through.

## Education and Social Class

When I interviewed Rosemary I learned how different education could be from one part of the Caribbean to another based on social class status, which reflected financial circumstances. Rosemary told me that, although she enjoyed going to school her high school experience came to an abrupt end at age eleven, just as she was about to settle into her studies at high school. She sat for the common entrance exam just as my brother and I did. And, just as we did, she earned a place at the very prestigious St. Joseph's Convent High School in Tobago. As she did not pass with very high marks, she did not gain a full scholarship as we did, so her parents had to pay a portion of the fees. Unfortunately, they could not afford to do this, so she was only allowed to attend the school until the money ran out. While Rosemary had Caribbean schooling to age fifteen, most of it was spent at the elementary school level where she would take the school-leaving exam at age fifteen and thus be officially entitled to leave school. She states: "I went to high school, but never completed that because of finances, I was not able to complete the high school part of it [my education], so there was a big break there [in my schooling]."

After hearing that Rosemary did not have an opportunity to complete her high school at St. Joseph's Convent, I inquired as to whether she had any opportunity to go back to school. She then shared this experience:

What I did was I went back to the elementary [school]. Rather than stay at home and run around and get into trouble with friends, I went back to elementary and just being in elementary [school] [I] just stayed in the highest, the last grade, which was grade seven.

As I reflected on this narrative, I got the impression that Rosemary was very frustrated with her situation of not being able to complete high school with her peers. The ending is almost a sigh that it was finally over. It must have been a painful exercise to be there with students who were much younger or were not successful at passing the national exams as she was. This, however, exemplifies the value and importance some people in the Caribbean place on education. As the following narrative indicates, one of Rosemary's teachers was instrumental in getting her back into elementary school. "I had a teacher who came home and got us out of the house and brought us back [to school]; she came home and said 'You come back to school'" (Rosemary, personal communication, June 21, 2004).

In some ways I sense the limitations that Rosemary experienced, and these exposed my own privileged subjectivity. However, these limitations were somewhat compensated by the accompanying drive and determination of which she spoke throughout our discussion. From Rosemary's conversations, I understood that while she did not complete her high school, she still had an interest in education and a dream of completing high school. The conversation also suggests that her parents felt schooling was important and they wanted her to get a formal education. My other conversations with her showed that within the home, the parents passed on informal knowledge to their children. However, the relationship between the parents and the community was such that each understood what roles they should or perhaps could assume in order to help children self-actualize. This is not to assume that all families functioned as Rosemary's did. I also cannot assume that all communities functioned similarly. Still, this was Rosemary's experience and in some ways it parallels my own.

With some of my other participants, such as Pamela and Errol, I saw another side of this community and communal endeavor toward the education of children. This is observed by what Pamela said when we spoke about the community and volunteering.

> In terms of being more specific to the question, I mean it was a good experience academically and in all ways, we had good relationships with the teachers and the community. We volunteered and so it is a rich experience that can match any. . . . We had school feeding programs. [She laughs.] I tell you I volunteered, but you know I ate some of that food, too. [I am happy that you mentioned those school feeding programs] because my aunt, Aunt Clemmie was responsible for that. All I know of my Aunt Clemmie is that she ran this breakfast shed [a midday food program] to feed people; the students in the community. My Aunt Clemmie and many of the other members of the Coterie of Social Workers understood that students needed to be fed if they were to perform well at school. She had two open air corrugated galvanized sheds in her backyard. These sheds had many rows of tables and benches. Whenever I visited her place, I observed women cooking a simple "rice and split-peas cook-up" dish in very large pots. This belief in feeding the body also extended to teachers in other schools that did not have direct access to community-school programs. In those cases teachers provided books and food to needy students.

## Formal Elementary School Experience

In the Caribbean, schools played an important role in the community and school attendance was viewed as a privilege. Much like Pamela, I can remember going through public schools in the Caribbean. Twice a day, on arrival at school in the morning and again after lunch, students lined up for formal inspection. The mornings were comfortable as the sun was not at its full intensity. However, after lunch, as we stood in the hot midday sun, usually perspiring from running around, it was a torturous exercise. I often wondered about its effectiveness. During those regimented occasions our uniforms were checked to ensure all the pleats were in place, our fingernails were clean, our hair was well-combed and brushed, and our shoes were shiny or clean if they were white.

School discipline and pride were enforced through the house system. We all belonged to a house (school team). For example, when I attended St. George's College I belonged to St. Patrick's House. We also had house colors. These were very evident during team events and on sports day. Each house had a representative, termed a prefect, in each class. The prefect system was part of many of our school experiences in the Caribbean. Prefects, who were elected by the members of the class in the respective houses, kept a meticulous log in which was recorded such things as punctuality, attendance, and neatness. He or she was responsible to the head girl or boy and performed such duties as rating the members who belonged to the particular house. The prefects were also responsible for assisting the other students in maintaining team spirit throughout the year. It was a responsibility that was taken very seriously. Ursula explains her memories of prefects:

> Well, I guess there is some sort of leadership qualities there I guess well you know how it is divided into various forms and you know it was a good experience. Because you get the respect from your classmates and with the other prefects you form a solid core of friendships. (Ursula, personal communication, July 16, 2004)

The prefects were peer role models and group leaders and they helped create a supportive school culture.

In the Caribbean, discipline was an important aspect of education. Students were expected to be well mannered, and there were consequences for breaking class rules. Spanking played a major role in our collective Caribbean school experience. Some teachers were known to be strict disciplinarians, and these included females as well. Miss Assay, who taught Standard 1, was such a teacher and it seemed she spanked students for almost anything and everything. I especially remember her making us redo our schoolwork if it did not meet her standards. I recall Miss Assay refusing to mark my exercise book and demanding that I do it over before she would mark it, because she felt my work could be neater. She was also my first sewing teacher, and was especially demanding regarding my sewing samples. The stitches had to be perfect and neat. Many of my classmates who did not obey her were spanked.

Alice's experiences were similar to mine. In describing what she remembers of her early school experiences, Alice, who went to school both in the Caribbean and Canada, compares the discipline of both these systems as follows:

> The principal and the teachers [in the Caribbean] had more influence on the children. There was more discipline, punctuality. . . . One thing I remember man, if you misbehaved the principal had options of spanking you or giving you licks on your hand.

Although Ursula describes herself as being studious, she also recalls the spanking culture of elementary schooling, making it a fearful place for her.

> I would say that for elementary I found it was really, really tough. I don't like to remember that part too much . . . and the reason for it is the spanking. . . . We got spanked for everything I chatted a lot and I still do and I got spanked for that. You get in spelling you get one [answer] wrong you got spanked for that.

While spanking has become less common in schools in the Caribbean, the education continues to be modelled after the colonizers' system, British in the case of Trinidad and Tobago.

## DISCUSSION

The participants' reflections illustrate some of the experiences in Caribbean education. For example, Rosemary's cultural understanding of education as a factor in social mobility was also borne out in her family history and socialization. On arrival in Canada she enrolled in night classes and completed her grade 12 and practical nursing certification. To some extent having experienced a culture of teacher involvement in the Caribbean, Rosemary was ambivalent as to what to say about Alberta's education system. As Rosemary expresses:

> I am not sure if the teachers here would actually come to you and help you unless you go to the teachers. They would always say they would help you if you need help. . . . Some might, but I do not know if they all will do that. In my time the teachers would actually put themselves out there. (Personal communication, 2004)

This and other findings from this research illustrate that as a collective Caribbean people support education, where teachers are a type of civil servant, and education is viewed as being necessary for upward mobility and as a way out of the second-class citizenship created through colonialism and slavery. The findings also demonstrate that while some families in the Caribbean were poor, they always valued the importance of education. In fact, one Caribbean mother expressed overwhelming satisfaction upon learning that her financially successful son had returned to school and succeeded in gaining his secondary school credentials. Errol, one research participant, recounts the following about his mother, "my mother she always said: Oh yes he is going to school now and he is doing well. He has gone back to school" (Errol, personal communication, 2004). This is another example of the educational cultural model of Caribbean families. An understanding of the cultural models of minority groups such as those from the Caribbean is essential, but this is one undertaking that eludes educators in many school systems in Canada.

Due to the lack of understanding and recognition regarding the cultural model of Caribbean youth, some experience ambivalence, operating in the spaces created by a "neither here nor there" [author's emphasis] identity (Hall, 2003). They operate within educational and social arenas of "radical configuration and cultural rearticulation [which] . . . have shifted the commonly held definitions of 'culture,' 'identity,' 'race,' 'nation,' 'state,' and so forth" (McCarthy, Giardina, Harewood, and Park, 2003, p. 459). At the same time, they do not see themselves represented in this changing national education discourse (James and Brathwaite, 1996).

## CONCLUDING PERSPECTIVES

From the narratives, it was evident that families in the Caribbean valued education and school credentials. Alfred's (2003) and Waters's (1999) research findings among Caribbean immigrants lead to similar conclusions. Black Caribbean families view education as being central to community and self-help, as a kind of job, and as a means of improving ones' social status and financial success in a drive toward self-actualization. An interesting question that can be asked is: How does this group define success? Having answered this question then there is a need to articulate this information to educators in school systems such as those in the United States and Canada. In addition, worthy of inquiry are the following. First, to understand if Caribbean immigrants face any challenges when they attempt to convey messages about their educational philosophy to educators, and for educators to understand how they can harness the cultural model that Caribbean youth and other transnationals bring into the schoolroom (Mitchell, 2001, p. 78); second, to understand if parents of Caribbean heritage students lack agency in schools or within the broader society. As Mitchell (2001, 2004) writes, groups with financial capital in a global economy can better influence their educational and social choices. This is a faint hint at the problems that poor minority groups might have, yet still they leverage their disadvantage in a cultural model of proschool motivations. In the age of globalization and increasing levels of social and cultural diversity, educators can better utilize minority students' cultural capital in the context of school processes and classroom pedagogy that promote achievement. Building on students' cultural stock of knowledge may very well be an important strategy for improving student engagement and developing a classroom and school environment of inclusion.

## NOTES

1. The term black has been racialized as pertaining to phenotypical characteristics (Wright, 2000); more recently, however, it is used to refer to a particular group of "people with family origins in the Caribbean and/or Africa" (Gillborn and Ladson-Billings, 2004, p. 3).

2. Also known as a cabinet-sécretaire, this piece of furniture is "a desk with a cabinet above" (Whiton, 1974, p. 185).

3. The 1710 map of Barbados was published by George Willdey (fl. c. 1695–1733) and sold at his business *The Great Toy Shop* next to the *Dogg Tavern*, on the corner of Ludgate Street near St. Paul's (www.antiquemaps.co.uk/chapter15.html).

4. The Walrond and Duke families figured prominently in the colonization of Barbados. Humphrey and Edward Walrond immigrated to Barbados sometime after 1645. Col. Humphrey, described as "exceptionally prominent and disruptive, in the early political affairs of

Barbados during the civil war" ("The Duke Family in Barbados," March 22, 2004), was president of Barbados from 1660 to 1663.

5. Cultural model is defined as "peoples' understandings of their world, which guide their interpretations of events in that world and their own actions in it" (Ogbu, 1992, p. 289).

# REFERENCES

Alfred, M. V. (2003). Sociocultural contexts and learning: Anglophone Caribbean immigrant women in U.S. postsecondary education. *Adult Education Quarterly, 53*(4), 242–60.

Alleyne, M. C. (2002). *The construction and representation of race and ethnicity in the Caribbean and the world.* Mon, Jamaica: University of the West Indies Press.

Appadurai, A. (2003). Disjuncture and difference in the global cultural economy. In J. E. Braziel and A. Mannur (Eds.), *Theorizing diaspora: A reader* (pp. 25–48). Malden, MA: Blackwell.

Bannerji, H. (2000). *The dark side of the nation.* Toronto: Canadian Scholars' Press Inc.

Barakett, J., and Cleghorn, A. (2000). *Sociology of education: An introductory view from Canada.* Scarborough, Ontario: Prentice Hall Allyn and Bacon.

Beckford, G. L. (1976). Plantation society: Towards a general theory of Caribbean society. In P. M. E. Figueroa and G. Persaud (Eds.), *Sociology of education: A Caribbean reader* (pp. 30–46). Toronto: Oxford University Press.

Berry, J. O. (1995). Families and deinstitutionalization: An application of Bronfenbrenner's social ecology model. *Journal of Counselling and Development, 73*(4), 379–84.

Bhabha, H. K. (1994). *The location of culture.* New York: Routledge.

Brand, D. (2001). *A map to the door of no return.* Toronto: Doubleday.

Brathwaite, K. (1996). Keeping watch over our children: The role of African Canadian parents on the education team. In K. S. Brathwaite and C. E. James (Eds.), *Educating African Canadians* (pp. 87–106). Toronto: James Lorimer.

Bronfenbrenner, U. (1979). *The ecology of human development: Experiments of nature and design.* Cambridge, MA: Harvard University Press.

Carby, H. V. (1999). *Cultures in Babylon. Black Britain and African America.* New York: Verso.

Clandinin, D. J., and Connelly, F. M. (1995). Teacher's professional knowledge landscapes: Secret, sacred, and cover stories. In D. J. Clandinin and F. M. Connelly with C. Craig et al. *Teachers' professional knowledge landscapes* (pp. 3–15). New York: Teachers College Press.

Codjoe, H. M. (1997). *Black students and school success: A study of the experiences of academically successful African-Canadian students graduated in Alberta's secondary schools.* Unpublished doctoral dissertation, University of Alberta, Edmonton, Canada.

Codjoe, H. M. (2001). Fighting a "public enemy" of black academic achievement—the persistence of racism and the schooling experiences of black students in Canada. *Race Ethnicity and Education, 4*(4), 343–75.

Dei, G. J. S. (1996). *Anti-racism education theory and practice.* Halifax, Nova Scotia, Canada: Fernwood.

Dei, G. J. S.(2008). *Racists beware: Uncovering racial politics in the post modern society.* New York: Sense.

Denzin, N. K., and Lincoln, Y. S. (Eds.). (1998). *Collecting and interpreting qualitative materials.* Thousand Oaks, CA: Sage.

Denzin, N. K., and Lincoln, Y. S. (Eds.) (2000). *Handbook of qualitative research* (second ed.). Thousand Oaks: Sage.

Fine, M., Weis, L., Weseen, S., and Wong, L. (2000). For whom? Qualitative research, representations, and social responsibilities. In N. K. Denzin and Y. S. Lincoln (Eds.), *Handbook of qualitative research* (second ed., pp. 107–31). Thousand Oaks, CA: Sage.

Foster, C. (1996). *A place called heaven: The meaning of being black in Canada.* Toronto: HarperCollins.

Friboulet, J. J. (2005). Measuring a cultural right: The effectiveness of the right to education. In A. Osman (Ed.), *Achieving education for all: The case for non-formal education* (report of a symposium on the implementation of alternative approaches in the context of quality education for all). London: The Commonwealth Secretariat.

Gillborn, D., and Ladson-Billings, G. (2004). Introduction. In G. Ladson-Billings and D. Gillborn (Eds.), *The RoutledgeFalmer reader in multicultural education* (pp. 1–4). New York: RoutledgeFalmer.

Gilroy, P. (1991). *"There ain't no black in the Union Jack": The cultural politics of race and nation.* Chicago: University of Chicago Press.

Giroux, H. A. (2003). Public pedagogy and the politics of resistance: Notes on a critical theory of educational struggle. *Education Philosophy and Theory, 35*(1), 5–16.

Giroux, H. A. (2005). *Border crossing* (second ed.). New York: Routledge Taylor and Francis Group.

Greene, M. (1978). *Landscapes of learning.* New York: Teachers College Press.

Hall, S. (1999). The global, the local and the return of ethnicity. In C. Lemert (Ed.), *Social theory: The multicultural and classic readings* (second ed.) (pp. 626–33). Boulder, CO: Westview Press.

Hall, S. (2003). Cultural identity and diaspora. In J. E. Braziel and A. Mannur (Eds.), *Theorizing diaspora* (pp. 233–46). Malden, MA: Blackwell.

Howard, G. R. (2006). *We can't teach what we don't know: White teachers, multiracial schools* (second ed.). New York: Teachers College Press.

James, C. E. (2001). Multiculturalism diversity and education in the Canadian context: The search for an inclusive pedagogy. In C. A. Grant and J. L. Lei (Eds.), *Global constructions of multicultural education: Theories and realities* (pp. 175–204). Mahwah, NJ: Lawrence Erlbaum.

James, C. E. (2003). *Seeing ourselves: Exploring race, ethnicity and culture* (third ed.). Toronto: Thompson Educational.

James, C. E., and Brathwaite, K. (1996). The education of African Canadians: Issues, contexts, and expectations. In K. S. Brathwaite and C. E. James (Eds.), *Educating African Canadians* (pp. 13–31). Toronto: James Lorimer.

James, C. L. R. (2002). *Beyond a boundary.* Durham, NC: Duke University Press. (Original work published 1963).

Kallen, E. (2003). *Ethnicity and human rights in Canada* (third ed.). Don Mills, ON: Oxford University Press.

King, J. E. (2004). Dysconscious racism: Ideology, identity, and the miseducation of teachers. In G. Ladson-Billings and D. Gillborn (Eds.), *The RoutledgeFalmer reader in multicultural education* (pp. 71–83). New York: RoutledgeFalmer.

Ladson-Billings, G. (2000). Racialized discourses in ethnic epistemologies. In N. K. Denzin and Y. S. Lincoln (Eds.), *Handbook of qualitative research* (second ed., pp. 257–77). Thousand Oaks: Sage.

Lather, P. A., and Smithies, C. S. (1997). *Troubling the angels: Women living with HIV/AIDS.* Boulder, CO: Westview Press.

*Macleans.* (2008, January 30). Toronto school board approves black-focused school: Critics concerned about "segregation." Retrieved March 10, 2008, from www.macleans.ca/education/universities/article.jsp?content=20080130_100311_584.

Maingot, A. P. (1996). Haiti and the terrified consequences of the Caribbean. In G. Oostindie (Ed.), *Ethnicity in the Caribbean* (pp. 53–80). London: Macmillan Education.

McCarthy, C., Giardina, M., Harewood, S., and Park, J. K. (2003). Contesting culture: Identity and curriculum dilemmas in the age of globalization, postcolonialism, and multiplicity. *Harvard Educational Review, 73*(3), 449–65.

McLaren, P. (2003). *Life in schools. An introduction to critical pedagogy in the foundations of education* (fourth ed.). Toronto: Allyn and Bacon.

Miller, E. (1976). Education and society in Jamaica. In P. M. E. Figueroa and G. Persaud (Eds.), *Sociology of education: A Caribbean reader* (pp. 47–66). New York: Oxford University Press.

Mintz, S. W. (1996). Ethnic difference, plantation sameness. In G. Oostindie (Ed.), *Ethnicity in the Caribbean* (pp. 39–52). London: Macmillan Education.

Mitchell, K. (2001). Education for democratic citizenship: Transnationalism, multiculturalism, and the limits of liberalism. *Harvard Educational Review, 71*(1), 51–78.

Mitchell, K. (2004). *Crossing the neoliberal line: Pacific rim migration and the metropolis.* Philadelphia: Temple University Press.

Nyerere, J. (1968). Education for self-reliance. In J. Nyerere, *Freedom and socialism: a selection from writings and speeches, 1965–1967*. London: Oxford University Press.

Ogbu, J. U. (1992). Adaptation to minority status and impact on school success. *Theory Into Practice, XXXI*(4), 287–95.

Palmer, C. A. (2006). *Eric Williams & the making of the modern Caribbean.* Chapel Hill: University of North Carolina Press.

QSR International Pty Ltd. (2004, May). *Getting started in N6.* Retrieved December 10, 2004, from www.qrsinternational.com.

Sleeter, C. E. (2004). How white teachers construct race. In G. Ladson-Billings and D. Gillborn (Eds.), *The RoutledgeFalmer Reader in multicultural education* (pp. 163–74). New York: RoutledgeFalmer.

Solomon, R. P. (1992). *Black resistance in high school: Forging a separatist culture.* Albany: State University of New York Press.

Statistics Canada (2008a). *Ethnic origins, 2006 counts, for Canada, provinces and territories for Canada.* Retrieved April 2, 2008, from www12.statcan.ca/english/census06/data/highlights/ethnic/pages/Print.cfm?Lang=E&Geo=PR&Code=01&Table=2&Data=Count&StartRec=1&Sort=3&Display=All&CSDFilter=5000.

Statistics Canada (2008b). *Ethnic origins, 2006 counts, for Canada, provinces and territories for Canada.* Retrieved April 2, 2008, from www12.statcan.ca/english/census06/data/highlights/ethnic/pages/Page.cfm?Lang=E&Geo=PR&Code=48&Data=Count&Table=2&StartRec=1&Sort=3&Display=All&CSDFilter=5000.

Stewart, J. (1986). Patronage and control in the Trinidad Carnival. In V. W. Turner and E. M. Bruner (Eds.), *The anthropology of experience* (pp. 289–315). Urbana: University of Illinois Press.

The Barbados Museum and Historical Society. (n.d.). *Barbados museum* [Brochure]. Barbados, West Indies: Author.

Thomas, E. (2000). *Culture and schooling: Building bridges between research, praxis and professionalism.* Toronto: Wiley.

Toronto District School Board. (2008, January). *Improving success for black students* (Report No. 01-08-1217, RTS No 212). Retrieved March 10, 2008, from www.tdsb.on.ca/board-room/bd_agenda/uploads/jan_29_2008/special_meeting/080129_africentric_1217.pdf.

Walcott, R. (1996). Beyond sameness: Thinking through black heterogeneity. In K. S. Brathwaite and C. E. James (Eds.), *Educating African Canadians* (pp. 284–301). Toronto: James Lorimer.

Walrond-Patterson, J. T. (1999). *Caribbean-Canadians celebrate Carnival: Costumes and inter-generational relationships.* Unpublished master's thesis, University of Alberta, Edmonton, Canada.

Walrond-Patterson, J., Crown, E. M., and Langford, N. (1998). *Welcoming diversity in the faculty of agriculture, forestry and home economics.* Unpublished manuscript, Employment Equity Discretionary Fund Sub-committee of the President's Employment Equity Implementation Committee and the Dean, Faculty of Agriculture, Forestry and Home Economics.

Waters, M. C. (1999). *Black identities: West Indian immigrant dreams and American realities.* New York: Russell Sage Foundation.

Westney, O. E., Brabble, E. W., and Edwards, C. H. (1988). Human ecology: Concepts and perspectives. In R. J. Borden and J. Jacobs, in collaboration with G. L. Young (Eds.), *Human ecology research and applications* (pp. 129–45). College Park, MD: Society for Human Ecology.

Whiton, S, (1974). *Interior design and decoration* (fourth ed.). New York: HarperCollins.

Williams, E. (1962). *History of the people of Trinidad and Tobago.* Trinidad, West Indies: PNM Publishing.

Wright, H. K. (2000). Why write back to the new missionaries: Addressing the exclusion of (Black) others from discourses of empowerment. In G. J. S. Dai and A. Calliste (Eds.), *Power, knowledge and anti-racism education* (pp. 122–40). Halifax, Nova Scotia: Fernwood.

# Index

Africa, 3, 35, 37–38, 44–45, 131, 139, 300,
301, 318; education, 131–46, 151–64,
169, 170, 172, 187, 204, 298
Asia, 22, 30, 39, 199, 203, 220, 231, 239–55

Banks, James, 8, 82, 89, 90, 95, 122, 244,
255
Bavaria, 8, 82, 85, 86, 87, 88–89, 94
bilingual, 103, 104, 112, 114–15, 173,
187–89, 195; education, 122–23, 181–82,
189, 191, 224, 230–31, 232–33
Buraku, 260, 261, 262, 263–65, 269, 270

Canada, 30, 117, 145, 151, 184, 243,
311–12, 316, 317, 320, 321, 325
Caribbean, 172, 297, 311–26
China, 22, 24, 103–25, 220, 223, 239,
240–49, 298
citizenship education, 8, 81–82, 83, 85–89,
91, 92–95, 96
colonization, 3, 5, 12, 23, 35, 36, 40, 46,
133, 134, 153–54, 158, 297, 299, 303,
314–15
community, 3, 9, 12, 25, 74, 82, 87, 95,
116, 132, 138, 143, 185, 213, 264;
involvement, 66, 91–92, 140, 152, 195,
203, 290–91, 292
complementary education programs, 8, 131,
132
culture, 112, 120–21, 168, 187, 192, 200,
230–31, 240, 291, 311–12; pedagogy, 6,
9–10, 11, 168, 317–18; teacher, 60, 74–75

curriculum, 26, 27, 28, 68, 77, 103, 104,
110–14, 115–19, 121, 131–46, 239, 244,
269, 277, 316

diversity, 7, 16, 59–78, 82, 85, 90, 94, 95,
96, 104, 112–14, 120, 239, 275
Dowa, 262–65, 269, 270
Dowa education. *See* Dowa

"education for all," 22, 103, 131, 219, 297,
298, 301–2, 304, 307
England, 59, 63, 65, 71, 172, 311. *See also*
United Kingdom
English-language learners (ELL), 11, 183,
190, 193–94, 196
ethnicity, 6, 15, 36, 46, 82, 103, 108, 116,
203, 240, 255, 261–62, 313
ethnocultural, 81, 82, 83, 85, 94, 95
environmental education, 103, 104,
117–19
European Union (EU), 7, 81, 84–85, 87

Germany, 22, 24, 42, 81–98, 188
gender and education, 27, 108, 110, 135,
154–56, 159, 160, 162–63, 202, 219–34,
243, 280
Ghana, 9, 23, 46, 131–46, 151, 153, 154,
155, 156, 160, 170, 172
globalization, 2, 3, 4, 7, 21, 23, 35–37, 81;
education, 1–17, 21–31, 60–62, 68, 88,
131, 199, 254, 298
*Gymnasium*, 85

# About the Editors

**Greg Wiggan** is assistant professor of urban education and adjunct assistant professor of sociology at the University of North Carolina at Charlotte. His research addresses urban education and urban sociology in the context of school processes that promote high achievement among African American students and other underserved minority student populations. In doing so, his research also examines the broader connections between urban school districts, globalization processes, and the internationalization of education in urban schools.

**Charles B. Hutchison** is associate professor at the University of North Carolina at Charlotte. Besides several articles, he is the author of *Teaching in America: A Cross-Cultural Guide for International Teachers and Their Employers, What Happens When Students Are in the Minority*, and the forthcoming *Teaching Diverse Learners*. He is recipient of Recognition and Key to the City of Boston, and has appeared on, or been featured by, several local and international news media. His research interests include international, cross-cultural cognition, and urban education issues.

# About the Contributors

**Ruth Ahn** is assistant professor of teacher education at California State Polytechnic University, Pomona. She was born in Japan to Korean parents and has lived in six countries. Her research interests include manifestations of the Korean Diaspora and their educational experiences in Japan, China, the United States, and other cultural contexts, and equity pedagogy.

**Stephen Bahry** has twenty years of experience as a teacher, teacher educator, and curriculum developer, largely in English as a second language and English as a foreign language, and at the University of Toronto English Language Program, and has also taught in both China and Tajikistan. His doctoral research is based on a case study of decentralized curriculum development at the local and school-based levels in a multiethnic, multilingual county in northwest China that examines perceptions among stakeholders, students, parents, teachers, and administrators as to what local knowledge, local culture, and local (minority) language(s) should be included in local (county-level) and school curriculum.

**Patrick Darkhor**'s research interests are in curriculum and education for global sustainability. He has worked as a public school teacher in Ontario, Canada, for several years and teaches courses such as "Global Issues and Education" and "Sustainability Education" at York University, Toronto. His research interests include UN mandated programs in global sustainability and environmental education, as well as research in global education, education for sustainable development, and teacher-education programs.

**Joan DeJaeghere** is assistant professor of comparative and international development education in the College of Education and Human Development at the University of Minnesota. Her scholarly interests include analysis of educational policies and practices related to ethnicity, gender, and citizenship. She developed and conducted, with Dr. Shirley Miske, the Ministry of Education and Training, UNICEF, and UNESCO in Vietnam, the design and analysis of a study on Ethnic Minority Girls' Transition from Primary to Secondary School.

**Linda H. L. Furuto** is an assistant professor of mathematics at the University of Hawai'i–West O'ahu. After completing her bachelor's degree at Brigham Young University in mathematics, she pursued her master's degree at Harvard University and doctoral degree at the University of California–Los Angeles in international education, with a focus on mathematics in the East Asia/Pacific region. During this period, she conducted dissertation research as a visiting scholar at the University of Tokyo. Over the past ten years, Furuto has collaborated with a number of international organizations including the World Bank, UNESCO, and USAID.

**Daniel Kirk** teaches at American University of Sharjah, United Arab Emirates. Born and raised in London, England, Daniel studied English literature at the University of Sunderland, achieving a BA (Honors) and Post-Graduate Teaching Certification before becoming a high school teacher. Daniel taught in the British system both in the United Kingdom and Qatar before returning to Sunderland to complete a Master of Arts degree. He went on to teach high school in Bermuda and Dubai before arriving at the University of Georgia where he received his PhD in language and literacy education.

**Jungmin Lee** graduated from Purdue University, Indiana, with a PhD in 2008. She is currently a research professor at Korea University, Seoul, South Korea. Before she came to the United States, she taught educational courses at colleges as a visiting lecturer and worked at the Korea Institute of Curriculum and Evaluation (KICE) as an assistant researcher. Her current research is on multicultural education in South Korea, specifically focusing on educational policy created by recent increases in international marriages and foreign migrant workers, which has resulted in diversity in Korean schools. She has examined school practices and teachers' experiences and perspectives in working with these diverse students.

**Jia Luo** is a member of the faculty in the Tibetan language and culture Department of the Northwest University for Minorities in Lanzhou, Gansu, People's Republic of China. His research focus is Tibetan society and culture, and the challenge of maintaining the best of traditional Tibetan culture while developing modern knowledge. His current research emphasis is on the use of oral history in generating culturally relevant materials for local curriculum. Jia Luo is currently a doctoral candidate at the Ontario Institute for Studies in Education of the University of Toronto.

**J. Lynn McBrien** received her PhD in educational studies from Emory University in 2005. She is currently assistant professor of social foundations of education at the University of South Florida. Dr. McBrien's research interests include refugee education, global education, media literacy, and the evaluation of teaching and learning enhanced by computer and Web-enhanced college courses.

**Luise Prior McCarty** is associate professor in philosophy of education in the Department of Educational Leadership and Policy Studies at Indiana University. Her areas of research include metaphysical and epistemological issues in the philosophy of Wittgenstein and contemporary continental philosophy, with application to multicultural-ism, feminism, and aesthetics. Other topics of interest are the philosophy of higher education, and European, Japanese, and comparative higher education policy. She has served as director of the Carnegie Initiative on the Doctorate (2002–2006) and was associate dean for graduate studies in the School of Education from 2000–2004.

**Obed Mfum-Mensah** completed his PhD in comparative, international, and develop-ment education at the Ontario Institute for the Studies in Education at the University of Toronto. He previously worked on the "community school project" under the supervision of Dr. Joseph P. Farrell. Mfum-Mensah teaches social foundations of education, comparative and international education, and multicultural education at Messiah College in Grantham, Pennsylvania. His research spans from complementary education programs, education in sub-Saharan Africa, and education of marginalized groups to influences of transnational advocacy groups on educational policymaking in the developing world.

**Shirley Miske** is president and senior consultant of Miske Witt and Associates, St. Paul, Minnesota. Her research interests and work are in gender and education in-ternationally, and in the improvement of the quality of national education systems, especially related to teacher professional development and literacy.

**Kwabena Dei Ofori-Attah** is an assistant professor of education at Northern Ken-tucky University, Highland Heights, Kentucky. He completed his doctoral studies at Ohio University, Athens, Ohio, in 1995. Soon after graduation, he received a teach-ing position at the University of the Cumberlands, Williamsburg, Kentucky. While teaching at University of the Cumberlands, he founded an online journal, *The African Symposium*. The aim of the online journal is to publish research reports on education in Africa. The online journal can be accessed at www.africanresearch.org. In addition, Kwabena is a research fellow for the African Educational Research Network.

**Debora Hinderliter Ortloff** is associate director for research for the Center for Urban and Multicultural Education at Indiana University, Indianapolis. She is currently prin-cipal investigator on a statewide inquiry into internationalization processes in Indiana public schools. Prior to her current position she worked with immigrant and refugee students in Germany. Her own research interests center on issues of comparative mul-ticulturalism, global citizenship, translational research, and qualitative inquiry.

**Theresa Perez** earned her PhD from Stanford University. Her research interests focus on the obstacles that prevent schools from modifying their curriculum and instruction as the needs and backgrounds of their student population change. Furthermore, her interest is long-standing and stems from the research she conducted as a graduate student, which resulted in a dissertation titled "In-service teacher education: A model for school change." A principal interest of hers is assisting graduate students to criti-cally analyze the challenges immigrant and non-English-speaking students encounter in mainstream classrooms.

**JoAnn Phillion** is professor of curriculum and instruction, Purdue University. Her research interests are in immigrant student education, multicultural education, and teacher education in the United States, Canada, and Asia. She has published extensively on her long-term narrative inquiry research in an inner-city Canadian school. She published *Narrative Inquiry in a Multicultural Landscape: Multicultural Teaching and Learning* (2002). She also coedited *Narrative and Experience in Multicultural Education* (2005) with Ming Fang He and Michael Connelly. She is associate editor of the *Handbook of Curriculum and Instruction* (2008) with Michael Connelly and Ming Fang He.

**Lan Hue Quach** is assistant professor and the program coordinator of the Masters of Arts in Teaching English as a Second Language program at the University of North Carolina at Charlotte. She has published in the areas of ESL, L2 Motivation, and teacher education. Her research interests include second language and identity development of immigrant children and critical multicultural education.

**Alicia Trotman** is a citizen of Trinidad and Tobago. Her work in teaching science and computer science to adolescents with severe emotional and learning impairments inspired her to pursue doctoral training at Michigan State University. Prior to her studies, she assisted international youth groups with their development through the Global Youth Action Network. Currently she is working on developing technology curricula, and pedagogy and assessments for middle schools.

**Jean Walrond** received her elementary and secondary schooling in Trinidad and Tobago. Her postsecondary education in Canada includes a PhD degree in education from the University of Alberta. She teaches in the Department of Sociology at Concordia University College of Alberta. Her research interests include cultural studies, sociology of education, multiculturalism, antiracism, race, gender, and representation.

**Yuxiang Wang** is a doctoral student in the Department of Curriculum and Instruction, Purdue University. His research interests are in multiculturalism and multicultural education in China and the United States, with a particular focus on issues of race, gender, ethnic conflicts, immigration, and minority cultures and home languages. He recently completed a project in a Chinese community in which he examined Chinese parents' involvement with their children's fight for language rights and equal education. An article on this project has been published with JoAnn Phillion in *Educational Foundations*.

**Kenneth Wilburn** is the director of undergraduate studies in the Department of History at East Carolina University, Greenville, North Carolina. He teaches history of Africa, Africa and Islam, history of South Africa, and a graduate course, "Imperialism: Theory and Practice." He recently codirected an ECU-Ghana Summer Study Abroad program and contributed to the creation of a new BA major and minor, the African and African American Studies Program at ECU. He is a web editor for SERSAS

(Southeast Regional Seminar in African Studies) and H-Africa. His research interests include African societies, Islam, colonialism, and the interaction between indigenous African populations and European imperialists. Late nineteenth-century South Africa, the Atlantic slave trade, reparations, and philosophies of history are current research topics.

LaVergne, TN USA
13 January 2011
212426LV00003B/29/P